The Mediati‹

MW00791059

Luce Irigaray

The Mediation of Touch

palgrave
macmillan

Luce Irigaray
Centre National de la Recherche Scientifique (C.N.R.S.)
Paris, France

ISBN 978-3-031-37412-8   ISBN 978-3-031-37413-5   (eBook)
https://doi.org/10.1007/978-3-031-37413-5

This Palgrave Macmillan imprint is published by the registered company Springer Nature Switzerland AG.
The registered company address is: Gewerbestrasse 11, 6330 Cham, Switzerland

Paper in this product is recyclable.

*May this book unveil to its reader the sensitive and transcendental
potential of the mediation of touch*

Acknowledgments

I thank the publisher for having welcome my innovative manuscript and the reviewers for having encouraged its publication by recognizing the worth of thinking and its originality.

I am grateful to Emily Holmes and Jennifer Carter too for having devoted time to reread my English version of the text.

Contents

1

Introduction: Expelled from the Nest

In his book *No and Yes*, René Spitz writes that the 'infrahuman animals divide into two main classes which manifest basically different feeding behaviours. These classes are named 'altricial' (in German *Nesthoker, in* French *nidicoles*) and 'precocial' (in German *Nestflüchter*, in French *nidi-fuges*). The definition of these two classes shows that the human being, which at birth is in a state of powerlessness and relative immaturity and which, during a long period, will need to be fed, helped and cared for belongs to the class named 'altricial' ' (*Le non et le oui*, Chapitre IV, p. 18; *No and Yes*, Chapter 5, p. 23). Thus it would be possible to conclude that humans are altricial beings upon which culture imposes becoming preco-cial beings, and without any transition between the two stages. Indeed, what is favoured by altricial beings is touch and warmth, whereas preco-cial beings favour sight and locomotion. And if touch intervenes for the latter group in the first time of nutrition, it is in a completely different way from that of the formers: a 'pushing pressure', notably of the head, (op. cit., pp. 22–3; op. cit., pp. 28–9) instead of the search for contact between the skins and mucous tissues of the infant and the mother.

Our tradition requires us to give up such a primitive touch for the benefit of sight. This means ignoring, even indirectly repressing, the first bio-psychic experiences and the first link between the body and the

© The Author(s), under exclusive license to Springer Nature Switzerland AG 2024
L. Irigaray, *The Mediation of Touch*, https://doi.org/10.1007/978-3-031-37413-5_1

psyche in the relationship with the other. What education do we receive to transform the first mode of entering into relation with the other? Who or what teaches us to cultivate this first link with ourselves and between us—notably to pass from a clinging to or even a spontaneous seizing to the caress and from skin to mucous tissues? And if sight and locomotion are necessary for precocial beings in order to feed themselves it is not the same with human beings. Why does our culture favour them? Could it be possible to maintain that sight contributes to the communication between humans more than touch? Instead, does it not necessitate the mediation of an object to the detriment of consideration for the intersubjective bond?

Would it not be the kiss, the caress, the embrace and the tactile communion which could represent a development of the first bond and emotions as a manner of communicating between us? This requires another way of conceiving of and of using negation—as that which ensures an intersubjective difference and not merely that which has to do with the adequacy or not adequacy of some predicates or 'object(s)'.

But why should the 'semantic gestures' and the 'verbal symbols' comply with a relationship with an 'object'—which in fact prevents us from discovering what can act as mediation between two subjects? Do we need an object to 'endow a gesture or voice production with a meaning'? (op.cit., Chapitre VI, p. 31; op. cit., Chapter 7, p. 39). And does the significance of the identification with or of the imitation of the other as an educational process not mean reducing the otherness of this other through apprehending him or her as a sort of object? However that may be, the objectal relationship is considered to represent progress in the development of the child and imitation to be a usual way of apprenticeship. The object would be that which allows children to surmount their narcissism.

The importance of the object could be explained by the passage from the one to the multiple, from the individual to the community. However, such a passage without a transition through the relationship between two naturally different individuals, which can preserve physical belonging and sensitivity, leads to a form of abstraction by which the incarnate subjectivity gets lost. Thus the latter will cling to an object to remain rooted in the concrete. But when the stress is put on the object, reciprocity between subjects is partly diverted, especially from the bodily level. And what is left of it could be limited to a kind of logical dichotomy: yes or no, good or bad, and so forth. What was decisive for our subjective becoming, that is, energy in/of communication, is not sufficiently taken into account nor cultivated. Due to the investment in objects, the relationship between subjects loses the complexity of its qualities in emotional communication and tactile communion and forces them to submit to an objectivity extraneous to their own. Hence, the extremely restricted and frustrating categories of which adults, including psychologists, will make use to interpret, and even shape, the behaviours of children (op.cit., Chapitre VI; op.cit., Chapter 7). Energy which is effective in communication with the other is misjudged. So, according to Spitz, the children identify with the object of love, which is then the supplier of their needs, which can prevent and blurs the existence of a loving relation and of the difference between subjects.

Instead of developing a culture of the first intersubjective relation, our tradition has substituted for it a logic governed by judgment and a truth for which it acts as the reference, and even as the purveyor. Such logic takes little account of the processes relative to intersubjective relationships, which, nevertheless, are subjected to it. Then the 'not', more generally the negative, does not serve the difference between sexuate identities and subjectivities, but it obeys the arbitrage of understanding concerning the suitability of the object(s). Thinking will be worked out from such a use of the negative, whereas the negative ought to be used to preserve the specific individuation of the subjects so that they could enter into relationship, even into a reciprocal relationship.

Undoubtedly, such a negative, which applies to subjectivity itself as particular and not universal, presupposes an additional stage in the working out of thinking. For example, instead of speaking of the mother as a lost object, one then devises a culture of the link with the mother which resorts to internalization. The internalized mother is not lost. She is in myself as a place where I keep her and can prepare a further meeting with her. I do not appropriate her, I appropriate myself to the possibility of a relation with her. This appropriation does not entail that I assimilate my mother to an object—for example to a bobbin, to allude to the Freud's forth-da. Rather it is a matter of maintaining her presence in me by the internalization of her smell, her voice, her touch, her smile. The presence of the mother exists for the children and it would be possible to help them to preserve it by bringing within their reach elements which evoke this presence: a cloth which keeps the mother's smell, a recording of her voice and so forth. In that way children are introduced to a psychic economy in which activity and passivity do not divide from one another—a thing which is crucial for the discovery of the touch which corresponds to self-affection and hetero-affection.

According to Spitz, the communication of infants with adults would begin with a 'no' that they would be able to assume from the sixteenth month. But does the 'rooting', the behaviour through which the newborn tries to be in touch with the breast of the mother, not correspond to a search for communication—to a 'yes' more than to a 'no'? To cultivate such a touch and to differentiate it from its initial dependence on need—assuming that it could ever be a question of a mere need—and from its reduction to the presumed quest of an 'object', would be decisive for the becoming, above all relational, of the child.

Moreover, the smile, which happens long before the sixteenth month, seems also to be a positive sign that the baby addresses to the other. The smile is perhaps the most universal communicative gesture between humans, and it intervenes between them without the mediation of any object.

It is strange that Spitz, and not only him, puts the stress on the negative regarding the first way of communicating with another human and that the latter is experienced by the baby as 'foreign', 'frustrating', 'forbidding', 'aggressor' and so forth. The smile, but also the babbling, bear witness to a really precocious and positive search for intercommunication on the part of the infant. And yet, there is no question of that in most of the authors, at least those whom Spitz quotes. Could it be because the smile and the babbling represent an intersubjective communication without the mediation of any object and that they mean a passage from the link dependent on a first food need to a more autonomous, psychic and even spiritual link?

As for Henri Wallon, he does not hesitate to assert that the infant has no relational life even though it succeeds in finding the nipple of the mother's breast, which it touches also with its hand, and not only in a tense way, while it sucks. Thereby a relational touch exists from the beginning of life, and the baby does not live in a closed world, as Wallon maintains. Touch is even necessary for its survival, which is dependent on touch more than on sight. And one cannot claim that the infant's way of touching is merely functional because it may let itself die of hunger in the absence of its mother, as has been taught by Françoise Dolto. For his part, Aristotle asserts that, for lack of touch, an animal will die.

What, therefore, does it mean, for a human, to sacrifice touch to sight? To remove the infant from its altricial destiny in order to transform it into a precocial being? At what cost? What have we sacrificed of our human life by favouring sight to the detriment of touch—and also the articulate language to the detriment of sensory and sensitive perceptions and gestures? Why would it be useful to separate the functional activity of the infant from its relational longings, as our education systems too often do? Why would the touch of the other have no function in human development, in particular that of uniting interoceptive with exteroceptive feelings towards the acquisition of the proprioceptive experience? Would this not correspond to the function of the caress, and even more of the kiss, in our longing for uniting with one another? Do we not exile the human being from itself or reduce it to the most elementary aspect of animality: the digestive function, when we fail to join together interoceptive and exteroceptive feelings? Then the human being would emerge as such through an aptitude for using articulate language and for a spirituality which, in reality, divides it into a somatic part and a mental part. Perhaps, some would say: into a part which has more to do with the genetic phenotype and another part with the linguistic phenotype—without a real unity of the human being, a unity of which amorous desire would be in search through a union, including a physical union, with the other which differs from oneself by nature.

Nevertheless the fulfilment of this desire requires a sensory, and more generally a sensitive, education, particularly regarding the connection between touch and sight or hearing. In one case, the relationship, especially the intimate relationship, with oneself prevails; in the other case, it is instead the relation with what is the cause of the perception. Thus there is less need for representation in the case of touch, since the meaning of what or whom one touches can do without the mediation of representation. This does not inevitably suppress intention, notably concerning reciprocity in touching, because the relational life already occurs at a more immediate and physical level, which can miss differentiation for lack of education—a thing which explains many errors and disappointments in amorous relationships, more generally in affective relationships, and the substitution of abstract rules, defined according to the adaptation to the sociocultural environment, for the regulation of natural affects existing between living individuals.

The entire emotional sphere is more often than not considered to be upsetting a more suitable activity and not an important aspect of human becoming. The description of troubles which are caused by emotions are multiple, but their role in the development of subjectivity and intersubjectivity is little treated (cf. Henri Wallon, *Les origines du caractère chez l'enfant*, pp. 44–61). Some theoreticians do not even hesitate to think about emotions as something which thwart our relational life because 'emotion consists only of dissociated, lacunal, disproportionate and chaotic reactions' (cf. J.R. Kantor cited by Wallon, p. 45). As for Darwin, he considers emotion to be a current survival of remainders of previous behaviours (op.cit., pp. 45–6).

According to Wallon, for Piaget and his school, 'the passage from childish to adult thinking amounts to the passage from an absolutely individual thinking, which knows only itself, to a thinking which, through becoming socialized, learns how to limit its own points of view as far as it would realize that they are incompatible with the points of view of the other and it would compel itself to use only those that the thinking of the other could use at the same time of it' (op. cit., p. 225). How could the child have this sort of thinking when it has not yet reached individuation? Why would the ideal model of adult development be to acquire a thinking that the other could use at the same time of oneself?— which does not take account of the qualitative elements of the concrete experiences of each, without even imagining that the qualitative could be more related to the transcendental than the quantitative, which in a way tries to substitute for it. And why should the rights of the child be those which are common to all? Could such an ideal of universal similarity correspond to the criterion which can assess the level of human development? Does this passage from the submission of the child to parents and masters to a submission to a current state of development and culture not amount to a model of evolution which is called into question by an intercultural era? Does the latter require us to acquire an additional aptitude for abstraction in relation to the sensitivity of the child or to have access to another way of conceiving of and living sensitivity as a possible mediation between all humans, even before transforming our specific words or objects? Is sensitivity itself not able to act as a means of communicating or communing with every human being if it returns to its original potential? And would the relationship with the other as different not be that which allows a culture of sensitivity to escape the alternative between automatic reflexes and representations? (op.cit., pp. 38–43). But the relationship with the other is practically absent from the analyses of Wallon and of many other theoreticians concerning the emotions.

And yet the one who has been conceived and begotten in the mother, and fed by her, prefers an interpersonal relationship to a relation to object(s). The same does not apply to the one who has been completely or partially conceived outside the mother. The mother is an internal incubator for the whole embryonic life of the human, which is not the case, for example, for the bird, a part of the embryonic life of which takes place outside of the mother, who sits on the eggs outside of herself.

Nevertheless, the bird is fed by its sires for a certain time but in the guise of an object not as the blood or the milk of the mother. Humans are thus more altricial than birds, at least a part of them, even if they were born in a nest. It is above all human beings which need the tactile perception of the mother and her warmth in order to develop during their embryonic life and to feed themselves after birth.

If it seems understandable that, in one case, an animal favours sight, locomotion and object in order to live, it ought not to be the same for a mammal such as the human being for whom the relationship with the other is that which ensures the survival and the development of life, notably through the mediation of touch and tactile movements, neither of which being in search of an object as such nor resorting to the muscular. Does the fluid which feeds the fetus or the newborn not amount to a link between living beings more than to a connection to object(s)?

Why has this link not been cultivated as that which gives life? Why did our culture not care about the evolution of this bond from a relation of dependence, in which needs prevail, to a relation of reciprocity in which desire is determining? This does not mean that touch, warmth and food are absent from our culture, but their nature and sense have changed. Has favouring the relation subject-object(s) over the relationship between living beings not thwart the development of our human existence? Why has birth been called 'a coming into the world' neglecting the importance of 'coming to the other' which, from the beginning, exists for the infant and that the stopping of the natural growth keeps, and even imposes, as the possibility of pursuing the becoming thanks to sexual desire strictly speaking but also the sexuate desire for a community life? Why do philosophers linger so much on the relation between the subject and the world and take less interest in the intersubjective relationship, especially as being at the origin of the world? Why is the word above all viewed as denomination and representation of the elements of the world and so little as a means of communication between 'I' and 'you' although it is in that way that the 'I' and the 'you' are formed or ought to be formed in order to have a human signification and status and the sense to circulate between them and beyond?

Indeed, is it not from that relation that speech originates and can remain alive without freezing in lexical terms more or less arbitrarily defined? Before it becomes more or less exact, more or less true, does not meaning form itself there as a relational means, as a current syntax underlying and justifying every lexical use? Is it not in order to enter into relation that sense must exist? Must it confine itself to a means of appropriating and exchanging objects, including those that the words designate? Does that not amount to stopping at needs—and only for certain living beings, not for human beings originally?

What has our culture done with this first truth? What has it done with the relationship between two human beings which allows us to come into the world and to have access to a more autonomous life? Why has our culture ignored, even repressed, the importance of such a relationship, subjecting the survival and the becoming of subjectivity to a dependence on object(s) more than to a relation to another subject? Ought not the subject to be first of all the guardian of such a relation in order to develop natural life and its spiritual becoming? Why have we been so blind to such truth, even though it is inscribed in nature itself? Are we really human beings, or merely surviving waiting to have access to their true life, if we do not take it into consideration?

There is no doubt that we come into the world by breathing by ourselves, and that this renders us autonomous apart from an environment, in particular a vegetal one, which provides us with oxygen. But we are not yet capable of procuring food for ourselves, beginning with the food that the milk of the mother represents. One way or another we are dependent on the other, on others, for our survival and development until we complete our somatic growing. It is the desire awakened by the dynamism of the germ cells which, then, will allow us to more freely assume our relationship with the other, an other which does not belong to our family genetic legacy.

Our culture seems to have cared about the somatic survival of the species without considering sufficiently the necessity of our more creative development at the psychic and spiritual levels thanks to a relationship between genders and germ cells which are different and are not only devoted to the reproduction of the species. In order to ensure its survival, humanity would have gone from an altricial to a precocial economy, from favouring warmth and touch in the relationship with the other to favouring sight and locomotion in relation to object(s).

However, by becoming presumably precocial, have humans not neglected to develop their ontological potential as altricial beings and thereby regressed to a phylogenetic submission? Human beings would have sacrificed the ontological potential of the individual to an evolution determined by a phylogenetic legacy, apparently more autonomous with respect to the mother but more dependent on the species, more rigid at the level of behaviours, less adaptable and self-modelling (*Le non et le oui*, Chapitre IV, pp. 19–20; *No and Yes*, Chapter 5, pp. 25–6), regulated by sight, locomotion and the research for object(s) more than by the relationship with the other, viewed in an 'objectal' way and not as a tactile communication or communion between two different individuals.

To become human would ask us to give up a fundamental sensitive relation with nature, in particular with our own nature. Instead of reaching the spirit which corresponds with our nature, have we not imposed on the latter structures to free ourselves from it and dominate it, the most important of them being language, a language which codifies the real in a more or less arbitrary way, and which worries little about connecting our brain with our body, about uniting, in us and between us, physical materiality with mental aptitudes, notably by a culture of the different areas of our brain: the midbrain, the thalamus and the cortex? Do our linguistic codes really take account of our memory? Of the connection between memory and affect(s)? Do they not instead aim at substituting themselves for it—leading us to remember words more than ourselves and other living beings?

Such a strategy has probably been imposed on us at a time of our evolution. Have we not to return to this failure in human becoming in order to regain the path towards our real blossoming? In order that we could find again the mediating resources of touch, not only to satisfy our needs as altricial beings but as a means of fulfilling our desire, especially towards the other which differs from us by nature—a 'roundabout way' or a 'provisory suspension' of our instincts by thinking being not sufficient to allow us to achieve that. Rather we have to subject the pretence to think itself to an *epoche* by compelling it to respect the negative which corresponds with the partiality of our natural being. It is not only a question of being capable of postponing the satisfaction of instincts or drives through thought and language but of admitting that our thinking cannot grasp the nature of another living being, that it has limits, in particular those that culture imposed on it.

In order to go back to our condition of altricial beings and its possible development, the existence of the soul can act as a guide. According to Aristotle, the soul is a property of the animal world, to which we belong as humans, which can evolve towards properly human qualities. The soul would be made of breath and touch, two elements which are essential to animal life, and which can grant it autonomy when they become internalized. Without breathing by itself and the ability to move to feed itself, no animal can survive. And Aristotle says that it is touch which can help the animal to find the food which is suitable. How could we not compare these words with the observations of Spitz concerning the search for the mother's breast by the infant?

But Aristotle has not considered how touch, associated with breath, can allow us to overcome the stage of a merely material food. In his time, the philosopher did not take an explicit interest in subjectivity.

Furthermore, the implicit subjectivity—the *upokeimenon*—of his thinking was masculine and it favoured the object to the detriment of the relationship between subjects. Now it is the latter which can ensure the passage from need to desire, from the search for a merely material food in order to survive to a food of another sort enabling us to have access to humanity. This more, both physical and psychical, ontological food could contribute to the culture of our belonging to the world of altricial beings, a culture which could exist and develop thanks to an interpersonal relationship, in particular between differently sexuate beings which do not share the same genetic inheritance. Aristotle's thinking about woman was an additional element which prevented him from imagining this specifically human evolution of the soul.

The resource that the Aristotelian soul represented for a culture of altricial beings thus little by little disappeared, and has even been forgotten, as well as the careful attention to breath and touch that it entailed. Hence, touch itself split up into a barely differentiated pathos, a passive experience of the elements of the universe, of the 'animal' world, of the lived ties with the mother, on the one hand, and, on the other hand, an active perception, especially by the hand, which can seize, finger, identify. Such a perception can be accompanied by an intuition, which functions as information about the action that must be carried out, an action in which form has a crucial role.

The relational and interpersonal touch between the infant and the mother, that the Aristotelian soul seems to remember, has disappeared. Our touch is no longer a means of entering into relation with the other in order to provide us with a material or an affective, an ontical or an ontological, food which human life needs. It has become a passive, and often unconscious, individual remembrance of a sensation or apprehension which has intervened in the active constitution of the world through its possible functioning as a tool. All that happens within the horizon of an autological, not to say autistic and solipsistic world, where activity and passivity henceforth are separated from one another notably because the mediating function of touch in the being in relation of different living beings no longer exists.

For lack of founding his world on an interpersonal relationship, man got lost either in a natural or in a constructed world. The environment which originates from the union between two living beings and which constitutes a horizon imperceptible in the present is lacking—a horizon which happens or exists only in advance or in retrospect for the subjects, none of them being able to create it only by themselves.

This horizon can be sensed or perceived but not appropriated by a single subject. From that results our splitting up in a world the various constructions of which do not take account of the union between two different living beings and two different worlds. Hence the world is lived as a barely differentiated nature or a universe which is made up of elements which are more or less arbitrarily gathered regardless of any living dynamism.

Such dynamism is basically relational. Each can experience it as the letting occur and being said in him- or herself of a relation more or less appropriate to their being. There is no doubt that the relationship between two humans different by nature is the one which most originally can act as the foundation or as the background of a human world. But it is not perceived as such and subjectivity attempts to weave relations with various elements more perceptible of the world in order to meet its need or desire for a conjunction. An ontological foundation is thus transformed into a multitude of ontical, material or spiritual, running aground. The stumble is original and every relationship is, then, in search of the one, both material and spiritual, of our elusive origin—an imperceptible energy foundation which is even more ontological than that of the white which, according to Henri Maldiney, joins all the colours.

This foundation is composed of dynamic exchanges between living beings from which singular bodies can emerge, notably thanks to a propensivity of different germ cells to unite with one another. Such an emergence is more problematic for the woman because, unlike the man, she shares with the other not only the germ cells but also the soma. This probably explains why she is likened to an earth which is nourishing but not fertilizing by itself. The forgetting of the conjunctive nature of our origin thus ended in a distribution between masculine germ cells and a feminine soma. Hence the tear that we endure between body and spirit and the fact that we long for a return to and within the maternal womb instead of acknowledging the conjunctive nature of our conception and its evolutionary and not regressive potential.

The relation to the environment then becomes determinant in our subjective becoming, which is fulfilled through a more or less dialectical process in relation to the environment and the objects that it includes. In such an evolution, the intersubjective relationship vanished as well as the crucial role of touch. And what ought to remain in the service of the latter substitutes for it. The subject-world and subject-object logic henceforth act as a background and a foundation for the subject-subject relation and the assumption of difference that it requires instead of adequacy, similarity, and equality serving as truth criteria and methodological markers.

Henceforth, we 'germinate' thanks to the sun which 'silently comes into us as a remote friend', Cézanne writes (cf. *Cézanne*, by J.Gasquet, quoted by Maldiney in *Regard Parole Espace*, p. 243). Human germination no longer is the result of the union between different germinal cells. The human being goes no further than a plant, rather than a vegetative germination of its nature, ignoring how its own conception happened, and it searches for incarnating its being either through its 'own will' or through an undergone 'bearing'—either through the activity of a demiurge or through the passivity of an embryonic life. It does not reach the link between activity and passivity that a desire shared with a different human being, even with every living being, can procure. And yet, does that not represent access to a properly human becoming, the foundation and ground of a human world taking place between those of nature itself and those of a divine universe?

Are we not too quickly resorting to the latter so that to assess its truth and depth and to overcome our own being torn between a natural and mortal soma and potentially spiritual and immortal germ cells, which bring to our bodily belonging an immanence and a transcendence which are not merely natural?

The germ cells are also the cause of forms which do not only amount to somatic limits or limits defined by sight but limits which have meaning by themselves. This meaning is not extraneous to the negative because the forms particularize the soma to which they belong, but they also transcend it and make it irreducible to an object. These forms express the nature of the material of the soma from which they emerge, a soma which does not remain a more or less inert and opaque mass. In their gathering, these forms address a sign or a call to the other—opened up to the outside through their outlines themselves, sources of energy through their apparently static permanence. The body as soma seems to be the support from which they arise towards a commitment to the world, in particular to the other, the difference of which arouses their dynamic potential, awakening them from a drowsiness due to a mechanical and neuter functioning.

Unlike sight, which generally fixes and objectifies what it perceives, touch prompts the existing forms to liberate the energy that they show to enter into relation with what or whom is outside of them. To transform touch into an analogue of sight (cf. Maldiney, *Regard Parole Espace*, p. 255) amounts to removing from touch the mediating function which is peculiar to it. It is to forget its germinating power, a power which has to do with a natural essence whereas the constructed essences are more dependent on sight.

Favouring the haptic character of touch to the detriment of its mediating potential amounts to viewing it within a metaphysical horizon in which seizure, prehension and apprehension are comparable to an operation of sight. But such a functioning removes from touch its intersubjective potentialities. To seize the other by our touch as by our sight runs the risk of being seized by him or her—as the words of Sartre and Merleau-Ponty regarding sexual intercourse prove. There is neither possible reciprocity nor possible communion by seizing. And if touch can individualize, it is through restoring to the body its natural properties and forms. It gets into contact and takes nothing but, rather, gives back nature to itself while giving it a human status—while individualizing it as human in particular thanks to reciprocity.

Touch has more to do with the origin of a genesis than with the seizure of a form, notably to identify it. And the genesis, or rebirth, that touch can grant needs a beyond or a underside regarding the foundation, the ground, the surface or the level already existing. But this beyond originates in an intimacy or interiority of the one who touches or of the ones who touch one another. It involves a bringing, or a bringing again, into the world in which matter and form(s) have to find, or find again, their organization, their mutual structuring.

In a way, there will never exist a thesis as far as a reciprocal touch is concerned. It always remains in the elaboration of a hypothesis. The union—what some call a synthesis—rests in the service of a foundation and ground from which definitive forms do not emerge but, rather, a never-ending reworking of the relations between matter and form(s) towards the accomplishment of the living who are in touch.

In order for an evolution faithful to nature to come true, living beings must remain different and more and more acquire their own singular identity. Their union must maintain and serve their difference, from which another world can arise. The negative relative to an original partiality not only must be respected and assumed but also kept alive. A culture of touch allows us to do that by individualizing forms and associating them with one another without cutting them off from the ground from which they are formed. Desire is that which requires and makes possible such a culture, a desire which longs for both limit(s) and limitlessness, individuation and union, immanence and transcendence. Such a desire arises from us thanks to the otherness of the other as a longing for transcendence which aims at a never-ending process of the evolution of matter. The bodily presence becomes sensitive interiority, which can be experienced and shared as the origin of a perpetual birth or rebirth. So the energy of each living being contributes to its own development, to the achievement of the union of the one with the other, especially as genders, and to the evolution of one's own species as well as to that of the world.

Part I

Merged with the World

2

Born of Soma and Germ Cells

Divided Between Two Truths

Nature itself includes a part of invisibility, its most important part, the one which is concerned with its original determination—its genotype—and the sap as existence, growth and relationality determining factor. Invisibility is not a matter of ideality, as Merleau-Ponty maintains. The dynamism through which nature ensures 'intra-structures and intersections' is invisible (cf. *La Nature,* p. 291; Nature, p. 228). This dynamism is also operating in intersubjectivity, when this is not more or less arbitrarily constructed. It permits the link between bodies and the actualization of their potential, notably thanks to desire, especially a sexuate desire. The inter-bodies relation of intersubjectivity, to which Merleau-Ponty alludes, seems to be the result of an artificial elaboration, of a coding extraneous to life itself. Its invisibility is not a real one; it bears witness to a lack of connection between the real and the coding.

Hence our body is torn between two truths: that of life that it incarnates and that of sociocultural encodings. Two languages correspond to these two truths: one wants difference and the other sameness. The first is appropriate to the relation between living beings, beginning with two

L. Irigaray, *The Mediation of Touch*, https://doi.org/10.1007/978-3-031-37413-5_2

different living beings, and the second is a mode of expression and communication between one and many, the one and the multiple.

Why has our culture imposed on us an artificial coding? Why has it attributed transcendence and its verticality to idealities, whereas it already exists in nature? Does not the sap raise vertically while also spreading out horizontally, for example to reach the other(s)? Is not the articulation between these two dimensions—the 'suture' or the 'joint' of which Merleau-Ponty is in search—at work in nature itself? In fact, verticality and horizontality need one another.

These two dimensions take part in our genesis as living beings. This consists in a conjunction. As living beings, we are not born of nothing but of a conjunction between two different beings. In such a birth, there is, no doubt, a rupture of continuity, which does not mean that our being originates from nothing. And in its origin, horizontality and verticality intervene: if to live entails to grow, growing is dependent on a conjunction, on conjunctions.

In fact, our totality is first natural—the result of a conjunction between two different elements which attract and penetrate one another. Why have we neglected this totality for the benefit of the whole that we form as a world and of our relation to this world? Why have we forgotten the link which originates our own being: the union between two different living beings, and wanted to reconstruct a whole by addition of many unities stepping over the conjunction of which we were born as a first whole? Why have we substitute for this totality, which remains open because it exists thanks to a difference and which is also fecund, a totality composed by addition of persons and/or things, which produces devices, and even nothingness, more than a real with a generative potential, at the natural and the ontological levels, and which, furthermore, involves the assumption of a negative and not its exclusion or rejection?

Inserting the negative in the constitution of the whole entails the desire to overcome it. This cannot happen through a solitary becoming but through a union with what or whom one is not. I want to unite with what or whom I am not not to become them but to become the one who I am thanks to assuming the negative that my particularity represents towards a union with the other. Contrary to what is generally imagined, notably by the philosophers, desire does not lack finality: it longs for uniting with the different both to surmount and to preserve the negative. Uniting with the other as different is a path towards the absolute which corresponds with the achievement of my being through its limitation, its difference and the permanence of its dynamism thanks to an insurmountable negative.

There is no doubt that if the other participates in my being or constrains me to subject to his or hers, instead of the difference between us being respected, I, and even we, fall into the facticity of mere being(s) again. I am then deprived both of the transcendence of my relation to my 'to be' and of my desire to unite with the other as transcending myself, that is, deprived of a triple transcendence: mine, that of the other and that of the union between us. If we assume the partiality of our 'to be', we can safeguard the unity of each and the possibility of a union with one another, whereas our falling back into mere being(s) causes our reduction to fragments of a unity which is not ours and in which we lose the possibility of a return to ourselves and a becoming of our own.

In order to preserve my unity, I must renounce incarnating all potentialities, especially as regards my sexuate belonging. This also contributes to maintaining the negative of a difference and the possibility of a union with the other—of a kind of intersection at the level of 'to be' which keeps other ways of evolving. Pretending to make effective all his potentialities amounts to the claim of one subject which wants only sameness and extends indefinitely until it becomes evanescent for lack of being questioned and fertilized by the meeting with a different 'to be' thanks to assuming his own particularity.

The Dynamism of the Germ Cells

Desire aspires after the infinite or the absolute more than after a totality. Born of germ cells more than of soma, desire aims at the beyond of the already existing—desire wants the transcendent in comparison with the vitalism of the soma. In a sense, it corresponds with the dynamism of the soul and aims at the entelechia of the 'to be'. The spirit, notably according to an Hegelian perspective, does not represent the accomplishment of our 'to be' but only of one part of it, which either contributes to such accomplishment or prevents its advent. Contrary to the claim of Hegel, ideas can amount to a weakness of nature. For lack of being faithful to nature, ideas can correspond to a for-oneself which is partially reactive.

Desire, as for it, supports the affirmative dynamism of a for-oneself, but it requires this for-oneself to be also a for-the-other and a with-the-other. Consequently, the structuring of my being is no longer a kind of reacting of a 'there is to be' to the environment. Rather it amounts to a gathering of my being that my desire carries out in order to approach the other, to present me to him or her, and make possible a becoming with them. Prior to any collective networking, our 'to be' must be structured in/through relating to the other, an other different from ourselves by nature. This can provide our being with an autonomous structure and preserve it.

In this basic relationship, the somas and the germ cells combine with one another, whereas they split up in the passage from one to many. Then the germ cells lose their potential and the supra sensitive ideals or the articulate language substitute for them in an evolution which has broken its link with the natural dynamism. To pretend that our evolution is possible from such dissociation leads to the disappearance of humanity. To evolve, this needs resources of matter and energy that a neutered individual no longer has. Our becoming then ends in a privilege of the mind and a robotization of the being, in which matter and energy are more and more separate and the living beings that we are are animated by a mechanism or an intention external and foreign to themselves.

How could we return to an evolution that we want in an affirmative way, and is not ordered by an outside or merely reactive, and of which we are capable as living? How can we decide on an evolution which preserves our human potential and its qualitative and not only quantitative development? This requires a return to our origin as living beings and a cultivation of our becoming which preserves our reserves of life, of energy and of desire, particularly at a relational level.

Must we speak of 'involution' on this subject? In that case, we must give to this word the sense of a return to recover and develop the living, lasting and qualitative nature of the evolution. Woman is probably more able to rediscover and promote such a movement, alternating with that of expansion which is favoured by man. Ignoring the resources of difference as regards sexuate identity and subjectivity amounts to depriving humanity of a suitable evolution, an evolution which would combine centripetal with centrifugal motions and would assure a dialectical process between the two. This would mean a return to nature in ourselves and a possible harmony with our natural environment. Being faithful to our sexuate belonging is crucial for such a communion with nature, in ourselves and outside of ourselves. If this faithfulness is not that which ensures its possibility and mediation, the risk exists of a falling back into the abstraction of a 'there is', a suffocation or a paralysis.

Too often we have imagined the evolution of living beings as quantitative in its cause and its effects. The importance of the qualitative dimension has been misjudged. The return to nature, to us as nature and flesh asks of us favouring quality over quantity. To assess evolution according to the number and a quantitative development little by little exhausts the living that we are—of whom many survive only as sorts of fossils of humanity. It is urgent to resort to other criteria of evolution and to consider the resources to be spared in order that this evolution should be possible. One of the first deeds which could contribute to that is to discover a manner of cultivating matter respecting its own forms instead of producing forms starting from matter only by ourselves. Our sexuate belonging is particularly relevant in such perspective because sexuation gives form(s) to our physical life while letting it be, and even allowing it to be, matter, a living and not only inert matter. It renders our body a place of possible affirmation, and not only reaction, including in its development, its evolution.

Henceforth our evolution is largely determined by a constructed environment, and humanity gets caught and frozen in a sort of merely phenotypical embodiment. It neglects, and even forgets, its genotypical resources, especially those of the pair of sexual chromosomes, the heterochromosomes, of which we were born. The relation between our organism and the world has prevailed in the way of conceiving of the evolution of living beings to the detriment of the resources that the meeting between different chromosomes represents, whereas these have to do with our origin and the possible link between the physical and the meta-physical, between us and the other(s), between us and the world. The evolutional potential of this couple of chromosomes has been underrated and its fecundity reduced to a mere punctual and natural operation, without questioning our power and our will on this subject enough. And when this happened, it was in a negative way: how to impede the fertilization and handle it with restrictive effects in mind.

In fact, the sexuate desire entails a sort of hypertelia, but this can favour incarnation or thwart it by calling the personal development into question. Desire has been used to support sameness, and how it can contribute to the human evolution by longing for a meeting between beings which are qualitatively, and not quantitatively different, has been misjudged, and even repressed. And yet this could render selection and mutation compatible without leaving them to a mere genetic fate. Could we not act on our genetic inheritance through a relational culture which has an influence on our chromosomal potential? Our evolution has been thought from an unique and not a dual origin. There would be an original type which would evolve by resemblance, mimicry and adaptation. However, we were born of two different beings. But this evolutional potential, which is probably the most powerful, has not really been envisioned. Why have we considered genetics as a natural determinism on which we could not have an influence in order to favour an evolution of humanity which would not be only dependent on the external environment but to which our will could contribute?

The Evolutional Potential of the Germ Cells

Our want to act on our evolution cannot be only solitary or communal, dependent on the will of one or of a community or a people. It demands a cultivation of the relation between two different germ cells, as it occurs in our own conception and that of other living beings. The question is no longer one of imitation and adaptation but of production or liberation of a still virginal potential—a real of the dawn?—to which we must give birth and we must cultivate. The researches on mutation and evolution generally confine themselves to a somatic reality, supposedly neuter and universal, without considering the role of the most important factor of transformation of matter: that of the germ cells.

Thanks to germinating cells, our organism is never closed on/in itself, which represents an evolutional potential and risk. For lack of taking account of it, we neglect one of the main causes of both our natural and cultural evolution, an evolution relating to quality more than to quantity, and that sciences and technology cannot guarantee—only what is living can be only qualitative in its becoming. To entrust the evolution to germ cells also means providing this evolution with a regulation of entropy that difference is likely to ensure thanks to the negative that it entails. The fecundity of the germ cells requires a spatial distance and a temporal interval to exist, and be maintained, which correspond to a difference that we attempt to overcome from the not yet come to pass of a union. Assuming a nothing in common, a nothing at present and a nothing yet is necessary.

When evolution is thought starting from the great number, the fecundity of the germ cells is not perceived as such and it might reappear under the guise of the purity of a race or another kind of sterilization of the germ cells in the soma. A discourse, a logos, concerning the germ cells and the union between germ cells as a factor of development does not yet exist. Before entrusting its, and their, origin and responsibility to God, it would be advisable to discover and care about that by ourselves.

Woman probably has a privileged role to play on this subject. She gives birth not only to the body but also to the spirit, at least potentially, through sharing her breath. She is and she gives flesh, and to give flesh is not only to give a body but also to give life to the germ cells—physically and also meta-physically. In fact the incarnation of Jesus ought not to mean a sort of fall or decay for God, as it is too often maintained. Woman gives flesh to germ cells which live on only thanks to her. In this way, she brings into the world not only a new human being but, possibly, another era of the spirit—she gives life to germ cells also at the level of thinking. The germ cells generate not only physical but also spiritual forms.

Flesh arises from a conjunction between germ cells and not by mere introduction of germ cells into matter. And germ cells which unite with one another in such conjunction are not of the same nature. As well as germ cells of her own, woman must provide a place welcoming this conjunction, which marks a break in the flux of life lacking in differentiation.

Besides her desire to unite with a fleshly fertile other, she must be a flesh receptive to this union and a possible fertilization. Could not the time of the Spirit—the third time, said that of the Spirit, in the Judaeo-Christian tradition—be that of flesh becoming spirit, woman being able to be the mediator in this advent, given her predisposition to interiority—man projecting himself more on/in the outside, in particular as regards flesh.

Man would re-open the place where flesh can take place, where woman can allow it to exist. There is no question of mere passivity on her part, rather it is an aptitude for joining together soma and germ cells, germ cells and soma. Has having access to humanity not to do with this task? For lack of acknowledging this role of woman, man attempts to appropriate it. He then falls back into the dissociation of form(s) from matter considering him to be responsible for giving form(s) to matter. So he suspends the work of life, including by a way of conceiving of religion which ought to contribute to its accomplishment. This would be possible only by respecting and favouring the union between two different incarnations of humanity, each bringing a specific part towards its achievement. The latter cannot happen through a mere coordination between the same ones or a subordination between the different. A decisive aspect of the union is then lacking: the spacing which allows two different elements to conjoin without being ever abolished. In this union two matters and two structures are linked together and give rise to a third element from which each returns to itself. Such a dialectical process, at work thanks to a nature which aims at its own development, permits a transformation of the sap itself. Could one imagine that germ cells themselves evolve while keeping their generative potential?

What compels germ cells to unite with one another is mysterious. How do they perceive one another as they are different and situated in different spaces? Could it be longing for meeting together? Is aiming at uniting inscribed in/on nature and the structuring which determines it? Could aspiring after transcending itself be a property of nature? Or are we wanting to reverse the process of our origin: I have been produced, thus I produce myself. Could it be a desire to experience the power of our body? Or the will to reproduce oneself in a supposedly same as oneself as a sort of demiurgic aspiration?

This last possibility could interrupt the work of generation in which we take part in a linkage between self-affection and hetero-affection. I search for myself through touching the other as a tactile mirror. However, this other is not really a mirror, it never reflects me in an adequate way; rather, it sends me back to me, to my self-affection in an endless motion. The touching the other, or from the other, has not the immediacy that Merleau-Ponty ascribes to it. If the other is perceived and respected as other, an insurmountable interval subsists between the other and myself in touch itself. This touch must be both active and passive, and it can be so only thanks to the assumption of the negative of a difference. Touching does not simply entail being touched while touching the other, and, besides, the other is not an object.

Yet a certain temporal interval can exist between the active and the passive when I touch myself. This allows self-affection to be also a mode of self-consciousness. Touch itself acts as mediation and its relation to immediacy is different from that of sight. Sight does not destroy the immediacy of touch, as Merleau-Ponty suggests, touch itself is already mediation. The touch to which Merleau-Ponty alludes seems to be a solipsistic gesture in a frozen world, whereas touch perhaps only exists in the reciprocity between living beings—including regarding self-affection—which presupposes a dialectical process between exteriority and interiority.

And it is not in the space of the world that I can perceive or feel my hand but through bringing my hands together or through touching or being touched by another living being. My hand, above all through its palm, makes me pass from the outside to the inside, from the inside to the outside of my body. It opens a passage between these two spaces or spacings corresponding to my body—and this passage already creates a first irreducibility between my body and this of other living beings. Assuming the difference between species creates another irreducibility, all the more insurmountable since such difference is specific, as is the case with sexuate difference.

Effects of Germ Cells on Subjectivity

Living sexuate difference as a structure which unifies and determines our being without, for all that, subjecting it to needs, could define our belonging to the human species. How to go from the sensitive experience that sexuate belonging entails to its being taken into account by consciousness? Ethics and dialectics which are needed to relate to the other as naturally different probably represent indispensable conditions. Such cultivation of the sexuate, and not only sexual strictly speaking, relationship makes conscious its sensitive dimension while keeping it sensitive. This supposes that the fact of being sexuate does not render identity more solipsistic but, instead, opens it up to new possibilities in the relationship with oneself, with the other and with the world, possibilities that culture must take into consideration. This also implies that sexuate belonging is not considered to be a mere means of reproducing our species but, rather, a means of accomplishing our humanity, notably by the way of living desire and union between two beings which are naturally different— thanks to the dynamism of germ cells.

What comes to pass in and thanks to such a union cannot happen in an experience which is only solitary or social. In the relation with the other as different, the ec-stasis due to the transcendence of the other gives rise to an in-stasis which contributes to our accomplishment. In the meeting between the two ec-stases and in-stases, our flesh becomes spiritual, it becomes incarnate as a modality of the transcendence of the spiritual after which we aspire as humans. Indeed, it is not true that the sexuate relationship, and even more specifically the sexual desire, are without entelechia— as, for example, Merleau-Ponty claims (cf. *La Nature,* p. 350; *Nature,* p. 282), but they aim, in particular as desire, at something which remains indeterminable, notably because they search for uniting with different germ cells, which are reducible neither to an object nor to a theme. Desire aspires after the absolute of our own fulfilment thanks to the relationship with a different human being. And this other can in no way amount to one's own 'image' in a more or less distant 'there'—as Merleau-Ponty asserts—rather it represents a for ever non-appropriable and insurmountable mediation in my longing for the absolute. Intending to appropriate this other not only abolishes the possibility of making one's own way towards the absolute, but also represents a murder concerning the other, who is not recognized in his/her otherness, and, more generally, in their own life. Unfortunately, this murder too often happened in our culture, and in the name of a supposedly universal reason.

The other must remain other as a recall to the truth inscribed in my own body, my own flesh, my own life—perhaps Merleau-Ponty would speak in this connection of the truth which 'lies in the secret order of the incarnate subjects' (op. cit., p. 367; This page as the following pages appear in Appendices of *La Nature* which do not exist in the Anglophone version). The desire for the other, a desire not only sexual strictly speaking, acts as a 'transcendental intuition' (cf. *Sharing the World,* 'The desire for the beyond') with respect to my own truth. Certainly, the other incarnates this truth in his or her own way, but they hold in themselves something of the mystery of my incarnation. The desire for the other is revelation of a mystery which can be unveiled only in the relation between us. It calls us in mind that we are nature—and not only 'in' or 'before' nature—but a specific nature, human and sexuate. This nature is revealed through the relation to and with the other who differs from ourselves by nature—a relation in which not only the soma but also the germ cells that the soma incarnates are present. Would the abyss which supports 'the great phenomenon of the world' according to Schelling (*La Nature,* p. 362; Does not exist in Anglophone version) not be the mystery that the conjunction between two different beings represents—a conjunction which reopens the horizon of each living world and of each vital solipsism towards the fecundity resulting from the meeting between different germ cells?

The respect for such difference amounts to an elementary respect for nature and its fecundity. This respect must begin with the respect for oneself as a naturally sexuate being. This natural belonging cannot be reduced to a 'bodily pre-constitution', to an 'earlier layer' or an 'original presence' of my being (op. cit., p. 366; idem). It must animate my present being here and now (op. cit., p. 367; idem). What it anyhow does through desire disguised in various ways by the philosopher as 'vital surge', 'intentionality', 'mystery of a natural teleology', why not through longing for ideals and the beyond. All these interpretations seem to forget nature that we ourselves are, a nature which aims at its fulfillment through a meeting, even a union, with a nature, with germ cells, different from ours towards its development and its fecundity.

By situating nature outside of ourselves or merging with it, as is often the case in the work of Merleau-Ponty, and by reducing humanity to consciousness, we have prevented our natural belonging from blossoming into a specifically human thinking—we have paralyzed life in and outside ourselves and we have gone out of ourselves and of the world. The desire for an other who differs from us can bring us back to us, to a natural identity buried under many more or less artificial cultural constructions. Only the experience of the irreducible natural difference of/from the other can return to us the innocence of the flesh. Living in nature with the perspective of a beyond sometimes can also leads us back to it. But of what can consist this beyond in order not to remove us from our sensitivity, our flesh, our life? Could it be the matter of a negative theology, or even a negative ontology? What path, what grace can bring us back to that?

Not to harm the process of becoming, the original determination of being must not close up into/with a final determination. The teleology which corresponds with our fulfillment must remain open. The desire for a qualitatively other permits that. The path towards the absolute is then determined but its objective, or objectal, finality is kept on hold in the union. In fact, the body itself is the keeper of a truth that desire expresses in a more or less blind way. This truth, as a sort of consciousness of the body, can be reduced neither to the unconsciousness of the mind nor to 'a first state', a 'black continent' (Freud), 'a labyrinth of the first philosophy' (Leibniz) or even 'a fog' (Eddington) (cf. *La Nature*, pp. 371–72; Does not exist in Anglophone version). And an ontology which takes account of our flesh cannot be reduced to a pluralism (op. cit., p. 370; idem). Assuming our natural difference with respect to the other sends us back to our being, gives us back to our being, and requires the assumption of a double negative: as regards the conjunction of which we were born and the relation to the other as different (cf. *To Be Born*, in particular the Prologue)

Touch as Mediation Between the Germ Cells and the Soma

A culture faithful to our human nature asks us to take root in it starting from a double discontinuity which cannot take place without an interiority in which touch has the main role. This touch intervenes at the most immediate but also the most elaborate levels between two humans who are differently sexuate. It is in that place that touch, above all a physical touch, as the one which exists between the infant and the mother or between us and the world, can keep its natural quality while being transformed towards a spiritual becoming. It is also there that the whole being can be experienced in a hetero-affection which corresponds to a communing between two self-affections. In such a hetero-affection, we can live the 'coherent structure' with which nature has endowed us (*La Nature,* p. 373; idem). This is not merely material nor merely spiritual but a linkage between matter and form(s) already present in our natural being, notably as sexuate.

By nature, we are already situated in a specific structure through the morphology of our body as well as through the relational context of our conception and of our birth, the two being determined by the species and by the genus. We must carry out their unity in the relation to ourselves, to the other and to the world. It is not at the same level that the two can conjoin: the species has more to do with the collective and the genus with the dual, which is wrongly confused with an opposition. The species more corresponds to the soma and the genus to the germ cells. The evolution of the species is slower than that depending on germ cells, which is potentially more active and spiritual. The genus is in a way additional to the species. It gives rise to it, but it also provides it with dynamism, it contributes to its development or paralyzes it, brings forms to it or distorts it.

The other as sexually different has not to be subjected to a master-slave dialectical process, notably through a confrontation of glances or a resort to a certain touch (see, for example, the words of Sartre, Merleau-Ponty or Levinas concerning sexual intercourse, notably in the first chapter of *To Be Two*). Rather, the other is the one who reveals me to myself, gives or gives me back to myself at a physical and potentially meta-physical levels. This requires this other not to be only an 'unspecified partner' (*La Nature,* p. 375; Does not exist in Anglophone version) but a partner who, while being faithful to his or her nature, lives it in a human way. The relation to the other as different corresponds to an at first not fixed entelechia of life that we must incarnate in a specific way to accomplish our humanity. The nature of indeterminacy is then different: it is no longer relative to the partner but to the both determinate and indeterminate way of living the relationship.

The importance of such a process is still inadequately thought. This results, at least in part, from the fact that man has considered himself to be in nature, perceiving nature and dwelling in it (op. cit., p. 379; idem) but not to be himself nature. When it happened that he considered himself as such, it was generally a question of a part of him, a part only passive and he had to surmount to become truly human. For example, Merleau-Ponty distinguishes between an actively and a passively feeling body, between two properties or faces of the body. This thwarts the communing with oneself, but above all with the other, which is possible because the active sensitivity is also a passive sensitivity and the passive sensitivity also an active sensitivity. I feel myself by feeling you; by feeling you, my sensitivity becomes itself actively feeling. And the fact that you feel me awakes the active feeling of my sensitivity—which makes useless resorting to incorporation. I perceive you as other thanks to touching you, and if I welcome you in myself it is to better perceive you, not to incorporate you in a sort of more or less spiritual cannibalism.

Thus feeling has nothing to do with a dispossession of oneself but, instead, is a means of cultivating our relational being. To succeed in that, we must become aware of it, which does not mean that it must be reduced or subjected to consciousness as we usually lived it, because it was more often than not the outcome of a misjudgment of the potential of touch. Hence it was difficult to unite in us a sensitive flesh with a flesh constructed regardless of sensitivity.

Why has our nature, as nature in general, been subjected to an artificial coding? Could the latter be required to dispossess nature of its own dynamism, as regards individual development or communication and interaction between living beings? Have we really questioned the means according to which nature can blossom by itself in each of us and we can communicate or commune with each other? And have we wondered about what permits both the growth of each and the constitution of the totality of the world? Before we intend to constitute it by ourselves, it would be opportune to question about how nature itself acts in such a way through air, sun, water, earth, and the interactions between living beings. Nature is neither a more or less opaque and inert matter nor a totality organized by some divinity, which brought dynamism and structure to a chaos, and it is not a whole composed by man either. Nature is a living organism already structured in itself and by itself—in a way the self-production of a meaning. And there is no doubt, in this connection, that sexuation plays both a generative and organizing role. If the soma can become inert matter, germ cells represent a dynamism which animates it, contributes to its development and its entering into relation with other living beings. If the soma could need the intervention of energy and structure external to itself, notably because it amounts to a merely individual totality, it is not the same with the germ cells.

Aristotle thinks that the natural mobility of bodies obeys a qualitative destination, but he does not question the difference between the soma and the germ cells on this subject. Sexuation obeys a qualitative destination which is not merely that of an atom or a simple individual, as Aristotle and the Stoics seem to imagine, but has a relational dimension. The soma could be compared to an atom, even a monad, but not the germ cells.

The germ cells have also the possibility of acting in and from the inside of our body—they do not leave the dynamism of such interiority and intimacy only to God as the Creator. The germ cells arouse an internal dynamism, a dynamism capable of surmounting the activity-passivity, teleology-ateleology, individuality-relationality, finite-infinite dichotomies. They are the cause of nature, give matter and form(s) to it, contribute to the production of its meaning and need difference to fulfil their potential. It seems to be relevant to say that the germ cells want difference, whereas the soma privileges sameness.

God too often has been of use to mask the importance of such difference, notably by being substituted for our natural origin as well as for the origin of our moving and its finality—hence a misjudgment of the ontological potential of the germ cells. Such misjudging has led to our reducing the amorous embrace to an energy release instead of living it as the deed and the place in which our natural, but also our spiritual, being comes true, and is not only reproduced. This achievement, but already this reproduction, of our being needs a natural difference between us. The amorous meeting in difference has an ontological dimension at the level of incarnation itself, whereas between the same ones it is more ontical, sending the origin of our being back to a beyond—a Being or a God. The desiring meeting between naturally different beings creates a space in which our being can come true as incarnate. Without such a space, this meeting takes place in the expansion of material or physical bodies without space being necessarily transformed into the subtle matter which is suitable for giving rise to our being and its dynamism.

3

The Space-Time of the Living

An Inhabitable Space

What unites our body with our soul is of three natures: the breath, desire and the flesh. Through the hospitality given to the desire for/of the other, our soul receives an extent—and even a material, Hegel would say. Opened by acknowledging the otherness of the other, it becomes also fleshly thanks to the physical dimension of desire, that is, thanks to the desire for/of the other as incarnate. The soul becomes a sensitive extent or material in which the other, and even the world, can take place as external to it. They are intimately perceived as living with some of their physical qualities—which permits a union of the soul with the body, in oneself and between the selves. Our tradition little wondered about the nature of this union and its effects. It thought of these elements as separate or composing a whole in which their specificity disappeared, but not as being able to unite with one another and act jointly. This perspective allows us to change our way of imagining the relation between matter and spirit, nature and divinity, and even unity and difference. Indeed, the desire between two humans who differ by nature allows us to overcome such dichotomies. And this shakes the horizon of the world in which we are, in particular as regards being and thinking.

L. Irigaray, *The Mediation of Touch*, https://doi.org/10.1007/978-3-031-37413-5_3

This also invites us to reconsider the nature of space. This cannot correspond to a mere formal intuition, as Kant would like, because it is also matter. And it must be perceived a such by living beings who communicate and commune in it through the air, the light and other sensitive perceptions. Some can even sense it as such through a spiritual perception which has something to do with the consistency of space itself. This represents another way of overcoming the matter-spirit dichotomy. Our tradition has too often imagined space as the result of a domination of man on nature, a nature not considered to be living as micro- or macrocosm.

The space in which we are is already a space shared between living beings—which does not call into question our individuation and our difference(s). We share something of life: for example, the air. Our ontological identity cannot exist without a belonging to the materiality of life. The human being cannot be merely anti-physical or meta-physical. Its finality consists in achieving in a specific manner its own nature in a suitable environment that it respects as such. This presupposes that it acknowledges its spatial dwelling as being material but fluid, permeable and open in order to concede a certain consistency and permanency to our being, which is neither merely physical nor merely metaphysical. If the space in which we live is more and more experienced as void, we need external limits to contain uncontrollable attractions and movements. The increasing abstraction of our modes of thinking and communicating renders our human being gradually more evanescent and unstable.

Space cannot be likened to a closed and void form, delimited by supra sensitive concepts. It must be habitable by incarnate living beings and must be open. This opening can be maintained, without harming our own unity, by thinking it not only at an individual level but also as being determined by natural relations between living beings. The space which, then, permits it to exist and that it produces is both dense and open.

In this kind of space, which takes root in and is determined by nature, a certain relativity exists, but it cannot be absolute on pain of neglecting the living and in a way incarnate character of space, at a material level but also a spiritual level—the spiritual being no longer imagined as abstract but as that which is endowed with a more subtle material quality, which can correspond with the psyche and with thought. This aspect of space must be present in the relation between two human beings who are differently sexuate. Can, for all that, this relation modify the quality of the space which enters in the constitution of the cosmos, as religious words suggest? Could the harmonization required by the relation between two humans differently sexuate spread into all the space? If it is not the case, what is the limit of its area of diffusion and radiation?

The way in which we appear to one another takes part in and modifies the answer to such a question. Does our presence amount to a construction extraneous to a natural efflorescence or, instead, does it correspond to a phenomenon expressing the real that we are? In this case, a natural energy animates our presence and allows it to fit into a living space within which it can radiate. If it is not the case, the constructed character of this presence could not only stop any radiation but also prevent the physical entering into presence of the other. And yet, this has been imposed on us by a society which was composed with neutered individuals and organized by laws foreign to natural laws.

The entry into presence of two individuals ought to respect the phenomenal aspect of each as both the material and spiritual expression of their beings. It ought not to amount to the face to face of two representations of the human being shaped by culture, which renders the physical entering into presence of the one and the other impossible, but also prevents their meeting from occurring in a natural environment—which does not mean in a 'wild world' as some philosophers claim, but in a living world. This living world has been described as 'barbaric' due to the incapacity to think of it. Philosophers too often have judged it in that way instead of questioning their own manner of thinking—their logos. As it is devised and built this logos, this logic, cannot express nature while respecting its economy.

A Living Being Among Other Living Beings

Sending nature back to an abyss, as Schelling does, perhaps could mean preserving it, as a negative theology does, but not yet thinking of it. The way of thinking and saying life is still lacking, notably because it lacks a thinking of *phuein* but also of sensitivity.

Nietzsche has certainly began to pave the way towards such thinking, but he has not sufficiently thought of himself as nature. He has not really cultivated his own *phuein*, in particular at the physical and sensitive levels. He used its living dynamism to criticize more than developing. And he wondered too little about the necessity of cultivating the relationship with the other to become the one he was, the one he wanted to become. He has been more spectator than actor—apart from a parodic actor of that which already happened. To cross the bridge between the old man and the new man he longed for reaching, he needed a feminine companion, as he himself acknowledged. This, perhaps, would have allowed him to perceive and develop his own nature as living without confining himself to perform various masks, characters or roles.

In fact, Nietzsche used perspective as regards what was already constructed more than as regards nature and himself as nature—which would have provided him with a method to cross the bridge between the old man of the West and a new man. Such perspective would even be of use to go from the immersion in nature to a coexistence with other living beings. It could also exempt from Kantian spatiotemporal apriorism by emerging from nature itself as a viewpoint allowing one to recognize being itself—neither pure objectivity nor pure subjectivity, neither pure in-itself nor pure for-itself. Perspective, then, can remain alive, fleshly, qualitative and keep a tactile dimension—whereas flesh cannot become merely visual, as even Schelling seems to believe. Perspective can arise from a love of life but not from its mastery. It opens a possible passage from the empirical to the transcendental: bridge, scale, transformation going from a material reality to a more spiritual reality without appropriation of/by representation. It corresponds to a means that intuition can give to itself in order that a mere physical sensitivity could become a spiritual sensitivity, notably through a carnal sharing. Nature that I am does not create only its object(s), it creates itself to perceive another real. This self-creation has to do with our *phuein* as living beings, on the one hand, and, on the other hand, with self-affection, that is, with a sensitive relation to ourselves.

Self-affection as a relation to/with oneself amounts to a pre-reflexive stage from a consciousness standpoint, but which can introduce into a self-consciousness capable of favouring our becoming as living as well as the communication or communion with other living beings. This implies us assuming our partiality, an insurmountable negative which gives access to a conscious perception of the living that we are and to its possible transformation. I must no longer only apprehend things in themselves, as Schelling wanted, which presupposes that they have an essence perceptible by me, but I must let them be and appear by themselves. Knowing something about them then requires me to consent to being overawed by them at a sensitive level while having an active consciousness of their presence in myself. Instead of attributing an essence to them from a subjective perception of what they are or would be, I let them reveal to me what they are through their apperception by my comprehensive, and not only visual or mental, being. In meeting them, I attempt to arrange a meeting between two lives, two sensitivities. And assuming the negative of a difference makes possible avoiding the often paralyzing, not to say deadly, stage of reflection.

Discerning and respecting the difference between every other living being and myself modifies my way of thinking and procures resources of energy for me in the meeting with other living beings. This also preserves my unity in a not sterilizing manner—I am but I am also open to, I am one but also porous, one but receiving myself from the other, from others, too. I am one, originally and finally, but I am a being in relation by nature and by longing for the absolute—situated in a space which exists as such and opening, reopening another, both natural and cultural, space in it. To be and to become demands me to differ from an original relation to the other and to the world without, for all that, giving up my natural belonging as culture too often forced me to do.

I must remain nature, which proves to be possible by differentiating my nature from the whole in which I am. I do not become my own nature by merely participating in a nature external to myself—as, for example, Merleau-Ponty seems to imagine—but by individualizing and cultivating the nature that I am. Most philosophers have spoken about nature as if they were not themselves nature. And, when they return to nature, it is often a return to a more or less opaque, primitive and original sensitivity and not to the nature that they are and they must individualize and cultivate as humans.

For lack of considering themselves to be nature, philosophers, even those said of nature, imagine that they must sink into 'a real existence' (cf. *La Nature,* p. 82; *Nature,* p. 55), immerse themselves in a primitive world, whereas the matter is rather of assuming their particularity and partiality as being themselves nature. It is necessary to perceive everything, and above all every living being starting from 'I am not that being'. This allows me to perceive other beings with my whole own being, including my flesh, and not only through my eyes and my mind. Then perceiving a thing, and even more perceiving the other(s), means accepting to be impregnated by them while differing from them, which cannot amount to having an image or representation of them. Instead the question is how to become capable of getting in communion with them, a communion that can be more or less comprehensive—the negative having to intervene the most rigorously towards what is closest to me, the human differently sexuate. As the other takes part in my birth or rebirth, this other is often mistaken for my own life. Hence the necessity of resorting to the negative to differentiate the one from the other. However, between an other living being and me something of life is shared, and I must constantly endeavour to distinguish what belongs to the other from what belongs to me.

Touch Between Natural Essences

The mistake of metaphysics is to have assessed difference in a mere quantitative or abstract way, to have intended to expel the negative from its horizon instead of taking charge of it to ensure a fundamental qualitative difference between living beings in order to perceive others as well as ourselves as living. Is it not the mistake even of those as Bergson or Merleau-Ponty who claim that they can use perception to surmount representation while using perception in a meta-physical manner? Certainly perception is no longer surpassed by representation, but it attempts to appropriate the living notably but not only by favouring activity and visibility—appearance over the real of life, image over the intimate imprint.

Hence the fact that they always return to an original, a primitive, a 'pre-human', a 'background of the real' a lack of differentiation from nature, instead of assuming themselves as a partial incarnation of nature. At the beginning, the unity of one nature would exist 'which would open out as a spray' (cf. a quotation of Bergson in *La Nature*, p. 88; *Nature*, p. 59) losing in that way its unity and its harmony. The fact that our origin is dual but we have to take charge of it as one(s) and, besides, we must constantly return to ourselves to weave between the origin that we gave to ourselves in the beginning and the origin that we give or give again to ourselves in the present is not taken into account by these philosophers in their conception of life. Then life is more uprooted than ever. Instead of communing with other living beings, they try to seize them no longer through a name, a concept or a representation but through an immediate perception without respecting their autonomy and their difference—hence a falling back into a basic lack of differentiation. Such a way of apprehending and mastering is almost worse than that at work in metaphysics and in Hegel himself. This is not at all surprising. Western man moved more and more far away from himself as nature, and it is not by grafting himself on the vegetal or animal world or through comparing himself to them that he can return to himself as nature. It is to his own nature that he must return and endeavour to cultivate it as living.

The way in which Bergson—but also Merleau-Ponty and even Michel Henry—imagine life is traditionally metaphysical. Life would be a neuter 'vital surge' which loses strength when taking form(s), above all a particular form (cf. *L'évolution créatrice*, p. 603, quoted in *La Nature*, p. 89; *Nature*, p. 60). From what arises energy of this vital surge? And why must Bergson resort to God in order for his thought to function? (cf. *La Nature*, pp. 93–4; *Nature*, pp. 63–4). In his way of arguing, Bergson takes account of species but not of genus. And yet, if 'the evolution of species is useful to life by producing new forms', this is still more true concerning the genus. And the forms are, then, source of energy and desire, which is more specific to human being than 'vital surge'. The particularity of these forms no longer paralyzes life but instead generates natural as well as spiritual life.

Furthermore, this particularity does not produce only external forms but also intimacy, a living intimacy. The determination of my body at the level of forms causes individuation, notably through a return to the origin of my energy, but it also causes desire for and of the other, which corresponds to another source of energy.

Western philosophers, above all those who claim to care about life, more often than not confine themselves to the soma without wondering about the germ cells as the cause of forms and energy, for all living beings and between them, but also as a unifying principle in each and between all. In fact, the germ cells overcome the split between our physical and our psychical belonging, between our body and our spirit. Germ cells want union whereas soma wants separation. Wanting union, germ cells also want difference, without which generation not being possible. And if the soma gives rise to a proliferation which can produce cancer, the germ cells regulate life through a generating process, and they can even improve it if the context is favourable.

The germ cells have not the materiality of the soma and, although they are physical, they do not decline like the body. They take part in the body but are, nevertheless, autonomous with respect to it—which allows them to unite with another body. This requires the mediation of touch, and even interpenetration. Touch does not lack logic, but its logic involves union thanks to the separation and difference due to individuation. Touch allows us to attempt to reconcile existence and essence, species and genus, origin and end. If the tree is, as humans we are not immediately, we have to become our 'to be'. And this 'to be' is not originally substantial as our soma. It is the union between two different germ cells—in a way two potential 'to bes'—which aim at re-forming an origin that we can never appropriate. For lack of taking that into consideration, our being does not know how to be confronted with nothingness and we fall back into a mere psychological interpretation and even being, forgetting our physical conception and/or merging with nature.

In a way, human being is not, it is longing for being, the achievement of which is not only dependent on it. Indeed, meeting and uniting with the other shakes its individual potential, at best increasing it. This questions our way of conceiving of space and time—it can no longer be a priori, be anticipated, be linear and capable of retrospection. Our space-time is neither merely natural nor merely constructed, neither merely objective nor merely subjective. It exists as natural, but it becomes and must be built as human in the respect for the macro- and the microcosm.

Once more philosophers, and more generally men, imagined space-time, as nature itself, as an outside of themselves without thinking of themselves as both objective and subjective nature, existing in space and time but producing them too.

What allows us to inhabit space and time is first our body as touch—*aisthesis*. However, as Husserl writes 'my eyes tend to define optimal forms (…)There is a teleology of the eye which is instinctively called by an optimal form of the object' (quoted in *La Nature*, p. 108; *Nature,* p. 75). It is thus our body, through our eyes, which creates essences. Privileging sight amounts to favouring a subject who is cut off from the world and considers the world as a spectacle, be it empirical or ideal.

Touch, as for it, wants to reopen forms but, given its repression by culture, it too often does that through breaking in a world which is structured by sight. Touch aims at contact, reciprocity and communion. The absolute after which it aspires is different from the one of sight. Sight spontaneously seeks to master. Perceiving by eyes, except sometimes in contemplation, amounts to removing living beings from their environment, to cut them off from their surroundings, by giving autonomous form(s) to them. On the contrary, tactile perception is in search of union, particularly of communion in the invisible. It is animated by a quite different energy and light.

The importance of touch did not appear because we have not truly differentiated ourselves from nature and from the world. We remain immersed in nature. We adhere to it, unless we situate it as an outside of ourselves, as something external with respect to ourselves. We do not think about ourselves as nature, which implies, among others, freeing touch from an immersion in nature or from an ec-stasis in a world supposedly only objective.

As we do not consider ourselves to be nature, we are not really capable of being a 'here' and of entering into relation with a 'there'. The relationship with another living being, especially another human differently sexuate, can give this possibility back to us. If I respect the other as other, I give to myself, and even to us, a center starting from which we can define a 'here' and a 'there'. For want of that, I remain, we remain, immersed in a universe without differentiation, that we wrongly consider to be natural, or maternal, whereas we have created this lack of differentiation.

I provide myself with a 'here' by assuming a world as my own, thus by not being the other. Hence, the natural truth is no longer 'originally' or a 'common original ground' (cf. *La Nature,* pp. 111–112; *Nature,* p. 78), it is in the present, in me and in my relationship with the other and with the world. It needs my access to my own being, a being of which the 'here' and 'now' cannot be substituted for any other, and cannot be universal.

Exiled in a Scientific Space-Time

Not only we remained merging with what we call nature, but in correlation with that, we accepted to be subjected to an abstract and neuter truth, to an alleged 'here' and 'there' allotted by a thought and a discourse which acknowledge them to be true only under the condition of their being common and universal. Hence the success of the scientist, who pretends to provide us with an exact knowledge concerning the natural truth without worrying about what structures his own perception of nature. And yet, the perception of nature in its objectivity, which the scientist intends to communicate to us, and the depositary of which he would be, includes a part of him, notably in the choice of investigations and methods, of which he does not take account.

The so-called scientific objectivity thus deserves to be questioned. Why does it remain always dependent on a conception of nature which favours only one viewpoint, a sort of univocal 'seizure' of what is supposedly natural without ever thinking about what happens between two naturally different beings? Why has such a reality been for a so long time ignored, notably by sciences called human, and more generally by all our culture? Even though we consider the words of the scientist to be an irrefutable testimony of a natural reality, he has already subjected it to a perception—to a perceptive device—which is his own and which neglects the numerous phenomena which result from interactions between living beings.

This is all the more important since the relationship between living beings produces a third element or world. A logic with three components—and not only a binary logic—is then needed in which each term is affected and in which it takes part. So, as far as human beings are concerned, each is a physical body, which could be at least in part objectified, but it is also a specific sexuate body and desire in interrelation with the other(s). Consequently, the bodies are already transformed into other than into objects which can be apprehended by the scientist or the philosopher.

Being myself already three and having in myself an aptitude for assessing that to which desire bears witness means that I am no longer subjected to the eyes of the other to have form(s) and existence—as it would be the case in amorous relations according to Sartre and Merleau-Ponty. I already gave them to myself by assuming my sexuation and through self-affection—which allows me to meet the other as other.

My sexuate belonging brings to my organism a structure which is both immanent and potentially transcendent, and which, furthermore, is turned towards the outside and the inside. I can perceive the other, especially the one whom I desire, outside myself and inside myself in a sort of internalization. This operation also corresponds to a kind of temporal articulation between the present, the past and the future that my desire allows me to carry out. I am no longer an object for the other nor can I be objectified by the other. I have become a subject which sends back to this other his or her own subjectivity, and even in a way makes it objective.

Nevertheless, such sending back can either freeze the other into an object—the words of Sartre, Merleau-Ponty and even Levinas about sexual intercourse show that—or restore their subjectivity to them. This modifies our relationship and shields it from a master-slave logic. This also gives to our relationship a sensitive transcendental dimension through a linkage between two different structures, which produces a qualitative event in the approach to the absolute. Such an event can constitute the horizon of a new world capable of sheltering, and even generating, a new human being.

This cannot happen without an elaboration of immediacy and of perception, and even their subjection to a dialectical process. Indeed, I cannot perceive the other as other without subjecting my perception to a double negative: with respect to my nature but also to my culture. And to keep immediacy in perceiving is possible only by freeing immediacy from any merely personal impulse and from any artifice due to a cultural construction. Immediacy in perceiving must be acquired; it does not amount only to a given, especially when it is a question of another living being, what is more of another living being different from us by nature.

How to gain a space-time suitable for such an elaboration of immediacy? Perhaps this can be obtained through a cultivation of touch. Our sensitive being is relational and it longs for reciprocity. Touch can grant it what sight is unable to bring to it. How can we live and imagine the space-time corresponding to touch? There is no doubt that living in nature is living in a context which appeals to our senses. Thus it goes for touch—we are touched by the light and the warmth of the sun, by the breath of the wind, by the rain. Beyond touch strictly speaking, nature appeals to our feeling. Nevertheless a real tactile reciprocity does not exist with the macrocosm. It can completely occur only with another human, and even a human differing from us by nature.

How can touch take place in space-time and have an influence on it? Are we sent back to solitude or solipsism when we are not in the same space-time—which can never completely happen? How can we touch one another in spite of such a distance? Through what process is that possible? Thanks to what mediation?

Does our favouring things in perceiving and comprehending not result from having neglected our sensitive being(s) and paralyzed our flesh for lack of a cultivation of touch and of its space-time? This ended in or reinforced a separation of the spirit from the body and brought about the impossibility of a real coexistence between living beings, in particular between different living beings. Hence the artificially ecstatic, and even a priori, character of the space-time to which living beings are subjected. Many interrelations and interactions between nature and culture, but also between exteriority and interiority, are then transformed into an objectivity and exteriority which do not really take account of their nature and of their evolution.

In fact, my own temporality and the temporality of another living being are never the same except if they are subjected to a mere cosmic temporality, on the one hand, or to a mere constructed temporality, on the other hand, which amounts to depriving them of properties and qualities of their own. If I want to return to the living nature of my relationship with the other, I must get through an experience of the negative. I do not live in the same space-time as that of this other. I long for the other, for the you that the other is for me, as for an additional existence, even for an additional being. However, to fulfil my desire, I must accept what appears to me as a less existing, as a limitation of my own existence. Perhaps, this could today represent a means of rescuing humanity. Indeed, living on a world-wide scale spreads out to the infinite, a bad infinite, our longing for the absolute. Accomplishing my being and my humanity compels me to give up such spreading. It requires me to work out my world as living before I extend it to the world as it exists regardless of my own living world, which leads to a paralysis of my becoming, a paralysis which, henceforth, threatens the human species. Hence the necessity of discovering a new way of joining natural belonging to human becoming.

This asks us to differently harmonize space with time or, rather, to discover how to combine the one with the other (cf. *La Nature,* pp. 139–152; *Nature,* pp. 101–106). Space and time are, at least in part, coordinated in nature. The space of the garden is not the same in spring, summer and winter, and space and time interact in it. My body behaves a little like a garden. As nature, it coordinates in itself space and time, but our culture too often destroys such a coordination. It can be found again and lived on the occasion of certain events—for example, an appointment or an amorous embrace. In the union, for which embrace longs and that it sometimes fulfills, a coordination of space with time can occur, which is destroyed when sexual intercourse are reduced to an energy release. Respecting a given word concerning an appointment also establishes a certain coordination of space with time, at both natural and cultural levels. It is not without some culture that the embrace as well as the appointment can re-establish a coordination of space with time. Starting from such examples, could it be possible to discover a means of carrying out such coordination in a lasting and world-wide way?

Self-Production of the Natural Forms

In fact, every perception involves touching and being touched. Could it be through us that 'Nature' re-touches itself, according to the discourse of some philosophers? Would it be our role, as humans, to be the guardians of the spatiotemporal order? Then we would not use our consciousness to dominate nature but to ensure its subsistence and its functioning. Thanks to our memory and our desire?

As for giving form(s) to nature, this is generally useless and, furthermore, prevents us from perceiving it. Nature provides its own forms and so becomes individualized by itself. Nature aspires to give form(s) to itself as the blossoming of life, a life of which we dispossess it imposing on it our forms. We must respect the forms that nature gives to itself but also the forms that it gives to us.

Accepting that nature takes form(s) in us as well as contemplating the forms of nature outside of ourselves contributes towards the advent of every 'to be'. To be does not happen thanks to a belonging to an immutable essence. To be is revealed, unveiled and becomes incarnate from the forms that living beings give to themselves, in particular by their germ cells. To be corresponds to the incarnation of a living being which, by coinciding with itself, takes form(s)—lets its 'to be' express itself and appears. What or who it is escapes a living being and cannot be mastered, and no more can an other apprehend it or apprehend itself immediately. The advent of 'to be' is irreducible to any seizure. It must be prepared by safeguarding one's own potential of life, a constant 'sensitive awakening', and a permanent 'activity of state' (cf. Whitehead, quoted in *La Nature*, pp. 153–165; *Nature*, pp. 113–122). These three conditions have something to do with and are in a way included in a self-affection, which can occur thanks to a relationship with a body of one's own.

According to Whitehead 'nature communes with itself'. Self-affection, through the touching one another of the borders of my body, is an attempt to commune with myself. By this gesture, I give to myself a more original and natural for-myself than that of consciousness. This for-myself results from the constitution of myself as a whole defined by limits. Through self-affection, I provide myself with a unity and I entrust to my memory this unity that I did not originally receive as a for-myself. Undoubtedly, breathing by myself contributes to such acquiring, but it is not perceived as my existence as a whole.

Through self-affection, I delimit the surround of an expanse—generated, I generate myself as a singular physical existence. Whitehead would say that I am the creator of the creature that I am (cf. *La Nature*,

p. 163; *Nature,* p. 121). Perhaps, it would be better to speak of generating, or to stress the fact that self-affection has a potential which is both generative and creative—which is important as regards the continuity of our becoming. Giving myself to perceive and remember my natural belonging, notably as sexuate, I give to myself a potential for growing, developing, and having a future. I am no longer only dependent on the other, on the world or even on God for such a possibility. I also create and generate myself by myself.

In such a way, by my existence, I can give or give back my 'to be' to myself. But this donation can only happen thanks to an original conjunction towards which the 'to be' that I give to myself aims as at its finality. This 'to be' cannot merely amount to a being, to an object. And it is through a negative ontology that I can approach it. Such a negative ontology is more complex than the ones which are already known because my 'to be' is basically relational. Henceforth, the negative does not apply to an object, whatever its status, but to the relation itself and to the subject who ventures into this relation—one could say that the negative has then more to do with syntax and logic than with lexicon and predication, at least as regards the attributes. How can syntax and logic contribute to approaching my being or removing me from it? What sort of relation is to be discovered, cultivated and shared to incarnate the 'to be' that I must be?

What space and what time can contribute to my incarnation, notably by their capability to combine projection and retrospection, these two processes being determined, especially physically, but escaping from the domination of my consciousness? There is thus through experience that I must clear my path and not through obeying an injunction of understanding, which a priori does not know my whole being, in particular my sensitive being. It is experience which, step by step, can reveal to me who I am. For lack of resorting to such a means to know myself, I search for myself in my origin and my end, through my nostalgia or my hope. A slow and wise process of incarnation could bring a content to such spatiotemporal quests.

My origin and my cause, forever elusive, cannot be blindly projected onto the future or onto the beyond, but they must inspire my manner of elaborating the becoming of my 'to be'. I must incarnate it from a conjunction that I will never succeed in mastering but which determines the one who I am. Between my elusive natural origin and my existence a kind of dialectical process must take place, which substitutes itself for the alternative between 'being' and 'nothing'. My 'to be' does not arise from nothing but from a conjunction between two naturally different beings which escapes my seizure and understanding. Mistaking elusiveness and nothingness, while intending to apprehend 'to be' through its attributes, is an arrogance of understanding. The origin and the end of my 'to be' occur without any predicate could be definitively attributed to them. They are and I am before they or I are something or someone already defined. I can experience something about the one who I am in the union with another 'to be' without this union being mastered by understanding. It is or it is not. To be is at stake or not. And our intuition concerning 'to be' or 'not to be' or 'nothingness' is perhaps dependent on the existence of a union between us. I conceive myself as 'to be' from the elusiveness of my origin and of our union.

My original cause as well as my final cause escape me even if I act them in a certain way. All what happens to me cannot be perceived and mastered by my consciousness—my life lives regardless of it. And I do not think that resorting to God could solve such an aporia. Life wants to develop and this living becoming cannot occur without faithfulness to the physical being that we are, thus also to a past which becomes true through a future. The dynamism of life intervenes before any decision or awareness from us. It makes us exist prior to and independently of any deliberate will. It wills us before and even without our willing it.

We take too little account of such a process. And it is even repressed in different ways, notably by comparing it with an operation of the unconscious, even with 'a dark continent' (cf. Freud) whereas it corresponds to a natural phenomenon which has nothing to do with a traumatic event of our childhood, of our story. If this phenomenon is lived in a negative way, it is because we underrate and even ignore its natural origin in the development of life in ourselves, be it a question of our own becoming or of our relationship with the world, with the other or with others.

4

The World of Human Beings

Generation of Forms Between the Genders

What theoretician really wonders about our relational potential? So I would like to ask Coghill and Gesell (cf. in *La Nature;* in *Nature*) of what consist, according to them, the relational embryonic tissues. Is not the behavioural development that they observe and interpret due to a relational motivation? What physiological tissue permits and accompanies its evolution? What tissues and forms are generated by sexual chromosomes? In what are they factors of and driving force behind our development? What corresponds with desire at the physiological level? And have the theoreticians noted what comes from the bodily 'I can' when it combines with the 'I can' of another body? What results, in that case, for the potential of my organism? And how, in a sexuate desire, are extension and expansion connected with particularity? Is it not the desire for an other as different which, then, produces both unfolding and individuation? Is it not such a desire which compels me to transcend myself while revealing to me the immanence of my potential, of my 'me'? Is it not my sexuate belonging which unifies me while opening me up to the outside? Is it not this belonging which awakens me from a sort of lethargy in a quasi-organic symmetry or from a paralysis due to a mirror image by forcing

L. Irigaray, *The Mediation of Touch*, https://doi.org/10.1007/978-3-031-37413-5_4

me to evolve because the asymmetry of a face-to-face with an other which differs from me by nature—an other which differs not only by sex, but also by subjectivity and the world? These strangeness and asymmetry with respect to my global being could make me sink into the deepest distress without the mediation of touch.

Touch both opens me to the other and holds me back in myself. In order to compensate for an asymmetry created by the meeting with the other, I unbalance myself to find a new contour or horizon and a new centring. My sight cannot grant me them, and going no further than sight ends in risking cancelling difference. If the latter is acknowledged and assumed, asymmetry leads me, and even forces me to discover another relation to form(s)—to the body and to the world—in which I live. My body and my world, which were almost at rest, must evolve and change in order to make the meeting between two different bodies and two different worlds possible. This means that these bodies cannot confine themselves to being merely physical, that they must become also spiritual, that is to say, become flesh.

Through the form(s) or the structure generated by the meeting between two different fleshes, I have access to a becoming in which touch is both a driving force and a mediation in my search for a personal absolute, and is determined by a desire for reciprocity in difference, which is the source of an absolute still more absolute. The totality, and in a way the autarchy, of my being gets in touch with another totality or autarchy, which compels me, compels us to a destabilization and an impetus opening to another structure, henceforth unstable and always open. However, to maintain this opening, such a structure needs a return, a repose in the one, at least partially symmetric, of a being of its own. Besides, things are more complex. Indeed, the touch of the other gives to me the possibility of feeling myself, thus of experiencing a totality which is reached thanks to a difference and an asymmetry—which is thus a more dynamic totality.

A mistake of our culture is to have considered sexuation to be a partial aspect of our organism and not a founding and structuring dimension of our being. This potential has too often been reduced to reproduction, to a mere physiological aspect, without being truly assumed and cultivated at psychic and spiritual levels, except in parenthood. This has in a way paralyzed, and even suppressed the dynamic power of desire. The child inherits a physiological dynamism, but it too often means the end of the dynamism of desire between man and woman—the child is the death of parents, Hegel would say. The desire between man and woman settles down and freezes in parenthood, which ought to represent a secondary aspect and effect of sexuation—the most somatic production of germ cells. Do the parents not contemplate in children the reliquary of their desire for one another as lovers instead of letting them live their own life and desire? The child stops the unbalance that desire arouses between man and woman for their evolution towards a new equilibrium. This unbalance, as a condition of their own becoming, breaks off in their care for the growing, and first the physiological growing, of the child, assuring in that way a family stability based above all on needs—on soma(s). But life exists only by becoming. When the latter is lacking, life becomes ossified, notably in habits, norms, stereotypes, institutions and so forth.

Such a sclerosis in great part results from a non-assumption of the specificity and partiality of their gender by each, which does not only amount to a mere deviating from a norm and a truth but to a qualitative ontological difference. The negative that belonging only to one gender requires us to take on is productive—I have not immediately at my disposal the potential which is mine and, besides, I cannot actualize only by myself this potential. Meeting with the other arouses this potential and its development, notably through participating in another potential. It is because we pay too little attention to this event, or advent, that we fall back into the subject-object configuration and logic again, which is more solipsistic and consuming at the relational level. The other and the natural world are transformed into objects, which diverts us from and hinders a development of life as such. Hence mind is privileged as well as the resort to information, which leads to an impoverishment and a fragmentation of our being. Then the latter appeals for a truth which would be common and, consequently, for rules, laws and customs which impose it on us. We, then, submit ourselves to a culture which is extraneous to the one that our life needs towards its own growth and evolution.

The relationship with the other different from us by nature can answer such a necessity thanks to an interaction which is assumed and wanted. In that kind of structure, the in-itself that a living organism is becomes a subjective for-itself without having for all that to give up a life of its own.

However, this in-itself and even this for-itself do not exist without the mediation of the for-itself and in-itself of the other. This means again that my becoming does not depend only on my own potential and that the latter varies according to my meeting(s) with the other(s).

Unfortunately, we behave, more often than not unconsciously, in a way which invalidates the result of such meetings. This happens, in particular, by reducing otherness to sameness, either ignoring the singularity of the other or nullifying it through imitation, domination or subjection, which amounts to suppressing the awakening and the resource that difference represents for our life—to subjecting the germ cells to a more or less inert soma. By neglecting in that way the dynamic potential of the germ cells and our assuming the negative that their specific and partial incarnation requires, we deprive ourselves of a means to have access to the positive aspect of our singular becoming and to that of the other and of our relationship.

In other words, it is by acknowledging, and not only undergoing, our difference, a difference which is not only physiological or organic, that we can keep ourselves living while becoming conscious. This difference transforms our body into a sort of dynamic 'animal' logos instead of this body being reduced to a sort of mechanism which is animated by an aim external to itself. This bodily transformation can correspond to an ethical imperative, but it is also and first needed by desire. As a passage or bridge between the material and the spiritual, the physical and the meta-physical, desire wants the maintenance of a difference, of an interval, between the here and now and an elsewhere and future, between me and the other, a difference or an interval the obstacle of and confrontation with which asks us to will an evolution of our lived experience but also of the substance of our living body. Its transformation into flesh?

Evolution of the World Thanks to Germ Cells

Desire also wants and needs an evolution of the world. It is in search of another world and it creates, at least in part, this other world. As subjective, it cannot content itself with a mere objective unfolding. However, if it closes up on a mere subjective dimension, the world also closes up because each subjectivity entails an objectivity. It is the relationship with other subjectivities, more generally with other living beings, which allows it to remain, and even to become, subjectivity, this having to stay alive and in relation in order that it could happen in that way. And there is no doubt that our sexuate desire keeps, or at least can keep, us living.

When our desire aims to modify the world, the undertaking is really difficult, notably at the level of energy, if it is faced alone with a world already objectified, one could say ossified. Our energy must combine with another living energy to remain itself alive. Only a living being creates or builds by itself a world which subsists and develops through relations and interactions with other living beings. The 'animal-machines' have not a world of their own; they react to defend themselves or attack the world by interacting with other living beings. Their way of being structured is incompatible with the creation, the subsistence or the development of a living world.

Building a world is a complex undertaking for a human being. It can neither build it only with its own substance—as the spider does with its web—nor in a manner which is completely extraneous to this substance. How can it deal with both nature and culture in the constitution of a world? The most interesting method, which is unfortunately the most neglected, is to create a world thanks to desire as an extension of the first dwelling that our body is. More often than not our desire puts a lot into abstract mental constructions and so denatures itself by building an artificial world which cuts us off from our natural belonging, which then subsists only at the level of needs, among which sexuality is classified. The main part of our tradition has been elaborated from such a split between nature and culture. This leads to a gradual disappearance of the human being as such. An alternative or a means to remedy this situation would be to consider desire to be capable of building a world both natural and cultural, individual and common. Such a world would transcend a mere material universe while remaining faithful to our nature, thus organic. It would favour coexistence between all living beings while safeguarding the specificity of the human being and the possibility of a sharing of desire between humans—without spending energy or devoting it only to reproduction, as is, perhaps, the case for some animals.

Sharing desire can stimulate our organism, help it to grow and even restore it. Through arising from a deeper level, notably because of more superficial lesions or cicatrices, desire can cure wounds (cf. on this subject words of Bertrand Russell quoted in *La Nature*, pp. 234–40; *Nature*, pp. 178–83). Through building a micro-milieu, reciprocal desires contribute to the development of our organism, also at the sensitive level. They create a sort of environment, in part a placental one, in which what remains embryonic in being can begin to exist. Reciprocal desires have a restoring, but also a regenerating, and even a generating, power, for each and for all. In an abstract culture or a merely constructed socio-cultural milieu, this potential is destroyed or anesthetized by an artificial stratum, a kind of cellophane or glass stratum, which separates the inside from the outside of the living being. The latter has no longer access to its generative or regenerative potential; it survives, partially paralyzed or asphyxiated. The milieu itself is no longer produced and fed by life and it can no longer be regenerated by interaction with living organism(s). This amounts to the end of a world that only an opening up to other exchanges with living beings can overcome towards the arising of a new world.

It is thus useful to reflect on the nature of the milieu itself in order that it should support our development at the physical but also the cultural and spiritual levels. Considering the individual to be a neuter entity is certainly not a suitable way of favouring the growth of life. An organic structure that each can incarnate in a manner which is singular but which also ensures a coexistence with the other, with others, more contributes to that. There is no doubt that our sexuate belonging is decisive in this connection, but its potential has been ignored and even repressed by culture. Hence paralyses happen in our becoming, which no longer finds how to develop for lack of a milieu which permits and supports our evolution beyond a mere physiological growth, this being in part unrecognized.

Indeed, what teaching accompanies the physical development of the child? Does an education exist which suits its sexuate belonging and its sexual awakening, as well as the disruptions of its puberty? Why are we surprised at the fact that sexual energy then expresses itself through violence, mimicry, domination or subjection, and a submission to the species often less culturally creative than in the animal world?

Amazingly, many scientists are interested in animal behaviours without much wondering about the impact of sexuation on them. However, some enigmatic aspects of these behaviours can be explained by sexual or procreative instincts that they do not question. In the same way, when they are surprised at the behaviour relating to objects, they go no further than the visible characters of these objects without wondering about the intervention of other senses or instincts and the interest that they arouse. Could the uncertain and disappointing effect of these objects not result from the fact that what is searched for is merely an image or a representation and not something which is necessary for the survival and the development of life, this process being stopped more than supported.

Another problematic aspect of the research of scientists is the little interest that they take in genetics. Most of their investigations concerning what is innate and what is acquired pay little attention to the genetic origin of the behaviours. And yet, if the genes are able to generate forms of our bodies, why could they not be behind modalities of our behaviours? Is not the specificity of some behaviours of a woman or a man at least in part related to their bodily forms and dependent on their hormones? Does the desire of the little girl for a doll obey a social stereotype or a natural instinct? Do our education systems—which maintain that they are in the neuter but, rather, are appropriate for masculine subjects—not amount to tools or modalities which paralyze or repress life? And does equality of women to men not mean imposing a kind of mimicry on women? Instead of developing their own nature towards a better fulfillment of themselves and of humanity, do women, then, not identify with those who are stronger, to those who, more or less aggressively, have appropriated culture in a sort of revenge on nature? In the animal world, is it not often the male which must seduce the female by his beauty and not the contrary?

How to Join Species to Genders?

The sexual, more generally the sexuate, behaviour represents a key to interpret many aspects of the passage from nature to culture. By paying greater attention to it, we probably will discover one of the main motivations of our evolution. Indeed, our sexuate belonging intervenes in the passage from the physical to the mental level through the relation to ourselves, but also to the other(s) and to the world. Beyond the fact that it can clarify what or whom a human being is and in what its becoming consists, sexual, and even sexuate, energy can act as a means of preventing and of curing certain illnesses—as I recently heard about Alzheimer's disease.

The sexuate dimension of the individual plays a crucial role in the passage from the inside to the outside, from the outside to the inside of the organism and of the subjectivity. Its embodiment requires the relationship between two different individuals to be respectful and reciprocal, thus it can represent a factor of community cohesion. We could even wonder whether this dimension cannot have a decisive function to interpret the symbolic order which governs the different cultures but also to elaborate a universal symbolic order capable of ensuring a better link between nature and culture in the construction of a world-wide community of living beings.

Sexuate belonging is so important that, in the absence of a partner of another sex, an individual of the same sex can compensate for the role of the other sex in the couple, as Jan Tinbergen notes about the animal world (cf. in La Nature, p. 258; Nature, pp. 198–99). The couple functions as an Umwelt without which living beings could not do. It functions as a mode of linkage between nature and culture, phusis and logos, which exists only in such a relation, such a configuration, in particular at the spatiotemporal level. For lack of the individuation which happens thanks to the couple, the living cannot develop all the potential of their being—this is cut back, fragmented, scattered, devitalized. Hence, the human being itself splits into nature and spirit, body and soul, and even subject and object, one and multiple and so forth according to a binary logic. It has lost the means to develop its life, which cannot correspond with a perception and a culture of life in general, as certain philosophers seem to believe. Such a culture can exist only as a culture of a singular life.

To speak of a unity of nature, of which we would be part—in a sort of assimilation of the inside with the outside, of the outside with the inside (cf. Merleau-Ponty in La Nature, pp. 263–68; Nature, pp. 203–208)— already implies our forgetting that each element of nature is a singular living being, that 'Nature' is not a whole of which every unity behaves only according to the functioning of the whole. This way of conceiving of nature is foreign to what the inside and even the outside of a living being are.

Humanity is generally viewed as species more than as genders, which amounts to a kind of inversion of our origin and cause. Indeed, species originates in genders and not the contrary. To put the stress on species leads to thinking of the human specificity by its differing from other species, and of the emergence of human beings as a phenomenon dependent on the environment—such an evolution would be above all reactive. If the stress is put on genders, a greater responsibility is incumbent on humans for their origin and their becoming. Hence, sexual desire, instead of being used above all for natural reproduction, can contribute to our individuation, also at the spiritual level, genders being a more decisive factor than genealogy for this sort of evolution.

Favouring species in comparison with genders is to grant us a mere ontic freedom within the limits of a basically ontological passivity and dependence. We do not give our being to us, we have fallen or have been thrown into being—or into Being, Heidegger perhaps would say. In that case, the dynamic potential of our nature—including in its ontological dimension—is destroyed or paralyzed. We are 'thrown' into an ecstasy from the real due to the forgetting of the ecstatic character of our origin: a woman or a man born of a conjunction of a woman with a man.

Privileging species in comparison with genders also runs the risk of differentiating human beings by their prevailing over other living beings—through a quantitative evaluation which does not really take account of their individuation and condemns them to a split between body and spirit. It is not through their physical strength that human beings prevail over animal species and if they claim to get the upper hand over animals by their spirit they risk being dominated at the physical level.

Genders introduce a split within the human species. If they are not only considered to be of use for ensuring the survival of the species, but to be a factor which contributes to our individuation, genders entail a division in the human species itself and a qualitative, and not only quantitative, assessment of the nature of human beings. At least it ought to be so if the intervention of a negative between the two genders in the definition of our human identity allows us to think of and to reshape our belonging to the human species in a more subtle and ethical way. Then it is no longer a question of superiority or domination of the human being over other kingdoms but of its ability to control itself, particularly with regard to its belonging to one gender, in order to elaborate a suitable culture of our natural difference, and of the assumption of the negative that it requires, towards the accomplishment of humanity.

A dialectical relation must exist between species and gender, gender and species, which allows the human being to acquire an identity of its own as man or woman without domination, if not over mere instincts. Such a dialectics grants human being the possibility of entering into relation with other species in a specifically human way, notably through assuming sexuation without reducing it to the reproduction of the species. So, humanity escapes a merely quantitative evaluation by its capability to adopt another mode of entering into relation, notably into sexual relations, thanks to a transformation of energy. The mediation of touch is a deciding factor to carry out this transformation.

Touch Does Not Stop at a Surface

Touch is not only, or primarily, an organ of prehension but, rather, of reception and communication. In a way, touch is the medium of every perception and communication—the means through which I can be in communication with myself, with the other(s) and with the world. However, touch as such is more than any other sense the medium of intimacy, the one which makes possible a communication or communion which is out of the other senses reach, because they are more subjected to exteriority and the necessary mediation of object(s). In that case, the communication between subjects needs to resort to sameness. According to Merleau-Ponty, what I can know of the other results from the fact that I perceive the same things in the same way, and that I communicate with this other through 'systems of equivalences', the content and the truth of our exchanges being dependent on a co-perception of one and the same world. Sameness is then the key which opens and closes up the possibility of a communication in which the other does not exist as other.

Entering into communication with the other as other can happen thanks to a communion which unites living beings with each other, the mediation of this communion being touch. It is touch which makes possible the passage from the outside to the inside, from the inside to the outside, of the body through self-affection and hetero-affection. But this touch does not stop at the skin, what is more a skin reduced to a surface, as most philosophers seem to imagine—it penetrates and unifies the whole being while remaining invisible and without any object, which does not mean without intention. To be effective as mediation, touch needs difference instead of sameness. As such, it is difficult to define it, furthermore a priori.

This touch seems to be ignored or misjudged in our tradition. When they allude to it, philosophers generally go no further than skin and inter-action between touch and sight, which prevents touch from being per-ceived as penetrating and acting beyond the skin. For example, Merleau-Ponty distinguishes between a language of the body as visible and a language of ideality as invisible. And yet, the latter is based above all on sight, at least in our metaphysical tradition, whereas the language of the body remains invisible as far as intimate feeling and communion are concerned. The most absolute of carnal desire and amorous feelings does not express itself at a visible level. It is lived and communicated or communed in the invisible thanks to the mediation of touch. Obviously, the other is and must stay outside us, but this other also touches us and addresses an invisible in us, where an amorous exchange takes place. A fleshly sharing corresponds to a communication or communion prior to discourse, even about the invisible. Does an articulate language not aim to subject to the visible what must remain invisible—to subject touch to sight?

We still lack an articulate language able to help touch to communicate or commune in the invisible. This is one of the reasons of our amorous distresses, but also of problems relative to the constitution of a commu-nity, notably a political one. Hence, we create milieus and environ-ments—kinds of *Umwelt*—which try to express that which we cannot communicate or commune between or among ourselves. Then what ought to contribute to an intimate exchange in some way exposes itself and freezes.

Consequently, the alternative between touching and being touched is not overcome by a passage to mucous tissues—as is the case in Merleau-Ponty's work. For him, it seems to be difficult, and even impossible, to be both touching and touched. Now, when touch has to do with mucous tissues, the two cannot be distinguished. Already, when the palms of our hands touch, they are both touching and touched. Undoubtedly, the passage to a mucous touching deprives the philosopher of being only active, and our tradition views subjectivity as activity. The subject would differ from the world by activity and not by a specifically human way of being passive.

Thus, for Merleau-Ponty, the fact that we can be both active and passive does not involve access to a most intimate of the self but a tearing of the self. The passage to a mucous touch as well as certain feelings, for example the amorous feeling, allow us to escape such a tearing because they entail both activity and passivity. It seems that, with regard to what is external to him, the philosopher knows above all relations to things but not to autonomous living beings, in particular to those which differ from him by nature—hence a lack of differentiation from the world, outside or inside himself, immersed in a world which is immersed in him. For Merleau-Ponty, the relationship with the other does not experience the communion between two living beings independent of one another. This relationship only exists thanks to sameness—I touch the hand of the other as I touch my own hand. Then I do not ouch the other as other but, at best, as a thing belonging to the same world as mine. The mediating potential of touch is thus deleted.

In order to touch the other as other, the 'natural symbolism' that my body is must be able to join together with a cultural symbolism—which does not mean with the 'conventional symbolism' of an already articulate language. I must perceive and recognize the other as a body speaking to itself and to me—an already spiritualized body. This does not happen through the sharing of 'systems of equivalences' but through perceiving my body and the body of the other as fleshes of their own.

To have access to such a mode of communication, which is not determined by similarity, socio-cultural agreements or supra sensitive ideals, sexuation seems to be a necessary structuring. Is it not a sexuate desire which allows us to link an indistinct and little differentiated physical symbolism with a linguistic code, and even a 'conventional language', so that we could communicate with one another? (cf. *La Nature*, p. 289; *Nature*, pp. 226–27). Thus they are henceforth two sexuate physical or natural logos which communicate with each other. However, is not my desire for the other naturally different from me which authorizes me to unite nature and culture, in myself and between us? Is it not this desire which makes my body the original place of a symbolic world in which a meaning for me can also be a meaning for the other? Does nature not find in it a kind of teleology and culture a non artificial origin and motive of existing? Is it not that which can allow nature and a 'wild spirit' to become incarnate in us and between us instead of settling in 'things' of the world for lack of having been able to do otherwise? (idem).

The Micro-Milieu of the Relation of Couple

To become incarnate means either taking form(s) from nature or imposing constructed form(s) on the natural life. In the first case, it is rather a matter of generation and, in the second case, a matter of creation. In generation developing remains possible from life itself; in creation, the development is often subjected to forms extraneous to the living from which life evolves indirectly or becomes paralyzed.

Generation has more to do with the potential of life itself which becomes actualized thanks to an event, a meeting or a crossing with other living beings in a continuum which is neither pre-established nor really linear. Creation, as for it, is often a solitary process the plan or intention of which interrupts the development of life itself, depriving it of the fecundity of the sap which permeates living beings. Human becoming is torn apart between these alternatives. The place of their possible articulation can be identified with difficulty; it is discovered little by little, notably on occasion of an amorous meeting. Then potentialities of life are reopened which need a creative contribution to develop and be shared. The revelation of such potentialities represents the origin of a not yet existing culture of which we are in charge as human beings. Being a human does not consist in joining a pre-established culture and world, but in constantly weaving together natural generation and contribution to its development, its blossoming and its sharing through creation. This asks an energy of which the aim—one could say *entelechia*—goes in such a direction. This energy is brought to us by life, but that is not sufficient if life is nothing more than a neuter flux lacking in differentiation. Life must become incarnate in singular beings and correspond with an intention which remains natural. Is it not there a question of desire, its most accomplished form being the desire for the naturally different other?

Does this desire not amount to a human means of pursuing the growing of life? Hence, the emergence of a specific living being generated by a relation, which can be also creative, between the genera or genders, each taking charge of the achievement of the species by a sharing of desire—an *entelechia* which rests faithful to a nature that we must incarnate in a true human way. Then the natural teleology no longer holds on to supra sensitive ideals with a view to a fulfilment of humanity which can only take place beyond our physical existence, but it aims, at each time, at an accomplishment of our being as human through the relationship between two different incarnations of humanity. In such a place, our natural and our spiritual potentials can be linked together. Going no further than a natural potential, confining ourselves to instincts or reproduction, or to supra sensitive potentials does not permit us to achieve the humans that we are. We must overcome such a split and it is desire which allows us to do that by creating bridges between the physical and the meta-physical, and between ourselves and the other(s).

Desire can also allow us to contribute to an evolution of humanity by freely assuming the natural determination that sexuation represents towards the fulfilment of the human species. If a selection exists, it is through the choice of what favours our development by a common creation, which less cares about eliminating than about integrating the properties and qualities which contribute to uniting our natural with our spiritual parts by the respect for mutual difference(s). In the evolution of the human species, it is no longer the impact of the environment and our ability to adapt ourselves to it which are more determining but our capability of liberating ourselves from a pre-given or an already constructed environment in order to create an environment which is more suitable for the becoming of the species. And what is mainly at stake is not the mere perpetuation of the species but its not yet happened accomplishment, in particular concerning what it can become taking account of the creative, and not only reproductive, potential of the genders. This leads to our wondering about the manner of carrying out such a potential. Contenting ourselves with one-multiple relations cannot succeed in that because this potential is first discovered and incarnated between two. Our culture more often than not does not cultivate, and even despises, this relationship, which amounts to depriving human being of a great part of its potentialities. Indeed, it is in this relationship that our natural belonging can become spiritual while remaining faithful to our nature. The natural and the spiritual unite their potentialities without sacrificing or subjecting the ones to the others if desire exists and is cultivated between two subjects faithful to their own nature, which they transform by their union. Such a work creates the ground as well as the space and the temporality which make possible an evolution favourable to an accomplishment of humanity in which physical belonging subsists while being spiritualized. This transformation brings about a modification of the relation to space by rendering matter more subtle. This solves some recurrent questions in the thinking of certain philosophers, among others Merleau-Ponty, about the spatial, the trans-spatial and the meta-spatial, and some perplexities regarding the difference between place and field (cf. *La Nature*, p. 307 and sq.; *Nature*, p. 243 and following pages).

To overcome the dichotomy between natural growth and cultural construction, we need a culture which corresponds with our natural identity. However, our evolution cannot be merely dependent on the existing milieu, it must also result from an evolution of being itself, be it individual, collective or environmental—which requires the contribution of the spiritual, but a spiritual faithful to our natural identity. We can reach it through our desire for another living being, especially a different human being.

The 'great number', which is presupposed to intervene in our evolution, cannot bring this sort of evolution. For us, as humans, the matter rather is of carrying out the qualitative transformation of the relationship between two humans who are naturally different towards their own evolution and that of humanity itself. This evolution can occur through an alternation of an opening up to the other and a withdrawal into oneself, which must first take place in the relationship between two different living beings. The evolutive potential of this kind of relationship is still misjudged.

Part II

Domination of Spirit over Soul

5

The Burial of Touch

Desire Aspires After the Beyond

Human evolution cannot be only quantitative, depending on 'the great number' or on a greater pressure of the environment. It requires the ability of the human being to act on the core of its original being and of its dynamism. The possibility of such an action, of such an inter-fecundity, exists in the couple as a relationship between two individuals but not between groups (cf. *La Nature,* p. 314; *Nature,* p. 248). Indeed, in this case, the split between nature and culture cannot be overcome. In the group, as in the community, the passage from the natural identity to the cultural identity cannot happen, as it can in the couple, because the relation to the body as a both natural and spiritual entity is dissolved or is transformed into cultural essence(s).

Adaptation as a factor of evolution also raises a problem with regard to the couple. What adaptation would be suitable? If it is a matter of an adaptation to the milieu, this could run the risk of not favouring the couple as such. And if it is a matter of the adaptation of one member of the couple to the other, the difference between the two, which has caused the desire, will disappear. Then man and woman long less for their union,

L. Irigaray, *The Mediation of Touch*, https://doi.org/10.1007/978-3-031-37413-5_5

notably as a feeling nostalgic for their origin and possible rebirth, than for an adjustment of their love towards its survival or its transformation into a parental relation.

The relationship of the couple must instead care about how to harmonize different desires, which requires faithfulness to one's self and modification of the aspiration, but without identification with or assimilation to one another. Desire must remain aspiration after a beyond to the self, after transcendence; it must adjust itself to both immanence and transcendence. It must also take account of centripetal and centrifugal forces and exceed their mere alternative or alternation by creating a relation between their ways of intervening in each. If the other can be a support of our longing for the absolute, this other cannot for all that incarnate it as such and the relationship must care about maintaining alive the longing for the absolute in each and between the two. The relation to the other must support the longing for the absolute without ever fulfilling it, at least completely.

The fact that our longing for the absolute is an important issue in our desire for the other can contribute to uniting our body with our spirit. The passage from the natural growing to the spiritual becoming is so ensured—or the 'joint', Merleau Ponty perhaps would say, between the physical and the meta-physical, thanks to our faithfulness to a 'primordial gestaltung' (cf. *La Nature*, p. 323; *Nature*, p. 256). What brings joy to us—joy of being and of sharing being.

For lack of discovering such a 'joint' or articulation, we stay at a genealogical level, either merely natural or transformed into a hierarchy of values extraneous to a real incarnation of our own. Hence, we approach the accomplishment after which we aspire only in an imitative way. It would remain out of our reach, and we would keep it on hold or entrust it to God or some other authority, without taking charge of achieving our human destiny. Consequently, our way of conceiving of our existence in its horizontal dimension becomes nihilistic, and we would be reduced to more or less homogeneous and autonomous atoms which lack a dynamism of their own—or the 'sublime absence of purpose' that experiencing life sometimes grants us. The vital and dynamic core of the human being no longer would be in itself, and its desire to provide itself with a finality corresponding with its origin. It would misjudge and cancel its own potential by extrapolating it into supra sensitive ideals.

And yet our sensitivity can help us to sense what our being could be and unveil something of it to us (cf. *La Nature,* p. 335; *Nature,* p. 268). But how could we contribute to this unveiling? Certainly this cannot happen by mistaking the world with a kind of external circuit with regard to our being, as most philosophers and still, for example, Merleau-Ponty, do. In such an exteriority, which sometimes invades or crosses us, we spread ourselves or freeze in a presumed objectivity. We lack a sort of short circuit in which we invest our being, a circuit that, in a way, it produces and which sends it back to itself—which the relationship with the other can represent. This relation allows us to pass from the inside to the outside, from the outside to the inside, in our search for our being, a being of which the in-itself remains inaccessible but can little by little be perceived through such a relation. Thanks to it, we can go from a physical to a spiritual sensitivity without, for all that, interrupting the continuum of our becoming. And the respect for the other as different from us also opens and maintains in us the space—the hollow or the cavity—in which this evolution can take place.

Such an evolution requires a constant passage from self-affection to hetero-affection. But touch to which Western philosophers allude does not give rise to a self-affection which reveals to us the being that we are— it is too external to our self and lacks the modes of touching-being touched that the mucous tissues make possible. So the touching of my lips, of my eyelids, of the palms of my hands and even of my feet has nothing to do with the 'figurative reflection' of which Merleau-Ponty and other philosophers speak about 'touching oneself', 'touching one another' or 'seeing oneself touching oneself', in which touch is already 'colonized' by sight. It does not act as the tactile as such can do.

On pain of reducing it to what it is not, touch is extraneous to sight. And when 'I see myself touching myself', it is no longer a question of touch but of the attempt to establish a phenomenology of touch in a traditional way. In this gesture, the fact that touch is both active and passive is called into question. The look, at least the one of which the philosopher speaks, is more active than passive and it impedes the mediating function of touch to be effective. If Merleau-Ponty considers the reciprocity between touching and being touched to be an access to humanity, why does he not favour this process without subjecting it to the reflection of seeing? Does he not sterilize in that way our becoming human? Whereas he seems to take interest in incarnation, does he not fall back again into a meta-physical supra sensitiveness to which his eye is, whatever his opinion, the accomplice? Does he not neglect a bodily morphology, and the mucous intimacy that it makes possible, to privilege visible forms which have more similarities to idealities?

Does Merleau-Ponty not miss the path towards the blossoming of sensitivity through its cultivation and its sharing? For lack of perceiving, cultivating and sharing a tactile mucous intimacy, does he not substitute for it a traditional metaphysical interiority? Hence, the exteriority of the self becomes, for him, a kind of more or less autistic parade (cf. *La Nature*, p. 337; *Nature*, p. 270) and not the amorous expression of an intimate awakening, of a secret efflorescence of the being in search of a reciprocity of touch. Such an interpretation differs from the one relative to stimulus and information that our tradition favoured even if it more mobilizes and unifies the totality of our being. Instead of being the result of a mastery— of the own self, of the other, of the world—by sight and the most cortical part of our being, it then happens through a comprehensive relation to and with the other, a relation in which the whole of our body as well as the whole of our brain are involved. Transcendence no longer corresponds to a domination of a meta-physical nature but to the respect for the irreducible difference of the other that even our organism can perceive.

What grants perspective to the immanence of touch is first the transcendence of the other. The action of touch cannot be completely interpreted by the higher brain, by understanding. Respecting the alterity of the other mobilizes a more comprehensive structure, both active and passive, sensitive and mental, and which is more able to value the relevance of touch—for oneself, for the other and for the relationship. This means having access to another economy of thinking in which order and regulation are not dependent on understanding but are required by the development of nature itself. The way of establishing meaning and the link between significations, but also the rhythm, the spatiality and the temporality are then different.

Henceforth, what determines the meaning, the logic and the unfolding of thinking is a question of structure more than a question of stimulus. And this structure is biface, turned towards oneself but also turned towards the other and towards the world. There is no ambiguity of meaning but a double meaning—a for-oneself and a for-the-other which do not unite a priori with one another, naturally or culturally. To bring them together asks us to clear our way towards a truth until now ignored. Desire is the transcendental intention which can guide us in our search of its unveiling, a desire which has more to do with touch than with sight.

Reciprocity of the Transcendental

Sight stops our thirst for the absolute by fixing forms, by objectifying, whereas touch revives and feeds it. It does not amount to an appropriation, as some philosophers would like, but, rather, to a sort of compassion in the longing for the absolute. It is an experiencing oneself that the other supports, unveils, without freezing it in exteriority, in fragments, in object(s) or representation(s). And if the other takes part in the perception of touch, this cannot be as a mirror, which merely reflects an image, but as an awakening, a recall, a com-passion or a communion. Touch reveals and builds an interiority that sight extrapolates into exteriority. The lover is, or ought to be, the conveyor between exteriority and interiority of the self. The lover ought also to be the mediator in the perception of desire and love as the objective, but not the objectal, embodiment of the subjectivity of being.

The lover is the one who brings us back to ourselves as longing for the transcendence that he or she incarnates for us. There is not an 'insertion in the world' which reveals to us our hand or our body, as Merleau-Ponty seems to believe, but a tactile meeting with the other. The mediation of touch, then, becomes a factor of transcendence, of distance.

A dialectics of sensitivity relative to touch has first to do with spatiality. It must join the closest to the most distant, the most intimate of the self to the most intimate of the self of the other and their conjunction in the transcendence of desire. This process no longer prioritizes a temporal relation to object(s) but a spatial relation between subjects. This takes place without any object or implement external to the body—for example a mirror or a phallus objectified as such—but only through resorting to the perception, a shared perception.

Through such a dialectical process regarding a tactile sharing, I shield my body from a lack of differentiation from the world by leading it to a communication, even a communion, between individuations. Tactile perception does not need images to become unified, it itself brings a living unity. Where sight analyzes, touch synthesizes; it searches for uniting or communing and not for capturing unless it is subjected to a traditional logic. Touch is without object—it searches for feeling oneself or one another towards being.

Sexuation represents a privileged structure and place for feeling oneself as it aims at uniting the inside with the outside, the mucous tissues with the skin—and even the matter with the form(s), the soma with the germ cells. It is in search of the blossoming of the self before being an instinct of reproduction or an aspiration after mere pleasure. It is mediation, revelation, unification and union as regards being(s). It has not another 'entelechia', which does not mean that it lacks finality. It leads the feeling to ecstasy without resorting to supra sensitive ideals. And it corresponds to a second consciousness, of which Freud contests the possible existence. It is, in particular, consciousness of the other in oneself (cf. *La Nature,* pp. 351–52; *Nature,* pp. 283–84), and above all consciousness of the necessity of uniting with the other as other—consciousness of the positive character of difference and an assumption of the negative to accomplish one's own 'to be'. Thus it gives up an immediate feeling in order to sense and to attempt to reach being as an ecstasy-instasy of a feeling which renounces any object to conjoin to a different subject. Hence sensitivity is no longer the occasion and the place of a solitary, not to say a solipsistic, appropriation, but of an awakening and a surge to overstep the closure of a body, of a self, without, for all that, falling into the lack of differentiation of the common.

Indeed, 'Nature' does not exist, only natural beings exist which have each a life of their own—if not they are no longer natural. And the cause of this life is not 'Nature' but a conjunction between two living beings— at least between two living seeds—that we, as humans, must assume as our natural origin. As such, this origin is also a historical event which is likely to evolve. It corresponds to a relation which takes place at a moment of history. Nevertheless, the memory of my natural belonging is not first reflexive, as Merleau-Ponty seems to claim (*La Nature,* pp. 365–67 in Appendices which do not exist in the Anglophone version), but it is dependent on a bodily imprint. My body remembers my nature, and if it was not the case I could not truly exist. My body also remembers the other as nature, which sends it back to itself. Understanding, as for it, is not really capable of doing that.

Nature is not a whole which lacks differentiation or a sensitive unity—it is a gathering of living singularities in becoming. Each singularity is unique and is not an other. Each natural being assumes the fact of not being the other. It exists while accepting not being what it is not. One could say that nature does not know nothingness, this substantivization of the not-being what each is not. Natural life assumes the non-being the other and develops from such limits. Natural beings have nothing to deny because they exist from their particularity, even their singularity. They must be faithful to them and concentrate, gather themselves together in their own being and becoming without indefinitely spreading, dispersing or altering. This permits their development without resorting to supra sensitive values, in which nothingness hides.

Natural beings do not need the unity that understanding provides. They exist as singular units, which develop according to forms which correspond to their materiality. Desire is that which allows us to coordinate them, in particular the desire for a naturally different human. Our natural belonging has an in-itself existence as it is living, but if this in-itself is objective it is not reducible to an object, notably because life is and moves by itself. In addition to that, human subjectivity possibly has the faculty for perceiving, assuming and transforming our existence as a whole. But, in order that this existence should not be artificial, it must conform to a natural belonging.

A dialectical process relative to the in-itself and the for-itself of our natural existence can be actualized in/through sharing desire with a naturally different human thanks to assuming this difference. Causality and totality are then reconciled with a finality which corresponds to our more or less conscious will to accomplish our species—humanity. Desire is either degeneration of our human belonging or its accomplishment. This cannot happen without a dialectical cultivation of the link between nature and culture that desire, in particular sexuate desire, can represent and can carry out. To contribute to the blossoming of our natural being, desire must take account of our being born of difference—of a conjunction between two different living beings, originally two different germ cells, that we cannot apprehend.

Our desire for the absolute in part arises from the elusiveness of our origin. This desire is dialectical in itself as it includes alterity, difference and negative on pain of not existing or being kept on hold by supra sensitive ideals. Desire also entails a complex, and in a way dialectical, relation to temporality. It exists in the present as in that which it transcends but it needs to become incarnate. Desire wants both to become incarnate and to exceed every incarnation towards a more subtle incarnation of our global being, especially as regards its relational dimension. Besides, desire makes more complex the present, as every temporality, by bringing to it, to them, a density likely to evolve.

Desire must also be subjected to a dialectical process between the one, the two and the multiple. A desire which gets lost in an interweaving of relations without any return to the self does not truly correspond to a human desire and to its potential. It dissolves into a plurality more and more disembodied, and it so runs the risk of becoming more nihilistic than its being put on hold by supra-sensitive ideals. Indeed, it is involved in their effects and other human constructions without keeping the dynamism capable of linking our natural to our cultural belonging.

Buried in the Common

Desire, as all which has to do with what is connected with flesh, has little been considered an objective reality happening here and now. From that results its assimilation to, not to say its disappearance into, a 'pre-constitution', an 'archaism' or a 'primitivism' of subjectivity or into the intention which, imperceptibly, animates consciousness. Its intervention, in a way its presence, here and now, as that which inhabits and moves subjectivity has not been really acknowledged. The body would be the cause of an 'I can' (*La Nature*, pp. 106–107; *Nature*, pp. 74–5). But the main factor acting in this 'I can', our desire, has been neglected. This probably results from the split between the body and the soul which prevents us from inhabiting ourselves, lost in a natural or a conceptual universal.

Without being faithful to what originates in us and re-centers us, while opening us up to the outside, we are unable to assume our individuation and to respect that of the other(s). Consequently, we ought to perceive, both ourselves and others, through the same artificially elaborate perceptive device, which objectifies and reifies what we perceive, including ourselves. Then we could perceive neither ourselves nor by ourselves another living being while respecting it as a specific self. It would be in the same way that we perceive a singular other and all others. An autonomy of living beings perceiving and perceiving each other thanks to a sensitiveness peculiar to each no longer would exist. To establish a reality of touch, it ought to be experienced as common. Thus the truth of the sensitive, never a priori common, would be sacrificed to constructed processes of apperception concerning truth itself. So a real disappears as well as its/the individual sensitive perception, in an 'earlier layer', a kind of earth-flesh 'pre-objective' occurring before the 'manifest being' as a sort of original existence or of a secret truth concealed in fleshly bodies—a 'natural layer in which the spirit would be in a way buried in the common functioning of bodies in the midst of the raw being' (op. cit., p. 367 in Appendices which do not exist in the Anglophone version). All that seems to be the still unthought admission of the flesh, and thus of the objectivity of an incarnate subjectivity, subjected to a presumed common existence in order to be apprehended.

Nature as well as human subjectivity are extrapolated from the living in order to be, next, subjected to an unveiling protocol regarding truth. Nature is reduced to an amorphous matter or content of which the common apprehension would reveal truth by giving form(s) to it. This forgets that every living being produces its own forms and that these are specific to a species, become incarnate in a specific way in each individual, firstly according to its genus.

Nature does not amount to a blind production, but it contributes to the birth and the growth of the individual being—vegetal, animal or human—towards the blossoming of its own forms. That is the teleology which animates a natural development. It is not pre-objective but it is difficult to apprehend it through the scientific protocols that we know. Claiming that what is common allows us to perceive such a natural process is reducing it to a moment of its becoming and subjecting it to another teleology than its own without apprehending and thinking of it as it truly is. A natural growth is never common, it is strictly individual, unless we assimilate it to what drives a robot or to the both undifferentiated and more or less artificially produced energy which animates the society.

Life as being cannot directly be grasped. It is only indirectly, through its manifestations, that we can perceive and say something about it. We can also let ourselves be touched by it and compare what a natural being—for example a tree—produces in us with what a fabricated being—for example a table—produces. Through perceiving this difference, we distinguish an animate or living being from an inanimate or made being. The relationship that we can have with the one or the other is not the same.

Some structures favour the relationship between living beings. The traditional privilege which is attached to sight does not go in such a direction. We more easily reach this relationship through touch, be this touch physical or even spiritual. Our sexuate belonging also implies being in relationship with other living beings. It corresponds to a natural morphology and dynamism which are often thwarted by constructed structures which fade perceptions, sensations and surges.

Our sexuate belonging longs for touch, and a reciprocal touch, which has something to do with the imperceptible growth of life. We long for touching one another to perceive us as alive and give life to one another. We also aspire after touching one another with our becoming in mind. Our organism itself includes a potential which compels us to exceed what or whom we already are. This potential originates in us but tries to become true through and with the other. Desire represents a teleology of nature which is in search of its development beyond the being from which it arises. This amounts neither to a mere mechanism nor to an idealist claim but to a process which joins the outside and the inside of the organism. Our sexuation and the morphology which corresponds to it means that the teleology which animates our organism is not without order. Desire does not attract us outside of ourselves without a regulative principle. If we listen to our desire as it arises in our body, we will note that it is in search of a becoming of life which cannot be depended on anyhow—it must participate in the development of life. In order to act in that way, it cannot only obey a spatial spreading, but it must also involve a temporal growing which respects the rhythms peculiar to a species but also to a gender.

Desire can also contribute to the evolution of the species by respecting the life of the self, of the other and of the world, which presupposes a certain economy of space and time. We can, and even must, constantly contribute to that evolution notably by taking charge of our being. The latter has too often been interpreted as a production of consciousness which would ignore or dismiss what concerns our bodily and sensitive belonging. And yet a consciousness of sensitivity exists. In the process of self-affection, the fact of combining feeling and felt means that I perceive myself without this perception, in a way conscious, obeying the criteria by which we usually define consciousness. I am conscious of my being but in a still indeterminate way. Thanks to the mould and material of consciousness, I also can perceive the other as sensitive, not because this other is the same as myself and through a system of equivalences, as Merleau-Ponty maintains, but because this other also has a natural belonging, a body and, thus, we can communicate as sensitive beings.

The most accomplished modality of such a relationship is probably communing, but this is possible only after recognizing the otherness of the other, which excludes fusion, incorporation, domination or subjection of the one by the other. Sharing communion seems to be the most achieved way of communicating between subjectivities, but it implies an economy of consciousness of which our tradition is still unaware or that it misjudges. It is the perceiving itself, a tactile perceiving, which, regardless of any externalization, objectivization or representation acts as mediation. So the other can be perceived by me—and sometimes better than this other can perceive himself or herself—and they can also perceive me. The communion between us takes place thanks to a complex articulation between the being that I perceive through self-affection and the being that the other perceives, as well as between the own being that the other perceives and the one that I perceive with regard to this other. If our traditional consciousness does not permit such an articulation, our sensitive consciousness sometimes seems to have access to it, perhaps thanks to the simultaneity between a skin touch and a mucous touch which establishes a connection between the different modes of being conscious.

A fleshly thought needs to resort to another consciousness than the one that we know. This cannot amount to a sending back to a Freudian unconscious which only exists as a complement of our traditional consciousness. A consciousness of flesh is a consciousness the meaning of which is determined by touch more than by sight. And this entails another economy, notably regarding space and time.

Such a consciousness also corresponds to another perception of the real. For lack of taking account of this other way of being conscious, we are unable to perceive the real as it truly is. We can reach that only through perceiving ourselves as what and who we are by a return to our sensitive self, especially our tactile self thanks to self-affection.

When to Be Becomes a Substantive

Heidegger's long comment in the beginning of his *Introduction to Metaphysics* concerning the question 'why there is being rather than nothing' mingles an affective dimension, which is not recognized as such, with an interrogation where it is groundless. Indeed, Heidegger's question supposedly concerns the status of 'to be' itself, whereas it takes place within a logical economy in which 'to be' is already transformed into a certain sort of being by the discourse. Hence the question is relative to this sort of being and not to 'to be' itself. It mistakes what is according to the logos for what is by itself or in itself. A fundamental logical operation focusing on the existence of 'to be' is then reduced to an element of discourse: a substantive—nothing, nothingness—or an adjective—disquieting, distressing, bad. The role of negation which is, or ought to be, to determine whether 'it is' or 'it is not' no longer exists. Thus it cannot be decided on what is or what is not. Being or not being are defined according to their status and situation in the logos and not according to the existence or not existence of their being.

On this subject, Heidegger speaks of the necessity of a 'leap' supposedly due to the parallelism between the real and the logos. It would be sufficient to give up the net that the logos is in order to try to rediscover the background or original sense that the logos claims to express, unless it resurfaces by itself. Sexuate difference which articulates the real and the logos, constantly accomplishes this leap or makes it useless. It crosses the distance between the real and its discursive expression towards a conjunction between two different beings.

The nature of being is not the same in the two cases. Perhaps Heidegger is in search of a real that the logos cannot express and for which it substitutes another real that the logos produces, notably through a logical articulation. Then the real remains ignored and only a 'leap' and an abandon to what exists prior to the logos would allow us to find it again. Does this search not transform 'to be' into a sort of thing, into a substantive, a name, even possibly into an essence, whereas the relationship between two human beings is in search of 'to be' as a conjunction? It is a colonging for 'to be' as a verb and not for a substantive. If Heidegger reopens, vertically, the closure of the logos by a 'leap' and the abandon to the substantive corresponding to an unnamed being, sexuate difference permits reopening horizontally this closure through abandoning ourselves to life in becoming between us that uniting with each other can bring to us.

Our being, even natural, does not correspond to a mere substance. It arises from a con-joining in search of an original conjunction. As such it cannot be held to be either a divine self-creation or the outcome of a relation to more or less appropriate predicates. It is in con-joining with another subject that something of 'to be' can happen.

In other words, Heidegger seems, unwillingly, to conceive of 'to be' as a substantive, a constructed essence, fruit of an unrecognized copulation, whereas sexuate difference permits the copula to save its status of conjunctive verb—to be. Through the maintenance of 'to be' as copula, the negation, as an adverb, recovers its meaning, but it loses it when 'to be' freezes in the essence of a substantive. Affirming that I am not the other which differs from me by nature has a meaning that speaking of non-being no longer has with respect to 'to be'.

Philosophy intends to worry about the totality of beings. In that way, it transforms our living being into an ontological construction in which 'to be' has lost its status and role of copula or conjunction between us and our self, us and the other, us and the world. When the truth at which philosophy aims and it maintains that it is the one of a people, or a truth inscribed on and conveyed by history, in fact this truth already amounts to a construction concerning 'to be' which no longer takes our living being into account. It results from a fabrication based on representations.

What happens when the other as naturally different from us stands before us there where the representation ought to be positioned according to philosophy? Either the other or philosophy loses a possible true existence—and even whatever real existence. That is the dilemma which faces us today and compels us to elaborate a logic allowing a dialectical process between the living being situated before us and the being corresponding with representation. How could the truth that philosophy pretends to discover and to pass on not be the bloodless product of the artificial transformation of the flesh of the other, and also of our own—a flesh only existing through its relation with another flesh?

How to acknowledge that the most original and radical questioning comes from the other and not from a historical horizon which sends back to us a sort of echo of what of our being remains unaccomplished in our productions and projections? How to return to the truth of this being not only by questioning the relation to our own origin, but also by letting ourselves be questioned by the other which is naturally different from us? Could this not be a path to recover a unity of our being which makes its becoming possible anew? Indeed the split between the body and the soul, which our culture has caused, has paralyzed the dynamism peculiar to the human being which can contribute to its blossoming.

The question for us today is not of simply going back to the body, to what is merely physical, but of discovering how to unite in ourselves and by ourselves the physical and the metaphysical in a constant movement towards the blossoming of our being. Indeed to be cannot be viewed only as to dwell, as Heidegger seems to think (cf. *Introduction to Metaphysics,* p. 27; *Introduction to Metaphysics,* pp. 15–6). *Phusis* entails becoming or it no longer exists—to be implies to become or it is not. However, this becoming as well as this blossoming are not necessarily visible. The opposition, even the distinction, between to be and to become is relevant only for the one who has already forgotten what *phusis* is, and who conceives of being and the world only as fabricated and animated by a becoming artificially produced. To be and to become ought to amount to a unique thing and to become be the gradual actualization of our natural and original potential.

The problem is that to be is more and more confused with being. Instead of considering to be that which has a dynamism of its own and becomes by itself, to be is said about a production at least in part fabricated and which paralyzes an original energy. A way out of this impasse concerning 'to be' would be to return to being as living. So we go back to our natural belonging, a belonging to which we must permit and even give an appropriate development.

The being without natural origin, but produced by a human making, traps us in a kind of labyrinth in which we no longer succeed in defining the difference between 'to be' and being. It only remains to us to interrogate being as such, so answering the question put by Heidegger in *Introduction to Metaphysics* (*Introduction à la métaphysique,* pp. 30–1; *Introduction to Metaphysics,* pp. 19–20), by considering this being a historical production which more and more conceals 'to be' from us, freezing it in constructed essence(s) for lack of acknowledging and cultivating its origin, in a way its essence, as living. On this subject, it is possible to distinguish two ways of thinking of essence: the transcendental and the ecstatic.

Animate and Inanimate

Increasingly, our culture mistook the animate for the inanimate, that is, what moves and develops by itself for what is fabricated. Then the questioning about 'to be', and even Being, confuses an interrogation relative to being as living with an interrogation relative to being as fabricated. And yet it is not a question of the same reality, and such assimilation leads to a confusion from which the philosophers, in particular those who attempt to overcome a traditional metaphysics, seem to be unable to free themselves. The distinction between Being—or 'to be'—and being, about which Heidegger never stops questioning, according to me, is based on a way of conceiving of 'to be' and being which makes this questioning insoluble. In what Heidegger designates as being something of 'to be', or Being, is already invested and paralyzed which, instead of being left to its own development—its *phuein*—is subjected to a supposedly unchanging accomplishment—to an idea concerning its complete un-latency. In fact, this questioning ought to be pre-cultural and returns to the origin of our living being. The question about being, according to Heidegger, is, or ought to be, a question about the evolution that our culture has imposed on the living—an evolution which, at the level of discourse, is expressed by the transformation of a verb, to be (in French 'être'), into a substantive Being (in French 'l'être') opposed to another substantive—nothingness—both being situated at the same semantic and syntactic level.

Indeed, the presumed existence of nothingness results from a double operation: the negation of a verb 'to be', not to be, and its transformation into a substantive 'nothingness'—which amounts to a sort of being. Assembling all beings in a totality engenders or presupposes a Being—Être—which opposes 'not to be' or 'non Being' or nothingness. And if a living being exists—for example, a tree—nothingness is produced by human being and results from its pretension to creating the 'to be' or Being of the whole of beings. A living being exists by itself, and it is not possible to establish the totality of beings because they are not situated at the same level of being and existing, and they have not the same link between them if they are living or fabricated—beyond the fact that the living beings evolve.

The creation of beings and their assembling in a world has been attributed to God, which has permitted confusing the living with the fabricated. The traditional way of conceiving of God, as well as the substitution of man for such God, has led to a nihilism from which we cannot free ourselves without thinking in a different way of the nature of being—and of 'to be'. This is possible only thanks to a return to our being as living, a living being not subjected to the creation of its being or to its subordination to some or other plan, project or model. This living being, engendered and not created, becomes or fades; it corresponds to a natural essence that it makes or not blossom. Its relation to other beings is what contributes to this blossoming.

The gathering of some beings can be made up only according to imperatives which are the concern of a culture of life. Being cannot oppose what permits and establishes bonds between the different living beings. Non-being challenges such links—hence the allocation of every being to a constructed identity towards the institution of other links. The negation applying to the 'to be' of the living determines the limits of each peculiar being, which allows it to develop as what or who it is. In that case, the negation does not apply to an already constructed being, as the one of which Heidegger speaks (op. cit., p. 35 and sq.; op. cit., p. 25 and following) but to a naturally engendered being on the existence of which we cannot decide by ourselves. On this subject, some philosophers appeal to God, and others to the power of man to arbitrate on the totality of beings. These two options deserve a questioning about another origin: that of a conjunction between two siring and that which we give to ourselves through our first breathing when we come into the world. Nevertheless, any of these origins is completely ours. It is not a matter for all that of waving between the one and the other—as Heidegger suggests about being (op. cit., p. 40; op. cit. p. 30)—but of assuming the non-being that I originally am. I am neither the conjunction of which I was born nor the cultural essence which is assigned to me as a woman, but I must ensure the existence and the development of my natural being. My natural essence is the result of a conjunction but this gives rise to the 'to be' that I am, and to which I must give existence. The question of my origin as being is what opens up to the space of a possible becoming of which I have charge.

To be must keep the status of a verb which tries, retrospectively, to determine the provenance of the subject. But this subject was born of a copulation, not between him and appropriate predicates, but between two naturally different subjects, and a copulation which happens between germ cells more than between somas. As a product of the union between two different germ cells, a living being must accomplish its own germination. To be, as a linguistic copula, takes part in this germination through the adequacy of predicates which are attributed to the subject. But the latter exists as such before this both retroactive and prospective process.

To be cannot concern the union between two subjects only at an ontical level because such a union already occurred ontologically. When the copula 'to be' or 'is' relates to subjects, they are already determined onto-logically, but they must actualize their potential, notably through ontical determinations. When 'to be' relates to a subject, it entails a dis-appropri-ation of 'to be'—or Being—as a general essence—I never am my species nor my gender 'in general'.

Every conceptualization relative to 'to be' involves a dis-appropriation regarding the being, but also the 'to be', that I am. This being aims, or ought to aim to accomplish the 'to be' that I am by the fulfillment of appropriate attributes but also by relationship(s) with other beings, if these are faithful to their own being(s). The being that I am today arises from my past and is turned towards a future, the present actualizing the potentialities of my being through their appearing and their transforma-tion—a transformation due, in particular, to both an active and passive meeting with another being which is. If the latter is a being without 'to be' or a 'to be' without being, nihilism is at work in my existing.

The meeting with an other, being his or her 'to be', represents both a resource and a risk of being led away from a becoming of one's own, because the being that one is then confronted with new forms that one could, wrongly, consider appropriate to oneself. Thus one is in a situation which could both allow one's own forms to be incarnate or to be lost, and even forgotten, which leads to the forgetting of the one that one is. Our passivity towards the other must be accompanied by an increased vigi-lance in order to safeguard the duality of subjectivities, their difference and also the search for a possible conjunction between them. The origin of the world, and not only of human beings, results from a conjunction between different beings able to be the ones that they are and not to be the ones that they are not.

6

Anesthesia of Soul by Spirit

A Universal Which Remains Particular

The partiality of our 'to be' does not know itself as such. At first, the sensitive perception that I have of myself can be lived as neuter and be merged into an abstract universality. Meeting with a human which is different from myself by nature and recognized as such can give back to this perception its immediate and concrete character. This does necessarily mean that I can perceive myself as sexuate only in the other but, rather, that acknowledging the otherness of the other sends me back to my particularity. The meeting with the other reveals the fact that the sense of touch can do without mediation. Touch is mediating by itself and, as such, it can stretch indefinitely, its sensitive quality gradually vanishing. It is the flesh of the other, as long as I feel desire for it, which stops the indefinite drifting of the sensitive touch. And this possibility results from the difference between two fleshes which compels them to unite with one another without ever becoming one.

It would be relevant to object to Hegel that if universal remains faithful to nature it is always also particular. Hence 'to be' has another meaning. So one could say about an oak that it corresponds to an essence which is both universal and particular. For humans things are more complicated because the universal is two: man and woman. Human being does not exist as an oak—it is man or woman. This determination of human being is not external to it but belongs to its being itself which cannot be reduced to an abstract universality. In that sense, human being, as man or woman, remains an *organon*, a sort of organism, and it is not determined by the outside by canons of truth which thwart its aspiration after developing endlessly (cf. Hegel, *Encyclopédie des sciences philsophiques en abrégé*, § 52; *Encyclopedia of philosophical Sciences in Basic Outline*, § 52). Hence the 'self-manifestation' of each being is not necessarily only subjective (op. cit., § 571). It is as much letting appear, for one's own self and the other, the objectivity of one's being with faithfulness to life and respect or desire for the other. This letting appear the objectivity of a being is also what contributes to a/its becoming absolute from a structuring of one's own—a sexuate belonging—and the development and desire that it wants and determines, not according to forms presumed to be neuter and universal which ought to define and finalize its modalities.

For Hegel, reaching the absolute amounts to being able to do without mediation. According to me, it is not the case. Desire always needs mediation when relating to a different living being. And the absolute cannot do without this relation remaining concrete; for lack of it, its objectivity is more or less constructed and abstract. But reaching the absolute in the relationship with a different living being necessitates a logic according to which subject(s) and predicate(s) give being to each other, or according to which the copula unites two subjects without reducing them to be alternately predicates for the other or for the community, unless one goes no further than a sum without link between them—hence a destructive potential arising from what has not been taken into account in their relation. In order that the latter could really come true, each subject must ensure their own predication—not only I am this or that and you are this or that, but I am myself and you are yourself. This self-predication is possible in the meeting between two different beings thanks to the mutual respect for their difference and the assumption of the negative that it entails.

What then happens from the union between 'I' and 'you'? In a mere sum, the difference is not taken into consideration and it will reappear in some or other way. The first effect is that returning to the self and to growth is paralyzed for both. In the subordination of the one to the other, the natural and ontological status of difference is not taken into account and this leads to the nullification of the being of each. A question remains about the meaning and the role of the copula in a predication such as 'I am myself' or 'we are ourselves' in which 'myself' and 'ourselves' are both subjects and predicates.

In order that such a relation would be possible with respect for the nature and subjectivity of each, it cannot be dependent on representation(s). It must stay at the time when each is still close to itself when expressing its intention of being close to that at which he or she aims. In other words, at the time when each is faithful to a natural belonging which expresses itself with a spiritual determination without any belonging reducing the other to an 'object', which would thwart a possible communion with oneself or with the other. This communion occurs only in a sort of dawn, a birth or a rebirth of our 'to be', which introduces it into another moment of its becoming.

This calls for the aptitude for a subjective interiority which lacks forms or images but corresponds to a self-restraint of intention, desire, and love, in order for one to be able to address them to an other in a suitable way without imposing on this other a singularity or particularity foreign to him or her. Such a self-restraint must not be dependent on consciousness or rules imposed from the outside, for example by morality, on pain of invalidating the presence of a natural sensitivity in the intention. Rather, it must result from a desire to commune with the other while communing with oneself. Besides, this self-restraint is sometimes more perceptible by the other than by oneself. Sometimes the other experiences me more than I experience myself thanks to a sensitive attention and welcome paid to my presence. This represents a means of harmonizing our intentions or desires towards a communion between us.

Such a communion must first take place in a relation between two, in which subjectivity can perceive the nature and spirit of itself but also of the other. When the other is perceived only as an other in a community—as an *allos* and not as an *heteros*—this possibility is generally lost. Thus an alive and concrete subjectivity is supplanted by an anonymous individuality, the unity of the individual being ensured by norms and laws which are presumed to be suitable for all mankind whereas they correspond only to a particular part of it. This stage can be considered regressive regarding the becoming of humanity, a return to a sort of vegetative existence and subjectivity—a milieu which is humanly elaborated acting as a substitute for the natural environment. For lack of having viewed how the human subjectivity can be constituted in its entirety, the human being is limited to a sort of vegetative survival or it is extrapolated into a supra sensitive life.

What allows human subjectivity to be constituted as a living whole, as an organic totality, and to be experienced as such, is the mutual recognition and desire between two humans differently sexuate. This requires otherness not to be lived in a hostile way and the positive nature of difference to be really perceived. Then difference is no longer envisioned only as what permits to emerge from a mere sensitive consciousness through the perception of an object and of its truth but as what gives access to a desire to unite with another subject.

Such difference implies that the other is not merely an alter ego in which I reflect myself but that the other sends me back to my global being and to life and energy which animate it. This means that this other returns to me a singularity which is both particular and universal, that is, to my natural essence. The latter is perceived with difficulty through a multiplicity of properties or its assimilation to an abstract essence but it can be perceived thanks to my sexuation acting as a structure, both particular and universal, unifying my material belonging and uniting it with my subjective existence.

The return to the natural being occurs in a privileged way between two humans who are differently sexuate. In this relationship the contradiction between particularity and universality can be removed, entrusting each with the responsibility for, but also the freedom of, joining them according to their own will and consciousness. Then being together with the other does not mean suppression or negation of the sensitive physical being but the opportunity to acknowledge, assume and cultivate one's singularity as a singular living being, which is potentially universal, as well as one's particularity regarding a supposedly human essence.

The Awakening of Soul by Desire

To be with the other provides me with a physical and meta-physical unity if this other is sufficiently autonomous and faithful to him- or herself to not appropriate me or mistake me for a part of their being—matter, form(s), energy and so forth—and recognizes me as an other with whom to accomplish humanity is possible, naturally but also spiritually. This requires each to assume its difference and the distress of an iunsurmountable separation from the other to incarnate the being that it is upon itself to incarnate.

Through such assuming and touching one another, as the one which exists between the two hands or the two lips, a flesh is created by their sending them to one another without merely reflecting one another. Indeed touch exceeds the potential of image or mirror reflection, revealing the existence of a flesh the presence of which evades sight. Our tactile approach to one another makes our body more than it was—it becomes flesh.

This flesh is sensed, it exists, but we cannot appropriate it. It is a simple carnal dwelling of space between us, and differently in us. We long for meeting and touching one another again to make it exist, but we toil to carry out the work of engendering humanity. We substitute for it the natural begetting of the child, more visible than the generation of flesh itself.

In fact, we must apply ourselves to differentiating the flesh which arises from our approach to one another, as a subtle and diaphanous matter still without qualities. First, we must agree to passively live it, to be affected by it in order to perceive something of it, but also to become impregnated with it and carnally transformed. We also must endow with a meaning that which has been passively felt without letting it become a merely neuter and abstract energy. And the concern with giving meaning contributes to perceiving the qualities peculiar to each and those resulting from the union between them.

Through the subjective passivity and activity intervening in the process of generating and sharing flesh, the freedom of each overcomes the limits of an only singular self and gradually becomes universal while preserving the potential of a natural energy in search of its development. In that sense, it is not only knowledge which is capable of ideality. The love of the other as other, the love which assumes the negative of a difference even better reaches ideality as energy and substance—or 'woven-material' Hegel would say. And, then, desire can be considered to be longing for ideality.

The awakening of soul and consciousness can result from both a physical and meta-physical desire for the other as other. This other plays a part, also physically, in the development of spirit, which does not happen only by itself, as Hegel wants, in a sort of parallelism between the body and the spirit. Neither the soul nor the spirit ought to exist independently of a bodily singularity. Rather, they must awaken and evolve in it and from it so as to cultivate the natural belonging towards a human becoming and sharing. And the soul cannot be limited to 'the sleep of spirit' (Hegel) or 'an only passive intellect' (Aristotle), but must be viewed as an awakened pneumatic substance on the move and in dialogue with a spirit less avid for imposing forms other than natural, for judging and categorizing until the exhaustion of all natural resources.

Perhaps one could suggest that the spirit wants to have, whereas the soul favours being. In order to seize, the spirit—for example in Hegel's work—must externalize to grasp before it internalizes. Hence 'object' is privileged as well as an objectivity dependent on the object more than the subjective perception as such, what is more a sensitive perception. The soul more easily accepts to be transformed by a sensitive impregnation without the passage through the externalization of an objectal perception, the only criterion of objectivity for the spirit. The soul makes its own internally, without situating outside itself what it experiences or situating itself outside its self to apprehend it.

The way of conceiving of the spirit perhaps explains why Hegel asserts that our sexuate belonging is perceived in the other. Instead of experiencing what it perceives of the desire of or for the other, the spirit would endeavour to seize something of it by projecting it in the externality that the other represents. Acting in that way, it nullifies the exteriority of the other and this other is no longer recognized as other, as a subjectivity different from one's own. This does not allow to cultivate 'the material of consciousness ', the substantial and qualitative nature of the soul (Hegel,

Encyclopédie des scieces philosophiques en abrégé, § 414 and 418; *Encyclopedia of Philosophical Sciences in Basic Outline*, § 414 and § 418). This is possible through a culture of intersubjectivity thanks to a dialectics of sensitivity (cf. *Sharing the Fire*) which avoids dividing human being into body, soul and spirit, private and public lives, feminine and masculine constructed identities, religion and philosophy and so forth.

Then 'I' is not determined by a relation to 'object(s)'. 'I' is determined originally and by nature, and it must make this determination spiritual, especially through a relationship with another 'I', which is different by nature. It cannot negativate this other subject and the latter cannot represent a mere object for it. It is faced with an elusive reality which cannot be reflected and, in the name of truth itself, it is sent back to sensitivity without being able to overcome it in a universality extraneous to sensitivity. Indeed, the latter has a share in subjectivity itself and it needs to be raised to an absolute which is universal in its particularity and is incarnate here and now thanks to the relationship with an other as other.

It is the maintenance of difference which prevents desire from being destructive and keeps alive its aspiration after the beyond of an immediate satisfaction. As originating in nature and aspiring to transcend it, desire cannot be satisfied with a relation to 'object', including as that which could solve conflicts between two self-consciousnesses. Desire cannot, for that purpose, amount to need, notably as principle of community organization, as Hegel would will. Rather, it must give up any mere satisfaction towards a sharing with the other(s) likely to forge links between members of a community. This entails one not destroying the immediacy of the desire of the other but each transforming immediacy of their own desire into a shareable immediacy so as to preserve the energy of desire while making it a factor or an agent of spiritual becoming. As such desire can contribute towards the formation and the cohesion of a human community in which each remains faithful to their singularity and their natural determination in order to cultivate their life and share it humanly. This cannot happen while the behaviour is limited at the level of mere needs but necessitates having access to desire.

Thanks to desire, we can remain living and elaborate a culture of life and of its sharing, instead of culture, in particular philosophical culture, being a sort of preparation for death in which an inanimate or a made-inanimate 'object' is presupposed able to act as mediation. The relationship with the other as different requires it to be objective without being objectal. I can neither appropriate such objectivity nor negativate it because it relates to a subject. I must acknowledge it as the objectivity of a subjectivity which is not mine and give up the idea that an absolute universality could correspond to my subjectivity—it can only aspire to the universality of a particular subject. Wanting to be capable of reaching universality, notably thanks to the relationship with an other faithful to the particularity of their nature, cannot mean that this universality amounts to both an objectively and subjectively unique universal, including for me. Indeed, in that way, I would negate a particularity of my subjectivity and natural identity that I cannot negate. As I am sexuate, and I am not an abstractly universal being, this determination particularizes my subjectivity in an irreducible way. And I can never be simply external to myself, the process of externalization being extraneous to a sensitive belonging, which is dependent on the body and the life.

I cannot negativate sensitivity as such but I can transform it so that it should become also spiritual. Such transformation contributes not only to my own becoming but also to the acknowledgment of the other as both a sensitive and spiritual being—as body and soul or spirit. And this acknowledgment is no longer merely formal, it is real. It is not only thanks to the respect for a traditional morality or logic that it exists but because of my desire for the other as other with my own becoming in mind. And desire henceforth aims at a qualitative and not only quantitative absolute, an absolute suitable for the evolution of humanity.

The Amorous Passivity of the Soul

There is not doubt that, by privileging the 'one' and the 'whole', Hegel does not take account of the desire for the other as the other of two—*heteros*—and, consequently, of a factor of the qualitative evolution of humanity. That begins at the level of the family assumed to form only one person, which nullifies the 'vital-corporal' dynamism of the desire between man and woman. And yet this desire can contribute towards the becoming not only of the couple but also of each member of the family if it is not reduced to standards of good behaviour which consider the carnal union to be the outcome and even the duty consequential to marriage and not its raison d'être (*Encyclopédie des sciences philosophiques en abrégé*, § 519; *Encyclopedia of Philosophical Sciences in Basic Outline*, § 519). According to Hegel, the naturally and culturally dynamic factor that desire between man and woman represents must be limited to an 'intimate subjective fervour', to a virtue which ensures the family cohesion, of which the begetting of children is required by 'the standards of good behaviour' as fundamental in the 'concluding act' of the marriage. Besides their natural birth, the spouses must procure to their children a second birth, a spiritual birth likely to make them autonomous persons.

What will the nature of such a spiritual birth be if the man and the woman, who have begotten these children, have not themselves spiritualized their desire for one another, notably through preserving their autonomy and difference towards one another? Does Hegel not abolish this desire instead of transforming it, making it the medium of the passage from nature to spirit in this founding relation of humanity? Is it not in that relationship that the totality and the unity of human being must be discovered and cultivated instead of being sacrificed to the supposedly organic totality of the state, of which family would be the basic cell? Unless it is sacrificed to the absolute spirit which searches for its truth through the exteriority of an objectivity, notably universal, which is already more or less arbitrarily constructed.

Could the absolute for which we long correspond to love becoming incarnate in human beings? Then the amorous relationship between two subjects who are naturally different, the coming true of love itself, becomes the place of reconciliation of the objective to the subjective. The communion between these two subjects no longer needs any 'object', any material external to it with a more or less necessary resort to some technique, but it is reached thanks to a transformation of the being of each, especially of their interiority, so that a communion between two different interiorities could exist. The exteriority of the other is not for all that abolished, and communion does not necessarily entail reconciliation. Rather, it happens thanks to the acknowledgment by each of their partiality, and the assumption of an insurmountable negative as well as the longing for an absolute which corresponds with this partiality but also its union with the other part of humanity.

It is the matter of a logic and a dialectics still to be discovered and applied. Indeed, the question is no longer of contenting oneself with an originally formal subjectivity, a subjectivity capable of dealing with negativity, and providing itself with an appropriate content by relating to 'object(s)', but it is now question of two subjects who are objectively determined and who assume the negative of their own partiality, thus a negative that they apply to themselves attempting to transform their particularity and singularity towards a communion of beings with respect for their difference. This requires sensitivity itself to be dialectized, and not only overcome by consciousness, notably to evade the alternative between goodness and badness. Such a dialectical process is necessary for the becoming of a subjectivity determined by its natural belonging to become, and not only through relating to 'object(s)' or an operation external to it. No doubt, these also have an impact on subjectivity but it can be only secondary on pain of paralyzing its effective becoming.

If subjectivity assumes its sexuate determination, also at the intimate level, it agrees to have its finiteness in itself as an insurmountable ontological limitation. This compels to resort to a dialectics different from Hegelian dialectics towards one's own becoming. The relationship with a living being different from one's own by nature offers such an opportunity, the coming true of which needs finiteness as a condition for freedom. Indeed, it is thanks to my partiality that I can have both a physical and spiritual relationship with an other different from myself by nature, which contributes to my perceiving and aiming at an absolute more absolute than the one after which I can aspire as an abstract and undifferentiated subjectivity. Of course the other is not an object and I cannot reduce him/her to that. In a way, the absolute is thus never reached but I can consider my contribution to the evolution of human subjectivity or intersubjectivity to be a progression towards the absolute.

Maintaining that sensitivity is that which human beings share with animals amounts to presupposing that sensitivity as such is not appropriate to human existence. It is true that this appropriation requires humans not simply to pass from individuality to community—from one animal to the herd—but to cultivate the relationship between two different humans, in particular two humans differently sexuate. It is not an insensitive or supra sensitive thinking which must humanize our relation to sensitivity, but our training of sensitivity itself, notably towards a sharing which is not merely 'animal' but takes part in spiritualizing humanity.

This cannot happen if our soul remains 'dull', 'dozing' or if the centre of our sensitive system is situated only in our brain (cf. Hegel, *Encyclopédie des sciences philosophiques en abrégé*, § 400 and § 401; *Encyclopedia of Philosophical Sciences in Basic Outline*, § 400 and § 401). In that case, the one who loves would be in a state of 'passivity similar to that of the foetus in the living womb of the mother'. This subject would be 'ill' and 'under the power of another subject, the hypnotizer', representing 'the subjective consciousness of a lucid individual' whereas the 'individuality of the sick person' would be 'a for-itself being void, which is neither present to itself nor effective' and is 'filled only with the other through which it feels, perceives, reads, hears' (op. cit., § 406).

The affective life would correspond, for Hegel, to passivity, a sort of paralysis, to a sleepwalker body governed by the lucidity of a hypnotizer, head or chief dominating and directing a living organism. Does all that not forget that feelings constitute the 'material' from which the spirit is supposedly formed? Is it not also to forget that the other is present in what I feel as a sensitive and incarnate being and not only as a mere lucid understanding? It is by becoming aware of and by spiritualizing the relationship between two sensitivities, two incarnations, that sensitivity itself can be spiritualized. This needs to discover the positive and, in a way, active nature of the passivity of touch—a touch still crucial in Aristotle's work but that Hegel neglects even when he quotes it—and that of difference, that is, of the otherness of the other, and not as an opposition, notably between the sexes, which ends in a split between the body and the head.

The Place of Transformation of the Sensitive Feelings

Our acknowledging and taking into consideration otherness by consciousness calls for faithfulness to a physical and psychic property like sexuation. This is both particular and universal but it is not perceived directly by us. It requires the mediation of desire for/by the other as different to become fully effective. Such effectiveness involves physical as well as spiritual, natural as well as potentially *ideell* dimension. It is revealed and becomes incarnate first between two naturally different living beings. It is the desire for uniting with one another which incites them to pass from a physical attraction to a feeling of spiritual nature, because that requires the transformation of a natural and singular energy into an energy sharable between two naturally different humans. Energy is then singular, particular and potentially universal. As such it can create links between the individual and the community without sacrificing one to the other.

It is not true, as Hegel suggests, that what is immediate is necessarily egoistic, and what is particular is necessarily opposed to what is universal. Indeed, desire arises as immediacy, but it cannot be satisfied as an egoistic need because it wants the relationship with the other as mediation towards the absolute. And, moreover, our sexuate belonging is a particularity which is objectively universal but of which each, he or she, must ensure the becoming effective from a singular destiny. In that case, ideality cannot be distinguished from a particular effectiveness. It is extraneous to the abstract structure of a subjectivity reflected in something or someone external to itself. It could correspond with the transformation of an original natural energy—Hegel perhaps would say a vital-corporal energy—into a more subtle energy which is compatible with the exercise of thought. Indeed, the latter cannot merely oppose the resource that natural energy represents, and cultivating it seems to be more suitable than destroying it by inflicting on the body a sort of calvary. In fact, the body itself aims at this transformation of energy, notably to surmount the gravity to which it is subjected. Beyond the fact that it can be appropriate for experiencing sentiments and exercising thought by shielding them from the heaviness of an egoistic singularity, natural energy can procure a sensation of levitation—for example, through enthusiasm, astonishment, and above all sexual, and even merely sexuate, shared desire. But this presupposes that our 'vital-corporal' energy develops and is transformed by the relation with other living beings, beginning with other humans. Instead of being repressed, expended or sterilized through externalization, physical energy contains itself to be internalized, to be kept, to grow and be transformed so that it should be suitable for a sharing and it should contribute to our comprehensive blossoming without immolating a part of us to another.

Perhaps such a process can be achieved thanks to a cultivation of the properties of the soul instead of subjecting it to the spirit. Made of breath and touch—as Aristotle acknowledges and also, indirectly, sometimes Hegel speaking of its 'tearing'—the soul is the place in which sensitive immediacy can be transformed. The soul does not lack truth, neither does sensitive immediacy lack truth, but this truth is different from that of the spirit. And if spirit cannot do without soul for its becoming, soul could do without spirit more. Indeed, it does not need reduplication or repetition to live on, notably to overcome contradiction(s). Perceiving an immediacy different from its own can contribute to the evolution of its feeling. So it can become more spiritual without leaving itself. Certainly the other is outside of the soul, but this can perceive and even commune intimately with this other. And it is no longer only between oneself and one's self that the relation is established but also between oneself and the other, and any of these components can be subjected to an absolute negativity.

The matter, for consciousness, is no longer of solving contradiction(s) between oneself and the other as autonomous but aiming at a same becoming. Rather the matter is of reaching a union between oneself and the other as different which contributes to the evolution of each and that of their union towards the accomplishment of human life. In other words, the matter is of reaching a relationship between two different and autonomous souls which takes part in the becoming of humanity, even of that of the whole world, through a generating process faithful to their natural potential.

Consciousness is no longer determined by an 'object' which must be subjected to negativity to correspond more or less adequately with the subject. Consciousness is determined by its natural belonging and must itself be subjected to the negative in order to make this determination spiritual, without for all that abolishing it, but by transforming it. This becoming requires consciousness to admit its partiality as particular, and to ensure a relation with a subject which is different without annihilating the one or the other.

Consciousness is not immediately aware of its determination. It is through assuming its self-consciousness as particular, and the respect for a living being with a self-consciousness which is different, that this determination can be revealed to it. It can also be unveiled by the specificity of its language and its works. But it expresses itself above all through desire, its issue and its qualities, the conditions of its effectiveness, notably in the relationship with the other. The nature of desire in the relationship with the other has been too little considered by Hegel. And the knowledge of the determination of consciousness by affects, in particular sexuate or sexual affects, is almost absent from his dialectics.

A real taking into account and a dialectization of perception independently of any 'object' seems also to be lacking in Hegel's work. And yet the sensitive perception determined by nature exists—for example, a touch without object—as a sensitive perception or consciousness of oneself but also of the other. If need necessitates a natural or spiritual 'object' to be satisfied, it is not the same with desire. Then perception more relates to the state, and the state has more to do with being than with having and can do without resorting to an 'object'. It is, perhaps, also the way through which the human being is the most capable of differing from other kingdoms, by an aptitude for deferring a reaction to what it experiences, and for modulating it.

A Sunny Soul

Warmth is an important phenomenon with regard to our states. However, when Hegel speaks of warmth, he mainly confines himself to physical aspect(s) without wondering about the psychical or spiritual qualities that warmth can have. This has perhaps something to do with his lack of interest in touch. When I touch the body of the other, for example the hand, this gesture first arouses an intimate perception of life thanks to the warmth of this hand. Obviously a conscious communication can exist but a communion between two lives first occurs thanks to the warmth which is experienced when touching one another. And my hand, before being the active tool that the western philosophers view in it, is a mediator of life in its various states. The perception of warmth is not provided only by the hand but also by other parts of the body, and by the soul itself. And warmth does not act only as that which can provoke a phenomenon of dilatation, as Hegel describes it, but also as a manifestation of life, including at the psychic and the spiritual levels.

Thanks to the warmth of life, the functioning, and even the content, of subjectivity become more fluid, less dependent on and fixed by forms and categories, and thus more likely to be communicated and shared at both singular and universal levels. To keep meaning, these communication and sharing must be appropriate, and the degree of warmth cannot be the same in a relationship between two subjects who are linked together physically and two individuals of a community. Between two subjects, furthermore who are naturally different and in fleshly relationship, warmth must take account of the suitable gravity and cohesion of the bodies for their union. It can cause neither their fusion nor their dissolution or their diffusion beyond what contributes to the becoming of each and the communion between the two. It must permit the return of each in itself as well as the perpetuation and the evolution of the relationship. This at least requires each of the individuals involved in the relation to have already achieved a unification between their body and their soul and a transformation of their physical nature and spiritual density so that they should be able to unite with one another in a way which is fecund for each, for the becoming of the two and also for that of humanity and of the world. And a more or less high degree of warmth is not sufficient to reach that. Besides, warmth must be qualitatively adequate to be suitable for the subjects in relationship. It must not diffuse in a manner that deprives them of their energy, of their life, and it cannot perturb the community order either. Indeed, the community cohesion calls for an economy of warmth which needs its partial transformation in light.

But light, no more than flame, is foreign to some materiality, a materiality being very subtle. Does that mean that they correspond to a 'physical ideality'? (Hegel, *Encyclopédie des sciences philosophiques en abrégé*, § 306; *Encyclopedia of Philosophical Sciences in Basic Outline*, § 306). Could ideality be considered to be of a more subtle nature, what is not to say to be abstract, in comparison with the gravity of a physical matter? Could idea, for Hegel, have a meaning different from that which it has for Plato? In a way, Hegel would be more materialist without for all that succeeding in thinking of matter and form in a manner that does not oppose them to one another?

This could result from the fact that the body is defined by a materiality and a cohesion different from those of ideas. But how to define their gravity and cohesion? Does Hegel question his own way of conceiving of them? Do thoughts not exist which have weight? Does the warmth of life only dissolve the physical cohesion or also make it possible, whereas the cold of death disintegrates it? Do we not need warmth to maintain the connection between the different parts of our organism? And is the 'internal warmth'—notably of the soul—not necessary to commune with another living being? Is it not a shared warmth which allows us to unite with one another—to establish a 'cohesion' between us thanks to a becoming more fluid of our fleshes? This requires their 'cohesion' to keep a density which lets warmth filter, and has not the stiffness of a corpse. Thus that flesh does not have the consistency of crystal but that of a porous matter which transmits warmth without dissolution, wasting or reduction to a mere ideality. That flesh has a density which allows each to hold in themselves while remaining permeable to the other and likely to be diffused in the other, or between one and the other. Could it be possible to say: that flesh keeps a soul?

Nevertheless, flesh must be edged, contained and limited by a structure that only sexuate belonging seems to be able to provide it with respect for sensitivity—a belonging which is not only one particularity of the self but determines subjectivity itself in a way which is irreducible at the level of singularity as well as of universality. This could logically be expressed as 'I am a woman' corresponds to the singular becoming effective of 'I is a woman'. In other words, I cannot allow me/it to subject all predicates to negativity in order to discover those which are most appropriate to my/its subjectivity because some predicates are already appropriate to me/it by nature: 'I' is originally determined in an irreducible way by its sexuate belonging. An equality to it is originally assigned to it that it cannot subject to negativity on pain of falling into a nihilistic idealism without any meaning.

An idea can neither completely express nor overcome the natural given. And, when it intends to do that, it produces an arbitrariness of meaning that any logical complexity or device can correct. Most of them probably aim to compensate for that which has not been taken into account of a natural identity and of an original predication: I am/is a woman, a particularity which is not merely one and which cannot be questioned as others in order to establish the subjective and objective identity of the 'I' who states the truth.

Beyond the fact that it is natural, and not constructed in a more or less arbitrary way, and it permanently determines subjectivity, this particularity also decides on the validity of some predicates—as a woman, I am not whatever one, and any objectivity cannot suit my subjectivity. No universality can subject to negativity this particularity of my being on pain of calling into question the value of meaning itself, of its mode of production and of its logical way of connecting. Besides, the fact that I am/is a woman renders the particularity of my 'I' capable of generating meaning in the relationship with another particular 'I', that of a man. The acknowledgment of the particularity of my sexuate belonging and of that of the other not only guarantees the validity or truth of meaning but it also supplies meaning. In order that this should remain faithful to the living being that I am, sexuation must be mediated not only by discourse(s) but also by the touch of self-affection and hetero-affection, which creates a space and a milieu in which communion in difference can take place. Such space and milieu are not foreign to the soul, a soul enlivened by the fire of desire.

7

A History Cut Off from Germ Cells

The Link Absent from Dialectics

If individuals who are different, as man and woman, are considered to be opposite, their relationship needs a mediation external to them and neutral regarding what opposes them. Hence, the resort to law, morality, custom and so forth, supposedly to be neutral, whereas they are often imposed by only one of the two sides. If the individuals are acknowledged as qualitatively different, the mediation has not to be imposed from the outside and be merely in the neuter. They are the individuals themselves who can provide the mediation by their want to enter into relationship with one another. This want can resort to the mediation of touch and the energy of a desire that each endeavours to modulate in order to unite with the other. Henceforth, what unites the two—notably the copula—is no longer dependent on a decision of understanding as an inanimate mediation; it is a dynamic process inspired by a will to become of life in a way suitable for humanity.

Then the subject is not in search of a this or that which he/she would be or ought to appropriate for being, but is in search of the way of becoming the 'to be' that he/she is. To be born becomes effective through a becoming, and this becoming cannot be subjected to the arbitration of

L. Irigaray, *The Mediation of Touch*, https://doi.org/10.1007/978-3-031-37413-5_7

opposing truths. Our being is animated by a vital dynamism which does not develop through oppositions and contradictions defined by an understanding by which it would be governed. This dynamism expresses a search for individuation and the desire for uniting which contributes to it—and it can give up neither the individual as living nor the transcendence of a becoming for a vital or abstract ideal lacking in differentiation.

In order not to be merely external to subjectivity but to correspond to an interiority, the universal must be also particular. Indeed, a neuter individual does not exist. An asexuate universal is thus a construction extraneous to the individual itself. The most radical confrontation between exteriorities takes place between two particular universalities, one corresponding with woman and the other with man. Nevertheless, these two universals are not opposed, they are different. Acknowledging this difference at the level of universality questions the relation between interiority and exteriority of both the universals. What attracts man and woman to one another is founded in nature, but it is also a longing for the universal and the absolute, which refuses the split between body and mind, particular and universal, and searches for the path of their reconciliation.

In their relationship man and woman, as different in nature and in spirit, internalize and spiritualize sensitivity, and externalize and embody thought. Their relationship is not devoted only to natural reproduction. To not weaken, it must contribute to a spiritual production, and not only for/by children (cf. Hegel, in *Encyclopédie des sciences philosophiques en abrégé*, § 521; *Encyclopedia of Philosophical Sciences in Basic Outline*, § 521), in which nature and culture generate one another and become indissolubly linked. This gives rise to new contents and modes of thinking, at individual and collective levels.

All that can happen only if gender, the carrier of germ cells, does not vanish into copulation or into the family unit, as Hegel thinks. The two genders cannot form 'a sole person' with a unique spiritual 'feeling' and whose 'intimate subjective fervour makes the union of marriage an undivided link between persons' (op. cit., § 518 and § 519). In that case, natural belonging as well as spirit run the risk of being paralyzed and not cultivated as human. 'Physical union' becomes a 'mere consequence of the link formed in conformity with standards of good behaviours' and the 'intimate fervour' is reduced to a substantiality 'which can only feel' and is 'subjected to chance and nullity'. It is according to such contingency that the family members enter into relationship as persons with consideration for each other (op. cit., § 522).

One can be surprised at the poorness of these analyses in comparison with the subtlety that Hegel shows in other respects. There is no doubt that they manifest one of the failures in Hegel's thinking, in his conception of subjectivity and spirit, in his dialectics. It is possible to suggest that the link which is lacking in the foundation of his phenomenology and his logic is desire as that which can join spirit to nature, in each and between all, in particular between genders. Gender does not represent a determination among others—it intervenes before other determinations and even determines them. Gender introduces a mediation which makes thought never merely immediate. It is thus possible and, furthermore, necessary to elaborate a concrete thinking of our natural belonging to a gender—this universal particularity determining our thinking even without our knowing.

Returning to ourselves as sexuate identities allows us to think in concrete terms about a culture of nature, and without subjecting our identity to a logical negation. Indeed, it is originally subjected to the negative by its natural particularity, and it is again by its desire for an other as other. And it is not true that one does not feel desire for what one does not know, as Hegel asserts (quoted by Jacques Dhondt in *Hegel, textes et débats*, Le livre de poche, p. 131). Desire between the sexes bears witness to that, unless it is reduced to a narcissistic issue, as Hegel seems often to do. It could even be possible to say that we experience desire only for what or for whom we do not know, because desire, contrary to need, aspires after transcendence. In a way desire subjects to the negative the ones we already are towards our becoming. But this generally remains unthought, notably by Hegel, who imagines that he can use the negative as he wants whereas the negative has already determined his thinking without his knowing. And he could be contradicted in some of his assertions concerning the 'beautiful soul', which could be applied to him. Does his way of privileging external action not mean a misjudgement of the internal operation that our evolution from nature to spirit requires? Does such evolution always need an external action for a human being?

And when self-consciousness withdraws into itself does it not find in this itself a presence of its natural belonging, of that of the other and even of that of the world, which are henceforth integral part of its flesh, instead of a mere 'transparent purity'? (cf. *Phénoménologie de l'esprit, tome II,* pp. 188–89; in *Phenomenology of Spirit, Tome II,* The Moral Conception of the World, II). Does the 'sinking' of a self-consciousness into the 'absolute self-consciousness' not result from a lack of consideration for the objectivity of the nature of its 'substance' which brings about the non-truth of it?

Undoubtedly, such objectivity is inner and escapes sight, but it exists. It is above all sensitive and tactile. Nevertheless, the objectivity of such dimensions lies in the self, and even in the weaving of consciousness, and it testifies to a presence of nature, of the other and of the world that consciousness cannot ignore on pain of fueling the non-truth of objectivity. In other words, exteriority has already objectively determined our being before we become aware of it, we can decide on the exteriority of an action with respect to ourselves, and we are confronted with the question of objectivity. In fact, the pretention of consciousness to being freed from the objectivity of its origin and from its weaving represents an absolute non-truth.

This is indirectly admitted by Hegel when he acknowledges that particular passions can have an impact on the rationality of history, and a dialectical process would be needed at that level between particularity and universality. Why does he misjudge that at the individual level? Is it not for lack of such acknowledgment that 'universal history' as 'image and work of Reason' (cf. *La Raison dans l'Histoire, U.C.G. 10/18,* pp. 117–18) henceforth offers a so much irrational spectacle to us? What would Hegel think about it? Would he consent, for all that, to interrogate the nature of consciousness, of idea and of reason, and to wonder about how they feed themselves? Would he still maintain that universal history is that which must fill the void of the 'hollow object' that self-consciousness creates for itself by refusing to be a 'thing' in order to preserve its 'interiority' from an 'action' and from a 'being there' at the disposal of the world as is today? Towards what history? Has it not come time for our consciousness to care about a self that it must preserve from being consumed by a historical unfolding which seems to have no longer any other purpose? In the name of what reason? The one which for centuries has sacrificed our life and our flesh to the demiurgic pretentiousnesses of an 'Absolute Spirit' which sucked the lifeblood out of them, including without their knowing? Is it not urgent to protect our remainder of flesh and to ask our consciousness how to cultivate and share it towards a human becoming other than a calvary in which it sacrifices itself in the name of a pretence which leads us to nothingness?

Overcoming the Master-Slave Relationship

Could viewing love as a communion towards bringing the human being into the world anew represent a mean of escaping the foreseeable disaster? To what self-consciousness could such love correspond? That of a carnal in-oneself which is a for-oneself but also a for-the-other and thanks to this 'for-the-other'? Have we the right to sacrifice such opportunity, such a germ of humanity, to a people which, henceforth, is more often than not without any really positive objective will? Or to sacrifice this opportunity to a reason which seems to have lost any freedom notably because of its subjection to sciences and techniques, which separate universality from particularity in a way which makes it difficult to subject interaction between them to a dialectical process and difficult too to detect a 'soul of the content' on either side? (Hegel, *Principes de la philosophie du droit*, pp. 90–1). Is it not to a living and dynamic content to which it would be suitable to return, and first to the one corresponding to the individual itself?

It is between two individuals that the master-slave relation ought to be first overcome by supplying both, beginning with the two genders, with a dialectics of sensitivity appropriate to their nature. This will permit that one no longer remains the guardian of life and the other of its supposed culture in an interdependence of which death is the referee and the master. It is up to both to ensure such a safeguard and to engender life from it. This asks them to consider their difference not to be an opposition resulting from a logic inappropriate to life but to be a natural difference which is a source of generation of living beings in their various components.

There are determinations, in particular natural determinations among which sexuate belonging is a part, that Spirit cannot delete 'to gain in this way a more rich and concrete determination' (Hegel, *La Raison dans l'Histoire*, pp. 197–98). All those who, today, attempt to abolish the difference between genders, notably in the name of Enlightenment, seem to have wrongly read Hegel. Indeed what 'more rich and concrete positive determination' could be substituted for sexuate belonging without incurring the risk of the disappearance of humanity itself? What would Hegel think about that in our time? Would he agree that sexuate belonging is only a means or an implement which serves a higher cause? (op. cit., pp. 47–9). What?

In what would then consist 'the union of the universal existing in-itself and for-itself with the individual and the subjective which constitute the sole truth'? (op., cit., pp. 110–11) Is it not sexuate belonging which represents the 'more rich and concrete positive determination' to be thought and incarnated in history—a determination which has always determined history itself without its knowing, and in an inadequate way, either because of hollowness or by default? Did, under the historical productions and under the constitution of peoples, not exist a sexuate, and even a sexual, difference acting in a subterranean way but which remained without consideration and spiritual becoming because it was reduced to the neuter of a supposedly universal truth? Must what appears today of this difference, in various and more or less chaotic manners, not be viewed as the necessary shaping of a new figure of Spirit? And does the latter not represent among others a resource towards the coexistence, even the union, between incarnations of Spirit in diverse peoples and cultures, given that such difference is universal?

This requires sexuate difference to be recognized as what it is: the existence of two natural, subjective and cultural truths founding and constituting humanity itself—a reality which is misjudged in most historical figures of the spirit, which, perhaps, explains and justifies their destruction and overcoming. Indeed, if it was really the flowering of nature, the spirit could develop without destruction but by transformation of/from a natural essence. But the latter is not one for the human being—we were born of a conjunction between two different beings and we must think of the human being in such a way. The new era of history, or the new figure of Spirit according to Hegel, does not represent only the outcome of a contradiction with respect to the previous era, rather it must mean a taking root in a real more real than the Hegelian real. To consider it to be the mere result of a contradiction would amount to agreeing that the negative is still at the disposal of a Reason which is not really universal because it is determined by a masculine conception of nature and culture. Henceforth, the negative must apply to a more fundamental level of the development of Spirit, this relating to the insuperable partiality of our belonging to only one gender.

To subject such belonging to a dialectical process will modify the nature of the spirit itself. The link of the passage from nature to Spirit is in a way absent from Hegelian thinking. And yet it represents an articulation between matter and form which allows their dissociation and even their opposition to be overcome. But, henceforth, it is not the spirit itself which is confronted with a tearing that it must surmount. What must be taken into account is the specific shaping of the spiritual according to each gender and how to make a conjunction between two different absolutes and universals possible. In other words, the spirit must subject to a dialectical process that which was considered to be the subjective, the objective, the absolute, the universal and even history starting from one subject only. It cannot do that without putting these past figures into perspective, a perspective which can exist only thanks to a subjectivity and an objectivity which exceed previous ways of viewing the world. It could even be possible to say the previous way of viewing the world, because the previous figures of history were produced by one reason only, a reason in the masculine—which has led history to the dead end in which it is now and to an indefinite destruc(tura)tion given its confinement in a horizon that it can neither leave nor transform.

It is possible for the spirit to overcome itself through elaborating an open and not closed world. Acknowledging that two genders exist and that it is necessary to respect and develop their respective effectivenesses, notably with their union and its fecundity in mind, offers this possibility. In such a perspective, they are no longer tools or aims completely external to subjectivity. Subjectivity itself is the tool and the aim, and the mediation of an object is no longer needed. The desire to commune in difference carries out the unity of each 'me', notably by the assumption of the negative and a becoming flesh, without for all that becoming a 'thing', except as a dialectical moment of its relating to the subject as 'me'—which does not really correspond to a 'thing'. The living and desiring body unites activity and passivity in the sensitive lived experience of a communion with the other which has to do with our 'to be', including as sensitive.

Such an experience exceeds what a solitary spirit can do only by itself. It is more absolute because it concerns, in the present, body and spirit, natural and spiritual, of each subject and of their relationship. It is also potentially more universal because it overcomes the natural and spiritual particularity of the masculine subject by conjoining the bodies and the spirits of man and woman in their difference. It also links instant and eternity in the accomplishment of events and advents which transcend the unfolding of the figures of the spirit in history. It is also the most absolute prayer addressed to a God who is creator and redeemer. This prayer takes on an intimate touch, and its risk, as a possible mediation between oneself and oneself, oneself and the other, oneself and God. It is an activity too which, instead of becoming a mere thing, assumes a passivity which, perhaps, corresponds to the most sublime activity—the ultimate assumption of the negative in order to overcome a supra sensitive nihilism substituting itself for a communion between us in which these categories vanish. Activity becomes itself passivity in order to reach its most complete accomplishment; it accepts to incur its annihilation, or at least its suspension, to experience the union of the natural with the spiritual.

Traditionally, activity, including the technical activity of man, substitutes itself for a natural dynamism of which woman would be, at least in part, the guardian through the evolution of nature in her body, her capacity for giving birth and her role in the family. But this safeguard of nature is, to a great extent, lived only in a passive way and not consciously willed, notably because the feminine 'destiny' ought to submit to the activity of man. The link between activity and passivity is achieved neither in man nor in woman if they do not assume their sexuate belonging as a natural and spiritual determination which must be perceived and cultivated for oneself, for the other and between one another.

This requires each to recognize the other as a being not only with needs but with desire, a desire which is both active and passive. In this way the master-slave relationship could be overcome otherwise than by a sharing out of tasks, of places, or of nature and spirit between both. Instead of imposing on the other the result of an unaccomplished dialectical process, and assigning to this other the role of nature or of a middle term, man and woman then would freely choose to enter into relationship with one another with respect for their mutual difference(s) towards the achievement of humanity. Thereby the cunning of Reason, which is attributed by Hegel to the feminine, would be transformed into an acknowledgment by man and woman of the particularity of a sexuate subjectivity which cannot merely impose, or be subjected as such to, the negative because it represents the presence of living nature and of its dynamism in the subject him- or herself.

In the Beginning, Difference Is

The relationship between two subjects who are different by nature entails a union which is never completely and once for all fulfilled—which keeps alive the becoming of life itself instead of paralyzing it in a system. And does a more valid objectivity exist than that of life that we must incarnate, develop and share as perfectly as possible? To carry out such a task, no particular subject can confine him- herself to the satisfaction of needs but must be fulfilled through their desire for a particular subject who is different in order to incarnate what could be a universal corresponding to human being.

The human being is presumed to represent the essence of humanity. This lacks meaning but that of the capacity for basing a being on a non-being. Indeed, the human being does not exist apart from a constructed ideality. No real identity corresponds to a human being—only genders composing humanity have a real identity. There is no doubt that speaking of human beings evokes a modality of begetting, a certain type of body, of physical and psychical competences, of specific needs, but all that does not relate to any self as identical to or different from one's self—no one-self corresponds to that and no self-consciousness. Human being as such just provides a sort of background from which the 'to be' of man and the 'to be' of woman can differ—and from the background and from one another. This presupposes a double process of differentiation, any of which amounts to an opposition. Another logic must intervene in which the negative is the condition of our 'to be' without our being able to use it as we please. The negative applies to the real itself in order to recognize and identify it first as human and, then, as man or woman. It is on such a condition that the truth concerning the human being can appear. Its true existence only results from assuming a double negative: I do not belong to an other species than human; I alone do not correspond to the human being. Only then a dialectics like the Hegelian one could intervene. But is it still a reason why it must exist? According to what modalities? Certainly not according to a logic of more or less as regards opposites, the quashing of which leads to a falling back into the lack of differentiation of a background if not as a questioning on methodology. As a woman, I am not opposed to another living species and I am not opposed to man either. It is only in relating to myself that these more or less can intervene as degrees, in particular qualitative degrees, in the accomplishment of myself, but not as modalities of an opposition between the other and myself. The other is henceforth situated outside me and is different from me but not opposed to me.

And if the end corresponds to the beginning, as Hegel maintains, perhaps it could be suitable to remind him that in the beginning difference is and it cannot come true through/in a sole universal or a sole absolute. In fact, the negative exists in the beginning, not as a difference between God and me, or my body and my spirit, but as a difference from which I originate and a difference from the other human being with whom I compose humanity. My natural existence entails a negative and I must take this original negative into account before I can pretend to use the negative. Could this be in that case a sort of unconscious mimicry of nature itself?

Is our use of the negative, following Hegel, not that of demiurges ignoring or misjudging the ones who we are—that is, our natural origin and identity? And if being can be 'void and without consistency' is it not because we forget them and our being is only an unconsciously narcissistic or abstractly defined production? The consistency and the reality of our being result from faithfulness to our origin and an original determination of its existence as such. Is the reality of our being not dependent on its being in accordance with a natural identity before it depends on the accordance of a being there—*Dasein*—with its concept? If 'the body has not the reality of the soul', does not the soul participate, at least partly, in the reality of the body? (*Encyclopedie des sciences philosophiques, en abrégé*, in Section A, *L'âme; Encyclopedia of the Philosophical Sciences in Basic Outline*, in Section A, The Soul).

Two structures intervene in our becoming human: one fits our natural belonging and the other is created by a culture which, too often, aims at dominating the first instead of respecting it and attempting to transform it spiritually. The second structure, more exclusively formal, is perhaps due to a sort of narcissism by which man tries to seize himself instead of letting him be the one he is. In this last case the absolute does not correspond only with identity to oneself but with a union with the other thanks to which the identity to oneself is overcome towards a human identity founded on an insurmountable difference—a difference, extraneous to a mere diversity, which determines our natural 'to be' and cannot be overcome through any contradiction. Anyway it is not contradiction itself which can be the cause of the development of life, as Hegel seems to imagine, because it already operates within a system which favours the identical, the one, the same; rather, it is the relationship with the naturally different other which can contribute to this development.

For the alternative between identity and contradiction, it would be opportune to substitute a logic based on difference and the desire to be in communion with the other towards the development of life (cf. *Science de la logique, II*, pp. 81–3). Such logic is founded on a negative imposed by nature itself and not a negative that we have at our disposal. Hence, the evolution comes from a natural energy which evolves thanks to one's own desire and the relationship with the dynamism of other living beings. The desire for the other as different by nature does not answer the need to fill a lack but a longing for a development which cannot come true without the relation with other living beings. It is difficult to agree with Hegel that 'something is living only as far as it contains contradiction in itself' (idem). The development of living beings does not seem to be dependent on contradiction(s) but on an environment which is or is not favourable to their growth and that they can or cannot handle in favour of their own being, beginning with the environment that the other natural beings represent.

The 'idealism of life' of which Hegel speaks (notably in *Esthétique I*, p. 153) does not exist, according to me. Life itself is capable of giving to itself an organic unity and of growing until its blossoming, a blossoming which must undergo death and rebirth or resurrection—to which, for example, the vegetal world testifies. That does not amount to an evolution from contradiction(s). It is true that contradiction, in Hegel's work, already acts at a constructed level—between a being and a nothingness already culturally defined. The negative at work in assuming the partiality of being a man or being a woman is quite another matter. It does not only operate between two notions or concepts which oppose one another, or at the level of two determinations of the same concrete being likely to oppose one another. It is a question of the determination which originally determines 'to be' itself and which makes specific the existence of each in an insurmountable way without for all that opposing it to any other. If, for Hegel, the essential difference corresponds to a constructed opposition, the difference which exists between the two genders corresponds to a difference of nature, to the particularity of a natural essence—a difference between sexual chromosomes.

The Spiritual Character of the Union Between Different Subjectivities

In the beginning, there is neither being nor nothing—neither Being nor nothingness—and a unity of their opposition either. In the beginning, a copulation exists between different beings, different germ cells, giving rise to particular beings of which each corresponds to one of the participants in the copulation of which it itself was born. As particular, this being, or better this 'to be', is accompanied by a negative, but the latter cannot reduce it to nothingness. Quite the contrary, it grants to it consistency, even if it is not just any consistency. The negative at work does not act as a more or less but rather as a limit allowing 'to be' to become effective. To be or not to be does not take place at the same level and cannot pass into one another as is possible when they are only abstractly defined.

In the same way, to be and not to be—being and nothing; Being and nothingness—do not abolish one another in the becoming, but assuming the non-being that the partiality of 'to be' involves is what allows its becoming. Each singular being is not contradictory, as Hegel would like, but it is particular and partial compared to all the existent beings, and its becoming is dependent on its relations with other existent beings. In other words, the existent being is limited from the beginning by the 'to be' that it is, and it is not only its mode of existing which determines it. Nor are its birth or its death likely to determine it qualitatively. It is first the determination of its being as sexuate which represents its irreducible qualitative difference. This difference is no longer a kind of logical operation over which we could gain mastery, it determines our global being as consciousness but also as qualitative modality or state of the matter that we are—as its shaping before any shaping from our part.

This determination exists independently of consciousness and it cannot fall into a binary logic in which 'to be' and 'not to be' confront each other and merge into a complementarity supporting the becoming. Nor can the other, likely to fill the place of non-being according to Hegel, come into such a process, either at intra-subjective or at inter-subjective levels. 'I am a woman' and, in a just as well necessary way, 'I am not a woman' cannot be acceptable sentences in a logic presumed to guarantee the truth of the living. And the other cannot appear at the same time to be a non-other either. In the two cases, a real resists such argumentation(s) and quibbling—a real, or a truth, which exists by itself and cannot be subjected to a dialectical process which does not take root in life itself. It subsists on this side or beyond the affirmation that 'only the spiritual is what is actually real' (Hegel, *Phénoménologie de l'esprit,* pp. 17 et 22–3). Unless the spirit is the flowering of the living human being and not a human construction which pretends to develop regardless of a natural belonging—privileging to do, or to make, to the detriment of being, the active and external deed to the detriment of a more passive and internal state.

If the internal state is truly considered, the relation to the other as other, and not only to me as other, is decisive. Hence, in the process of reflecting I must take the other into account and not only the other but also my relationship with this other. However, to think about the other is a complex operation because in such thinking I am anyway also present. Certainly, I can try to imagine something of the other from what appears of him or her through their gestures, words and ways of behaving. But I run the risk of reducing the other to object(s) if I do not wonder about whom or what is the cause of all that. If a thinking about then can exist it is only as a sort of matrix which welcomes what I perceive of the other without ever being able to objectify this other. To think about what happens in the relationship between the other and myself is perhaps a means of making subjective what I perceive and welcome of the other, and of succeeding in rendering in a way predicable that which can exist between us.

If my reflections concern my relation to and with an other, I cannot subject them to the negative in order to become. My own subjectivity must agree to be transformed in order to render the relationship possible. My thinking about the other cannot be merely speculative either, it must be also fleshly. It is from the state that the other arouses in me that I can modify my way of being with the possibility and the quality of a link with this other in mind. Then the becoming happens without contradiction. It is the development and blossoming of life which are at stake and the search for their possible modalities, which needs a certain structuring, but cannot close up in a system.

Art could play a main role there as mediation between the body and the mind, in us and between us. Transforming us into works of art for one another is also a manner of making spiritual a fleshly sharing. And if every loving relationship is basically religious, mediating it through art is a way of humanly incarnating the divine between us. According to Hegel, Greek art represents 'the highest expression of the absolute and Greek religion is that of art itself' (*Esthétique II,* L'art classique, II, L'art grec comme réalisation de l'art classique, p. 163; *Aesthetic II,* The Greek Art as Incarnation of the Classical Art). For that very reason, Christian art represents another era of efflorescence of art that Protestantism will suspend by resorting to a supposedly more spiritual relation to God. Hegel joins together the eviction of art by Protestantism with that of the figure of Mary who, according to him, is the most achieved figure of the union between the human and the divine thanks to love. Protestantism would challenge or give up this figure of the absolute as sentiment in maternal love for a more exclusively mental approach to the divine, which would be more spiritual. Is it not to neglect the fact that the absolute of love is not limited to a sentiment but entails the spirit itself—something to which the Annunciation probably bears witness in the Judeo-Christian tradition and the strange word saying that the conception of Jesus in Mary depends only on the Holy Spirit?

Could it be possible to suggest that the amorous desire between lovers is even more spiritual than maternal love and that the importance of grace in Protestantism is, perhaps, what substitutes for or announces the possible fulfillment of amorous desire as the most accomplished modality of the union between the human and the divine?Hegel does not say anything about the relation of this desire with the absolute and the divine, and he subjects it to the 'good behaviours' and to procreation in the framework of marriage. He also interprets the figure of Jesus as incarnation of 'the idea of love in its universality, the Absolute, the spirit of truth in the elements and form of the sentiment' (cf. *Esthétique II*, L'art romantique, Chapitre I, II, c, p. 288; *Aesthetics II*, Romantic Art, Chapter I, II, c) without truly alluding to the physical and sensitive dimension that incarnation is presumed to mean and to which the Gospels abundantly testify, notably by the importance of touch in various forms in Jesus's life and work. Even the maternal love of Mary is evoked as purity of a 'sentiment' without referring to the bodily and fleshly link existing between Mary and Jesus. However that may be, privileging the maternal aspect of love amounts to avoiding wondering about the desire between lovers and assuming the negative that it involves, as a figure of the divine incarnation of Spirit.

When he broaches this subject, Hegel speaks of 'sensual pleasure', 'subjective interiority of sentiment', 'complete fusion of consciousness with that of the other', even of 'a feminine abandon or abnegation' representing love in its full beauty (op.cit., L'art romantique, chapitre II, II L'amour, p. 313; Romantic Art, Chapter II, II, Love). Torn apart between a natural belonging, which is itself divided into 'sensual pleasure' and 'subjective interiority of sentiment', on the one hand, and the absolute idea of love which is incarnated in Jesus, on the other hand, love, in Hegel, is neither that which can unify body and spirit nor that which could incarnate a figure of the absolute in which subjectivity and objectivity make only one. Love remains a sort of stage in human becoming which would not succeed in overcoming the split between nature and spirit. This probably results from the fact that love is thought as a solitary affect but not as the possibility of truly incarnating the relational dimension of our being. For Hegel, love is either the abandonment of one's own subjectivity to that of the other or the 'passage of one's own subjectivity into that of an other' (op. cit. pp. 312–13; idem) but never the union of two subjectivities which differ from one another by nature—which requires another relation to the negative and another dialectics than the Hegelian.

The Absolute of Love

Hegel does not view love as a stage towards the accomplishment of Spirit, nor as a figure corresponding to the Absolute. Love, for him, rather is a kind of subjective fancy without a truly objective foundation, unless it serves great causes, as is the case, for example, in Greek tragedies. Generally, love clashes with the interests of the state, the love of country, or the service of family. For Hegel, love between lovers obeys individual, narcissistic or intensely close interests in which each is in search of itself through the other.

In fact the conception of love according to Hegel appears to be quite nihilistic: the choice of the partner is often a matter of chance, faithfulness between lovers seems to be uncertain and the amorous feeling incapable of universality. The objectivity of love and of its sharing as a path towards human accomplishment seems to be unknown to him. As is the case with the relational dimension of subjectivity, with the ontological importance of the difference between the sexes and with the crucial role of the mediation of touch? In Hegel—as in other philosophers as Merleau-Ponty or Levinas—if there is a question of fusion as a negative relational aspect, the positive aspect of intersubjectivity that communion represents is ignored. An yet this way of sharing touching one another plays a decisive role in the human becoming and allows having access to an absolute corresponding to an infinite subjectivity, which, for Hegel, could be reached only by the spirit—'only Spirit imparts reality to the absolute as an infinite subjectivity' (op. cit., L'art romantique, Chapitre premier, III, L'esprit et la communauté humaine, p. 291; op. cit., Romantic Art, First Chapter, III, Spirit and Human Community). Could love not be substituted for spirit in such a statement? Beyond the fact that it can carry out the union between the body and the spirit, could not love represent a figure of the universal and the absolute in which individualism and egoistic subjectivity would be overcome? Has neglecting this stage in human becoming and having confined it in the private domain without a suitable cultivation not deprived the individual, but also the collective, spirit of becoming incarnate in a more accomplished absolute and universal? Has having gone, without transition, from the individual to the community and, consequently, having subjected the individual to the collective, not ended in taking no account of the irreducible difference between man and woman? Hence, does this difference, which takes root in nature, not resurface as differentiations, generally quantitative, inside an already constructed whole? Only an impetus arising from longing for the absolute would be able to reopen the closed system that not only such a whole, but also the individuals then form. If that is the way it is, is it not because the former as well as the latter ones are developed regardless of life itself? Life is not without forms, but these forms do not constitute a whole closed on itself because life is in perpetual evolution, and even in perpetual communion. Only the individual constructed according to speculative norms and a world constructed according to modalities of cohesion more or less artificially conceived correspond to closed entities that spiritual or community imperatives, which are also more or less arbitrary, must afterwards reopen. A dialectical process can take place between these closing and opening but it remains inside a system by which it is determined. Only what it did not take into account can reopen it—by explosion, fragmentation, destruc(tura)tion for which philosophers as Hegel feel a particular sympathy.

What would happen if the community was composed of living beings which prevent any totality from closing up by their growing, but also by exchanges, notably dialogues, between them? If they are only constructed entities inside a closed world, what could be the meaning of such exchanges? To strengthen the validity of the whole of which they are prisoners? To contest with one another until they submit themselves to one another because they have been defined as opposed to one another? Is it not the case as far as men and women are concerned?

For Hegel, holding a dialogue is a less perfect modality, the embodiment of a more spiritual dialectics which takes place inside one and the same consciousness, as a logical process aiming to reconcile into a unity supposedly antithetic aspects of being. As Hegel himself writes 'I am the fighting' before any fight with anyone. It is in himself that 'sometimes he divides and splits up, sometimes is reconciled or reunited with himself'. For lack of acknowledging the radical difference of the other outside of himself, Hegel perpetually conflicts with himself. It is in that way that he provides himself with limits, unity, and identity by differing from himself to reach what he considers the most absolute self. He indefinitely struggles with himself between being and non-being until he finds a place where this quest draws to the best close. He has not acknowledged the non-being of himself that the other represents—the insurmountable difference which resists his dialectics and has more to do with a negative onto-theology than with a calvary. He has not admitted the partiality of his subjectivity and of the use of the negative of which he is capable only by himself, an operation that finally exhausts him instead of leading him to the discovery of his full being.

According to Hegel, the individual could turn to history and claims its owing from it. Indeed, history captures in its evolution all that humans project onto or abandon to it without their knowing. They unknowingly and unwittingly feed a world which little by little deprives them of their substance and exiles them from themselves, in particular from their sensitivity, their desire and their flesh. Henceforth, they form a sort of undifferentiated magma in which no one keeps one's self-control, is responsible for oneself, for one's will and one's longing for transcendence. The world and history have appropriated all particularities in the name of a Reason presumed to be capable of taking account of them, of organizing them and ensuring their cohesion and durability as a sort of divinity who would know what is suitable for each but is out of its own will and knowledge reach.

Reason would feed itself on the life of each of us and would transform it into a collective spirit from which the truth of being and the rules of 'good behaviour' could be defined. In what this Reason has its origin and its legitimacy to intend to govern us? To what has it led us today? How could we recover our own 'to be' and the way of developing and sharing it in our era, given the 'global spirit' which, henceforth, lays down the law on us? How to stop such a world-wide evolution which seems to conduce the world more and more to its ruin? How could we oppose our consumption in order to fuel it? What energy remains to us to do that, and what self-consciousness which corresponds to a real self and not to a construction which already removed it from us? What dialectical process, what conflict(s) could still return to us our subjectivity from such entanglement of subjectivity and objectivity in which it becomes alienated because of our unconscious submission to Reason? How to find our natural belonging again in the cultural evolution and mixing of cultures more and more mediated by techniques which substitute for human beings? How to regain our path in a supposedly vital flux in which Spirit has already assimilated, confused, fluidified and sterilized our individual desires to entrust them to a universal history, which forgets that the universal lies, first an in an irreducible way, in our natural identity itself?

Part III

The Question of Being

8

Confusion of the Living with the Made

Being That There Is

If logos is considered to be that which takes place in itself, by itself and for itself (cf. Heidegger, *Qu'appelle-t-on penser?*, Deuxième partie, V; *What Is Called Thinking?*, Part Two, Lecture V), how can we ignore the difference between the words which originate in/from a masculine natural belonging or a feminine natural belonging? How does such belonging express itself in predication assuming that the logical process allows it to express itself? And how to get a dialogue going between two differently sexually determined subjectivities? Could it be necessary to remove them from their natural belonging, to put them in the neuter, not to say to castrate them, in order that a communication should be possible between them?

This makes us wonder about the use of the word 'to be' or 'is' (op. cit., Deuxième partie, V and VI; op. cit., Part Two, Lectures V and VI). When I say 'human being is', the use of 'is' is already the result of a construction. Strictly speaking, human being is not, only men and women are. There is no doubt that some predicates permit us to affirm that the human being corresponds to a certain entity, but it is not possible to say that 'human

L. Irigaray, *The Mediation of Touch*, https://doi.org/10.1007/978-3-031-37413-5_8

being is' as 'the apple tree in flower is' or 'this woman is'. We never are really in the presence of a human being.

The question concerning being—and first the use of the word 'is'—supports and undermines all the construction of western metaphysics. Indeed 'to be' is originally used by the Greeks to designate beings which objectively exist. Then 'to be' is a word which both acknowledges the existence of these beings and integrates them in a logos so that we as humans should remember them, construct a world to which they belong and communicate about them. Already the 'to be' of being—for example of this 'apple tree in flower'—is removed from its life and its growth by a mental appropriation by the human being. Nevertheless, this 'apple tree in flower' still refers to a real thing. As soon as logos produces generics—the tree—reality corresponding to 'to be' or 'is' becomes more problematic. Indeed, what reality corresponds to the word 'the tree'? A great part of that which we consider to be real results from such an use of the word 'to be', which refers either to a real existing by itself or to a reality produced by the logos. Wondering about the relations between generic, particular and singular can enlighten us about the possible ambiguity in the use of the word 'to be' or 'is'.

Such questioning can also help us leave a confinement in a discourse which cuts us off from the real. As Heidegger writes: We are in a world which is constructed by a certain use of the word 'to be'. How can we emerge from that world in order to be situated in a universe of living beings not yet transformed into words among others? How to recover the breath and energy which not only animate us as living but also circulate and are shared between us? How to make our sojourn, our home among living beings and not only among words which designate them? How to return to such a place on this side or beyond the spoken words—an on this side and a beyond which are not already determined by the logos? (op. cit, VI, in particular p. 171; op. cit., VI, in particular pp. 177–78). And how do these 'on this side' and 'beyond' relate to what happens between us as naturally different? What place is created by this relation, what possible sojourn from which we do not stop freeing ourselves, although it is probably the one which allows us to become humans? How to open, reopen that place, that clearing in spite of our alienation, notably as living who are different, by a history, a culture, a community which constantly negate this difference as an irreducible physical and psychical determination?

What or who has appropriated the place which is opened by and between us by our difference? Has something of that place not been assimilated, stolen and hidden in the neuter of a 'there is' which appears to us both as an opportunity and as an obligation which give to the neuter a mysterious meaning which fascinates, seduces and removes us from our being and our destiny? What real is concealed in the apparently ingenuous presence of the 'there is'? To what reality does it refer according to whether we are in a natural or a cultural place? It is not the same. But Heidegger does not take account of such difference although it distinguishes Greek culture from his culture—the 'there is' from cosmos from the 'there is' from logos. He does not seem to acknowledge the cultural hospitality that nature as such offers to us, a nature that we ought to appropriate, and appropriate to ourselves, including thanks to poetry, so that we should dwell in it. The 'there is' about which Heidegger speaks would be already constructed. By whom? For whom? And in accordance with what necessity?

It is understandable that Greeks endeavour to reach the objectivity of a 'there is' in the neuter. But how is it possible after acknowledging that subjectivity is the cause of meaning? Does the perception of nature not differ according to the subject who perceives ? And if it is still possible to say that the natural environment gives me to be, does that remain true when it is a question of a cultural environment? Would the 'there is' due to the elaboration of culture by men only be capable of 'putting things in their being and keeping them in it'? (op. cit., p. 179; op. cit., pp. 188–89). Of what things is it then a question? And what could be said about the one who would be capable of putting a subject in his/her being and keeping this subject in his/her being? Is it not necessary to resort to the intervention of another subjectivity and the respect for the difference between subjectivities?

Does the presumed lack of terrestrial measures, to which Heidegger alludes (op. cit. p. 182; op. cit., p. 195), not originate from a failure in the respect between living beings due to neglecting, even forgetting difference between their belonging to 'to be' on the one hand, and their way of developing—*phuein*—on the other hand? Hence violence arises and pseudo beings emerge as the result of the absence of consideration for beings really existing, and existing by themselves, and for the relationship between them. It is not only heavens which give measure to earth, it is also interrelations between living beings with respect for the life of each—each giving to each and receiving from each the possibility of becoming the ones that they are.

Respect for the difference between living beings acts as a structure from which the 'to be' of being, as well as the relations between beings, can develop. This asks to acknowledge and assume the invisible part of living beings which escapes our mastery. Indeed, if a living being is before me, I cannot for all that imagine it as living. What I see and can represent of it corresponds neither to its life nor to the core of its subjective potential—either I subject such parts of being to the logos or I admit that the logos is unable to truly express 'to be' as such. What logos can express is not only ambiguous, as Heidegger thinks (op. cit., p. 189; op. cit., pp. 201–202), it is also partial and does not correspond to the saying of 'to be' itself but only to its appearing.

How could logos ensure the safeguard of the 'to be' of being whereas, to say it, it cuts it off from its living origin? It cuts it off—Heidegger would say 'picks it off'—to keep it. Heidegger even says more 'When we take into our care that which is lying before us, we keep respect for its 'being lying before'. 'Through this respect, we gather ourselves around what is lying before, and we assemble what is kept under our guard' (op. cit. p. 193; op. cit., p. 209). It would thus be a matter of gathering ourselves together around what is put down before us, which we afterwards intend to gather. This presupposes an interdependence—a hermeneutic circle?—concerning the assemblage of being(s) as a world, as logos or the human self, which prevents from any possible continuity of a becoming of one's own as a peculiar becoming.

The Non-existence of the Generic

There is no doubt that we can, and even must, help another living being, in particular another human, to be and persevere in its faithfulness to iself. This is possible only if we are each capable to gather ourselves together in such a faithfulness—which needs to maintain a free space between ourselves, open by the acknowledgment of our difference relative to 'to be' and the way in which it becomes incarnate. In other words, it is necessary that each can gather itself together independently of the fact of being gathered by the other, all the more so since the being of each does not completely appear to the other. In reality, it does not completely appear to itself either, but each can perceive something of it in particular through the gathering itself together that self-affection and its expression by the middle voice can provide. I have not merely to actively gather myself or let myself passively gathered by the other, I must endeavour to gather myself together so as to perceive something of the one that I am. I must attempt to keep guard on myself through perceiving the limits of my body touching each other—which individualizes me with respect to the other(s) and to the world.

Such taking into one's care must be watchful, in particular as far as sexuate belonging is concerned. This is from the outset as much a for-the-other as a for-oneself. The latter is even often perceived through the desire for the other. Nevertheless it must also be preserved as a for-oneself to safeguard desire itself. The for-oneself cannot become alienated, together with that of the other, by/in procreation either—which ends in the death of parents according to Hegel. For lack of each keeping effective and alive the for-oneself-for-the other corresponding to their respective sexuate belonging, man and woman lose their identity and subjectivity in the parental function of reproduction. Intending to be more spiritual, they become slaves of a natural reproductive potential without making blossom their sexuate potential for themselves and between themselves.

An other means of paralyzing such potential is to invest it in cultural or civic values extraneous to its purpose—which our culture, in particular our philosophy, has done. This has been made possible notably because of a lack of consideration for the impact of sexuation on discourse. In other words, because of the forgetting of the fact that a physical logos determines, independently of our consciousness, the metaphysical logos, which does not recognize that which really exists in what it considers to be true, although that could be one of its main causes.

The living being is its 'to be'—at least it ought to be so. Of course, it cannot be it completely in the present. In the present it is being its 'to be'.

A living being moves by itself through becoming its 'to be', through becoming the one it is. Its presence is a manifestation of the one it is at present, but not of all the potentialities of its 'to be'.

Living beings, in particular the human being as living, depend on relations to/with the other living in order to be. Their being themselves cannot amount to actualizing an essence—a being defined once and for all as their ideal being. Being is a process to make effective their/our 'to be'. And the relations to the other(s) need a constant distinction between that which corresponds to the 'to be' of the other and to one's own 'to be'—in the present: between the being of the 'to be' of the other and the being of one's own 'to be'. Paying attention to the becoming of each living being has been put on hold by generics, ideals, constructed realities which interrupt or lead astray their moving by themselves. Hence living beings are no longer present as being by themselves but as being the result of a making and an objectifying which thwart their development and their relations to/with the other living.

Often the reduction to object is implemented by resorting to constructed transcendences which are substituted for transcending oneself to become one's 'to be', on the one hand, and for entering into relation with beings which are different, on the other hand. However, transcendence ought to get true through these gestures without ever coinciding with already objectified ideals. Desire and love ought, at each time, to produce transcendence that humans need to become the ones who they are.

In such a process, the incarnation of subjects and their belonging to living beings could overcome the traditional subject-object split. This probably results from conceiving of subjects as abstract beings which search for recovering something of living through the consistency of object(s). Wanting to be of an ideal nature, subjects lose the dynamism that they need to exist. It is by appropriating and overcoming the object(s) that they get moving in a way that already results from the way of conceiving object(s) in a metaphysical way.

Returning to life itself is that which allows us to go out of such a mechanism which functions in a more or less artificial manner. But this requires another interpretation of the nature of being. According to western thought being is interpreted as a sort of incarnation of its ideal—or of its Being—which makes it dependent on an objective extraneous to life.

Returning to the living demands that presence is no longer conceived as the appearing of an ideal essence but as the current manifestation of life (*Qu'appelle-t-on penser*, in particular Deuxième partie, X; *What Is Called Thinking;* Part Two, in particular Lecturer X). In other words, 'idea is no longer the face through which something at each time shows its aspect, looks at us and so appears, for example as a table' (op. cit., p. 205; op. cit., p. 222). But the living being that, for example, a tree is is revealed to us according to a face which corresponds to the moment of development of the living that it incarnates. The same does not go for the living as for the made, and it is not by chance that Heidegger refers to a fabricated object—a table—to comment on presence in a metaphysical logic.

If Heidegger does not resort merely to an idea in his comments on presence, he conceives of Being as a sort of generic process which is not totally foreign to it, notably in his manner of interpreting the words of Parmenides: *Chre to legein te noein t'eon emmenai.* It would be possible to propose another interpretation which avoids the tautology *eon eon.* Then the question would be of suggesting that *emmenai* could amount to a middle voice and that the sentence could be interpreted in a way almost opposite to a metaphysical interpretation as: being is the present being of its 'to be'. Such reading of the words of Parmenides sends present being back to its living origin instead of extrapolating it into a Being as a result of a cultural elaboration. In that case, being partakes of the 'to be' that it is by nature and not of an ideal essence.

Living Being/Fabricated Being

It seems that the life itself of beings has been trapped in the construction relative to an external world—which, perhaps, reflects a sort of ideal narcissism at a subjective level. There is, above all in the conception of being, an assimilation of beings being by themselves to fabricated beings. And yet the formers have their being in/from themselves, whereas the latter ones receive it from whom and even from what have made them. It is not a question of the same sort of beings in the two cases and they are not liable to the same sort of predication. But the logos—at least as Heidegger views it—aims at assembling them into a whole, attributing to Being that which exceeds, compensates for, palliates by/in putting on hold such an assembling by man. Consequently, Being is presupposed to have various and even opposed meanings, notably that of the 'to be' or natural essence of living beings and that of the essence of fabricated beings. In the word 'Being' are thus confused that which has to do with life, on the one hand, and that which has to do with a human conception, on the other hand.

This gives to Heidegger's thought a magic character and a coefficient of indeterminacy which results from an inextricable combination of an economy corresponding to life and an economy corresponding to the logos. For example, Heidegger quotes as beings, to support his argumentation: the mountain, the house, the tree. Now these three beings do not belong to the same sort of beings. How is it possible to assemble them into a whole? How could the same whole integrate them and let appear each according to its 'to be'? How can they relate to one another in such assembling? What perception of them can we keep? And could resorting to Being give back each to itself? Does this not, instead, capture them into a constructed world in which each alienates its own existence, its own truth and an origin which irrevocably determines it?

It first matters to acknowledge that predication cannot obey the same logic when it is a question of living beings, which have in themselves their own dynamism, and of fabricated beings. Their way of relating to space and time is different. For living beings the question is above all of acknowledging the ones that they are and how they can become, whereas fabricated beings can be more subjected to imperatives external to them concerning their matter, their manner of being made, their use and so forth. The way of relating to saying and to thinking as well as their articulation cannot be the same in the two cases. And if a living being can, ultimately, do without articulate language to exist, the same does not go for a fabricated being—it is somehow or other the result of a saying.

Of course the conjunction of which a living being, and particularly a human, was born can be considered a sort of exchange of saying between two beings, but it is the saying of the body or of a fleshly desire and not that of the constructed logos which distinguishes itself from them, notably by resorting to judgment and representation. Such operations are not mostly useful towards the union of two living beings, in particular of two humans who are different. And if Heidegger speaks of the necessity of a leap to seize, by a translating, the nature of the link between *einai* and *emmenai,* could it not be possible to suggest that it is rather a question of a necessary transformation in order that two living beings should bind to and unite with one another?

Once more, has not man considered the relation between *einai* and *emmenai* to be something external to him but of which he could be the agent? He did not sufficiently wonder about the process through which he could gather himself together and unite with another living being, notably with a subject different from himself. This needs a trans-formation of the one and the other and not a translation of the one into the other.

Presence has too often been thought as the result of a deed of man, notably thanks to the logos, and not as the appearing in the present of a living being. Thus would come into presence that which or who separates in the present from the assemblage that the logos implements. The present being would also emerge from the Being resulting from the constitution of the totality of a world by the logos. The present being would become separate from Being to appear to us and, then, would return to Being. It ought to take off the veil in which the logos keeps it and return to/in it.

A truly other interpretation of presence is possible: being gives itself to be seen in the present as the appearing of the one it is. More exactly, one could say about being that it is itself—*emmenai*. Indeed, for lack of being by itself, of being itself, being cannot appear to us by itself through a present moving of the 'to be' that it is.

These two conceptions of presence correspond to two different views of the world between which Heidegger seems to waver. Perhaps he attempts to find the first again starting from the second—which the examples that he proposes would prove. And yet, that is not possible. Such a confusion also appears in the way in which Heidegger defines the objectivity of being. This would result from the standing in front of him of being regardless of the objectivity of its own existence, which does not necessarily appears to us. So the fact that being is itself appears to us only indirectly and is not dependent on us. And yet it is from that that the one that it is can appear to us, particularly as living. Hence its appearing-disappearing corresponds to an alternation between exposing itself outside and withdrawing within itself that the becoming of life entails.

Anyway such moving is not solely dependent on us and does not truly appear to us, but it exists. And to ignore or misjudge it means leaving to technique the production of presence—the first technique being logos itself.

Every presence is either appearing of life by itself or the result of a technical production. Heidegger does not sufficiently distinguish one production from the other. He himself lets us glimpse that in some of his statements (see, for example, *Qu'appelle-t-on penser?*, p. 216; *What Is Called Thinking?*, p. 235). Of course the Greeks do not yet wonder about that because their culture is still faithful to cosmos and not dependent on logos. Their culture still speaks of living beings more than of objects which are fabricated, notably by logos itself. No doubt that their culture concerns itself, at least in part, with what is situated in front of the speaker, but that still amounts to elements of the cosmos, to beings living by themselves and that are not made by man somehow or other, including through representation. The passage from a culture relating to cosmos to a culture dependent on logos is expressed in the first intervention of the chorus in the Sophocles tragedy Antigone—and more generally in all this tragedy. Antigone is the figure who announces and denounces this transition.

Two Modalities of Presence

In a cosmic culture, the speakers are part of a living whole that they endeavour to say. They do not yet distinguish themselves from it. Gradually they will become products of the logos as the other elements of the cosmos. Each is then deprived of relating to its own life as well as of living relationships with other living beings. What could maintain a living link between beings of the new world was probably the link between subjectivities. But, beyond the fact that subjectivity as such does not yet exist in Greek time, the link between beings has been subjected to a discourse external to them, a discourse privileging denomination and information to the detriment of communication and communion. From that results the objectivization of every being, including of subjects themselves, an objectivization depending on the sovereignty of logos and not on the objectivity of the being of everyone or everything and on the relationships between them.

Perhaps logos could take another path or adopt another logic, for example starting from the sentence of Parmenides: it is necessary to say and to think that being is being itself. It is necessary that all words about knowing correspond to the being present in its 'to be'—that life of each be not subjected to the economy of a certain discourse but that this attempts to say and keep every life in/as what is its own, notably concerning its relationships with other beings.

They are two quite different ways of conceiving of presence. This can be viewed as the present appearing of life according to a specific natural essence—for example, an oak is not whatever tree. Presence can also mean the unveiling, in its appearing to us in the present, of a being the essence of which is dependent, at least in part, on a human making, notably through the logos. The call of which Heidegger speaks, can be a call for/of life towards its safeguard, its growth, an invitation to living being to express itself towards communication or communion or it can be a call for a search for being—perhaps Heidegger would say for Being—on hold in the logos. The call is then of a different nature, as is also the transcendence which must be considered. It is not a question of the same call nor of the same way of answering it, either by thinking or by the mode of saying. And if the call, or recall, concerns somehow or other our desire, it is not a question of the same desire in the two cases—the desire for living and sharing life here and now does not amount to a desire for being— even for Being—resulting from a saying of the being(s) by the logos. The duplicity of the Being of being, of which Heidegger speaks, could also be different in the two cases. It could be a matter either of the present appearing of the 'to be' of a living being or of the re-appearing to us of the idea relative to the being of a living being through a linguistic and logical construction. Heidegger's thinking seems to waver between these alternatives—hence the difficulty in approaching it.

Heidegger writes that the call or 'the recall which re-commends our being to thinking' 'allows it to be free—and in a so decisive way that 'That' which calls us for thinking donates, for the truly first time, there is freedom of the free, in order that we could build in it a human dwelling' (*Qu'appelle-t-on penser?*, p. 232; *What Is Called Thinking?* p. 133).

According to Heidegger, we dwell, as humans, in what is to be thought. It does not exist, for him, a dwelling built by our relational being—a dwelling built by desire and love.

There is no dwelling in nature either, whatever his need of it, his attachment to it. Heidegger dwells in logos, which has been substituted for dwelling in cosmos in the Greek epoch. But the whole that logos represents is not the same as the one cosmos offered—a gathering of living elements which interact with one another. In logos, these elements are appropriated by man and deprived of their own origin, their own breathing, their own life—it is a whole in which they are included without being able to leave it. The relations to themselves and to others are determined by an order external and foreign to their beings. According to Heidegger, thinking could restore a space of freedom to human beings trapped in logos. But does this space not remain somehow or other inside logos? Could Heidegger's thought return to us our physical and sensitive origin, and the dynamism of our desire for one another? Of what desire is it then a question? Does logos, as it is already structured by Greek thinkers, allow us to continue to shape ourselves as living beings, and to place us in relation to our natural environment and other living beings?

Does not the hermeneutic circle in which the Heidegger's thinking moves—between Being of being and being of Being (op. cit., p. 261; op. cit., p. 227)—not cut us off from us as living and from our relations to other living beings? Is not then misjudging, even forgetting, an other possible interpretation of being, that which means the present state of the 'to be' of each living in accordance with its natural essence. The word 'essence' here must be understood as a specific modality of incarnation of life—for example my way of being present as a woman as well as the way of being present of an oak. Is it then a question of circularity or duplicity between being and Being or of a difference between a verb in the infinitive and a present participle? Does not such linguistic observation send us back to simplicity, especially that of our being, but also to the undertaking that our becoming as living represents? This becoming has to do with many other realities than those which are put before a living being but starting from which it can discover what or whom it is. Heidegger asserts that 'man finds himself in what is put before him' (op. cit., p. 257; op. cit., pp. 205–206). Does not human being rather find itself, or ought to find itself, through realities which cannot be put before it: intimacy, touch, interiority, development and relationality as such, invisible as a part of the real with which it has to do and so forth.

Does that which Heidegger calls thinking, and which requires a putting before oneself, not neglect a great part of the real which constitutes, or ought to constitute, our being as humans? Why? Because that is dependent on a view of man concerning the real? Thus is dependent on a privilege of sight, what is more of the way of seeing of man, which is accompanied by a more or less animal acumen (idem). The being of subjectivity, even of identity, of man as thinker is, moreover, determined by that to which he attends (op. cit., p. 260; op. cit., p. 215)—by the impersonal form of a 'That' or 'there is'—and not by what would be basically his own by nature.

Hence the question arises about the link between 'Being'—or 'to be'— and 'being'. Either the matter is of considering this link the present appearing of the 'to be' of each as being—this apple tree of my village appears to me flowering in that way in the current April month—or the generalization of such a presence—the apple tree generally appears covered in flowers in April. In the first case, the 'to be' of the apple tree is flowering when I meet it; in the second case, it appears, or reappears, to me from what I know of it through the logos.

Entering into Presence

In the latter sense, presence as such does not exist. Does this way of conceiving of 'to be' as presence not amount to substantivizing a process of putting into relation which assembles, in us and between us, different elements? Does what is called 'presence', and which is supposed to define being, not amount to a standstill on the appearing of a configuration which has no being as such? It is only the—visible?—expression of a possible incarnation of life, in us and between us. And to fix one's will on such a present figure, instead of devoting this will to becoming, can arouse resentment and revenge. Indeed, our energy is then paralyzed and is no longer at our disposal if not as an 'it was' without any possible 'it will be'. To be has always to do with an assembling, which appears or can be seen or perceived, in some or other way, according to the moment of its development. Only a robot can always move in the same manner, animated by a program which suits it once and for all. In a way, it is outside time because without becoming—a sort of artificial presence to which our culture would like to subject us through the discovery of an algorithm which is appropriate to us. But, if we remain alive, such an algorithm constantly changes depending on what we perceive, we receive, we assimilate of our environment, in particular of the other, of others.

The presence corresponds to an act which continuously evolves if we remain in relation to/with nature, in ourselves and outside ourselves, and we keep a certain degree of freedom. Resentment arises when we can no longer act in accordance with what or whom we are with our becoming in mind—when we can no longer actualize our 'to be'. This proves to be possible as long as we take charge of our incarnation and of the evolution of our natural being—a being in a way immortal as sexuate, but we must incarnate this sexuation in/by our particular existence, including our physical existence.

Resentment and a spirit of revenge perhaps result from our refusal to be the ones who we are more than a totality abstractly constructed. Willing to be ourselves as sexuate beings presupposes that we overcome a mere 'it was' while remaining faithful to the growth of our natural being. This is always developing as living—it is consistent and in becoming, and its permanence is due to its nature and is not the fruit of a mental elaboration. If nature is cause of our permanence, this wants difference without confining itself or returning to sameness, if not as to what originally determines us.

So I am a woman and I must become the woman that I am while constantly transforming myself notably by my relationships with different beings, particularly with other human being(s). Our will can be free only if it is truly our own, that is, if it is faithful to our natural origin. I am free to be as a woman. Whatever the obstacles culture sets against me, freedom is then mine and allows me to evolve while remaining faithful to the one who I am: a woman.

Heidegger wonders about the relation of Being to the being of man and that of the being of man to Being (*Qu'appelle-t-on penser?*, p. 81; *What is Called Thinking?*, p. 106). But does this Being exist if my being, as a human, is founded in my natural belonging, my original 'to be' and my relations to other living beings with respect for mutual differences? We cannot appropriate our origin as human beings, notably because it lies in a conjunction. Have we not transformed the original conjunction, from which our being arises, into many relations of subordination to attempt to appropriate, even to give to ourselves, our 'to be'? Has not the copula 'to be' or 'is', which originally means a conjunction, been used by our logic in order that the subjectivity of only one and the same being could appropriate our being born of two different living beings? And is it not such a basic mistake which generates Being as keeping on hold a conjunction because of the non-acknowledgment of the difference that it involves?

Besides, such a conjunction is unspeakable—thus extraneous to the logos. Only a certain use of syntax, of logic, can prepare its possible occurring, an occurring that we can recognize as being without ever seeing or appropriating it. How could we appropriate the intimate link between two different living beings? Could it be this impossibility which has caused its denial, even its oblivion, by our culture? And have we not transformed the desire, which invited us to remember it, into a relation of appropriation through/by subordination? Hence, desire no longer corresponds to a longing for being, to an intuition concerning the path towards being our to be. Rather, it becomes an aspiration, even a need, relative to a possession, to assets. As such it contributes to the destruction of our 'to be' but not to its accomplishment.

What is still to be thought, what is necessary to think is how our will can be transformed into a desire which gives us to be. This requires desire to unify us and unite us with the other(s), desire to give us to us and open us to the other(s), desire to be a bridge between the inside and the outside of us, but also between the past, the ones we were originally, and the ones we have to become.

If thinking is a work of hand, according to Heidegger, and if relating to matter is what prevents it from sinking into 'the void of its activity'—as is the case with the joiner concerning 'the relation to wood'—then it is rightful to ask Heidegger if a thinking unconcerned with our physical belonging is not a thinking which 'sinks into the void of its activity' (cf. *Qu'appelle-t-on penser?* p. 88: *What is Called Thinking?*, pp. 14–15). And yet is logos, and its current incarnation as technology, really concerned with our natural belonging? Does it pay a true attention to it? Is not its most secret claim to substitute for nature, in particular as far as the being of human is concerned?

So, if moving by itself is one of the most basic properties of the living, what is to be thought about the energy prosthesis that technology henceforth represents? Is it not transforming the human being into a sort of inanimate product that a technique ought to set, or set again, in motion? Where can then the being of humans withdraw? Has it not destroyed itself by its own productions—beginning with that of a language which does not accompany the development of the natural belonging?

If life never exists once and for all as complete forms, is not the challenge of technology to constantly subject us to finished forms—to enclose us in forms in spite of the perpetual becoming that the living beings that we are need?

9

To Be as a Conjunctive Verb

The Subject Before the Apple Tree

Things are still more complex when it is a question of the subject. Either this is an impersonal and abstract mechanism—a sort of technical device—to and through which all appears or reappears from a timeless and unchanging definition by the logos—through Being?—or the subject corresponds to a living being and the one it is, and even what it wills, in the present. The status of the being 'apple tree' but also the status of the subject who looks at it are different in the two cases, as well as that of their relation to 'to be'—or to Being—and being and their articulation. If the subject, as the being that he meets, place themselves, or have to be placed, in relation to their status in the logos in one case, in the other case they always are and are met for the first and sole time, and each must be perceived, but also created, in the present in accordance with the meeting. At least it goes this way for the subject as long as he or she remains living and responsible for the becoming of his/her life, and more generally for that of life itself. In that sense, two living beings can appear to one another on the condition that they gather themselves together in the invisible intimacy of their beings. What they let appear of themselves is necessarily accompanied by the maintenance of each in the invisible of the one it is. The meeting between the two is always a sort of dawn where they unveil themselves to one another for a first and sole time. What language provides us with such saying? And if it tries to emerge, how not to cover it again with a logic or a syntax which takes no account of the gathering of each in the particularity of its being?

In a certain way, Greek language, at the dawn of our western culture, is still a kind of parataxis. Logos has not yet assembled all beings through a syntax which cuts them off from their natural beings. Afterwards, logos imposes on beings a meta-physical assemblage and gathering instead of an assemblage and a gathering which take their physical belonging into account. And yet this sort of assemblage exists and it requires another gathering of beings between them. So sexuation of human beings acts as a way of physically gathering them together which corresponds to a certain syntax. This is different for a man and for a woman. Subjecting the two to the same syntax and pretending to gather them together by this syntax amounts to removing them from their own origin and relational beings.

Respect for difference between the sexes makes us differently wonder about relationship and proximity. A proximity respectful of difference obeys another logic than that which ignores the negative which permits the assemblage and gathering of living beings. This negative allows each to assume itself while opening up to the other as other—a deed which is not necessarily dependent on judgment and representation. It intervenes at a more physical and sensitive level where the development of life and its sharing can act as guide—provided that 'absence of limit of the same' has not imposed on 'thought its most curt limitation' (Heidegger, quoted by Granel in his Introduction to *Qu'appelle-t-on penser?*; cf. the Introduction of the French version of *What Is Called Thinking?*).

Indeed it is difference between two beings which allows them to approach one another. This proximity cannot happen without distance. But it is not necessary to go abroad in order that it should exist—respecting the other as different and belonging to another world is sufficient. Such difference must take root in a natural belonging so that the approach to the most intimate should take place. It only happens in a fleshly and spiritual relationship with the other which differs from us by nature thanks to the mediation of touch.

Touch, and the intimacy it makes possible, in that way can overcome the distance created by a culture which privileges sight. Then in my appearing to the other I separate from myself and cannot unite with the other. Favouring sight is one of the causes of the lack of intersubjectivity, already in Greek culture. The Greek thinker looks at the world and attempts to say it, including in its appearance. Each is so removed from itself and is appropriated by the other. And duality between two beings no longer exists.

One could suggest that the master-slave distribution already takes place in this way: one contributes to the becoming of life and the other enjoys this work by appropriating its result through appearance. Such appropriating of the work of natural growing occurs from the part of man from the beginning of our culture. Instead of working on his own natural development, man enjoys that of others, particularly that of woman and children. Moreover, he believes instead of growing, deferring his own becoming as a natural being to supra sensitive ideals. For lack of contributions and exchanges regarding natural development, this resorts to artifices: make-up of the body or imposition of inappropriate cultural forms, more or less inspired by a narcissism which drains the natural sap.

We do not yet, in particular as Westerners, have the means of becoming and becoming together in accordance with our natural belonging. We waver between maintenance or relapse into an amorphous naturalness and paralysis in forms extraneous to our nature. In these alternations, we lose the always immediate property of our natural life and of our desire for the other, an immediacy which must be cultivated to be shared, especially through a mutual respect between beings which differ by nature. For want of that, we are deprived of experiencing proximity because of the lack of differentiation between us or the confinement in our mirror image and its cultural substitutes.

Such deprivation also comes from a lack of memory resulting from a fusion or a shortage of difference in relating to the other, or from an exile due to our being captured in reflections and projections. All that thwarts our access to ourselves and that to a relationship between us as beings. We have lost the memory of our own being. We can recover it through our desire for the other, a desire both physical and meta-physical. This desire sends us back to ourselves as to that which has still to be fulfilled of our being, notably by thinking. We remember because we desire (*Qu'appelle-t-on penser?*, p. 21 and sq.; *What Is Called Thinking?*, p. 4 and pages down). But that for which we desire never merely stays in front of us and cannot be represented.

That for which we desire, at the level of being, has withdrawn into us and stays retired within us, even retired from us, unless the spark of the awakening of desire reminds us of its existence. Even then we cannot grasp to what we are called. This can be neither objectified nor represented, but it is. And it is not through a leap that we can approach it, as Heidegger suggests, but instead by withdrawing within ourselves, there where the memory of the conjunction of which we were born and we want to rebirth has been buried. We are summoned to this withdrawal by that which mysteriously touches us. We are summoned to return to the touch, which is withdrawn within us and even from us, on this side and beyond any object or any representation relative to the reality in which we stay. We are summoned to relate to being, in ourselves and between us. How could we answer such a call, or recall, and all the history which, then, turns towards us—a history which could cover us with all that which has been substituted for this being, has buried it under more superficial realities, and has even forgotten it? How to emerge from a tradition which has favoured our sight, our mind and the object to the detriment of touch, in us and between us? How to welcome the part of being which comes back to us without subjecting it again to a language and a logic which make it turn away from us again?

The Path of Beauty

Heidegger writes that 'beauty is a destiny of the being of truth, where truth means the unveiling of what is veiled. Beautiful is not what pleases but what falls under this destiny which happens when the eternal non-appearing, that is, the invisible happens in the most appearing

appearing' (op. cit., pp. 31–2; op. cit., pp. 19–20). And he suggests, also by his own relation to Hölderlin's work, that the poetic word can be a path towards unveiling Being through beauty. He also gives us to understand that *poiesis* and *techne* will share the destiny of thought in the West, the development of the second into logistic contributing more and more to the withdrawal of Being—or 'to be'?—from thinking (op. cit., pp. 33–4; op. cit., pp. 21–2), in particular from a thought caring about the living. Hence not only the desertification of the Earth, that Nietzsche foresaw, but also our own 'desolation' which diverts us from remembering the forgetting of Being—or 'to be'—notably by taking the path of beauty.

Is it not beauty which could preserve us from the disappearance of any relation to the world? Is it not beauty which maintains, in us and between us, a place that the sciences could appropriate with difficulty? This place is both physical and meta-physical and it allows us, as such, to stand on the edge of the horizon determined by our traditional logic, notably because beauty cannot be merely objectified, that it radiates something of the life of the flower or of the interiority of a human being who is neither reducible to an object nor appropriable by a subject. Beauty in a way is visible but it cannot be subjected to the norms of our predicative systems for all that. Beauty does not correspond to 'a representation which fits its object' (op. cit., p. 40; op. cit., p. 39). Something of another life, as a sort of autonomous 'subjectivity', is already at work in beauty.

Beauty is foreign to Schopenhauer's conception of the world in which the world amounts to a 'representation'. Beauty is an autonomous word of the one who produces it—a word which touches us extending the horizon beyond a visible which can be objectified. Beauty touches us as a sort of grace, regardless of any information or given datum which would be right, exact, could be verified, and technically reproduced. Beauty is a sort of through the 'That' of Being—a path to a recall—provided that it does not submit to a technique: make up, mere artistic production, reduction to scientific assessment and so forth.

To be the emerging memory of Being—or 'to be'—beauty must escape any mastery from our part. It must radiate from being without turning into it, it must remain transcendent to being without separating from it for all that. Thinkers of our tradition have often ignored this sort of transcendence. Sometimes it became incarnate in art, in particular in Christian art, but its radiating in/from presence seems almost unknown by thought, which then became a sort of science neglectful of Being. This perhaps results from our being unable to express in subjectivity a development and a transformation of life—which sometimes emerges as a sort of spark in the awakening of desire between two humans who are naturally different. The call for being that this awakening represents is a call for transcending oneself through a body—a call that the other incarnates, but that he/she must send back to us as something which transcends them. Perhaps Nietzsche alludes to that when he speaks of the difficulty of forgetting him.

When the call towards the other finds an echo in this other, we must be able to disregard the being that this other already is or appears to maintain wide-awake the transcendental dimension of desire. The call launched by desire can never be satisfied. The one who desires and the one who is desired must each for the other, and each by the other, preserve the call for the beyond that desire represents. This call cannot confine itself to overcoming the traditional man. This would amount to incarnating the 'overman' from an already past being. The call rather is intended for a not yet being, the appearing of which is radically unexpected. What can support its advent is the acceptance of his own partiality by man and of the possible existence of another world beyond the one which already exists, not as past or future but as the world of man—as being and the way of conceiving of Being, or of 'to be'.

We cannot anticipate that which can result from such an acknowledgment, and above all from an insurmountable negative; we can only know that it cannot correspond to only one being and only one Being—or 'to be'. More than criticizing the old man, including through criticizing oneself, it is thus a question of letting be this being still unprecedented that the human is—a being which is conceived not by only one but by two humans and two who are naturally different. Passing from 'animal to overman' asks for much more than criticizing the being that man is or was. This requires us to become aware of the unforeseeable of a conjunction between two different beings, a conjunction the outcome of which we cannot anticipate but only prepare a possible advent by transcending the ones we are towards a future arising of Being—or 'to be'—from the union with a naturally different being—which never appears unless secondarily, and not as Being, or 'to be', itself.

It is true that man is an animal not yet determined, as Nietzsche asserts, but the determination that he lacks is of conceiving himself as a being for and by an other and not only in itself and for itself. Considering our being as sexuate is crucial for such a discovery. Indeed sexuation is a for-oneself-for-the-other or a for-the-other which is also a for-oneself. This really particular and, in a way, unique character of sexuation involves, to acquire a human status, our assuming a negative. And this negative does not apply only to an object but to a subject and to his/her original being. Crossing the bridge between the old man of the West and a new man does not first of all ask man to overcome the revenge spirit. This in a way is only the result of his pretension to incarnating human being as universal. Rather the matter is of man accepting his own partiality and difference from the other and envisaging the relationship between two naturally different beings as the possibility of such becoming. Then it is not really a question of a bridge going from a place to another. Indeed, if there is a departure regarding the two places, there is not a unique and foreseeable end of the transition. And the will is no longer willing something but a willing oneself that cannot be carried out without the will of the other and the conjunction between two different wills.

To Be as a Verb

The question of Being is not merely 'a question of history' (Heidegger, *Introduction à la métaphysique,* p. 61; *Introduction to Metaphysics,* end of Part I). It also has to do with our provenance and the saying about it. Being says that we are, without saying how we reach the ones we are. The origin of the fact that we are is sometimes attributed to God, sometimes to nature, sometimes to a mother or a father and even to language. Any of these interpretations wonders about the copula or link between two living beings of which we were born. And yet in that perhaps lies the enigma of the signification of our 'to be'. Before I can say 'I am', to be ought to be able to indicate the origin of this 'I am'. However, it does not do that. Being does not question about the fact that 'I am' is first the result—the 'is' or the 'was'—of a conjunction. Being conveys a meaning that it does not unveil. Is it not from that that the fictitious, or magic, character of presence results?

As copula, 'to be'—or 'is'—generally is of use to ascribe to being, in particular to a living being, its determinations: he is young; she is clever; the squirrel is brown; the tree is in flower and so forth. Thus 'to be'—or 'is'—is used to determine and, in a way, incarnate being. Only one predicate can really be said of 'to be' as such—he is a man; she is a woman. Man or woman, as well as all other living beings, are before any predicate is attributed to them. But this does not indicate their provenance. For example, 'he is a man' presupposes that 'he is not a woman'; nevertheless, he is conceived by a man and a woman—which does not appear. In fact, man, as human being, is the result of an insurmountable logical contradiction. Hence our mystery regarding language—and also the difficulty in bringing together being and Being. We are and we are not a man—and even not a human being—contrary to what a famous syllogism asserts. It seems that to overcome such contradiction we have been split or we have split into two: the having become a substantive—a soma?—and the 'to be' of a verb—germ cells? But if 'to be' henceforth can put up with a substantive, it less puts up with the activity of a verb. It remains a 'to be' which longs for the infinite—in the infinitive. We would be a being defined by the logos, not by our natural being, in search of the infinite— torn between two aporias: the one of our origin and the one of our end, the two having something to do with soma and germ cells. For lack of considering our potential as living beings, we resort to death as limit.

As living, we are always limited but we do not perceive that. It is touch, and above all the re-touching ourselves, expressed by the middle voice, which can provide us with the perception of a living, thus moving, limit of our being. The 'I am myself' of self-affection allows me to be a limited growing—*phuein*. Such self-affection grants me to stay in myself, to perceive myself without any addition or construction from the outside. It is not my difference from a non-being in general which can help me to perceive myself as a singular being but, rather, my non-being the other— the other genus, the other germ cells.

Presence, then, becomes the manifestation of a 'to be' but also of a doing. But it is not at an appearing that it aims—it is a 'to be' that in this way becomes a verb. Self-affection which allows us to be does not aim at appearing but, instead, it institutes an interiority which lets 'to be' show through. To be as *phusis* or *phuein* does not appear except indirectly and it is neither unchanging nor stable, it is as long as it becomes. Self-affection as mediation between one's self and oneself brings limits and a dwelling in which 'to be' can appear as existing and can develop. It procures to it a sort of earth of flesh for its growing and blossoming. It creates an environment in which being can become incarnate and develop.

However, this being also longs for going outside itself especially to unite with the other. If the only stake of appearing was *phainestai*, it would stop the becoming of being—which has occurred in our tradition since Plato. Being has cut itself off from its origin and development to show itself, stopping in that way becoming as being, happening as being. But it is not above all through struggling against the world that being becomes its 'to be', it is by being faithful to its own origin—which privileging appearing does not. It is true that being faithful to one's own origin entails separating from the other while remaining bound to this other. The most original fight is there, and it is also the most subtle—I separate from the other to desire this other as other. It is in that way that I determine and accomplish the 'to be' that I am.

If 'to be' corresponds for some philosophers to that which lacks determination—which does not mean its non existence—one could say that 'to be' corresponds to 'to live'. Experiencing life as indeterminate is possible. Nevertheless, in order to be I must determine life. 'I am' does not amount to living in general unless I confine myself to a linguistic or logical assertion regardless of the real. I am provided that I am and only am my own 'to be'—which presupposes that I am faithful to my origin in its particularity. And they are my faithfulness to myself and my difference from the other which allow me to have access to my ontological status. For lack of that, I am only empirically determined by the context, notably the historical context, of my existence—at best with my being as a *Da-sein*. To be truly human such *Da-sein* must become flesh, which happens in particular thanks to relating to the other which differs from me by nature. Unless I entrust that to a religious tradition? But, then, what does flesh mean? And what happens to its horizontal incarnation, instead of its vertical being taken on hold by supra sensitive ideals?

Moreover, this is required by faithfulness to a dynamic and not only a static meaning of 'to be'. To live, to grow, to blossom while appearing and to remain faithful to myself in the present are possible only thanks to a sexuate belonging and a relationship with the other which differs from me by nature. This relationship can help me to exist beyond an organic growing that in a way I undergo; it is what allows me to say 'I am' as living. It is also that which lets and even makes me grow and blossom, in particular by arising and manifesting myself beyond any aspect merely physical while remaining natural. It is that too which grants me to dwell in myself in faithfulness to my own being.

The split between Being and being results, at least in part, from a lack of cultivation of this relationship. Then 'to be' only represents an original potential which is projected onto the infinite of a future for want of its becoming incarnate being possible. And, moreover, this 'to be' gets bogged down, freezes in a growing, an appearing, and stances which no longer have to do with the living. Hence its paralysis in one or various beings, its artificial becoming and its wandering in search of its real destiny. Our to be is also searching for itself in genealogy, in God or in supra sensitive ideals without ever appearing as the one it is.

When to Be Works Out the Gathering

It is true that 'to be' never appears merely as such: it exists and develops towards its blossoming while remaining. It is but never simply appears. The same goes for life, desire, love and what they produce as relationship between us. They are, but they are not merely present. Does the void of which Nietzsche speaks and about which Heidegger questions concerning the junction being-Being not come, beyond the forgetting of 'to be' as copula, from a misjudgment concerning 'to be' as an invisible reality and the substance of which is apparently undetermined? What Heidegger would sense when he says that Being is both the most undetermined and the most determined. And if 'to be' is perceived as void, is it not because the philosopher has deprived it of its meaning—in a way, as 'we have killed God', according to Nietzsche? Is not 'to be' that which our logic did not succeed in reducing to its categories? Does 'to be' not convey a meaning which eludes our tradition?—which does not mean that it lacks meaning.

Heidegger also says that the other of 'to be' can only be its negation: not to be. What does such an assertion mean? What 'to be' is it then about? And what 'not to be'?—which is also called 'nothingness'. Has Heidegger not too often transformed the verb 'to be', and its role of copula, into a substantive? And has not the negation applied to the copula also been transformed into a substantive: nothingness?

What does 'to be' mean as copula? It has been envisioned only as articulating a subject with an attribute. The fact that it could only express the 'to be' of the subject has not been truly contemplated—unless when it is a question of God who is the one who is. God would be what or who he is regardless of any attribute. He would synthetize all the positive attributes without them being named—absolutely undetermined and yet determined (*Introduction à la métaphysique,* La question sur l'essence de l'être, en particulier pp. 90–95; *Introduction to Metaphysics,* 'The Question of the Essence of Being' in particular pp. 85–91 Part III, 1 and 2). It is so much so that, to escape nothingness, we must be somehow or other similar to him. This conception of God has something to do with the Platonic idea, of which God would be a substantial complement. Does such a way of conceiving of God not stop at his attributes without considering God as a subject? In fact, 'I am what I am' does not yet amount to saying 'I am who I am'. To make such assertion possible, we must resort to another logic in which the negative does not apply to the attribute(s) but to the subject as such: 'I am who I am' and 'I am not who I am not', that is, another subject. The meaning of 'to be' is then quite different. If meaning refers to the attribute(s), it is more material and objective, even objectal, whereas if it refers to the subject it is above all ontological and has to do with 'to be' as origin and provenance of meaning, which can include a substantial and formal limitation. The first meaning presupposes an undetermined subject who is defined by his/her attributes, whereas the second meaning implies an originally determined subject with a specific ontological relation to himself/herself and to other subjects.

Then 'To be' corresponds to the in-stasis of a subject and/or his/her in-stasis among other beings, in particular in relation to a subject who is different—the place in which a habitable space occurs. Such in-stasis comes from an origin but it is experienced through a multitude of relations, and not only objectal relations. The mistake of metaphysics—and still that of Heidegger?—is to too quickly fix them in a substantive—being or Being— instead of wondering about their function as a verb. This contributes to privileging 'is' to the detriment of 'I am', 'you are' and so forth.

If one questions about the function of the verb 'to be', one observes that it can be used with almost all the prepositions—it has the most extensive potential. Only 'to live' could perhaps be substituted for 'to be'. The possible extension or generalization of its role of copula gives to 'to be' the comprehensiveness of its meaning. The latter cannot be fixed in any substantive; it acts as a mediation between substantives and not only between them. It shows that the most basic meaning is relational. What is still to be unveiled of 'to be' is that it is relation, and that the most meaningful relation is the one between two different subjects.

Our tradition has almost ignored such a meaning. It has focused on object(s) as means of constituting the subject and has neglected the role of the intersubjective relation. It has even transformed 'to be' into a sub- stantive in order to objectivize it. The meaning of 'to be' as a union between two different living subjects remains little-known—hence it searches for its meaning in procreation. And yet its first meaning has to do with 'to be'. But such meaning cannot be objectivized, it is the non representable cause of meaning. Instead of lying in the objectivization of a being, even as God, the 'to be' of being is then in the subject and in the conjunction between subjects. It is because these subjects and their con- junction exist that 'to be' arises, including without being objectivized.

To be is gathering. You as other give me to be by gathering myself together. Your difference does not constitute an opposition to the one I am, it represents a difference in relation to my being. We do not discover our true being by overcoming an opposition between us, mastering in that way a non-being. Rather our being emerges by acknowledging and assuming our not being the other. It is our difference which allows each of us to be unified in itself and for itself but also for the other and to unite with the other to generate and create our being.

How can we distinguish our 'to be' from the 'to be' of the other and from 'to be' in general? This question is still on hold. It is in this connection that the universal and the most immediately singular of life and of human destiny must be interrogated. What happens in the conjunction between two human beings? What is generated between two living beings made of body and language? How then can be asked the question concerning transcendence and the absolute? Indeed, such a meeting can either lead to a falling back into a mere physical facticity or be the opportunity of its transformation into a transcendence of flesh and its sharing.

To Be As Such Is Not Visible

If 'to be' implies the gathering of the self, it does not necessarily amount to appearing. On the contrary, this gathering happens in the darkness of the earth or of the fleshly intimacy. The becoming of 'to be' does not necessarily happen towards a visible blossoming, and it requires an alternation between visibility and invisibility. This becoming is not linear and does not obey a simple teleology. Moreover, 'to be' has not the same meaning in all the ages of history, which is not only due to a forgetting. For example, interiority is not determining in the Greek time, but it became so later, given the development of subjectivity and the impact of Christianity. Thus 'to be' could no longer amount to appearing; and to accomplish the ones who we are needed as much, perhaps even more, giving up appearing as a criterion of blossoming of our being. Then appearing can correspond to the radiance of an internal state which occurs without searching for it as such. And if becoming is inseparable from 'to be', the same does not go for appearing, which can be a mere means of accomplishing ourselves, notably as a mediation in the relationship with the other or an unintentional manifestation of blossoming.

The importance of appearing can also mean privileging sight to the detriment of the gathering of various elements of the being. This contributes to freezing the 'to be' of being in appearance(s) by cutting it off from the development of life and its flowering, which cannot be limited to appearing. It is even possible that, for the human being, this flowering rather requires to renounce appearing, as a negative theology and ontology give us to understand. Anyway, to blossom as a human cannot be reduced to become completely visible.

Greek culture has favoured a saying of the visible, which, historically, has needed a theology as far as the invisible was concerned. But the bridge between the Greek world and the Christian world is still to be built. Human blossoming demands a culture of the invisible, whether this is physical, psychical or spiritual. Regarding truth, the Greek philosopher has focused on the visible without considering the partial veiling that the truth entails and the non-unveiling that the appearing of living beings involves. This philosopher has also taken little account of the interaction, in particular between the living, in the way of conceiving of truth.

Privileging sight is probably a means to which the Greeks resorted to emerge from a lack of differentiation from nature and the maternal world lived as nature. Seeing was, for them, a means of coming into the world, of opening up to the world. This way of opening up to the world has ended in a new immersion in nature. But nature was henceforth viewed and mastered, at best contemplated, by human, and even by masculine, eyes. Man had not become sufficiently autonomous to coexist with the natural world: in himself, in the other(s), in the world itself. He remained trapped within only one horizon, including by his seeing.

The Greek world still lacked the interiority that a later religious culture tried to provide, often to the detriment of the natural world, by focusing on the invisible. The sensitive and fleshly world was not cultivated for all that; they were the sensitive values which were considered to be necessary to the development of human being, including and paradoxically in the Christian tradition.

In fact, Greek culture does not yet represent all the truth. And if this truth seems to be sensitive it is because it takes root in the vision of the living, but it does not yet cultivate the sensitive living we are. What is seen is then transformed into appearances to which a kind of autonomous life is attributed either by brilliance or by permanence. The being of the subject is also projected on/in what is seen for lack of being cultivated inwardly. The space of our interiority, its extent and its content are projected on an external visible world and are confused with it. This deprives as well the world as the subject of a life of their own—of a being of their own. Hence all belongs to a system which is not acknowledged as such and in which meaning, the other(s) and even life are subjected to more or less arbitrary decisions and attributions.

What allows escaping this general systematization is a return to the particularity of each being as living a life of its own—which involves assuming an insurmountable non-being. But the latter is no longer applied to an object or/and its attributes but to the subject, in particular in relation to another living being—I am a human and I am not an animal or a plant; I am a woman and I am not a man.

Without respecting the natural origin of beings, we enter a universe in which non-meaning and non-being are generalized. To be is confused with not to be, and it is not a debate or a conflict between subjects which can decide on that. In fact, nature already has decided and any logic is hypothetical if the natural truth is not respected. Nature gives a first meaning to beings, a meaning which is not dependent on appearing or naming. This meaning can express itself externally, but it comes from another meaning which exists, develops and acts inwardly. It is not a question of a meaning which comes to appearing and, then, disappears, but of a meaning the invisible presence of which appears only partially, either in space or in time. Human being does not blossom as a flower. Its visible blossoming depends on the flowering of an internal world. Human being must beware of not projecting itself on/in the outside and of being caught up by the outside. It must preserve an internal space in which a world of its own can be elaborated from which an external world can be both approached and considered. The internal space no longer is the outcome of the idealization of an external reality, according to a Platonic method and some of its religious avatars, but of a relation to this reality which acknowledges it as other and allows entering into relation with it as such. Hence the connection between ontical and ontological comes up—even folds up—differently. It involves a return to the origin of life—to life as origin—and not a projection of it on/in the beyond—or the 'there is' or a 'That'.

Assuming the negative makes such a link possible—an 'I am not the other'. If I were the other or the world, such an operation would not be possible; and the same would go if I would be equal to or the same as the other. Another space or another relation to space is opened, or reopened, by assuming the particularity of my being.

As human beings we do not flower only externally. We also flower inwardly, notably by welcoming the other as other in ourselves. This asks our being appropriate to non-appropriation, a process which is perhaps peculiar to nature itself. Is it not noted that being pregnant makes a woman blossom? And does not any natural being blossom only by preserving its singularity?

10

An Ontology of the Living

How to Free Ourselves from a Traditional Ontology?

We lack an ontology of our living being—in a way a fleshly ontology which can result neither from a merely mental construction nor from an exclusively active shaping or conceptualization. Between the traditional ontology and our traditional way of living sensitivity, something is to be discovered the form of which is both given by the being as living and developed by us, in particular through our relationships with the other living being(s). In that kind of shaping, touch is more important than sight. Touch delimits in the present the relation to oneself and to the other(s) without fixing form(s) which would be suitable once and for all. Touch respects, gives and gives back forms produced by life itself, but it also makes them evolve. This does not happen without a certain passivity, an active passivity.

Sensitivity cannot be limited to a mere undergoing, it is also a means of becoming. It accepts and it permits a shaping which does not depend only on the mind or on neurons. Our whole being is involved in this constant shaping in which form obeys physical and not only meta-physical requirements. One could say that forms have to do with organic and not only neurological givens. And yet our logic is based on a neuro-muscular economy which is presupposed to correspond to our global being. This gave rise to our subjection to various technical, technological and electronic processes which today intend to govern us—not without exhausting our vital potential from which they originally borrow energy. Now this energy is not extraneous to our physical belonging, whereas our brain rather functions according to a mathematical logic.

Subjected to such a logic we can be freed from it by what could be named 'grace'—that is, by a divine or human relational mystery which touches us and awakens or reawakens our global, including physical, being. Such a grace is assumed to come from God, the one who is not without being conjoined with/in himself, but it can also come from the other as other. How to articulate these two sorts of grace? God unites with us, whereas we unite with one another, which asks us to modify a merely individual energy. From that results the question about what would be the most accomplished of the two graces.

Does a religion of incarnation not open the path towards a union with one another which could be of divine nature? This union can bring us back to our own nature and asks us to redeem it from its claim to become divine before accomplishing our humanity—which cannot happen without a union with the other. This entails a communication, even a communion, between two self-affections and not only the elevation of only one self-affection towards an absolute of divine nature. Indeed, can the latter maintain the immediacy of affect that a union with the other as different can preserve? Then does not this better prepare an availability for grace while keeping a fleshly sensitive quality? Indeed grace does not correspond with an abstract reality, which a solitary becoming runs the risk of becoming in its quest for ascending towards the divine. Hence the meaning of incarnation is unrecognized, even denied, and we fall back into a will to become God without accomplishing our humanity—without becoming a divine man or a divine woman. Grace is a path towards the becoming divine of human being. It ensures a passage from the body to the spirit, implements a sort of transubstantiation of our physical belonging which neither neglects nor disowns it but invites it to transform itself, to transcend itself in order to humanly blossom.

Grace acts as a mediation between the absolute and a human being as it is here and now. It can also ensure a mediation between humans, uniting them while respecting their singularity. They are united by the mediation of grace without this union amounting to a fusion, a lack of differentiation, the abolition of the one or the other, the subjection of the one to or by the other. The touch of grace corresponds to an energy which allows us to gather, while remaining different, in a unity independent of each and irreducible to a totality.

It is between beings which differ by nature that grace has the most creative and transcendental role of mediation, notably because it acts above all inwardly. Between those who are the same, its external, sometimes spectacular, mode of intervening is privileged in comparison with an intimate touch—even the form of the body prevails over the flesh and an invisible touch. Hence one rather wrongly resorts to sexuality as what could help get into contact, whereas it too often destroys it. Sexuality strictly speaking ought to intervene only after a sensitive awakening of flesh. Sexual attraction calls for a touching, in particular a physical touching, which needs a site being prepared in order that it can take place without abolishing its role of mediation between two fleshes. This asks us to observe what such a touch produces in us and to cultivate a suitable interiority in order that we could welcome the gesture of the other without reducing it to an 'object' external to ourselves. Thus the visible aspect is not the most important, and it matters less than the tactile impact and the generation of forms which are invisibly perceived. In fact, it is the 'to be' of the other which touches us and not only the being he/she is in the present. We lack words to say such touching of 'to be'. Hence it is unrecognized and even forgotten whereas it represents the most decisive link regarding the incarnation and development of human beings—a link which exceeds visibility, opening up to being and compliance to all norms to reach an intimacy unknown to us but that the other can reveal to us.

Touch can carry out union in difference and not only unity in sameness and between the same ones, according to the philosophical and religious ideal of our onto-theology. In an economy of sameness, the self-affection of each is not preserved and what it entails as link between the active and the passive in each in order that it should ensure its individuation and its singularity. Now the matter is of respecting each being as it is without subjecting it to being in general, or to Being, as Heidegger wants (cf. *De l'essence de la vérité,* IV, in *Questions I,* p. 176; *On the Essence of Truth,* 4, in *Basic Writings,* p. 125). If we take difference between beings into account, including as far as we are concerned, each of us is already 'ec-sisting' and 'exposed' with respect to the other, without needing an additional gesture from us as humans if not the acknowledgment of that which is.

The Autonomy of the Living

Heidegger seems to assent to a totality of being(s) with respect to which our freedom would allow us to ec-sist. But why constitute such a totality if not in the name of an ec-sisting of human being which forgets that human being as living is already situated among beings with which it shares life, without this being a question of totality? By including us in such a whole, Heidegger, as many western philosophers, deprives us of a freedom with which he next intends to endow us in a more or less artificial way. In fact, our freedom corresponds to an ability to become the ones who we are, including in a relational union with the world and all that and those which surround us. Freedom is that which grants us to stay in ourselves and to develop what and whom we are, instead of ec-sisting outside of a world built by ourselves. And if freedom asks us to 'abandon ourselves to being', it is to abandoning ourselves to the ones we are that it ought first to apply. Indeed, this abandon lets each be the one it is without an 'ec-sisting' in relation to the world being necessary.

The work of Heidegger is ambiguous concerning what he calls 'being(s) in totality' and the fact that he discovers himself as *phusis* in that way (op. cit., IV, p. 177; op. cit., 4, p. 126). Indeed he does not conceive of this totality as the cosmos of the Greek time but as a world already constructed by the logos. The *Dasein* to which he refers does not allude to a human being in the cosmic universe of Greeks—if only because it is imagined as lacking in differentiation and in the neuter, unlike the living world. Does Heidegger's insistence on 'veiled' and 'unveiling' not result from a substitution of a more or less opaque construction, which makes living imperceptible as such, for the invisible growing of the living and its visible efflorescence? Could that correspond to the 'beginning of western history', to the fact that human belonging has begun to be determined by history more than by nature, which was accompanied by misjudgement or denial of the importance of the natural evolution—an evolution amounting to Greek *phuein* (op. cit., IV, p. 178; op. cit., 4, p. 127). In reality the *phuein* of each living being makes a breach in the totality of the world. This is true for each human being if it remains living, ec-sists in the present with respect to the totality in which it is situated but also, and first, with respect to itself as a whole. The ec-sistence about which Heidegger speaks can be only secondary in comparison with the constant ec-sisting of the living, unless it nullifies it, notably by unconsciously miming it, so cutting the living off from a real growth of its own. The active mood of a human being in its opening up to being also represents a sort of reversal with regard to all that which it already has received from living being(s) to subsist. Thus the question is not only one about the confusion of appearance with truth, but about the freezing of 'to be' in a constructed essence instead of letting it be in relation to a living which is always in becoming.

As growing, a human being needs limits. Unlike other living beings, these limits cannot be determined only by nature. Its natural forms do not define, for a human being, the limits of its possible evolution, as is the case with vegetal beings which unfold according to their material forms, increasing them but without transforming them. If the efflorescence in its physical forms is a decisive stage in the development of the living that human being is, its becoming cannot be limited to it—at least it ought to go this way, including at the bodily level. However, this becoming cannot be kept in abeyance by supra sensitive ideals either. It is desire which can ensure to human being a development which is neither merely physical nor merely meta-physical, a development that touch is likely to support and accompany with the help of limits provided by self-affection and hetero-affection.

Thus it is not a question of the only passive and in a way unconscious mood—*Stimmung*—towards the totality of being(s), about which Heidegger speaks. Rather it is a question of both active and passive perception of the sensitive, physical and fleshly dimension of the living being by itself and/or in its relation to the other(s). Such an emotional attitude is not without relation to life and to the soul, which Heidegger despises a little because they cannot aspire to an essence and do not relate, notably historically, to being(s) in totality but to particular beings.

There is not only a technique which can bring us back to the perception of some or other being but the respect for living beings and the peculiar characteristics of their world—a perception which has nothing to do with a revelation of being dependent on 'a conscious leveling of a knowledge which is no longer more than knowledge' (op. cit., V, p. 181; op. cit., 5, p. 129). Indeed paying attention to the living nature of being cannot conceal from us a possible glimpse into the totality of being(s), but builds a place in ourselves where we can question about the way according to which beings relate to each other. And it is obvious that living beings and fabricated beings cannot be put together to constitute a totality which does not take their difference into account. The way in which human being relates to living beings, with which it shares and from which it even receives life, and to fabricated beings, cannot be the same and it cannot include them in only one and the same whole. Such a mistake, such an abuse, obscures thinking and prevents it from perceiving each being in its singularity and how beings can, notably by themselves, be joined to each other in a whole. Could it not be opportune to cultivate, beyond care, the main affect in Heidegger's work, astonishment, admiration and respect for the particular nature of each living being and the persistence of the 'mystery' that life itself puts forward, and even 'objects' to us in this being, first and above all as human? Is not privileging sameness a means to which man has resorted to avoid to open up to another living being—and the breach that it makes in all totalities constituted by man himself according to his sole arbitration?

Heidegger maintains that we can exist as humans only from our 'ec-sisting' in relation to being as such. But he does not seem to take account of the 'in-stasis' in the natural being that he is nor of the fact that the latter already determines the way in which he relates to whatever being. Still he leaps over a stage of human becoming. Hence the necessity for another 'leap' to return to it—what is impossible. Indeed, this attempt to return to the self takes place from a belonging to a culture which does not allow him/us to return to the experience of and the in-stasis in a natural being. The *Dasein* of which Heidegger speaks is already extraneous to inhabiting the natural being that we are and its manner of co-existing with other natural beings.

From that the wandering of man happens, a wandering of which opening up to the meeting with a living being different from himself can make him sense the nature of a mistake other than a mere wrong judgment. Only acknowledging the mystery that a living being which is different from him represents can provide man with limits through the perception of a structure and a world which allow him to assess the edges of the horizon in which he stays and moves. The non-unveiling of the being of the other sends man back to his own mystery as living and to the way according to which this mystery could be in harmony with that of another, human or non-human, living being. This cannot be dependent on a decision of judgment only, but on a more or less appropriate yearning. Indeed, desire reveals human being to itself, and helps it to develop in a way which exceeds natural growth and to enter into relation with what oversteps its own horizon but for which it longs to ensure its own becoming. This desire for the other which differs from oneself by nature has perhaps something to do with 'the letting be of being as such in its radical original aspect' (op. cit., VII, pp. 188–89; op. cit., 7, p. 134), an originality which is not necessarily relative to history but to a natural origin to which we must always remain open.

Irreducible Singularity of Living Beings

Such letting be questions about 'being in its totality' (idem, p. 188; idem, p. 134) in order to turn to the 'to be' of living being in its particularity and singularity. Then the question which must be asked is what word can be shared with this living being before we can decide on the one which fits 'being in its totality'. In linguistic terms, perhaps one could say that the latter privileges utterance, and the saying of or on being, whereas the former privileges enunciation and the saying to or with the other. Obviously, this is only a first approach from which it could be suggested to western philosophers a non-fixed 'fulcrum' to re-found philosophy in a way which does not free itself from thinking and respecting life, as far as themselves but also any other are concerned, including at ethical and political levels. Thus the question is of returning to a thought of nature based on the real and which is not bent, from the very beginning, to a difference between being and Being from which it would be difficult to go out by 'stepping back', as Heidegger suggests. Only the existence of another world and another subjectivity can lead us to put into perspective the world to which we belong, to reopen its horizon and to adopt another logic.

What most efficiently can allow us to perceive the limit of each living being in its singularity is the fact that it cannot be subjected to a totality because it belongs to a world of its own and a world in becoming. Besides, it is in that sense that, at least originally, the world of man and the world of woman are not the same. This still appears quite clearly in Greek culture but, surprisingly, Heidegger does not take account of it, notably in his 'stepping back'. If our culture more and more privileges subjectivity, it still misjudges the difference of subjectivities between the sexes. Rather, it tends to increasingly neutralize under various pretexts—which opens the pathway to the power of technique. However, stepping back is not truly possible, as far as the neutralization of subjectivity is not questioned. Indeed, such stepping back happens starting from some a priori, which distorts the truth of what is discovered, the most decisive of them being the presupposition that living beings can be thought and organized in a totality by the human being even independently of its thinking of itself as living. What is considered the 'background' producing the totality of being(s) then already amounts to a fiction elaborated by consciousness.

The same goes for being conceived starting from a presupposed universal thinking, unless one agrees that it is perhaps still to come thanks to a logic which takes account of our global being, including of its physical and sexuate dimensions. Hegel considers very little such a being and no logos until now has been able to ensure its foundation (cf. *Identité et différence,* La constitution onto-théologique de la métaphysique, in *Questions I,* p. 292; *Identity and Difference,* The onto-theological Constitution of Metaphysics, in Third Question). Why does man intend to found the 'totality of being(s)' without first respecting the origin of beings themselves, in particular, but not only, that of living beings? Why make living beings and fabricated beings dependent on a human will which removes them from their own reality? Why does the human being aim at appropriating being in/through an ideal essence instead of considering it in the development of its own existence?

This asks us to remain faithful to our own global being without making it dependent on a more or less artificial construction which takes little account of its physical and sensitive belonging and of some of its properties, notably regarding memory. Indeed, this cannot be merely neurological or somatic without becoming pathological and harming the living organism for lack of an articulation between all its dimensions. And yet this has something to do with the functioning of our culture and the reason for it forgetting of Being, or of 'to be'—either metaphysical logic taking no account of that, or that being of a nature other than metaphysical.

For example, even at the level of sight, metaphysics fails in considering the optic chiasmus and its effects on memory—without yet alluding to its little consideration for affect in the definition of the truth. In other words, it would be possible to say that our metaphysical tradition neglects the tangible aspect of the truth even though it is decisive in the perception of the living nature of being and of the forms and modes of apprehension and memorization of its truth. One could also say that our culture separates our head from our body without thinking about the role of the thalamus in its conception of truth—of being and Being, or of being and 'to be'.

Hence Being and being are separated from one another—the metaphysical from the physical. Is it not to ignore that the 'to be' of a living being is physical, that it is what persists and becomes true on this side and beyond all the present incarnations and underlies their existence?

To be and being are really different as the permanent is distinct from the momentary, the invisible from the visible, and life from its manifestation. They differ but they belong to the same real and cannot be divided between what exists by itself and what is constructed by human beings as far as the living is concerned. And no 'stepping back' is necessary to perceive this difference. In a way, it is never perceived if not through an evolution, originally natural, of the appearing of 'to be' in being, an appearing which ought to happen by itself and does not last. All Heidegger's considerations about veiling and unveiling, the gap between Being and being and their possible conciliation in presence, the difference between universal being and supreme Being, seem to result from a construction which ignores the difference between 'to be' and being as regards natural essences themselves. Does that not mean that the work of life itself is unrecognized and is, secondarily, attributed to the logos, as the background from which could arise the 'totality of being(s)'? There is no doubt that a new conception of 'to be' results from the subjection of being to the logos in its various historical modalities. But it cannot be substituted for the reality of the living being on pain of distorting the discourse about truth.

To prevent such a distortion, 'to be' must be incarnate in being, which itself ensures its relation to 'to be' in a double temporal movement challenging the linearity of discourse. This is both projective and retrospective; it unfolds towards the future in faithfulness to its origin without ever fixing meaning in/on one and only one presence. Indeed, a living being becomes and it cannot correspond to only one appearing—this only amounts to one moment of the existence, or ec-sisting, and of being in relation to 'to be', a moment which incarnates 'to be' in a more or less appropriate way. 'Stepping back' does not necessarily reveal that because that is not, at least not always, visible. As in metaphysics for example, it can be a question of method, of the way in which being remembers 'to be'. Does such memorizing happen inside a world already constructed by logos, or does it depend on the memory of that which founds being as living? In the first case, memorization is more mental and metaphysical whereas in the second case it is more physical and the concern of sensitivity.

Heidegger does not wonder about this difference of memorizing and about what is maintained forgotten but is, nevertheless, acting in his conception of 'to be'—or Being. Such 'to be'—or Being—could be founding being and founded by being, according to him (op. cit., p. 303; op. cit., idem), which is both possible and impossible as far as a natural being is concerned. This has an origin which cannot be modified by being—a natural origin that no existence can challenge.

Besides, this natural origin cannot be subjected either to a logical universal or to a supreme Being. It is singular for each being, which logos as a background cannot express. Then being—or Being—is extrapolated from 'to be' in a limitless horizontal or vertical extension: universal or supreme (op. cit., pp. 304–5; op. cit., idem), the criterion of assessment of which being quantitative and not qualitative. The general economy is then more mathematical than physical, more merely neurological than physiological on the whole, without any link or compatibility between the two organizations.

From that results a split between the physical and the spiritual that even a theology of incarnation did not truly succeed in overcoming. Hence also the aporia, the aporias, of an ontology which intends to found being from a common background and its insertion into a totality in which all beings would take part (op. cit., p. 305; op. cit., idem). Such an economy, such a logic are extraneous to living beings, difference between living beings and their way of relating to each other. Indeed, each of them is 'founded' in a singular manner of which their introduction into a totality must take account on pain of cutting them off from themselves and from their becoming. In fact, each being is *causa sui* as living and it is only if it is subjected to an origin or totality other than its own that it is dependent on a cause external to it. If it remains alive, being as such is its own cause. And it is at another level that a God can intervene in its existence.

A living being can be reduced neither to an image nor even to a representation. It is not perceptible as living from a surface; it corresponds to a volume. As living its forms differ from forms which are privileged by metaphysics, more generally by our culture, and it is by touch more than by sight that it can be approached. This is true notably because a living being moves by itself and that any moving on our part can contribute to visually perceiving its volume. Thereby it is the contact, even the impact, with another volume which teaches us something about their respective limits, thus about their volumes. Such knowing is dependent on a touching of which we can try to have a representation but from a phenomenon which is not visible.

This way of knowing is more easily memorized than that, resulting from the sole sight, of forms reduced to images or representations. These are memorized by processes of apprenticeship or kinaesthetic protocols which have an influence on our perceptive mechanisms, rendering them physical and not only mental. This does not return for all that their material density and their weight to living beings and is only the result of a comparative evaluation between movements and speeds of various visible elements.

The Non-perception of the Living by Sciences

It is surprising that the works about perception—for example, those of Piaget and Paul Guillaume, but also, differently, those of Merleau-Ponty—take so little interest in the perception of living physical beings. However these pose specific problems, notably because their visible forms are dependent, at least in part, on an organic structuring unity which is not visible. Nevertheless, it interacts with our own as perceiving and even could, ultimately, compose a unity with it, as it sometimes happens in love life. Such interaction is envisaged by Guillaume only by the introduction of stimuli, for example of electric charges, in material bodies, but not as an energy potential of bodies themselves, which, beyond their own limits, generate a 'field' or a 'world' of their own because they are living. These interactions and 'field' or 'world' do not result from mere neurological processes dependent on external stimuli. They are produced by the dynamism which animates living beings and compels them to enter into relationship with other living beings—which can be facilitated by a physical or energy proximity more than by a formal resemblance.

If scientists little broach the question relative to the shaping up of living bodies, they still less wonder about the forms and distortions produced by relationships between living beings. The relation of the observer to an object is almost the only one which is considered. The relationships between living beings are tackled at best in the field of psychology, or even of psychoanalysis, that most scientists refuse to acknowledge as scientifically valid.

A domain of perception is thus ignored, even repressed. Nevertheless, it is really important as regards the dynamism of living beings and their relationships. But this dynamism is often conceived as solely mental, mechanical and dependent on external stimuli, and not as a manifestation of life itself and its incarnation. Then human beings more and more turn into robots for lack of consideration for their own potential and their own flesh—which cannot be reduced to a natural organism, on the one hand, or to the acquisition of cultural norms and imperatives, on the other hand. In that case, they miss a structure capable of assembling their physical and psychical belongings in a way which also ensures their relationship with the other(s) and with the world. This could mean their failing in taking account of their dynamism as living, a dynamism which both unifies them and unites them with one another in a manner which differs from a totality constructed by the logos. Indeed each living being is autonomous but it takes part in an organic whole from which it cannot be separated on pain of declining, and even dying. This whole is substantial and not only formal, it is dependent on elements which constitute the living—earth, air, water, fire—and it is dynamic at a relational level, which requires each to keep a structure of its own.

And there is no need of 'threads' or other more or less material or cultural techniques to join together all the elements of the whole; life takes charge of that (cf. Paul Guillaume, *La psychologie de la forme*, p. 323; cf. The Gestalt Psychology), provided that it is assumed by each with respect for the life of others.

There is no doubt that for human beings, more generally for living beings, touch, be it immediate or mediated and from a distance, is a unifier, conductor and even producer of energy. If it can undo formal structures, it can also bring back living beings in their physical structures, whereas imposing formal structures can disintegrate organic structures.

What today happens to living beings and the universe looks that way. If we came to that, it is because humanity has not wondered enough about the conditions, not only organic but also dynamic, of its development—as far as each living being but also the relations between living beings are concerned. Our tradition has favoured the static in relation to the dynamic—the soma in relation to germ cells?—which thwarted the necessary evolution of the living.

In fact, nature is finalist—it aims at its own fulfilment, its own blossoming. But such becoming is not independent of that of other living beings. One also can note that nature favours a certain asymmetry contrary to a more formal economy. And difference is source of a natural evolution more than similarity, parallelism or reversibility. And yet such criteria are essential in our culture, which paralyzes, at least partially, the evolution of the living which do not obey the same principle of organization or the same finality (op. cit., pp. 38–9). It is all the more so since the theory of the solids prevailed in our culture, which took little interest in living bodies which have a unifying structure quite different from that of inert solids. This does not prevent Guillaume from comparing 'the movements of our members' with those of 'pieces of machines' and from affirming that 'all that which has just been said about material forms can be applied to the sphere of life' (op. cit., p. 40). However, these words seem to contradict some of his comments on physiological forms (cf. op. cit., p. 40 and sq.) regarding to which he often confines himself to peripheral reactions without taking account of internal reactions, at least those of flesh. And yet they are less mechanical than those more exclusively nervous. They are also more dependent on processes which take part in the relationship with another flesh and can be observed in it more easily than by the intervention of a technique which frequently interrupts the functioning of the organism as a whole. Sight also can act in that way, which favours the maintenance and repetition of the same form rather than its evolution. And the traditional privilege of sight leads to a quite partial conception of what is envisaged too, including by the scientific experimentation, as 'immediate experience'—all that which belongs to the field of sensation or affect is generally considered extraneous to the reliability of the scientific domain. And the scientist does not hesitate to support 'a subjective experience' with only the 'retinal image' (op. cit., p. 49) and the cerebral process which corresponds to it, without alluding to the whole organism. He also endeavours to discover isomorphisms and similarities between phenomena and cerebral processes (op. cit., p. 113), which is more difficult to be found out for the whole organism in which 'a qualitative irreducibility' is more obvious (op. cit., p. 114). Besides, the organism has its own structures and shaping and it cannot be compared with 'a pure sensitive and chaotic diversity' (words of Kant quoted by Guillaume, op. cit., p. 204).

But the perception about which the theoreticians speak is generally a perception of 'things' and it takes place inside a subject-object logic which is little appropriate to relations between living beings, and even between subjects—unless perception is reduced to a visible perception of behaviours with formal properties comparable to objects (op. cit., pp. 206–7). Something to which the reduction of the human being to a neuter individual can lead.

However the relationship between two living beings, in particular two human beings who are differently sexuate, provokes reactions the shaping of which remains sensitive and cannot be limited to a visual perception—they belong more to the field of touch. Nevertheless, it is not a question of introspection but, rather, of internal forms or imprints about which it is difficult to distinguish perception from sensation, in particular if what is experienced is not appropriated as one's own but relates to the other who is its cause. In that case, must acknowledging the intervention of the other be considered to be a matter of intellectual nature or, instead, must we admit that there exists an economy of sensitivity still underrated and which has to do with the too little envisaged subcortical zones of the brain or the thalamus—as is the case with immediate or mediated by the other phenomena reliant on touch, merely physical or transformed into affects? Such phenomena stand between little differentiated sensations and more systematic, even conceptual, forms. They do not lack structure, but this acts at another level and with properties which differ from those which are more dependent on sight and more exclusively mental. Their logic is still little-known, which hinders a part of our subjective and inter-subjective development, at the individual and collective levels, an insufficient attention being paid to desire and the shaping it can carry out. The passive aspect of the perception that we experience, which touches us, and which takes place before any activity on our part is also little considered. And yet, before we are actors, we are receptors.

For example, before we perceive form, we perceive colour, which touches us without any process of formal abstraction being necessary and which has more to do with our whole flesh than with only sight. For scientists, this often means that such perception is of a lower nature than the perception of forms (cf. Janet quoted by Guillaume, op. cit., p. 219). This underestimates the potential of sensitivity at the level of meaning but obeys requirements of similarity and mimicry as well as the subject-object logic favoured by our tradition.

Such an opinion also privileges exteriority in relation to interiority—which does not amount to introspection—expression in relation to impression, activity in relation to passivity, solid in relation to fluid, man in relation to woman and so forth. And even if Guillaume stresses the possibility of different structures and of a progress between the phases of evolution, he takes little interest in the internal structures of the psychism or the organism. However, they have a more evolutive potential for the living than external structures, a potential that anyway has an influence on memory and the structuring of current perceptions, and perhaps all the more so since they are organized in a less definitive and systematic way, as an uncompleted task can be.

The theoreticians of perception, notably those of Gestalt theory, miss what concerns the articulation between external and internal structures as well as the level of their fleshly integration and sedimentation. Therefore, they also miss the articulation between visual and in part auditory perceptions and touch as such—a question about which culture, notably education, ought to wonder, in particular to surmount the dualism between matter and form, body and spirit. There is no doubt that touch is the more intimate bodily sense while keeping a spiritual potential, to which the religious language bears witness. However this potential is underestimated, which harms the development of human subjectivity and intersubjectivity, but also the relation of human beings to other living beings and to the world in general. The mediation of touch, in its various modalities, can favour a greater harmony between all the elements of the world and prevent their reduction to objects or tools, notably to serve the ambition of human demiurges.

To such an attitude can contribute an education which stops at a stage of our evolution without taking account of the dynamic potential of touch still present in children. Unfortunately, adults wrongly repress activities of children motivated by touch, underestimating the importance of touch as mediation between living beings. This explains the privilege of sorts of structures and forms different from those that touch can generate, which are more physical or fleshly and more flexible towards exchanges and the sharing of what can arise from them.

The Lack of a Culture of Sensitivity

The lack of attention paid to a culture of sensitivity, of affect and inter-subjectivity is frequent in theories concerning the development and apprenticeship of children. For example Piaget (cf. *La représentation du monde chez l'enfant; The Child's Conception of the World*), like Spitz and many others, considers the constitution of object(s) as an essential stage in their evolution. The logic based on subject-object relation greatly prevails over the subject-subject logic, which does not contribute to the blossoming of sensitive and sensory qualities, in particular those relative to touch. This is often reduced to the seizure of an object without paying attention enough to the effect produced by touching the other or being touched by the other and the issue that this represents in human evolution. And yet the subjective development is quite different according to the privileged logic: more active, visual, mental and motor, in the one case, and more attentive to the positive role of passivity, to emotion and the fleshly belonging, in the other case; or either: more solipsistic or more relational, more abstract from life or more immersed in the living world and so forth.

According to most theoreticians, individuation acquisition requires breaking off the sensitive tie with the mother without a cultivation of the affect which goes with it. The constitution of the object and its mastery ought to prevail over the persistence and the development of original affects, the existence of the object(s) over the presence of the other, beginning with that of the mother (cf. Freud's comments on the language acquisition by the little Hans). In reality the dependence on objects is substituted for the dependence on the mother. Then it is in the name of morality, religion or politics that the relationships with the other(s) will be assessed and trained but not towards a global blossoming suitable for human being. Its sensitive belonging, its fleshly belonging will be structured by laws, duties and customs which have to do with the collective order more than being perceived as a part of the individual real-lived experience, which requires the greatest attention and care to gain a truly human subjectivity.

According to Piaget, the function of perception is even 'to insert each particular object or event into frameworks which can integrate them and aim at reducing the real to deductible and convertible structures' (op. cit., p. 445; op. cit.). Then the knowledge provided by perception serves to 'connect' at each time what happens in the present to operative systems and diagrams in which actions or operations, on the one hand, and particular object(s) and event(s), on the other hand, take part (idem). The here and now perceived is of use in a process of abstraction and generalization which makes its contribution to operative and transformative systems possible. The sensitive knowledge as such is not really considered if not as what lacks structure. However, what we perceive of another living being remains without structure only if we reduce it to a passive and solitary sensation. As soon as the other is acknowledged as other, what is more with reciprocity in view, perception becomes structured. This domain of structuring of sensitivity is little-known and it is as pathology that it reappears. For lack of having been considered and treated, this field of perceptions brings about psychic and physiological perturbations, but also the decline of our intellectual potential as well as of our way of conceiving of truth. Besides, thinking becomes mechanized, one could say automated, and the mental functioning diminished and is without any creative dynamism, in particular at the intersubjective level.

Instead of such being turned into robots, why is the impact of sexuation on perception not acknowledged? If the subject intervenes in the perceptive mechanisms, as Piaget himself asserts, why ignore the role of sexuation in the 'perceptive structuring', which then acts between a mere sensitivity and the transcendental dimension at work in the respect for the natural difference of the other? This would solve some dichotomies between matter and form, body and spirit, sensitivity and intelligence, and even sensation and perception. Indeed sexuation operates as a specific structure between those of the living organism and those reliant on mental constructions. Moreover, the organization of the relationships with the other as other requires the intervention of perception, but also of reason as a means of regulation allowing a relationship in difference to take place, beginning with that of the relationship between two human beings differently sexuate.

Hence the structuring depending on the subject will no longer be only a matter of 'genetics', in particular the one relative to the soma, and of modalities of relating to 'object(s)', but it will incarnate the conscious or unconscious presence of the sexuate belonging of the subject—of the germ cells—notably in the perception of other subjects but also in the perception of objects and of the world. And their presumed objectivity would be questioned by the peculiar perception of different subjects and the possibility of debates regarding their nature. So the properties of the subject would be taken into account and not only those of the object—which needs a double centring and not successive decentring from the subject with respect to objects.

If the perceptions relating to touch are almost ignored by the theoreticians of perception, they are also misjudged by those who take interest in sexuality strictly speaking. For example, Jean Rostand speaks of the sexual awakening of puberty in merely physiological and even somatic terms. That corresponds to his speciality, one could object. It is true, but it is nonetheless true that he comments almost exclusively on reproductive organs—as it is more often than not the case in education—without alluding to the awakening of the desire for/of the other whatever its possible impact, even on the production of sexual hormones. Once more there is pathology, notably thanks to Freud, which arouses interest in such an aspect of the problem, given the existence of psychosomatic troubles. The possibility that delay and troubles of puberty could be due to a depressive state of the adolescent is not envisaged by the presumedly true scientists.

The fact that puberty inaugurates the passage to another sort of development, less merely somatic and more psychic because of the awakening of desire, a development capable of differentiating the human being from other kingdoms if it is not reduced to reproduction of the species, is not considered either. And, for example, if Rostand acknowledges the influence of sexual hormones on emotions and their expression, on mood and character, he does not really analyze how they act on the development of the adolescent, in particular on its relational aspect.

Moreover, it is only today that one begins to imagine that desire, in particular sexual, and more generally sexuate, desire, can prevent and even cure some illnesses. However, even if the scientists now take interest in the effects of hormonal insufficiencies on the physiological and even the psychic equilibrium, they do not seem to suppose that the reverse is possible and the importance that relational life can have in this connection. And yet would not humans be living beings devoted to be in relation to the other(s) for their becoming, particularly to the sexually different other? Perhaps, this could explain the slowness of their organic evolution and its limitation in favour of the importance of the sexuate dimension—of the germ cells?—in human life.

Part IV

Feeling Nostalgic for the Dynamism of Germ Cells

11

What Desire Grants Us Life?—Beyond Laughter and Tears

The Artificial Ecstasy of Supra Sensitive Ideals

We have paralyzed our desire either through an investment in various beings, various 'objects' defined by our cultural tradition, starting from which we relate to the other(s) as members of a community, or through leaving it suspended in supersensitive ideals or in divine figures. These had the virtue of partially preserving the transcendental character of our desire, but they dissuaded, and even prevented us from fulfilling it.

Wanting to expel from our world the non-being, we became slaves of nothingness. The ec-stasis through which supra sensitive values kept our desire in abeyance exempted us from taking care of a double ec-stasis being the cause of our desire: the ec-stasis relative to our own origin and the ec-stasis regarding the other as irreducible to ourselves. We drew back before taking on these two cuts, voids, negatives or not-being, thanks to which we can exist as humans. Instead of understanding that the possibility of fulfilling our 'to be' happens only starting from these ec-stases in regard we made Being what called us for transcending ourselves—for example making God a sort of supreme Being instead of considering God to be a possible supplier of our 'to be'.

© The Author(s), under exclusive license to Springer Nature Switzerland AG 2024
L. Irigaray, *The Mediation of Touch*, https://doi.org/10.1007/978-3-031-37413-5_11

In reality our past transcendences made us fall from our 'to be', deprived us of its perception and its becoming towards our real accomplishment. Indeed, longing for the other as other and for incarnating the between us, asks us to be faithful to our 'to be'—furthermore faithful to our 'to be' as ecstatic with respect to being(s) but nevertheless determined, especially sexuately determined. It is this ec-stasis and this determination that allow us to dwell and to inhabit ourselves. They are also what grants us a return to the dawn of the unhurt—a return to the innocence of the dawn, to which both Nietzsche and Heidegger allude. Such a return permits us afterwards to let us reach us what comes to us (cf. Heidegger, in *Letter on Humanism,* in *Questions III,* pp. 71–154, in particular p.147; *Letter on Humanism* in *Basic Writings,* pp. 213–265, in particular p.147) and to be able to say 'yes' or 'no' in accordance with faithfulness to our 'to be'.

I cannot exist the 'to be' of the other. I must assume this impossible being in order that my existence will not be undermined by nihilism. Overcoming nihilism does not amount to avoiding nothing of being but requires us to think it as what is beyond our possible. What Nietzsche, but also Heidegger, do not consider is that such nothing lies in nature itself: to be a woman presupposes not to be a man. Thus to be born as a human presupposes a nothing of being already existing, an ec-stasis with respect to what constitutes our origin. We really come into the world if we accept that we exist from a nothing of being—I could even say a nothing of 'to be'—except the horizon of desire and love which made our conception possible. But it does not always exist.

It is up to us to give ourselves our 'to be' by freeing ourselves from all the sorts of beings in which our life is paralyzed from the beginning. However we need unity for living, for incarnating our 'to be'. We need a place, a dwelling in which to stay to live on. As our destiny is ecstatic, we long for a Being ecstatic in relation to ourselves. And thus we imagine a transcendence beyond our terrestrial existence forgetting that this existence is, itself, ecstatic. Perhaps we ought to pay more attention to the fact that our desire corresponds to longing for what transcends us. The best guardian of our 'to be' is then the one who pays attention to the meaning of the desire which calls us to him or her. The one who listens to the ec-stasis involved in desire and preserves it from being annihilated notably by the being that he or she is at present or that we project onto them. The one who agrees with being the companion of such an ec-stasis, by keeping it alive and in a state of innocent simplicity, without either becoming paralyzed in a being already existing—even transformed into a sort of Being by means of a cultural attractive but subjecting creation—or being lost through expending energy arisen from desire in a nothing of 'to be', that we generally confused with the climax of sensual pleasure. The one who perceives that my desire is longing for transcendence and not for falling behind with regard to the 'to be' of which I am in search and in charge, and of which my desire itself embodies the quest. The one whose desire, as different as it may be from mine, endeavours to pave the way for discovering, incarnating, cultivating what or who he or she is so that our 'to be' as human finally finds a shelter between us—between our arms, our words, our lives—where, sometimes, it can exist while reposing before starting its always infinite quest again, which springs from nothing but the desire to be. This must not be mistaken for a desire for Being, not even a supreme Being, because the latter might be a mere artificial being, of which, furthermore, we ought to ensure the safeguard and embody the existence.

Now we cannot share in the same Being. We have been subjected to that by our culture, but, beyond the fact that this Being perhaps does not truly suit our human destiny, it does not correspond with the destiny of all of us in the same way. Indeed if the essence of a vegetal being—for example, of an oak—is in continuity with its origin, with its roots; if ultimately we could speak of one Being about an oak, it is not the same for us as humans, notably because as such we do not participate in one and the same Being. Our truth and the blossoming of our becoming do not correspond to one human essence, but to the 'to be' of a man or the 'to be' of a woman, in a way to a non-essence. Hence our attempt to develop thanks to supra sensitive ideals with a presumed essence held in the beyond of ourselves instead of lying in our origin.

For What Ecstasy Longs Our Desire?

In reality, 'to be' for us as humans only sometimes occurs between us through the fleeting advent of a conjunction in an ec-stasy for which we long and which unites us, making our human 'to be' exist by taking on the not being, but also the not to-be, a mere human being, that our being a man or being a woman involves. Without taking on this negative with respect to a supposedly human essence, we cannot become humans and we cannot desire and love one another, not even live as human beings.

What desire charges us to do is to assume the nothing—or the nothing yet. Desire is a phenomenon of the dawn. Desire arises before the sun rises, unless because of modesty or lack of courage we defer it until an imaginary future. In reality, this is impossible and it is still thought starting from a cultural background and a milieu which does not consider us to be both living and human.

A truly human desire enjoins us to assume a cutting-ourselves-off from the being which already exists, breaking a mere continuity with it, so that we could turn back to that which we can contemplate as what or who really is and, perhaps, love them as they are. Desire requires us to turn to ourselves and take charge of the ec-stasis that our origin represents in order to be able to get in touch with the other in their own ec-stasis—without reducing this other to us, appropriating them, making them somehow or other an object—and bring back and entrust to them their own life. This makes possible a communion between us—a communion always ecstatic for each, that is, irreducible to a mere being, but which meets what our desire wants: a longing-for before which too often we draw back, unable to suit it, and dooming ourselves in this way to indifference, to boredom, to despair. Desiring grants us life if we agree to give up remaining merely in continuity with life itself in order to correspond to it as humans.

Desire arises to save us from the paralysis into which a wrong relation to our origin plunged us, from freeing us from mistaking our origin for the environment or milieu where our infancy took place. We too often confuse the surroundings and humans who assisted our incapacity for caring for ourselves, who compensated for our immaturity, with our origin, so becoming trapped in being(s) without a possible perspective and freedom with respect to it, and also to them. Desire calls us back to our transcendence provided that we do not use the energy that it arouses to return to a mere natural belonging, furthermore that we did not cultivate, but we live it as an injunction to remember our ecstatic destiny regarding the entire world in which we stay.

Desire invites us to return to our natural belonging not as to a mere facticity but to achieve our transcendental component by making our desiring flesh a mediation between body and soul, body and spirit. Far from being the opportunity to go back to the familiarity of a wrong origin, with which we provided ourselves for avoiding taking charge of our human destiny—a mistake which, no doubt, has been the source of wonderful literary texts but did not allow us to fulfil our human fate—desire questions such security. It is the event which enjoins us to give it up in order to incarnate the origin, or absence of origin, which corresponds to our human condition. Indeed our own origin is the one that we gave to ourselves by breathing by ourselves and by incarnating our own sexuation, an origin of which we are in search and sometimes we approach and share in amorous desire. Given that we are in a way responsible for our own origin, it is incumbent on us to live it in a human way, calling into question all what diverts us from our human accomplishment.

In reality, the work to be carried out, the work that Zarathustra intends to undertake is not the giving up on happiness, about which he weeps and that he confesses to his animal companions. Nor is it only to give birth to further books or children with renunciation of his own felicity, his own blossoming. Such a choice was unworthy of Nietzsche's aspirations and, in fact, left him lacking in energy to fulfil his desire. The work to be carried out is above all the one of giving birth to ourselves. This ought to be our first creation as humans, our first work of art. To such a work we are assigned as to our most demanding creation, a creation which requires of us the courage of a hermit or an eagle (*Ainsi parlait Zarathoustra, Quatrième partie*, 'De l'homme supérieur, 4, p.348; *So Spoke Zarathustra*, Part IV, 'About the Overman', in 4). It also asks us to go beyond our personal suffering and distress and experience what is meant by 'getting pain in human being' (op.cit., 6, p.350; op. cit., in 6).

This work is not carried out without tears, nor without laughter either, especially at ourselves. And it cannot be completely achieved independently of the desire of the other—desire for the other and desire from the other—because the ec-stasis or transcendence that such desire represents in relation to that which we already are invites, and even forces us to become what or the ones who are not yet through a constant return to the innocence of the not-yet-happened of the day, of what has not yet seen the light, has not yet come into the world.

The meeting, indeed the union, which occurs in this 'not yet' is the chance of giving birth to our 'to be'. No doubt it is that for which we are longing but before which we draw back because this means acknowledging and sharing a nothing of being. Our traditional metaphysics tried hard to exclude such a trial from its horizon, it endeavoured to avoid this hardship for us by keeping in abeyance the nothing, in particular through supra sensitive ideals.

Nevertheless, this nothing reappears or returns to us as the transcendental opportunity that sensitiveness itself offers us. In *So Spoke Zarathustra*, we find these words 'Never a great love wants love only, it longs for more' (op.cit.16, p.355; op.cit., in 16). It longs for acknowledgment of and reference to transcendence that it entails, not that of a presumed being, or Being, kept in abeyance in ideals beyond sensitiveness, but the one which is needed by love itself in order for it to be lived humanly. Assuming such transcendence in relation to what or who we are, and we are to one another, is that which allows love to exist between us, but also us to be as humans.

Overcoming Nihilism Through a Fleshly Transcendence

This cannot happen without a transformation, a sort of transubstantiation of our flesh, of our energy, which then become more subtle, more ethereal without losing their carnal nature. It is perhaps what Nietzsche attempts to tell us when he invites us to give up every heaviness, not to say gravity itself, and to be light, to dance, and even fly above and beyond ourselves, that is, to discover a physical density which could be in harmony with transcendence—as far as we but also the between us are concerned. Indeed, it is a condition for us being able to love one another as humans.

But this does not occur without laughter and tears. We do not always keep the same density of flesh, of energy. Hence our falling into more material and heavy states again, due to our physical gravity, a gravity that desire sometimes overcomes. This can provide us with opportunities of laughing, but can also bring suffering to us. We feel lost, disoriented, abandoned, including by ourselves, above all if we believe that the change in density that we feel is caused only by the other and that it is not our relation to and with the other which produces it in us. We are thus capable of living such change of density of our flesh, of our energy. Even if the awakening of our desire for the other was the cause of such transformation, we experienced it and it is up to us to be in charge of it, to cultivate it as a potential of our own being.

Something that we neglect, of which we are even unaware. And more often than not, instead of being grateful to the other for having aroused our desire, we hold our loss of lightness against him or her without wondering about our participation in it. We turn, this way, the increase of energy against ourselves and it becomes hate and heaviness where lightness of desire took place. Which prevents us from becoming what and who we are.

Questions can even be put to Nietzsche himself on this subject. Are not the nastiness, cruelty and contempt that he sometimes shows or promotes, and tries to justify, features of the old man of the West? Do they not participate in one polarity of the dichotomies to which our logic subjected us? Do they not contribute to our heaviness and gravity? Do they not result from resentment? No doubt they bring some ice in comparison to the fire of desire. But how will this ice favour our growth? Will it not, instead, lead us to a regression, to our decline? As far as life is concerned, what or who does not grow dies. And freezing does not protect the development of life; it only prevents what is dead from deteriorating, from decomposing.

Could this be the becoming to which the new human being must aspire—to protect itself from decomposing through an eternal return to and of the same? Is it then a question of another plan than freezing the old man of the West waiting for a new conception of human being? Could this new human being not be, on the contrary, the one who no longer depends on the blossoming of only one into forms which last and are immutable, that is, the one who corresponds to a ceaseless becoming, because life cannot dwell into definitive form(s)? Could the new human being not be the one who sometimes can be born and exist thanks to the *kairos* of a meeting with another living being? Such momentary in-stasis or repose is, then, a sort of landmark to carry on our path—a path which is neither linear nor marked out by mere visual markers, but is opened by a transformation of our energy, of our physical matter and of their manifestation, which amongst others result from our perception of the other through our various senses. How, indeed, can we turn towards an encounter and a union with the other if, from this other, touch, tone, flavour and even smell do not appeal to us? Would human being be so much lacking in such qualities that its longing would prefer to give up a sensible or sensitive transcendental and its sharing for a subjection to supra sensitive ideals? Perhaps these keep in abeyance a part of our energy and prevent it from being expended without moderation, but they do not allow for its cultivation as a living sap necessary for us to become—an undertaking which no longer would give rise to resentment if we really get down to it. Indeed, resentment bears witness to an idle energy or an energy of which the deeds do not contribute towards our global blossoming, of which the deeds do not venture to become, but go no further than what already exists without caring about life, which does not last without evolving.

Hence the fact that loving the other always entails renouncing loving him or her only as they already are, but helping them to be born as the ones who they are not yet, letting be what could occur this way. This requires us to keep our desire concerned with paying attention not to be fixed on any material or spiritual object, to remain wide-awake, aiming at what is human but also at its beyond-leaning with one hand on the bottom of the valley and hanging with the other on the highest summit of the mountain, in an impossible division between the body and the soul, which both participate in desire and are essential to our becoming. This becoming indeed has not much to do with understanding and our past logic, but rather requires our courage, a courage capable of joining in us what our tradition had divided, and thus paralyzed: our body and our soul or spirit. A courage which teaches us to question not about a truth presumed to be already established but about the conditions of our becoming, a becoming other than a repetition and an increase of what already exists, but which cannot regain its resources without innocence, humility, desire for the 'nothing yet'.

Giving Birth to One Another Anew

This is often accompanied by a return, a shameless return, to infancy that we sometimes attain very late, and that we must ourselves conquer without letting it be stolen by parents or masters who assisted our human prematurity or immaturity while subjecting and paralyzing our transcendental potential, especially with regard to our breath and our sexuate desire.

Returning to infancy must mean an opportunity to regain innocence or virginity at the level of sensory perceptions, of sensitiveness, but also of thinking. It must be an opportunity to have access to a silent naivety which renders us able to recover our freshness in the perception and the assessment of what we have to live, to think, to love. Which brings us back to the freshness of touch, a touch which intervenes in all our perceptions, and that a linguistic and logical teaching intended to replace, so taking away its living resources.

Now in order not to indefinitely wander outside of ourselves, taking root in sensitiveness, in sensory perceptions, especially in the most fundamental of our senses: touch, is necessary. Intersubjectivity can take place between us only if we succeed in linking the ec-stasis which corresponds to our human destiny with the physical world thanks to which we exist. Our human condition asks of us to unite in ourselves the most transcendental with the most tactile and not to remain torn between the summit and the valley, as Nietzsche says, not even between sky and earth, the deities and the mortals, according to Heidegger. We must assume such a human fate not only with our own development in mind but in order that intersubjectivity should become possible between us. This probably is the means of overcoming nihilism not by avoiding facing the negative, the nothing, but by taking it or them on in a constructive and fleshly way. The space, the place opened by the interrelation between our subjectivities, subjectivities developed in accordance with their own nature, is that which can provide us, as human beings, with a taking root which respects the nothing of being that we are originally and the nothing in common between us.

Our desire must reckon with these two ec-stases in order to be really human. However, it is such a path that our tradition never stopped blocking by subjecting us to genealogy, notably to a divine genealogy, and by leaving sexual attraction between us uncultivated at a transcendental level. The questioning of nihilism by Nietzsche and by Heidegger, but already its approach by the Hegelian dialectics, neglected the importance of these two ec-stases starting from which being as human can be founded, can be rooted, and they did not consider the transcendence which originally makes possible our existence as humans. They favoured our 'to be' as word more than as life. They did not question the articulation between word and flesh enough—which gave rise to a being undermined by nothingness, by a construction, a creation of our 'to be' which is extraneous to life and based on a plan of man that did not wonder about the not-being for which human beings are responsible.

In fact, the matter is particularly complicated for man. The ec-stasis which his existence represents with regard to his origin renders problematic the articulation between life and word. Even Nietzsche thinks about becoming as a passage from the old man of the West to a new man in a comparative way with respect to what is already named, more than as the search for a word which gives life and allows for its growth, that is, which goes back before the origin that he already gave to him. He imagines that a new man can occur, can exist without radically shaking the linguistic ground which supported the existence of the old man. Indeed going from one contradiction to another and exacerbating them does not yet permit us to free ourselves from remaining locked into the logical patterns which have generated them.

And if Nietzsche refers to Being, and perhaps even 'to be', as to something which is evanescent, as a 'smoke' or a 'vapor', it is because he does not think about our 'to be' as the possible blossoming of a cultivation of life thanks to another word. If Zarathustra often keeps silent, if silence and sleep play a great part in his search for a new humanity, if he talks a lot to himself, and in every possible way, even whispering or in a under-tone voice, if he holds dialogue with imaginary animals which embody various aspects of himself, he does not allude to a possible birth of a new human being thanks to the word of the other giving rise not only to a physical child but to a new existence through which we get closer to incarnating the 'to be' that we are. There are many different others in the journey of Zarathustra, but these others are people that he judges, he masters, that he tries to dominate as the stages of his becoming, that he tackles with their overcoming in mind.

There is no time when the word of the other enriches him enough so as to clear the bridge between the old man that he no longer wants to be and the new man that he is not yet. The word that he lacks for such occurrence, for such an advent to happen is the word of a desire which determines the becoming of our 'to be', its development towards a more achieved human being.

In reality, to get angry at Being, especially at humans subjected to Being, as Nietzsche does, seems to be, from his part, a misapprehension of the fact that the 'to be' of man does not yet exist, that it has not yet taken place because no word has allowed an incarnation of human being in its wholeness to happen. Only desire, a desire embodied through a sharing with an other different from us by nature, can make our develop-ment progress towards a new humanity, because only such a desire can renew in us nature and word towards a becoming human still to come. The word that, then, we tell to one another is that of our flesh seeking to transcend itself thanks to the desire for the other, longing for sharing our destiny ecstatic with regard to a merely natural belonging.

The Word of the Other

Zarathustra-Nietzsche does not imagine that the sign, or the omen, he is waiting for can come from the other. He seems even not to expect it, including as a mere chance or hazard. If he feels nostalgic for meeting 'true men', beyond his love for true animals, he does not tell a word about his hope of meeting a true woman whatever his needing a woman as a condition for pursuing his work. But it is perhaps giving up such hope that leads him to shed so many tears and to renounce his good fortune in order to devote himself only to his work—to what he calls his children, children to which he will give birth alone without passion or compassion except longing for his work, a work for which he finally will walk down the mountains again.

Besides, does not Nietzsche affirm that 'fundamentally one loves only one's child and one's work' and that where a great love exists for oneself it is an omen of pregnancy. And, by the way, he does not seem to worry about the gravity or heaviness of this pregnancy. The love of the different other does not appear to be what induces Nietzsche to give birth to children, but only the love for himself, and perhaps for humanity. Moreover, to become his companion one must be a 'co-creating and co-celebrating of Zarathustra' and 'to write one's will on his tables'. One must share the same ideal and aim at the same perfection—which looks like a Platonic plan at the relational level. The only desire for love that really concerns Nietzsche is this of getting lost for his children. But his companions and children are those that he creates so that they should correspond to his hope.

Nietzsche does not care about, or renounced, being available for welcoming the hazard of an unexpected meeting with a different other coming towards him. But did he not give up this way his good fortune, because according to his own confession this fortune is a woman? It is difficult not to hear in such words a possible sort of wisdom, but is this wisdom not dictated by resentment, especially against the time which passes, because they are words attributed to the afternoon of his life. And they probably show an enclosure in an eternal return of the same from which he did not succeed in freeing himself. Indeed making oneself available for the other runs the risk of no longer being able to close the circle of the return, of finding oneself higher or lower than the alignment of the borders or sides of the encircling. The return to the same is then impossible as is the illusory serenity that it brings. Because life never comes back to the same and the energy that it grants is not sustained by repetition.

Life does not grow, and even lasts, without leaving the horizon which already existed, the forms already produced. And, as humans, only the desire for infinity that an amorous longing brings to us can provide this opportunity. It is not without reason and grounds that the defenders of supra sensitive values have misjudged or condemned the strength of such desire. Amorous longing is the only energy capable of substituting for the power of supra sensitive values. It is our sun, the one that sometimes we can make arise between us, if we care about the carnal density which allows it to rise, and to bring warmth and light to us. And it is not here a question of metaphors, as is still too often the case in the discourse of Nietzsche. Instead I am alluding to a cultivation of energy that the 'hazard' or 'chance' of an amorous meeting requires, and also to the work that it needs to incarnate the 'spark' or awakening that this meeting provokes. Such a task is probably the most difficult to carry out, but it is also the most indispensable in order that a future of humanity should be possible.

We cannot give rise to this future without laughter and tears, without renouncing the old man of the West by becoming new human beings thanks to a birth or a rebirth of ourselves that we can grant to one another through amorous desire. Did we not decline enough? Did desert not sufficiently spread? Is not the dusk, not only of past idols but of humanity itself, fallen enough so that we grab the chance that perhaps is still left to us of welcoming and cultivating the gift, not to say the grace, of energy and light that an amorous sharing can grant us? Have we not for quite a long time wandered from one conception of truth to another and suffered from the heaviness of guilty feeling, to which a thinking subjected to judgment condemned us, or waited for living beyond our terrestrial existence, when our 'to be' finally would be disclosed to us, so that we understand that this 'to be' can be discovered and take place between us, that it exists thanks to our union as the advent of a human 'to be' that no one can appropriate? Would the time not have been come of our paying attention to this chance of reaching our being humans instead of wasting this opportunity through an extension and dissipation of our existence into an indefinite proliferation or multiplication of beings? Which, perhaps, amounts to a way of compensating for our lack of taking root by needs which more and more exile us from ourselves instead of attempting to attain a desire suitable for our global being and shareable as such between us as human beings.

To Conclude: The Ecstatic Meaning
of the Copula

Such desire allows us to return to the copula in which we have our origin, a copula through which two subjects long to unite with one another whatever their difference(s) may be, instead of each trying to be fulfilled only by itself through a logical copula ruling on the adequacy between a subject and a predicate, a subject and an object. And I am not here playing with words but referring to a truth before which we draw back with a mixture of irony, fear and even distress because it obliges us to assume once and for all and permanently, without any possible overcoming, our non-being and impossible sharing in a common Being, in order to attain a humanity which exists only through the union of our different potentials.

These potentials have too often been of use for rendering us slaves of one another or for subjecting us to values extraneous to each and which aimed to conciliate our differences, unless we used them for the sole purpose of reproducing without considering the additional energy to which they give rise, an energy which could be the cause of a human becoming which is not only natural while being faithful to our nature.

We ought to pay more attention to this source of energy as to a call for reaching our being as a human one. We ought to attend not to waste it for a pleasure leading to the 'petite mort' of which Freud speaks, but instead to keep it, to cultivate it and to share it, that is to pool it towards its increase, its concentration, its transformation so that it brings us to another stage of our development and, sometimes, to our transfiguration. This can happen through a sharing of energy which can provoke an enlightenment, a sort of transmutation of fire into light.

Such phenomenon can occur between us only if we are able to acknowledge and to assume the two ec-stases which correspond to a lack of an origin of our own and to the partiality of our human 'to be' entailing a transcendental difference in relating to the other. This transcendence between us, which is based on an insuperable negative, makes us able to unite with one another as humans. And the path towards such a union is less that of a gift, the gift that Nietzsche-Zarathustra intends to give to us, than the path of the search for an amorous sharing that he finally abandoned.

Anyway what present Zarathustra-Nietzsche intends to give us, he who considers Being to be smoke, a vapor without substituting another 'to be' for it? With what guilty feeling does he want to weight us down for having himself unilaterally received? Does such a gesture correspond to the love that he claims to feel for humans? And does he not say that one must be grateful to the other for receiving that with which he is bursting? Does not the acceptance of such a gift amount to a risk of being diverted from our own becoming by locking ourselves within the circle of the eternal return of the same?

Note

To understand this chapter it would be suitable to read some passages of the Prologue of *To Be Born* which clarify my words:

> Unveiling the mystery of our origin is probably the thing that most motivates our quests and plans (…)Now such grasping proves to be impossible. We become existent by cutting ourselves off—by ec-sisting—from our origin. Indeed, we were born as one of a union between two. We are the fruit of a copulative link between two different beings (…) of a meeting between two humans—one masculine being and one feminine being—who gave birth to a boy or to a girl. We are for ever deprived of an origin of our own (…) The origin of our being is in suspense in a connection between two terms which escapes any prediction and predication. And yet we are there—presence of an 'is' without any 'to be' originally identifiable. We are in charge of being (…)The ec-stasis with respect to our origin leads us to wander outside ourselves.(…) We search for ourselves in a common world already existing, and yet it is the one which prevents us from discovering our own 'to be' and the path towards a possible conjunction with the other as other. Rather we must listen to the desire of the other which attracts us beyond a horizon defined by sameness and the already common, a desire which remembers the ec-stasis from which we exist and calls us back to the question of our human being. (*To Be Born*, pp. v–vii)

12

'My Dear Little Soul'

A Hylemorphic Path

Heidegger immersed himself in being(s) in order to clear a new meaning—he immersed himself in *ule* in search of a new *morphe*. But this *ule* was already shaped by a technique, the logos, except when he went back endlessly to walk in the country paths next his chalet of Todtnauberg. There is no doubt that, by the stays and walks there, he tried to provide himself with a viewpoint on being. However, the heavens of Todtnauberg and those of metaphysics are not quite the same. If the ones still take part in nature, the others are dependent on culture, and they already result from a technique that Heidegger did not detect sufficiently. Whatever the efforts and the 'leaps' through which he attempted to free himself from it, he remained blindly captive to it. Hence his inescapable relation to the poetry of Hölderlin, who endeavours to tell nature, especially that of his country.

According to Heidegger, 'Every essential and great deed arises from the fact that man has a home and is rooted in a tradition' (cf. *Réponses et questions sur l'Histoire et la politique,* Interview avec *Der Spiegel, p. 47; Only a God can still Save Us,* An interview with *Der Spiegel*, in Thomas Sheehan, *Heidegger, The Man and the Thinker*, p. 57). After he tried to give himself

L. Irigaray, *The Mediation of Touch*, https://doi.org/10.1007/978-3-031-37413-5_12

a home through resorting to politics, has Heidegger not resorted to nature and poetry as places from which he could make his thinking exist? But he never succeeded in reconciling them because he could not liberate his nature from the logos which had moulded it. Indeed, the home of Heidegger is indubitably the logos—and the German language. Staying in language, his 'house of language', prevented Heidegger from returning to himself, to his own natural belonging.

Heidegger points out as one of the etymologies of the verb 'to be': to dwell—*bauen*—and all his work could be viewed as a constant search for a place where he could dwell. It is always a question of where and how to dwell—thus, for him, to be—be it the matter of his chalet of Todtnauberg and his endless walks in the country or of his concern about the earth, of his desire to work on a national unity of Germany, of the necessity of being rooted in a tradition, of his conceiving of language as a house in which to live, and even of *Da-sein*. One could even say that, by making efforts to leave a metaphysical exile, Heidegger attempted to transform the language into a sort of *ule* in which he cleared a path in search of a meaning at which he could stop to dwell. But what he tried to clear towards an original meaning was already artificially constructed. Searching for himself through the *ule* of language, he went into exile from himself and 'ran aground into being(s)' (op.cit., p. 52; p. 58). Heidegger did not succeed in dwelling in himself. His search for himself through several love affairs probably resulted from that. However, to have sexual intercourse, in particular within the horizon of a patriarchal tradition, is often a manner of being absent from oneself. On the contrary, to inhabit a sexuate body can provide us with a dwelling thanks to the structure—the natural logos—that a specific belonging supplies. But that requires us to accept the partiality of our human destiny—to be a man or to be a woman and not to be a human being—or a *Dasein*—in the neuter.

If Heidegger fought against fragmentation and disintegration, if he refused to content himself with a mere criticism, without for all that consenting to remaining in a whole formed in a meta-physical way, he has not understood that the return he had to achieve was a return to himself, within himself, in order to discover how to gather with himself. He searched for himself too far away in space or time—spread too much in search of his being. He wanted to be very great in order to be in a position to think according to his time, whereas the matter was of going back to the humility of his flesh so that he could perceive in it a truth of being still to be unveiled.

But it is difficult, even impossible, to unveil such truth only by oneself. It is thanks to a sharing with another flesh that this truth can be revealed. And that has little to do with mere sexual intercourse, procreation or parenthood. Rather, the question is of giving oneself up to the mystery of the meeting between two subjectivities which are different, a difference which is not merely ontical, as it can be in the meeting between two persons belonging to different cultures, but is also ontological, that is, which corresponds to a meeting between two different natural beings. Then the word 'ontological' regains a meaning that it generally had lost, except when we allude to vegetal or animal essences. For example, we speak of trees to designate the essence of a vegetal species among which an oak has a specific essence. Humanity has the particularity of comprising only a species but which is divided into two genuses which correspond to different 'essences'. Indeed, unless we reduce the female genus to an 'accident', as Aristotle does, we must acknowledge that it belongs to an 'essence' which differs from the masculine one. Obviously, it is not a question of an essence such as a supra sensitive entity, or an ideal being, but of a natural essence to which particular constitutive properties correspond: physiological, morphological, genetic, but also psychic and even linguistic.

No Western philosopher until now admitted that the human ontological identity differs according to the gender. Not recognizing such truth gave rise to a culture in the neuter which exiles the human being from its living existence and its real being. Hence it is running aground into being(s); moreover, being(s) which are already made and without a life of its/their own.

The thinkers are endowed with an energy other than that which is used by most of the humans in their everyday existence. This energy feeds their desire to overstep the limits of the world in which they live. They hope for succeeding in changing the world, unless their aspirations hold on to the transcendence of an ideal or the belief in another life. One of the motivations which led Heidegger to be interested in politics probably lies in that. But, as he himself said: the one who thinks on a large-scale, also can be mistaken on a large-scale. The awareness of his having been mistaken, of having or having been run aground has probably paralyzed the enthusiasm of Heidegger regarding his desire to change the world and sent him back to the running aground into being(s) that *Da-sein* in a way represents—a first *Da-sein* from which it could be possible to free oneself little by little according to him. To be helped in this progressive emancipation, Heidegger resorted to nature, to the poetry of Hölderlin as a shepherd of nature, even of nature as his home, and to the expectation of a god.

But what god can exempt us from being humans? And about what have we still to think concerning this 'being a human', especially regarding our sexuate belonging? What have we to discover about our desire for a human differently sexuate as a longing for a transcendence always still to come and unspeakable? Could we substitute the desire for a god for the desire for another human? How could we join these desires to one another? Does the desire for a god not run the risk of shutting again the ontological, and self-logical, circle which Heidegger tried to leave, if it precedes the desire for another human?

But of what nature is the desire for the other? What question relevant to our being asks us this desire? Does the desire for the other not involve a double, and even a triple questioning about being?—who am I? who are you? who are we to call each other for being? Why am I incited to leave myself to step up to you? Why does there exist such a prompting to meet you, even to unite with you? Of what being is there a question?—a being which corresponds to a verb again and not to a mere substantive: a being. Indeed, the question that my desire asks, the overstepping from myself towards you that it compels me to achieve is an act, a development, a transcending myself without dwelling in whom, and above all in what, I already am: a 'being' or a 'have been' as in a sort of 'cover', Heidegger wrote (cf. *Qu'appelle-t-on penser?*, p. 135; *What is Called Thinking?*, p. 120) or in an essence which would develop only by itself, as is the case with a tree, which does not need another tree for its growth.

Heidegger did not wonder sufficiently about such a question concerning the relation between 'to be' and 'being'. At least not in connection with the desire for a differently sexuate human. At least not in his work. And yet this would have perhaps brought to his thought other than a desire, or a need, for thinking on a large-scale, as a spreading in space and time, but instead a desire for thinking of the truth as far as the human being is concerned—an inescapable task regarding 'being' and 'Being'. Or 'being' and 'to be'?

Heidegger has not thought about the call of the other, in both a subjective and objective genitive. If he paid a careful attention to the call of the country paths, to the call of nature and of its main poet Hölderlin, to the call of thinking and to the call of a god, he seems to have remained unfamiliar with the call of the other, at least at an ontological level—a call which would have given back a fleshly and sensitive quality to the meaning of the words. Strangely, Heidegger, who is so much concerned with language, does not wonder very much about the gender of the words. He avoids the question by favouring the use of the neuter. But, in this way, he neglects the impact of the subject who produces the discourse on the wording and the statement, and on what occurs at the level of meaning and truth according to the subject of enunciation. For him, meaning would be, and ought to be, irrespective of the subject. It would happen by itself regardless of the present intervention of the subject—which perhaps corresponds to Heidegger's desire for a return to the Greek thinkers way of saying the world thanks to the logos independently of subjectivity. We would have become the result of such an attempt to appropriate the world so as to presumedly safeguard its being(s).

But what about the being(s) which would be safeguarded in that way? What would be the mode of safeguarding the world and ourselves as living subjects? And what could signify the connection between being(s) and Being? Was the Greek attempt to appropriate the world through the logos not the outcome of a more or less conscious will to emerge as human beings, above all as men, from the whole that the cosmos constituted? Were not the ones who named and assembled the world by the logos already subjects—subjects being still lacking in self-awareness and determination(s) as such, at least apparently. Indeed, they were determined in the way, in fact the masculine way, of placing the world before themselves and gathering it together into a whole by their saying.

The Soul of Heidegger

Even when it is a question of the soul, Heidegger speaks about '*Gemüt*', of 'an internal gathering', of a 'being collected (*An-dacht*)' or 'remaining constantly collected', of 'gathering through/in a permanent belief' (op. cit., pp. 146–47: op.cit., pp. 140–41), and even of 'acknowledgment and gratitude for something' (op.cit., p. 149; op.cit., p. 143), but not about the diaphanous space of self-affection arising from a touching one another of the borders of the body—for example, the lips or the palms of the hands. This would be more similar to the Aristotle's way of conceiving of the soul, without the subject-object split that will become a key operation in our western logic. For Heidegger, the soul is not a sort of tactile dwelling where he could gather himself together but a possibility of faithfully 'retaining', of being 'obeying thanks to a meditative listening' to 'That which is our lot' (op.cit., p. 147; op.cit., p. 141). And this lot does not seem to have amounted to a fleshly belonging and place in which he could hold himself and welcome another flesh, not as an 'object' but with a communion or union between beings in mind.

If Heidegger agrees to give himself up to a gathering already consti-tuted, to a 'That which is his lot', he does not seem to agree to confide or abandon himself to an other, especially a feminine other, to a presence which corresponds to a gathering or a world different from his own, even if the words with which he titles the letters that he addresses to his wife are often 'My dear little soul'. He is grateful for the gift of thinking which is, according to him, 'the highest gift that is granted to us, a gift which truly lasts and will remain our being, with which we are endowed so that it is only thanks to this gift that we would be the ones who we are' (op. cit., p. 149; op.cit., p. 142). However, he does not acknowledge that the other could be the cause of 'That' which gives to think, which wants 'to be thought and, consequently, originally requires a faithful thought'. He does not know the withdrawal into oneself as a 're-touching' oneself, as a gathering with oneself which allows one to open up to the other as other, and not as a call for a repetition or the safeguard of something to be remembered and for which we must be grateful.

If Heidegger maintains, in a comment on Hölderlin's poetry, that we need to go abroad to experience our home as our own, he does not, for all that, admit that the other as other could be a path to know oneself and build a world of one's own—to be revealed to oneself. He ignores such questioning about a return to himself, to his own being. He spreads far and wants to be 'great' in search of what is to be thought without opening an interval of space and time to think of himself—also in order to perceive what or who could be the other in himself without mistaking the one for the other in a 'That' or a 'there is' which lacks difference and negative, if not the one of a non-intentional forgetting. And yet, they would have allowed him to better differentiate the far from the close, the different from the same, the other from himself, the appropriation of the other from appropriating himself to the other and so forth.

For lack of a thinking of difference, Heidegger gives way to technology, the embodiment of a thinking in the neuter which substitutes itself for the sexuate living. Those always imply the existence of an other who questions them about their being and invites them to welcome and gather his or her own through both passive and active gestures, guardians of a truth that none can appropriate—a truth concerning being, in particular being a human.

Perhaps, this could correspond to a function of the soul, according to Heidegger. However, does he not contradict himself when he distinguishes the human being from the living being? This seems to be the case in a sentence as 'To think of man as a human being and not as a living being' (op. cit., p. 151; op.cit., pp. 148–49). Or also in the sentence 'There is a major difference between taking into consideration this trait of man as a living being and considering the relation to what is to be the fundamental trait of the human being that man is—the initial proposition, the one which provides the trail' (idem). Does this not mean that, for Heidegger, a major difference exists between being living and being a man? Could that give rise to the neuter of a 'That', a 'there is' or 'it gives'—even of a *Dasein*—and to a Being which both exceeds and fills this difference? Could this Being then correspond to the memory of our determination as being living, thus sexuate, the forgetting of which would be safeguarded under the cover of the neuter—a neuter which gives, gives itself and gives us to think what would be the most to be thought?

But what happens when you give me to think about the impossible thinking of a difference between us? Is it not from the real, but unthinkable, existence of this difference that the neuter of a 'there is to be thought' is extrapolated, which sunk into oblivion but recurs to us under the guise of an alternative or a split between 'running aground into being(s)' or being kept in abeyance by/in Being? Is it not that which is presupposed by the fact that, for Heidegger, the feelings and longings of human beings are 'disposed by' and 'in accordance with' what is, which means being somehow or other dependent on an 'object' or an objective which moulds them? There is no allusion to the objectivity of subjectivity, to intersubjectivity nor to a mood which is shaped in order to be in harmony with another subject.

For Heidegger, the beginning which hides from us our origin is a sort of 'envelop' or 'cover' and not the fact that we correspond only to a part of this origin even though we are full-subjects. This modifies our logic, frees it from a totality in the neuter. It is true that, in the early Greek, some ways of expressing intersubjectivity exist—for example, the word *heteros* meaning the other of two, the middle voice and the dual forms. What conceals our origin from us is a logic of representation in the neuter and all that is kept in abeyance on this side or beyond what our thinking can signify—which is extrapolated from it and kept on hold in/by Being. In the dialogue between us as different, I cannot imagine what or who you are; but I can endeavour to sense your presence, to let myself be 'disposed' by it without being reduced to it or reducing it to me. Assuming my partiality grants me this possibility, preserves the 'weaving' of my sensitive being, Hegel would say, and contributes to a gathering of what or whom I am which is likely to enter into presence with an other, who is also gathered with him- or herself. Then the logos at stake is concerned with what and how to tell you about myself, but also about you, more than with saying something about something regardless of a true exchange between us.

What I have to say to you about myself or about you can be neither imagined in the neuter nor be reduced to a merely mental or speculative activity. My, and our, comprehensive being are in question in such saying, and if our soul must ensure the mediation between us, this soul must recover all the properties, notably the physical properties, that Aristotle still attributes to it. And yet the relationship of the soul with the body is almost absent from the Heidegger's thinking. Even its relationship with life seems to be almost nonexistent—except, perhaps, as a self-defense process. But we know very little about the way in which Heidegger's soul suffers, and even feels. It seems to be almost entirely devoted to a metaphysical concern—at best subcortical, as memory and gratitude, but already submitted to thinking, the sensitive belonging of which seems to go with the neuter.

Unless we question the difference between a logos in the masculine and a logos in the feminine in connection with that, one favouring the subject-object relationship and the other the subject-subject relationship. Heidegger does not take interest in such a question, as is generally the case with the western philosophers. And the different function that is then assumed by the copula 'to be' is not considered by him although it is behind the way of conceiving of truth in the West. The fact that I am as a woman remains outside of that which is viewed as having to do with truth, including when it is a question of life—and of the soul -, and it does not seem to concern the philosopher. At best he shows interest in the intellectual qualities of the soul, leaving to the woman its sensitive and bodily qualities from which he intends to free himself as a man.

Torn Between Things and Words

Sensitive properties are also entrusted to things—notably by Heidegger—things the materiality of which is of use to embody notions. The soul of Heidegger settles on/in things for lack of being able to join with the body and with another living being. It also settles on/in the words, which are compared to beings. Hence it is valid to wonder about how this soul relates to motion and sensation (cf. Aristote, *De l'âme*; Aristotle, *De Anima*). How does it move and what does it experience when it is reduced to an intellect extraneous to the body and is exiled from life itself? What enlivens a thinking indifferent to the body from which it arises, and is in a way always external to itself? Could it be only the need to increase in order to apparently continue to exist? Or a need to appear, to show itself? Could it also be what brings to mankind that which the vegetal being receives from the air and the sun? Indeed, it is from an outside of himself that Heidegger waits for 'That' which is to be thought—notably 'Being'. Would he attempt to be faithful to *phusis* in that way—even to mimic it? According to him, the essence of mankind would correspond with resorting to and obeying the pressure of 'That', of 'Being', in order to fulfil his destiny, although/as he is exiled in history and an environment which is made up by the past, the present and the future notably from such an exile. Has not this gesture something similar to the 'calvary' that Hegel considers necessary to reach the absolute Spirit? With the difference that the Heidegger's work remains open to questions, to the need of a thinker 'greater' than him and, above all, to the expectation of a god—a god who, in spite of all, seems to be less metaphysical than the God of Hegel.

Nevertheless, Heidegger's soul looks like a sort of exile in an impassive intellect. As if this soul never had been really moved by an other, by an affect which united it with a sensitive body, but also with another body. Heidegger's soul seems to lack a fleshly awakening—except, perhaps, when he relates to nature. But Heidegger, apparently, did not completely know what the sharing of a carnal desire could be. And yet is not desire that which, most originally, sets the soul in motion?

Desire cannot be viewed as an 'accident' as regards the soul. Is it not in a way its principle itself? Desire is that which allows the human being to pursue its becoming beyond a mere physical growth. And that is possible because the soul takes over from it when a merely natural growing stops. But the soul does not move only by itself or through its own body, it is also moved by the desire of the other: the desire for the other and the desire of the other for itself. The soul is the place thanks to which the unification of our being can occur as well as the union of our comprehensive being with a being different from ours—a union that the desire can achieve, a desire for which the soul must safeguard a freedom of choice and thought, which distinguishes it from a mere instinct or drive.

The soul acts as a place and a mediation. The latter is both passive and active—the soul is sensitive and appetitive. The soul is also the place where the one can become the other without a dividing from one another so that one could be attributed to the feminine and the other to the masculine—one becoming 'anima' and the other 'animus'. As well the woman as the man must have a soul both sensitive and appetitive and be capable of joining the one to the other. And it is less the proportion of sensation and desire which can differentiate a woman from a man than the way of linking both together. Could I suggest that the woman is more actively passive and the man more passively active, which would correspond with a way of achieving their beings but not with a quantity or a mixture.

All that is just a first approach to the question, which must be developed not only in connection with objects but between subjects, between living beings animated by a specific soul. This presupposes a particular relation to touch. Man has too often reduced the latter to a tool with which to master instead of making it a means to transcend himself thanks to a property of touch and what it is able to set in motion. The soul would be the agent and the intermediary, susceptible to a certain touch and its trending towards a growing, a becoming. The soul would mediate the sensitive, preserving it from an immediate reaction, on the one hand, and from the capture by the mental, on the other hand. The soul would transform the sensation into a possible quality, a possible light, warmth, tonality or colour of the flesh.

The way of conceiving of the soul seems to have evolved from a more substantial nature to an almost exclusively formal nature. One could say: from an emanation from the body to a production of the spirit—with a frequent distribution between the feminine and the masculine. Such evolution means that a more sensitive soul has become a soul which is more cognitive, above all at the formal level, which is accompanied by a change of the kind of desires, going from more sensuous or affective to more intellectual desires. The simultaneous existence of the two kinds of desires, and their passage from the one to the other, is generally lacking. Is it not the relationship with the other as different from us by nature which could solve this aporia by requiring nature to be provided with appropriate forms? This would need a present and horizontal relation between the one and the other instead of being dependent on a vertical relation, which asks for renouncing matter to the benefit of form(s)—thus giving up making blossom our being as living. Then our soul falls back into a vegetal or animal existence without ensuring what is truly human: being capable of transcendental appetites and of a fleshly thought as well as of their sharing. This allows the soul to leave a body of its own and to return to it, in it, enriched, also spiritually, by its meeting with another soul. So the soul would be endowed with the four faculties that Aristotle allots to it.

But what language could be accountable for such destiny? Has the conceptual language of metaphysics, and its way of dealing with being, not rendered that impossible? Is it not, henceforth, incumbent on us to invent another language, another logic—another logos—which could be of use in different cultures, for example, in both Eastern and Western cultures? (cf. on this subject 'D'un entretien de la parole' dans *Acheminement vers la parole*, pp. 85 à 139; The dialogue between Heidegger and a Japanese master in 'A Dialogue on Language', in *On the Way to Language*, pp. 1–54). Indeed, the function of 'to be' cannot be limited to join a subject and a predicate or an 'object', causing in that way a separation between two different subjects unless they submit to the same objectality. What is thus at stake is to discover another use of the word 'to be', or 'is', which could unite different subjects with one another. The question is not of giving up resorting to the word 'to be' but of wondering about its meaning and its function as copula—notably as a verb and not as a substantive.

The Amorous Interlacing

How can the copula 'to be' contribute to the becoming of our natural belonging—or natural essence—without subjecting it to a metaphysical essence? What can be the linguistic properties and the use of that copula which could put us into relationship with one another as different without subjecting us to one another, or reducing the one or the other to the status of an object, instead of leading us to a reciprocal intersubjectivity? What truth can support, unveil and develop such a use of the copula, preventing us from falling back into a background—a *upokeimenon*—which is lacking in differentiation or is kept on hold by/in metaphysical idealities? What language, what logic can allow us to speak to one another without this language moulding us in a way that destroys what we have to say to one another? (op.cit., p. 90; op.cit., p. 4). This language is certainly not the one which views the meaning as supra sensitive and the sound or the letter as sensitive (op. cit., p. 100; op.cit., p. 15); that is to say, a language which is strictly speaking metaphysical. Rather, it is our sensitive existence which needs to be thought and still lacks the suitable language. Even the gesture, in particular of the hand, is considered in the West a means of seizing, or even palpating, which does not fit an exchange between us—it does not favour the presence of each in its own being.

What happens in that kind of exchange, especially of amorous exchange, is a change of nature of the sensitive itself. It no longer amounts to an immersion in what lacks thinking—as a mode of running aground into being(s)—but to the transformation of what we lived in an only passive way into an active perception and search for transcendence. Lingering on what the other reveals to us at a sensitive level, without for all that wanting to seize, understand or appropriate it, modifies our relation to sensitivity. Nevertheless, the matter is not of passing to a supra sensitive level, which does not allow us to perceive the other in his or her living otherness, but to have access to a perception in which feeling and thinking no longer divide from one another or are prioritized with respect to one another. Such a perception happens in a place that is unknown to us or forgotten by us—a place intermediate between our body and our spirit which could correspond to the heart or the soul. It is in such a place, the language of which is still to be discovered, that we could meet together and unite with one another as different. This place has certainly more to do with breath and touch than with the visible and the object, including the conceptual one.

Obviously, it is then a question of a touch which differs from the one that is generally acknowledged as such in the West (op.cit., p. 101 and p. 107; op.cit., p. 16 and p. 22). In 'A Dialogue between a Japanese and an Inquirer' (in *On the Way to Language*, pp. 1–54), the Japanese master alludes to what this touch could be but even more to what it cannot be. It is from a culture in which subjectivity as such in a way does not exist—except through gestures?—that the teaching comes. How could we, Westerners, return to it or have access to it? Perhaps thanks to the 'clearing' that our desire for the other who is sexually different from us can open in our culture. The natural *Gestell* that our sexuation represents provides us with an opportunity to perceive otherwise than through the sensitive-mental split that past metaphysics imposed on our subjectivity.

Our sexuation does not make us necessarily available, but it (re)opens in us a possibility of uniting sensitivity and thought in order to be able to meet and commune with an other different from ourselves. The position of the Japanese master rather evokes a faithfulness to the natural world from which subjectivity little differs except through its ability to act—in a way as is the case in the Greek world. As Westerners, we have to free our subjectivity from its subjection to our traditional metaphysics in order to grant it another status and allow it a new unfolding by a conscious and assumed consideration for our natural belonging—an opportunity that our sexuation offers to us. Taking such a dimension and its cultivation into account could liberate our subjectivity from a meta-physical authority and give to it a meaning, in particular a relational meaning, until now little-known, which can reveal to us a still hidden truth of our being and bring us energy to implement it.

Our mode of being and thinking lacked dynamism—hence it froze in being(s) instead of contributing to the becoming of our 'to be'. The split between Being—or to be—and being, which represents one of the basic aspects of Heidegger's thought, perhaps results from a failure in the dialectical relation between passivity and activity in regard to our way of being. Certainly, to be sends us back to a state, but why must it be assimilated to a destiny which is assigned to us rather being understood as a way of being to which we can contribute? We cannot come into the world only as a 'being' except, sometimes, in the eyes of our parents and of people around ourselves. We were born as a peculiar living being which had to be thanks to our first breathing. There is no doubt that our entering into presence transforms us each time into a being, but it is up to us to emancipate ourselves from it, freeing ourselves from that momentary appearing by continuing to become as far as we but also our relationship with the other(s) are concerned. Hence the task which is incumbent on us is to join the 'to be' which is ours, including potentially, to the one that we actualize in the present—that is, 'to be' as a global potential to 'being' as a momentary unfolding of this 'to be'. Could that which is extrapolated in Being not result from a failing to be our original 'to be' more than from a failing to correspond to that which humanity has not—not yet?—incarnated of our human being in history, from which a part has been kept as a potential of culture—in an inextricable mixture of matter and form(s)?

That which contributes to such being kept on hold by/in Being is our tending to fix, above all through naming, the unfolding of life, to paralyze in substantives—in beings—the dynamism of a verb—to be. This can give rise to a hermeneutic circle the language of which—the logos—is supposed to be the main agent and guarantor. But this language is already meta-physical, at least in the West, as Heidegger himself acknowledges, and it ought to try, with a greater modesty, to serve life instead of having the pretension to replacing it. Even our poetic language cannot express all the sensitiveness of life of which our physical belonging is the carrier and the mediator. Does this language not already transform to be into being(s) when it attempts to say our feelings?

A 'to be' Lacking in Words

Could we join life to words without falling into the transformation of the living into beings? Could figurative languages, as those which are in use in Eastern cultures, be more able to express life? Do our Western languages, which are coded in a more or less arbitrary way, not force us to resort to representation to understand and share meaning? What happens with life in that case? Is it not the other, then, who can give signs, or be a sign, of it to us, without subjecting life to metaphysics provided that he or she remains faithful to their natural belonging? If the other escapes being trapped in appearing and enters into presence in order to achieve his or her being, does this other not call us for living, notably by entrusting the safeguard of life to us? It is up to us to send back this other to the most original of their being through liberating him or her from all the appearances or beings in which they became trapped. It is up to us to return them to the experience of their being as living instead of subjecting them still more to a culture of representation.

It is also up to me to unveil to the other what or whom he or she is at their most intimate level and they cannot experience without my desire and my thinking. It is up to me to bring the other into the world again, a world which is suitable for him or her and they can discover, or rediscover, from a gathering that I can carry out and reveal to them through a non-appropriating perception of the ones who they are. It is up to me to pay attention to their gestures as to a sensitive and meaningful manifestation of their beings that they themselves do not know— gestures which touch me, question me, are not merely visible but tell me what words do not succeed in saying.

Our desire opens a sort of hermeneutic place with regard to our being, a place where sensitivity expresses itself without our being able to tell it except, sometimes, through loving gestures. In such a place, representation is not always operative and it is more between our souls that we confide in one another, as long as we understand the soul as a sort of subtle emanation from life, through which we continue to be born thanks to our breathing and our relation of desire for and love of the other, in which touch can act as mediation, freeing us from a logic of representation according to which only the subject-object relationship is really effective.

Then our constant coming into the world, our appearing and our becoming correspond to a flowering more than to the result of a cultural construction. They are an 'un-sheltering' of our being by the return to a beginning in which the living being that we are longs for its unfolding. There is no doubt that desire can lead us to an unlimited unfolding in which our being little by little fades, unless it hangs on supra sensitive ideals. Desire must be both a revelation which calls for being and a gathering, an incentive to flower and a return to the source—a motion in which what appears is only a moment of that which is originally, the being of which cannot be perceived objectively. One could say that no phenomenon could exhaust its truth. Being to which desire aspires never completely amounts to an appearing, and the desire for the other, or the desire from the other, sends back our longing to an irreducible difference, thus to a limit of/in being, which always remains to be assumed by each one in faithfulness to its origin.

In other words, the 'openness without withdrawal', of which Heidegger speaks, does not belong to the living being—life as life does not appear if not indirectly. For a human, it is desire which prompts it to blossom, which does not necessarily amount to a becoming which is visible. This becoming is more perceptible by a touch, the nature of which is not a conscious touching by the hand as it is traditionally imagined in the West. Rather, it is a question of being moved and put into motion towards what we need in order to be revealed to ourselves and continue to develop without forgetting the limits of our own being, without completely giving ourselves up to the 'void of the heavens' that the Japanese word *kohou* expresses (cf. op.cit., p. 127; op.cit., p. 41).

The perception of the other who is naturally different from us can preserve us from such a danger and takes us back to the 'earth' that our natural belonging represents. From this earth, it is possible to live the transports of delight without going into supra sensitive raptures (op.cit., p. 130 and sq.; op.cit., p. 44 and sq.). This delight can result from the fact that the other has touched us at the most intimate level but has not removed us from ourselves. The desire, which is then awakened, calls us for going towards the other from a withdrawal into ourselves and a gathering with ourselves which must be preserved to make it possible to approach that which has delighted us. The grace which arouses this awakening is always instantaneous and unique; it does not repeat itself—this would amount to submitting it to the traditional domination of the sensitive by the intelligible. This grace touches our global being, reveals it to itself through a call for being appropriate to the one it is in order to answer the call of the other. It is an inclination, exempt from representation and objectivation, which can attempt to fit the grace or the spark of such an appeal.

Such an inclination cannot be satisfied with the appropriation of an object or the achievement of an aim. If it suits the clearing that the desire for the naturally different other opens, the desire for the most intimate of us that the call coming from the most distant awakens, this grace will be the revelation that the appeal of the other is a call for being ourselves, and that the desire to unite with one another is inseparable from the assumption of an insurmountable distinction. But the latter wants to be overcome through transcending oneself towards the other. The desire for the other does not involve a need to be assuaged, an instinct in search of satisfaction. It is a desire for a beyond as for what can contribute towards our becoming.

In reality, the desire for the other has something to do with the Heideggerian remarks about our opening up to the unfolding of the word. Does it not act as a 'lightning', which 'opens and lights up' a wideness in which 'an unfolding of the word can get to appear?' (op.cit., pp. 138–39; op.cit., p. 53). And could one not say that once more Heidegger substitutes the unfolding of the word for the unfolding of the natural life? And even that he uses Greek terms—for example *phusis* and *phuein*—with a meaning which differs from the meaning they have in Greek culture? Hence one of the difficulties that the interpretation of his thinking entails?

The fact that the desire for the other has something to do with the unfolding of the word can also be heard from the need that the 'spark' which 'opens up to the perception of the unfolding' has 'to be soothed' in order to give rise to a possible being appropriate to or fitting in—as desire needs love to be lived and shared. But it is then a question of the unfolding of our comprehensive being and not only of that of the word, to which it cannot truly be compared. Has Heidegger not entrusted what he could not live of his being, in particular of his flesh, to words, on the one hand, and to things, on the other hand? Does this transposition not exile the human being from the development of its own being—henceforth split between a meta-physical language and an inanimate matter? Is it not then deprived of a soul as a unifying agent of the 'animal' life? As his soul has become above all mental and it is so separated from the body, without sensitivity and appetite except regarding mind, does not Heidegger search for giving back to himself some materiality or substance through the hyle which could be conveyed by language?

13

The Dynamism Necessary for Our Becoming

The Other as a Source of Evolution

The soul of Heidegger—as the soul of Hegel and of most of the western philosophers—ends in being a merely capturing structure, a sort of technical device without life. For lack of being the soul of a body, it amounts to a kind of structure in search of what can ensure its functioning. And its ability to move, henceforth, is dependent on an artificial energy production and not on the power of a living body. The act of which such a soul is capable is extraneous to a potential which is its own—as it is the case with a mechanism searching from what and how it could become operative. Hence, the soul spreads indefinitely without a return to a natural body being possible, a body from which it could receive its own power.

Indeed, a soul cannot exist without a body, but it must correspond to the body which is its own—it cannot be the soul of whatever body. Thus the soul cannot be neuter—the soul of a man and the soul of a woman are not the same and they cannot substitute for one another. As for what can unite them with one another, Aristotle speaks of begetting as 'a participation in the eternal and the divine' and even as a possible 'communion with the divine' not in 'an individual identity, but in the unity of the

L. Irigaray, *The Mediation of Touch*, https://doi.org/10.1007/978-3-031-37413-5_13

species' (*De l'âme*, II, Les facultés de l'âme, 4, L'âme nutritive, p. 39; *De Anima*, II, The Properties of the Soul, 4, The Nutritive Soul (415 a-b)). Aristotle does not allude to a possible generation of the lovers by one another thanks to a communion with one another. This would imply that he acknowledges the generative power of difference at the spiritual level and he does not leave the potential of the germ cells only to the divine for the benefit of the unity of the species.

However, Aristotle maintains that we can feel and feed ourselves only as different, the other, beginning with the other gender, being the main cause of our feeling and feeding. In other words, the other would be a source of life whereas the similar would contribute to a preservation of life but not towards its development, which entails an evolution. Thus if knowledge only takes place between those who are similar, it cannot be an element contributing to life itself, according to Aristotle. Nevertheless, he distinguishes the sensitive faculty from the cognitive faculty while considering them to be dependent on one another as power, on the one hand, and act, on the other hand. He reflects very little on the cognitive potential of sensation and the sensitive potential of knowledge and their respective and reciprocal ways of acting. This ends in paralyzing human becoming by the domination of life by its presumed knowledge.

Such a paralysis also results from the fact that Aristotle—and not only him!—imagines the other as opposite and not as different, which would mean that this other represents a different life and a possible fertilization of one life by the other, as it happens at the physical level. Besides, if Aristotle rightly notices that touching—differently from seeing, hearing and smelling—does not require an external medium for being effective, he does not wonder about the existence of another flesh as a medium which is external in relation our own. He does not question the fact that a flesh is never anonymous either, even if it has not a specific name as such, and that it is the touching of the other which allows most the passage from 'power' to 'act' of each flesh and its determination.

Aristotle seems also to ignore what takes place in touching another flesh, and in the touching one another of two fleshes. And yet this creates a medium which favours the unfolding of the flesh itself. Such a medium is produced and partially limited by the relation between two different fleshes. One flesh must be moved and in a way affected by an other in order that that should happen. The communion between these two different fleshes generates a flesh which belongs neither to the one nor to the other but is the fruit of their union. Aristotle, as many other philosophers, does not recognize that this potential flesh can contribute to the development, including the spiritual development, of the human species through the union between two different germ cells. At the logical level, he also misjudges the fecundity of the difference in comparison with the opposite, one remaining connected to life whereas the other is situated within a constructed and closed system. Aristotle neglects too to think about what can correspond to a real proximity or intimacy arising from a reciprocal touch. Hence, the cultural fecundity of this touch is buried in an uneducated naturalness which is accompanied by an aspiration after a life beyond our terrestrial existence in which our being could finally reach its accomplishment.

Aristotle affirms that the human touch can distinguish a human being from other animals because it 'surpasses all of them by far in acuity'—what makes the human being 'the most clever of the animals'. However, he does not worry about how a culture of touch could help us to blossom. Nevertheless, he indicates that touch is the sense which can determine the ones among the humans who are well or poorly gifted: 'the ones who have a hard flesh are poorly endowed with intelligence whereas the ones who have a tender flesh are well endowed' (*De L'âme,* II, 9, L'odeur et l'odorat, p. 56; *De Anima,* II, 9, The smell and the sense of smell (421 a-b)). This message has been very little perceived! As is the case with the one regarding the fact that living beings are sexuate, that most of them have a voice, and that by their voice as well as by their sexes they are sexually different. But this does not prevent the philosopher from favouring a culture of sameness without really wondering about the importance of the other and of difference for the living, and about the need to take account of the latter at the sensitive but also the mental levels.

The part that the other plays in the actualization of the flesh is not treated, nor is the fact that, as not just any body can fit a given soul, the choice of the other in the sharing of the flesh cannot be just any one. One flesh cannot go together with any other—putting into act their relation asks them to be appropriate to one another, which does not mean being the same. At an elementary physical level, it could not go this way because as far as touch is concerned the dry needs the moist and the cold needs the warm in order that they could be perceived and tasted. The same goes with sensation, which requires the different as a source of motion and a cause of actualization. If our intellect wants the same to be able to appropriate the 'object' at which it aims, it is not the case with the natural life. It does not develop without the intervention of the different. It becomes sterilized and fossilized in a relation and an environment which are comprised only of the same ones.

The Union Between the Same and the Different

As humans, we need to be in relation with the same and with the different, and to have an environment in which they can harmonize with one another. Perhaps, it could be to that that touch both aspires and contributes. But what is then at stake is above all an inner milieu—the flesh, the heart, the soul. Besides, we must be capable of containing this milieu inwardly, which assuming our sexuation, on the one hand, and loving the other, on the other hand, can ensure.

In fact, the potential of our touch has been kept in abeyance by a culture which favoured supra sensitive values. Sharing this potential asks us to return to touch as such and learn how to cultivate it as humans. This cannot confine itself to a merely solitary undertaking. A relation to the outside of us is necessary to make operative the inner space which allows touch to exercise its mediation. And as only an appropriate food can awake our taste by its flavour, an appropriate other is needed to make effective and give meaning to our touching without destroying its potential.

How could this other be recognized, be defined? What allows two human beings to touch one another without destroying the potential of their own beings? How can touch contribute towards their evolution? And how could we avoid becoming the other while touching, or being touched by, this other? Could it be by not contenting ourselves with a mere passivity—for example, by making touch a means to assemble and gather together what and whom we are, the one and the other? The experience that touch arouses can give rise not only to a passion but also to an action—uniting power and act in each and between those who touch one another. Touch is a means of concentrating our sensitive potential and of giving form(s) to it, not only at the physical level but also at the spiritual level. Touch can give us back to ourselves while making us capable of relating to the other—the one and the other being both agents and patients in such a relationship.

Touching one another as human beings who are naturally different allows sensitivity to ensure a passage from the body to the spirit. This does not take place through a quantitative progress but thanks to a qualitative evolution, which does not disown the natural forms but transforms, transmutes them in order to render them shareable with a view to a human becoming. Touching one another can be a means of giving meaning to our natural belonging, of making it a path towards the accomplishment of our being through a perpetual giving birth to one another as bodies and souls.

Through its immediate action on flesh, touch permits a relation between different beings, which cannot exist without it, while preserving each natural belonging. Touch brings about a feeling and passes on both a physical and mental information that we interpret with difficulty given the split between body and spirit that our culture imposed on us, a split that our soul would be able to overcome, according to Aristotle. Moreover, the meaning of such an information results from a meeting between two different beings, and our logic does not allow us to interpret this sort of union—of 'synthesis'. Touch can surmount a double division: one between the body and the spirit in the same being and an other between different beings. But a culture of our tactile potential, which can lead us from the most empirical of our bodily belonging to the most subtle transcendental, is still lacking. Hence, we resort to supra sensitive ideals, which deprives us of the possible actualization of our natural energy potential. Indeed, the latter becomes operative only with the awakening of an inner emotion that touch is capable of arousing. It can move us at the source of our being instead of attracting it outside of itself, of inciting it to project itself towards the impossible appropriation of what or whom it is by means of forms extraneous to sensitivity.

Touch calls us for achieving our entelechia starting from the most intimate of our living being and not from abstract forms which would be likely to sublimate our materiality. Touch reaches and awakes, even gives rise to, forms inscribed in nature itself, and that the desire to unite with what or whom moved us prompts us to animate and render more subtle in order that their connection or communion should be possible.

This asks us to have access to another way of thinking. Indeed, about what the other gives me to experience, the question is no longer of linking the present and the permanent (cf. Aristotle, *De l'âme, I,* 3 Critique de la théorie de l'âme motrice d'elle-même; *De Anima, I,* 3 (405 b–407 b)), but of distinguishing and succeeding in uniting what I feel of myself and what I feel of the other—which means in joining the same to the different. Aristotle, and Western philosophy in general, claims to be impossible something which can happen thanks to properties and truth of sensitivity that they did not manage to think, notably because of their manner of conceiving of the truth. Hence the fact that the other is imagined to be only a cause of alteration, even of annihilation, of the same. And yet, the other is necessary for the accomplishment of our being. Why? How? Because the other compels us to actualize it, to incarnate it, in particular by evolving from the need for a food to merely survive to the desire for a more psychical or spiritual food. Not being merely altered by the other, not becoming the other by its/our touching, constrains us to a transformation of ourselves in order that touching one another should become fruitful and not destructive of the one or the other.

The relationship with the other can neither be lived nor be cultivated by resorting to a traditional dialectics only, which presupposes the existence of a single truth, even of essences, that the one and the other ought to share. Rather, it requires an economy of thinking in which the sensitive, which feeds it, is not sacrificed to the supra sensitive. The difference between us produces feelings that are necessary for our evolution and cannot be neglected, but they entail a becoming which transcends the present—that is, a sensitivity being aware of the transcendental, and which compels sensitivity itself to evolve without being put on hold in the supra sensitive.

Instead of sensitivity taking place in only one subject, it becomes embodied between two subjects and even between their becomings. Then that which puts thinking into act is not only an 'object' which is mentally defined but a subject who is bodily and spiritually different. Hence the distinction between the potential of matter and an intervention, notably technique, making this matter effective, cannot really subsist (*cf.* Aristotle, *De l'âme*, III, 4, L'intellection et l'intellect en puissance; *De Anima,* III, 4, Intellect and the Potential of Intellect (429 a-430 a)). Indeed, the other is not merely a potential matter, and this other is not merely a potential at the level of the intellect either. The accomplishment of our being needs a relationship with the other, but this cannot happen without each of us having already actualized, at least in part, the matter and the intellect which are our own.

For lack of such actualization, a relationship between man and woman cannot come true, the latter remaining a potential matter that the former ought to put into act. Thereby a relationship between two subjectivities cannot be fulfilled, each being too dependent on the other for its achievement. There is not in each either a soul capable of producing forms, 'objects' or aims so that it can be responsible for itself and can enter into presence and unite with the other. Undoubtedly, each receives from the other the means of more fully blossoming, but this can happen only if it is already capable of assuming itself. Otherwise, the relationship with a different other can end in annihilation and not in blossoming. The act through which we can produce one another cannot completely be substituted for our producing ourselves. In the two cases, desire intervenes as a driving force. But that for which we long is now less an 'object', be it transcendental, than a path to evolve towards our accomplishment (cf. Aristotle, *De l'âme,* III, 9, La faculté motrice; *De Anima;* III, 9, The Driving Force Property (431 b–433 a)). And this path can be cleared only if each is capable of returning to itself, of dwelling in itself and of remaining founded on/in itself—if each keeps in itself its driving force.

The Driving Force of the Living

Our driving force is more able to unify our being than our intellect can do only by itself, notably because such a force is concerned with the different parts of our soul. Furthermore, as corresponding to this driving force, desire can not only unify us but also unite us with the other. The early Greek language used the middle voice to express such a process. In that case, it is no longer the existence of opposites and their possible overcoming which is the cause of the motion, but that which favours the development of our natural belonging, a development which is too often paralyzed by a logic in which sensations and feelings are subjected to the arbitration of the understanding without truly taking account of their impact on our global being. And yet the evolution of the latter is more dependent on the creative or destructive impact of our sensitive perceptions than on the overcoming of opposites. Thereby paying attention to what we feel, to our states and to the assessment of their contribution to our becoming is needed. This is particularly important when it is a question of a relationship with an other living being. The way in which this being acts on us and we interact with one another cannot be reduced to a mere alternative between what is good and what is bad, which neglects, or even neutralizes, the perception and the effect on our subjectivity of a wide range of qualities.

Desire has too often been imagined, already by Aristotle, as above all physical, and not as a bridge between the body and the psyche, the mind or the spirit, and its opposite cannot be aversion, as this philosopher claims, nor its aim, satisfaction. Desire has more to do with the transcendental, notably with regard to time and space. And it is the main agent of our evolution and transformation, which are not achieved in relation to opposites, the objective of which is rather to maintain the stability of the intellect. Indeed, it is not because of opposites that desire sets us in motion, but because of attractive qualities or properties after which it aspires. These can be multiple but, as our driving force must keep a unity, desire must be preserved as such by favouring the ones which contribute to maintaining its dynamism at the service of the development of our being.

Thus what is desirable cannot be something that we could consume or appropriate but that which keeps our desire alive as the driving force of our becoming—hence the fact that it is concerned with supra sensitive values. However, if these can prevent desire from falling back into the facticity of satisfaction, they paralyze its dynamism as belonging to an incarnate human being. It is rather the relations with another living being which maintain this dynamism on the condition that it escapes its reduction to a need or the reduction of the other to an object.

By keeping the desire wide-awake and in motion, both moved and moving, reason serves sensitivity, and the appetitive and cognitive dimensions of our being—and of our soul—can be linked to one another towards the achievement of our human destiny. In order that no dimension should supplant the other, that they will remain moved and in motion jointly, the difference of the other and its transcendence must be respected—including when the complementarity of the parts of the body or of the soul could cancel the duality of the persons (cf. Aristotle, *De l'âme*, III, 11, La faculté motrice et autres facultés; *De Anima,* III, 11, The Driving Force Property and Other Properties (433 b- 434 a)). As Aristotle calls us in mind, nature wants to grow and it is up to us to contribute to this growing by our desire.

The development of nature asks us, as humans, to distance ourselves from an original immediacy. How can this distance be operative without bringing about a separation from our physical belonging? What mediation can make this process possible? Must it be carried out by us? By the external environment? By an interaction between the two? Which? And does it take place mainly between the subject and an element of the environment, or between two subjects? Why? How? What component of matter or of spirit makes that possible? On what condition(s)?

If a touching from a distance exists, does this not mean that touch can act as a means to transcend itself? Its immediate operation could serve as a mediation towards its own overcoming. This would allow a becoming which is founded on sensitiveness without resorting to supra sensitive idealities. Then transcendence itself shelters touch, differently from a mere exteriority—it transforms it, transmutes it, while keeping it sensitive. A matter, the nature of which we do not know, then arises from our touching one another in a sort of transubstantiation of the flesh of the one and of the other. This implies a communion without consumption—a global and mutual perceiving and knowing which remains sensitive.

According to Heidegger, the human being is the being which is pointing out that which is (cf. *Qu'appelle-t-on penser?* Première partie, p. 28; *What Is Called Thinking?* Part One, Lecture 1, pp. 9–10). Could I suggest that, according to me, the human being is the one who is capable of transcending itself—is a being capable of not getting stuck in the facticity of being(s), but can distance itself from it/them. How can it succeed in that without cutting itself off from its global being, as it happens with the supra sensitive ideals? The desire for a living being different from itself seems to be able to grant that to it. And it is not necessary, for all that, to resort to a Being which cancels the negative of a difference. Acknowledging the difference of the other procures the space which is required to open a transcendental perspective with regard to an empirical and lacking in differentiation experience. The human being would be truly human when it is capable of assuming its difference with respect to another living being, especially capable of experiencing and respecting this difference at the level of the feeling of sexual attraction to a human different from itself. To be a human would mean to be able to transform what is experienced with a view to its sharing with another living being. In that case, the distance which was created by the transcendence of Being, or of supra sensitive values, returns to base itself on/in the respect for the natural life instead of on/in its non-acknowledgement or its oblivion.

And if temporality can help us to respect our natural life thanks to the part that desire and memory play in the relationship with the other, supplying our immediate experience with a perspective, temporality does not represent for all that the most decisive element in the constitution of the human being. Besides, the importance that we attach to temporality is, perhaps, the result of a lack of consideration for the movement itself. It would be, at least partly, a transfer to and an extrapolation in temporality of the complexity of the moving and spacing out between the sensitive bodies. In them and between them, an attempt to articulate and balance the gravitation and attraction forces constantly exists. If the solar attraction seems to prevail over the terrestrial attraction in the blossoming of a vegetal being, the same does not go for a human being. This stands at the crossroads between various forces: solar and terrestrial attractions, bodily and spiritual attractions, but also the attraction that desire for another living being represents, in particular the sexual attraction. And to all these attractions, a sharing of the forces which relate to work, to public life, etc. must still be added. The human being is not a merely physical being—even acknowledging that matter itself is endowed with forms of its own.

It is incumbent on the human being to carry out or to ensure the passage from an energy which is merely physical to an energy which is also psychical or spiritual. This allows it to overcome the traditional dualism between matter and forces, body and spirit, nature and freedom, etc.

Almost all is still to be worked out regarding such possibilities—the development and exercise of which have something to do with touch. Indeed, the latter contributes to the energy awakening and its sending back to a bodily and specific source. Touch both marks and oversteps the limit(s). It brings us back to and within our body but also induces us to have a relationship with another body. It makes us perceive the boundary of a difference and blurs it with the energy arising from a relationship between different living beings, between which it mediates. It provides human beings with a surplus or a complement in relation to that which the natural elements—the water, the air, the sun—bring to a tree for its growing. The human being needs the other(s) to develop. Touch is the main mediation to actualize this relation and to regulate the alternation between interiority and exteriority which is required, especially at the level of the strength or energy capable of animating and transforming the bodily matter.

Touch also allows us to overcome the split between subjectivity and objectivity—which occurs when, in the relationship between two different subjects, the necessity of resorting to an object is surmounted without our giving up objectivity. Something objective takes place in the touching between the subjects but this phenomenon is irreducible to any object. Something exists, is effective, but remains elusive, foreign to a definite form or object. It amounts to a production of life, a life neither anonymous nor being lacking in differentiation—a life which is, without being reduced to the neuter of a 'there is' or a 'That'. We are the cause of this life, the generation of which does not appear, if not through its effects and sensitive perceptions. This life remains a sort of tactile energy, extraneous to the inert nature of matter. Some philosophers would even assert that it is merely form(s). However, it is not the case, unless we admit that all nature is form(s), including imperceptible forms. Perhaps we have here to do with a generation or a creation of our germ cells and their ambiguous status between matter and form(s).

Natural Dynamism and Mechanical Energy

Energy arising from a meeting with another living being is accompanied by a limitation of our own energy. Source of an additional energy, the other living being also restricts an indefinite energy expansion. Limited by the determined forms of each, energy is also limited by the relations between living beings who are different. Taking this further shaping into account could exempt us from resorting to the regulation of energy by and between opposite poles. Then the energy economy has not to deal with a balance between attraction forces and repulsion forces, as it is generally imagined in the time of Aristotle and even formulated by him, but with the harmony between attraction forces and retention forces, which permits a relationship between different living beings while maintaining each in itself. Holding in oneself entails the ability to keep oneself within the limits of one's own forms, which the attraction forces overstep and that we must recover in order to respect both the other and ourselves and pursue the relationship. Such an energy economy preserves a natural dynamism which favours the generation of a new life, whereas energy going backwards and forwards between opposites does not allow such development.

Relational energy must contribute to the evolution of each, to that of the relation itself and that of the environment, thus of the world. This requires energy not only to remain free while being limited in its expansion but also to increase in a way which is compatible with the development of living beings. For these, to become must surmount the inertia, for example of gravity or repetition, but also that of the indeterminate attraction or expansion of the volatile. Becoming requires us to evolve, including as relational beings, while remaining ourselves.

This asks us to acknowledge, assume and combine the various forces which interact in us. For example, if we do not take account of the gravity force, we let fall its load on our body, left to the heaviness of a quasi corpse. Not taking account of the solar attraction acts in the same way. Ignoring the impact of desire on the materiality of our body deprives us of a means of uniting in ourselves and between us material with spiritual forces, and the body with the soul and the spirit. However, all these phenomena are too little acknowledged and assumed in their natural and psychic, objective and subjective, dimensions. Hence, what belongs to one dimension is sometimes attributed to an other not without some contradictions. So the woman, who is traditionally compared with nature or identified as the guardian of the natural life, is supposed to suffer from an inertia that the man ought awaken and animate. And yet, it is rather natural life which is endowed with an energy of its own, which expresses itself through culture without the latter more often than not admitting that. Such misjudging locks man and woman in a closed energetic system—hence the necessary return to homeostasis by energy release in sexual intercourse, according to Freud. From that also results the paralysis of our human development, for which our contribution to the persistence of our species through procreation would compensate.

The fact of aiming at, or contenting oneself with, the formation of a finite and closed whole—at the objective and subjective levels—amounts to a solipsistic conception of the existence which impedes its development. As relational, every living being is an open whole likely to evolve, in a world which is itself evolving, especially by its relationships with other living beings, both autonomous and having part in a sharing of life.

Hegel, and not only him, considers nature to be imperfect and lacking freedom in comparison with reason. But do the perfection and freedom in question not fit in with an ideal of closing up and withdrawing of each and of the whole? What then happens with the surplus of dynamism and being arising from the relation between each other, and between each and the world? And does the Hegelian perspective not involve a contradiction because only what or who which is withdrawn would be free? Is the freedom that the concept grants us not accompanied by a breakdown of the link between the elements which make up the whole, unless this is dependent on reason? Is the latter an emanation of nature and of its way of flowering? Is it not instead a sort of parallel to nature or a reflection of nature which supposedly would aim at improving its functioning?

Has Hegel sufficiently wondered about the fecundity of the bond between the natural beings and the supplement of life which can result from it? Did he wonder enough about that which interrelations between living beings can bring to the development of each and of the whole that all form?—a development that reason can neither cause nor check. And does nature not answer the Hegelian objection regarding its inability to reconcile its diverse products by the conception of a new living being? It can do that and it constantly reopens in this way every constructed totality. Such a whole is exceeded by the strength of growing arising from life, but also by the energy resources that desire, will and thought represent and which contribute to the becoming of the human being. In this an interaction of forces takes place which has been traditionally kept on hold by resorting to, more or less artificial, cultural regulations like supra sensitive ideals, morality or customs, the imperative of reproducing, the reduction of desire to needs etc. As it did not think of itself as nature, the human being has not constructed itself according to its own living dynamism but by subjecting itself to the same energy as a made product—be it a product or a creation of God or of humanity itself. Then forces of inertia developed as a resistance to constructed forces which impeded a natural dynamism. The human being became also integrated into a world extraneous to nature, which prevents it from returning to itself as a living being and from relating to/with other living beings.

The movement coming from the inner self, from the natural dynamism, returns to this self as forces of/from the outside in which energy peculiar to each has been integrated. Each has become foreign to itself, without any perception of its self, of the strength, affects and will of its own. It is also deprived of an energy resulting from the communion between living beings. All that matters to a culture of the state of the human being is almost ignored, and this leads to a paralysis of becoming, a resistance to the environment, decline, illness, even death.

Besides, the sciences presumed to be objective and in the neuter, are determined by subjective parameters, in fact generally masculine, which are unrecognized. For example, porosity, fluidity and communion are almost absent from the argument of the scientists, notably with regard to the properties of matter and force. Their underlying logic is limited to the subject-object relation, with a subjectivity which amounts to a sort of abstract mechanism and an object which inherits, and in a way is a substitute for, matter. Only one subject, which is artificially constructed, is confronted with the physical properties of the world, which he treats as if they were external, even foreign, to him and through which he tries to give to himself consistency again. It is especially the case in the Hegelian work. However, if Hegel criticizes others, particularly Newton, for reducing physics to mechanics, does he not behave in the same way towards subjectivity itself? Is the Hegelian subjectivity other than a mechanism able to deal with negativity—notably as a technique opposing the gravitational force? Does something physical remain in Hegelian subjectivity? Of what does this shortage deprive subjectivity in order that it may develop as that of a living being? And how can such subjectivity enter into relation with other living beings?

Does this way of conceiving of subjectivity not prevent Hegel from subjecting to dialectics a great part of the real, a real that he does not acknowledge as such, in particular in its physical dimension? Hence the fact that he must resort to the negative to define entities, to provide them with limits, without making use of more physical properties—notably thanks to touch. Is Hegelian logic finally not similar to a mechanics, especially because he does not take the physical and natural strength or energy of the subject sufficiently into account, above all the one arising from his/the sexuate belonging? This dynamism—which determines, unifies and unites the subject(s)—is little considered in the dialectical process which is presumed to lead us to the absolute after which we aspire, and it is a sort of logical mechanism which is substituted for it, at least in part.

In reality, Hegel wavers between natural forces and spiritual forces without succeeding in establishing a continuity between them. He even imagines that nature could conform to the laws of the spirit instead of the contrary. Hegel, like most philosophers and not only them, misjudges or forgets the abstract—meta-physical—character of the logos and the fact that it is not completely extraneous to a mathematical code. How does such coding treat or transform the living, including the living beings who we are, into lifeless objects? How to bring physical nature, that is, life again in the discourse is a question which does not sufficiently arise. And yet it is a determining question with regard to the conservation of a natural dynamism, both outside of us and within us. What language allows us to take account of it? What concept is likely to truly contribute to the blossoming of our nature and its sharing? Perhaps, a sexuate language could begin to answer such questions. Is it not the one which could send us back to our identity of living beings and to our difference from other living beings?

Part V

Emergence of Germ Cells at Individual and Collective Levels

14

The Touch of Grace

Meaning of the Word 'Grace'

Before developing the argument relating to the theme I must treat, I often check, in the dictionary, the generally acknowledged meaning of the keywords relating to it. I did that for the word 'grace' and I have been surprised by the number of significations which correspond to this word. They range from the most physical to the most meta-physical, passing through the political and the social. If the word 'grace' seems at first to allude to an intervention of God himself, it also expresses the enchantment caused by physical forms or movements, thus by that which from nature, in particular that of the woman, appeals to us and arouses in us, including at a carnal level: her sweetness has grace, her gestures are graceful as is her youthful abandon. It is not only a question of nice forms, something more plays a part in meaning which moves us differently. So we already went from the favours that God sometimes accords to us to the awakening of desire that the charm of a body, in particular of a feminine body, can arouse, a desire that we could receive as a sort of grace to help us carry on our path and not as a temptation aiming at our shirking the divine grace.

L. Irigaray, *The Mediation of Touch*, https://doi.org/10.1007/978-3-031-37413-5_14

Between these two apparently opposite senses, we find political or social uses of the word. For example, at juridical or political levels, we have: a grace period; the queen graced the event with her presence; as an act of grace, the judge freed the person from their debt. And at a more social level: to be in someone's good grace: to do something with good grace. Without forgetting: to say grace.

I wondered what meaning united all these uses of the word 'grace'—at least in French, in English and some other languages—of which in fact I quoted only a few. I think that it is always a matter of a relationship between two subjects, or at least two living beings—for example, a flower or certain animals can have grace—a relationship which happens without the mediation of an object, a relationship which is positive provided that it includes a part of reciprocity and that it concerns the global being and not only an aspect of it. Besides, this relation one way or another underlies all the other relationships, be they of love, desire, forgiveness, gratitude, demand etc. and it has something to do with touch. This touch is more or less physical or meta-physical, more precisely transcendental, as it presupposes beings which are different, and, through its mediation, two persons or two living beings are linked in a way that is mysteriously radical but unfamiliar to our usual manner of thinking, deciding and acting in a conscious way. There is, something exists, but, perhaps, as a remainder of a state prior to our present human existence, which subsists but from which we moved so far away that it has become impervious to us and occurs only as an extraordinary phenomenon which oversteps our human lives and possibilities. More than ever we would need such a 'grace' to be able to take up our human becoming and pursue it.

Wandering Outside Ourselves

For lack of natural roots, we run the risk of expending our dynamic potential in an unending quest outside of ourselves or an unending dissipation of energy thereby losing our ability to develop as living beings. Grace is, perhaps, that which is capable of returning it to us by bringing us back to our flesh through its touching. It will be up to us to turn the action of grace towards some embodiment or another.

I think that grace, in particular a divine grace, corresponds to a touch of our comprehensive being and not only of our soul, notably understood in a sense that favours intellect to the detriment of feeling, of perceiving by flesh itself—as Thomas Aquinas seems to conceive of it. I can no more agree with him about his claim that grace is neither physical and sensitive nor natural and it serves above all the intelligible, as he explains concerning the essence of grace (cf. the volume devoted to grace in his *Summa Theologica*).

Besides, Thomas Aquinas contradicts his affirmations a little when he stresses the importance and meaning of grace in the New Testament, which results from the incarnation of the divine, that is, from the fact that Jesus is endowed not only with a divine nature but also with a human nature and that grace acts through him in a way that is physical, sensitive and natural. We have only to read or reread the Gospels and note the manner in which Jesus accomplishes miracles to be convinced of that. It is through touch that grace passes from Jesus to the one who needs recovery. Such a touching can occur by words which move but also by a contact between two bodies.

In this connection, I would like to suggest that it is often maintained nowadays that Christianity has prevented Platonic philosophy from reaching us whereas it is as much, and even more, right to claim that we interpret Christianity in a Platonic way. This can probably explain why the most revolutionary contribution of the Christian message is passed over in silence, especially regarding touch and the way according to which grace works. There is no doubt that some elements of the Gospels are acknowledged as challenging our onto-theological tradition, but few of them allude to the revolutionary ferment that the incarnation of God, and hence the importance of touch, represents, a ferment which continues to be repressed one way or another by Christians themselves. And, perhaps, Nietzsche is not completely mistaken when he says that only one Christian has really existed and he died on a cross.

The position of Meister Eckhart concerning grace seems to me more in accordance with the Christian message, at least in part. And it is not by chance that some of his affirmations have been condemned by the ecclesiastical hierarchy, always quite traditionalist. Could the wisdom of Eckhart regarding grace result from the fact that he addressed feminine monks, a thing that Thomas Aquinas had not the opportunity to do? Eckhart adopts a mode of speaking and arguing which concerns being in its comprehensiveness and attempts to touch it as such, that is, as a whole. For Eckhart, what matters is to reach 'union', and this requires him to lead the persons he addresses to discover how to gain their unity. To succeed in that everything can and even must be tried, including freeing oneself of God. Besides, Eckhart asserts that 'If I would not be, God would not be. I am a cause of the existence of God as God' (cf. in the Sermon 'Pourquoi nous devons nous affranchir de Dieu même?'; in the Sermon 'Why must we free ourselves from God himself?'). The purpose is to free oneself from one's own will as well as from that of God, and to return to the time when nothing of that yet existed, prior to birth, when 'the soul does not receive anything either from God or from creatures because what it holds is only itself' (in the Sermon 'Comment l'âme suit sa propre voie et se trouve elle-même'; in the Sermon 'How the soul follows its own way and finds itself'). And when 'the soul begins to experience itself it is able to make its own path and it no longer is in search of God', 'the soul discovers that it was in search of itself without getting what it wanted' (idem).

Nevertheless, afterwards, it is necessary that soul leaves itself in order to return to itself and come to know that God and it are only one. As the Song of Songs states 'If you do not know yourself, ho! you the most beautiful of women, come out of your dwelling'. According to Eckhart 'the soul must leave itself to reach its inner self and the knowledge of itself' (idem). God is hidden in the soul as is the beloved of the Song of Songs. Time as well as multiplicity, which is peculiar to what is created, have concealed God in the soul and 'more the soul liberates itself from multiplicity, more the realm of God reveals itself to it' until it discovers that 'soul itself is God'. The soul and divinity are one and the same thing. The soul is 'the realm which corresponds to God' (idem).

One will think: What an arrogance these words show! But Eckhart teaches us that 'the height of the divinity is nothing else than the deepest of humility' (in the Sermon 14; in the fourteenth Sermon). Thus, without humility, we cannot meet God and unite with him. But once he is 'truly humble, man can have control over God' (idem). In reality, for Eckhart, 'God is a creation which amounts to a will of the creatures but not of God himself' and 'the greatest honour that the soul could do God is to leave him to himself, to free itself from him' (in the Sermon 'Comment l'âme suit sa propre voie et se découvre elle-même'; in the Sermon 'How the soul follows its own way and finds itself') to follow its own way.

I can only agree with such words. And without wanting to be arrogant or to imitate Eckhart—which would run the risk of losing my own path and the possibility of reaching divinity, I could suggest that what I say about the touching one another of my lips, my eyelids, the palms of my hands and even the soles of my feet in order to recover my integrity has something to do with a means to which a soul can resort to find itself again. It could be the case at the very least for a soul which is not yet separate from the body—as is the soul in the treatise *De Anima* by Aristotle.

Cut Off from the Touch of Grace

At first sight, such a way of conceiving of grace could correspond with that of Eckhart. However, it differs from it at least on two points: (1) When Eckhart asserts that what is physical acts only from the outside, whereas reason acts from the inside and that 'the beatitude of God himself is dependent on an operation of reason' (in the Sermon 9; in the ninth Sermon). Rather, I believe that which fits what is most intimate with us is flesh, that it is flesh, and not reason, which favours the mediation of touch and that flesh is thus a better receiver and vehicle of grace than reason. (2) Nor can I agree with Eckhart when he says that man must be in conjunction with God, a conjunction which is a sort of 'almost' or 'as' dependent on an action and evaluation of reason and which allows us to have access to 'the place where the eternal Verb of God dwells in itself' (idem). After he invited us, more precisely he invited women because he addressed feminine monks, to discover our/their own unity, does not henceforth Eckhart maintain that we/they must obtain beatitude through a conjunction with the divine Verb, there where God himself experiences beatitude because 'his knowledge there hangs continuously in itself' (idem)? From such a viewpoint, does not the soul lose both its unity and the dimension of touch that it needs to reach this unity? I think that Eckhart can make this sort of remark because he remains inside of the horizon of a logic of sameness according to which what he calls conjunction is limited to a comparison which does not allow a union to happen without the abolition of the one or the other, generally of the smaller in the greater—thus of the soul in God.

Obviously, we are then in a completely different perspective from the one on which I previously lingered, a perspective according to which the most important thing for the soul was to discover its own path. In reality, Eckhart does not succeed in keeping separate the existence of God from the existence of the soul between which it is a matter of achieving a union through grace. That which Eckhart calls a conjunction means a more or less accomplished approach of the soul to divinity. The human soul has lost its autonomy and its properties, in particular those corresponding to sensation and perception, properties among which touch is the most necessary and the most universal because it participates in all our perceptions—and it is also the best receiver and mediator of grace.

For lack of a carnal mediation, grace takes us away from ourselves. The accounts of the mystics tell us about this removal, in an exemplary way those of Therese of Avila. But is it then really a question of the action of grace or, rather, of the result of a lack of cultivation of touch in the onto-theological tradition which is ours, a lack which results in the forgetting of the sensitive, thus the tactile, dimension of the soul? Hence its subjection to supra sensitive ideals. In the treatise *De Anima* by Aristotle, the soul holds a link with the body, notably with its tactile properties, and even in the work of Plato the soul remains dependent on the thymus, the gland which regulates our moods. But the soul has been removed from itself by traditional metaphysics and it has become a sort of slave or a sort of mechanism being in the service of supra sensitive ideals. The soul has lost its own dynamism, its faculty for experiencing and acting in its own way towards the becoming and the comprehensive accomplishment of the individual. The soul has been paralyzed, removed from itself and, henceforth, it became sterile. Perhaps one could say that it became rigidified or fossilized in a sort of privative virginity which cut it off from its becoming woman, a state that Eckhart himself considers higher than a mere virginity and which asks, according to him, that 'the soul liberates itself from any obligation and rests always close to itself'.

The soul, our soul, is, henceforth, waiting for a touch which awakens it, restores to it its potential of life, of energy, of sensitivity, and its ability to perceive, especially to perceive grace. Could all that happen thanks to a mere passivity yearning for a divine grace? Would gaining a living relation to touch and cultivating it not be a more appropriate path? There is no doubt that the matter is not easy to carry out in our times given the state of our culture which brings to us more death than life. However, without touch 'no animal can survive', Aristotle writes in his *De Anima*. And this touch cannot become effective again through an additional and excessive intensity, as Gilles Deleuze seems to imagine, because that ends in 'destroying touch as a necessity for life', as Aristotle also maintains. The touch that we must regain is the one which brings back life to us, notably by our rediscovery of the sensitiveness of our flesh, which is both the receiver and the mediator of our relation to touch, and thus to grace.

Awakening to the Innocence of Flesh

Returning to nature and to the ability of perceiving through all our senses seems the first initiative to be undertaken. Besides, in certain Eastern traditions, which remain closer to nature, the cultivation of the sensory perceptions is used as a method with spiritualizing of energy in mind (cf. *The Yogasutras* by Patanjali). The argument that I would put forward against such teaching is that it also aims at reducing duality to unity. It is true that the duality in question is that of the subject and the object. But Patanjali does not think about substituting the relation subject-subject for the relation subject-object. And yet, the relation subject-subject requires a cultivation of our perceptions which aims not only at increasing energy but also at transforming our manner of perceiving. In Patanjali's perspective there is no reciprocity between the one who perceives and what is perceived. The touching which takes part in the perception is thus still capturing and appropriating, if not an object at least energy, and it is not a touching which corresponds to a sharing or a passing on of life. Unfortunately it is this kind of touch which is favoured in our tradition, which considers touch as a means of seizing more than of entering in communication or in communion. In that case, our hand, more generally our body, becomes a tool to appropriate or build a world external to us and it no longer belongs to a flesh which receives and passes on energy, sometimes divine energy, between two living beings. In other words, one could say that our flesh is no longer the medium which is needed for the reception and the action of grace. By subjecting touch to a subject-object logic, our culture—could it be because it is predominantly masculine?—deprived touch of its aptitude for transmitting grace to us, and between us, notably because that involves both passivity and activity, an active passivity.

In fact, the grace after which we aspire is, probably, above all that of a reciprocity in touch. Have we not deprived ourselves of the possibility of receiving such a grace by transforming it into a sort of object between a donor and a receiver in a genealogical or hierarchical situation—God and creature; parent and child; master and disciple or slave; rich and poor; man and woman etc.—or by abolishing the duality of subjects through a fusion or other modalities of cancellation of the irreducibility between two different subjects? In order to recover touch as a receptor or receiver and a mediator of grace, we must give up that which favours the subject-object relation, but also the one, the same, the identical as our onto-theology has defined them and which take part in such an economy. We must discover what is entailed by a logic of difference, which evades any reducing to quantity as well as the assessments or orders decreed by understanding or of which it claims to be the guarantor. We must practice a sort of negative onto-theology until we reach the not-yet-happened of the dawn—to which Nietzsche, but also Heidegger, allude—one could say nothing if not the life of what or whom is just born, as Eckhart in his own way maintains. We must succeed in returning to the innocence of an early infancy that, sometimes, we reach very late when we achieved freeing ourselves from all the truths, the duties, the imperatives that our parents or masters have taught us and even imposed on us when we were not yet able to provide for our needs and were dependent on them for survival. We must win an innocence which does not amount to privation of anything but to the recovery of a potential of life and transcendence with which the newborn is endowed, but that is neither acknowledged nor cultivated as such because of the subjection of the newborn to its needs.

We must reach an awakening of our flesh which makes it virginal at the level of sensory perceptions, of sensitivity in general but also at the level of thinking. And this presupposes an artlessness to which we consent, humility and also desire for that which has not yet happened rather than desire for repetition, increase and even improvement of that which already exists. There is no question of repressing flesh or subjecting it to the privilege and the authority of reason but instead of restoring to our flesh its function of intermediary between the body and the soul, between materiality and spirituality, exteriority and interiority, in ourselves and between us. This requires resorting to a negative ontology that the respect for the difference of the other can help us to carry out. Obviously, it is then a question neither of a constructed difference as it exists, for example, in a given culture, nor of a quantitative difference but of a natural and qualitative difference as is, or ought to be, the difference between sexuate identities.

The Advent of the Beyond of Which Desire is the Messenger

The first path to recover the freshness and receptiveness of our flesh, especially with regard to touch, is thus in some ways a solitary one. The second path, which presupposes the first but cannot be substituted for it, is an intersubjective one between living beings which are naturally different and endeavour to have a relationship with mutual respect. We are then constrained to put in question again what we considered to be the truth of our perceptions, be they sensitive or intellectual, a perceiving by our senses, by our flesh, or even by our reason. We must admit that our way of perceiving is particular and cannot be imposed on the other without running the risk of destroying the possibility that our souls touch one another. For lack of first assuming a nothing in common between us, due to our natural difference, we cannot have access to a comprehensive communion between our living beings. Such communing is an event or an advent of the beyond of which our desire is the messenger. It is desire which compels us to leave our self to go in search, beyond our own world, of the companion of our soul, the one who is capable of bringing our soul back to itself, in itself, thanks to touch. The fact of being touched, that desire itself already means, yearns for also being touched by the caresses and the words of the other.

As I tried to underline in the beginning of this chapter, grace is a phenomenon which occurs between two subjects, or at least two living beings, and which unites them in a positive way provided that there exists between them a reciprocity which allows grace to pass from the one to the other. If that really corresponds to grace, the conjunction between our desires, as longings for the beyond that we represent to one another, is the privileged place of the advent of grace. It is there that grace can happen, become incarnate, diffuse in the one and in the other by a touching one another of our fleshes. Such an event presupposes that touch occurs as a sharing of transcendence and gives rise to an in-stasis rather than to an ec-stasis which amounts to a rapture outside of our self. The grace which springs from an encounter, in particular from an amorous encounter, calls for our being touched, our being moved and led to make our way towards a beyond of what already exists, and of whom we already are, although it has its source in us and between us. The amorous meeting is a source and a way of grace if it is born of our natural belonging in search of transcending itself, while remaining carnal, through a sharing of desire with the other.

In order that grace should then happen, we must recover the tactile innocence of our flesh, being careful neither to reduce the other to an object nor to make the other the only origin and end of our desire. We must dwell in ourselves and live the desire which compels us to transcend ourselves towards the other as a path of grace with the accomplishment of our becoming in mind as well as the becoming of the other with whom we share desire and that of the world. The point is not to give up our flesh and the world, to relinquish the sensitive mediation of touch, which can be a path of life and grace for us, but to gradually transform them into an approach and a communion more subtle and reciprocal, and thus more fulfilled. It is a matter of incarnating as well as we can freedom between ourselves, leaving to God his own freedom.

Calling into question metaphysics from touch has not been considered sufficiently by masculine philosophers, and also by most feminine philosophers, or they did not really succeed in broaching the matter. They probably imagined that such a subject does not deserve careful thought from them, unless they did not find how to restitute to touch its worth, notably at the transcendental level, so that it should become the means to leave our tradition without for all that abolishing it but in order to care about a more achieved blossoming of the human being. There is no doubt that the way in which Sartre, Merleau-Ponty and even Levinas allude to sexual intercourse shows that they ignore the transcendental potential of touch and reduce it to a means of seizing the real and appropriating it, this real being living nature, the other and even themselves. Even the words and way of acting of Merleau-Ponty regarding the touch between his two hands seem to be a means of separating him as well as his world from a contact with any sort of alterity, including that with his left hand which his right hand seizes more than touching it. In reality, meeting with the other, above all with the other as woman, remains subjected by these philosophers to a form of master-slave relationship which has little to do with the sharing of a human destiny, which ought to happen in the amorous union. One can observe that, even in the discourse of Levinas, the caress does not aim at a sharing with the feminine partner but, rather, at an attempt at making her fall into infancy again, or into animality or perversity, whereas Levinas, as a man, returns to his metaphysical or religious transcendence once he has achieved his carnal duty (cf. on this connection *Totalité et infini*, Chapitre sur l'érotisme; *Totality and Infinity*, Chapter on eroticism).

Such a way of conceiving of an amorous touch is obviously unacceptable and demonstrates the failure of our tradition concerning a thought and an ethic of our becoming incarnate and the way in which living beings enter into relationship with one another. But is it not starting from its lacks and its aporias that a tradition and its horizon can be exceeded? Touch is, perhaps, that which allows us to radically criticize metaphysics without for all that falling into a worse nihilism than the one that our past tradition implied. It is touch that, perhaps, can still save us because it allows us to acquire an additional individuation and to discover a sensitive transcendental without being reduced to a mere immanence after the fall of our idols and giving up our being subjected to supra sensitive ideals.

Touch enables us to achieve our individuation but also to have access to a sharing between two different individuations without reducing one to the other. This is possible because touch provides us with the perception of a whole which is still undetermined—either through our lips, our eyelids, the palms of our hands or the soles of our feet touching each other or through a touching between us. Such a touch can send us back to the transcendence of our coming into the world, even before we come to light, be it a matter of the coming into the world of each of us or of the rebirth of both thanks to a transcendental relation between our fleshes from which we become incarnate anew, notably through our breathing and our sexuate belonging.

Because of the specificity of our sexuation, touching one another requires us to assume a negative—as sexuate, each of us represents only a part of humankind, and we can neither reach our individuation nor enter into relationship with one another without taking on our partiality, that is, the fact that we do not correspond to the totality of the human being—and allows us in this way to escape nothingness and a certain negativity. Indeed, I can forget, cover, conceal in myself what it means to experience touch, but I cannot subject this experience to a Hegelian dialectics because the other takes part in that touch. I must undertake and undergo another dialectical process in which the becoming of each of the subjects and its fulfillment are bound with those of the other and also with the evolution of the relation between the two. In this process, touching ensures the mediation between to be and being. Touch is irreducible to any being, as is the difference between us as sexuate, but it is also irreducible to a supra sensitive absolute to which each, and even both, ought to submit. Touch is exactly the place where grace can act—between to be and to exist.

If we remain in the horizon of a world which favours sameness, the nothing corresponding to the particularity of each soul or the nothing in common between souls is difficult to be reached, especially because it is a question of a nothing which challenges the whole that God ensures. Indeed, it is precisely God who underlies and supports all the onto-theological structure of our tradition. But if we adopt a logic founded in/on difference, the nothing exists from the origin and it even represents the beginning of our making the way towards the other. I make my way towards the one that I will never be and I cannot appropriate, and such an other forces me to change, to free myself from my paralyses, from drowsiness, from habits, repetitions, stereotypes which thwart becoming, becoming being that which characterizes living beings. There is touch which can act as mediation in such evolution—from the most physical to the most transcendental, from the most distant to the closest. It can be a touching, and touching one another, by the hand, by another gesture, by words, but also by a manner of being, even a touching of/by the soul. We have only to be moved, to be touched so that we should get going.

By Way of Conclusion

To maintain the connection between touch and motion—a connection of which an Indian tradition reminds us when it considers Vayu to be the god of both touch and wind—the difference between those who touch one another must be preserved as well as the desire for touching as such and not as the means of seizing and making one's own a material or spiritual object or another subject. Desiring to enter into relationship with another living being thanks to touch must live on, a desire for the event or advent which happens by touching one another. This remains inaccessible to manifestation but is behind any manifestation—touch is the threshold between what can manifest itself and what eludes manifestation. It acts as a reminder of the existence of a beyond of my flesh, of my soul, of my world. It is a call to pay attention to opening myself to, and sometimes to sharing, this beyond. Touch invites me to go outside myself, to leave a self which already exists and within which I am partly trapped, in order to search for myself in the beyond through whom or what appeals to me outside—which could correspond with an interpretation of the Song of the Songs.

From the call for coming out of the place where I dwelled, I receive a new unity which allows me to relinquish my past confinements to carry on my path towards my blossoming. Nevertheless, I am not able to completely define what attracts me, what compels me to get going—which would represent the occasion to close up or to withdraw into myself again. The cause of what moved me and incited me to go outside myself is perhaps a longing for immersing myself with he other in touching one another and the grace that this can bring to me, to us. However, such a touching remains irrelevant to an object, be it material or spiritual, which could be appropriated, even if it is at the source of our life. It is a touch which escapes any sort of capture, by our senses or by our mind. It is a touch for which we yearn but in which we cannot stay. It conveys the event and advent of a grace which reawakens us and gives to us the impulsion for continuing on our way towards our fulfilment.

15

From the Individual to the Couple and to the Community

Communication Between Sensitive Identities

Thought and politics are nowadays more critical and reactive than affirmative. A positive foundation is lacking for both the development of thinking and the conduct of politics. It is not by merely encouraging citizens to be in the opposition that they are allowed to be responsible, including for themselves. And neither is it by reducing them to a social and partial identity as workers or heads of the family, or by considering them according to external properties: fortune, possessions of goods, even of cultural goods. What above all matters, particularly these days, is to invite, even to constrain, them to be themselves through cultivating self-affection and hetero-affection, as well as to care about an environment which supplies them with what they need to develop in their whole while relating to one another. This requires them to be concerned with their environment as well as with a lasting growth not only regarding various elements of the world but also human beings themselves and the desire which can unite them with each other.

To be has been defined, notably by Heidegger, in opposition to becoming, appearing, thinking, or having. But what does to be mean as such? How to define it positively and not only as opposed to something other?

L. Irigaray, *The Mediation of Touch*, https://doi.org/10.1007/978-3-031-37413-5_15

Perhaps it is possible through a return to our natural belonging and its development in accordance with its specificity, thus by taking into account its difference in comparison with other living beings. This difference entails our assuming a negative that any opposition could reduce and which corresponds with the preservation of a being of our own. It is not by being the opposite of the other that I can discover and incarnate my own 'to be', including with its limits, but by attempting to be faithful to what or whom I am.

This asks me to return to my own nature which, as sexuate, is also for the other. This for-the-other needs to be cultivated and be subjected to a dialectical process in relation to a for-myself, without being reduced to mere inter-physical linkage, to empathy, to fusion or to domination and subjection. In these behaviours, the mediation of touch is exploited instead of being respected, really effective and cultivated. The experience of touch then gets lost. Touch can act as a mediation between different beings and it needs this difference in order to preserve itself, in particular from the ascendency of sameness and sight.

Self-affection can keep as invisible the power of touch: the invisible of the flesh, the invisible of life and of sensitivity. Self-affection also restores the perception of the self, thus the possibility of a relationship between different fleshes, different lives. To protect itself from a lack of differentiation and from neutralization, self-affection needs a different structure from that of a simple body image or perception. Sexuation can provide such a structure and allow self-affection to be a touch already endowed with qualities and to be a for-oneself longing for being a for-the-other so as to experience and develop oneself as singularity, but thanks to relations to/with the other.

However, such an 'inter-being(s)', Merleau-Ponty would say, cannot happen at first. It entails our assuming a negative applied to our natural origin and a mediation which remains physical. Our sexuate belonging can ensure such a function. Sensitivity must be differentiated to be experienced in a lasting way. All the degrees and hierarchies that we institute regarding our feelings perhaps represent a means of leaping over a relation to sensitivity without cultivating it as such. We transform what we experience into connotations instead of wondering about what it is and what it means for/in our existence and our being or our becoming human.

For such a questioning, we must shield sensitivity from a lack of differentiation and a mere neutralization—'there is sensitivity' or 'that is sensitive'—and be capable of perceiving it as such by distinguishing ourselves from the whole of the world. Neither do I correspond to this whole nor to an undifferentiated part of this whole—I am a woman, that is, a specific human being. And by applying the negative to my natural belonging, I do not become this 'being intimately woven by negativity' (cf. Merleau-Ponty, *La Nature*, p. 275; *Nature*, p. 212) because I have assumed my difference from the other living beings. Thus I would not speak, as does Merleau-Ponty, of 'nature to which we belong' or of 'nature in us' but of nature that I am, and the partiality of which I must acknowledge and cultivate in the relation to myself, to the world and to the other.

This nature, which I am and the other is, remains hidden from my view and I can experience it only by touch—as a touching of life itself. They are not idealities which are invisible, nor philosophy as consisting of idealities, as Merleau-Ponty would like. These seem to escape our sight only because our gaze is not acknowledged as the cause of idealities in a sort of keeping in abeyance touch and life.

This makes our self-awareness extraneous to us because it is not founded on/in a singular self-affection. And such strangeness of our self-awareness cuts us off from our potential to be, to become, to think and to love. Hence, our presumed potential is imposed on us by laws, rules, norms and customs external to us and which prevent us from developing in faithfulness to a being of our own. Rather the latter is revealed to us through a process of self-affection and what it opens up in us as a longing for entering into relation with an other, particularly an other who differs from us by nature, through a desire for hetero-affection. There is not, as Merleau-Ponty maintains 'only one world' or 'only one nature' but a gathering of living beings which coexist and long for entering into communication, even into communion, with each other (see notably op.cit., pp. 198–204; op. cit., 148–153).

Such a communication or communion can be achieved in various ways by touch, the heart being, according to Aristotle, the organ which is capable of centralizing and organizing them (cf. his treatise *De Anima*). Our touch can perceive not only the shapes but also the qualities of the other living beings which we touch or by which we are touched and so assess what compatibilities and reciprocity are possible between us. For example, touch can assess if we have only to respect them as different or we can enter into an affective communication or communion with them so that each of us and our relationship itself could develop.

Our flesh is the milieu through which touch can exercise its mediation. We can perceive something of the nature of touch by its way of being at work in self-affection. The flesh is then a diaphanous milieu corresponding with touch—which differs from the one regarding sight, of which Aristotle speaks in *De Anima*—that we must preserve so that we should be moved, livened up to our becoming, the one of the other and that of our union with one another. We must perceive and cultivate flesh in ourselves. We must also attempt to share it outside of ourselves—which needs first sharing it with another living being which is different from us. We must care about preserving the mediation of touch, that is, that which makes it possible for us to unite with each other, something which varies according to whether it is a matter of two persons who share fleshly relations or individuals who partake in a community of citizens. Self affection can act as that which provides us with an internal space, with a place in which we can dwell, but also with a kind of protective horizon-membrane which allows us to enter into relationship with others without losing the perception of ourselves.

Individuation and Individualization

Touch seems to be limited to a mere immediacy—and it has generally been considered in that way, including by philosophers. In reality it is not the case, but these philosophers have not taken a great interest in the potential of touch which allows it to exercise its mediating properties. Moreover, they little wondered about the nature of the flesh itself and the role that self-affection, hetero-affection and the heart play in a cultivation and a sharing of flesh—that is, in a communion with oneself and with the other(s) in order to create a world of living.

Such a world cannot exist without an appropriate individuation of each, man or woman, which permits a communication or communion to happen between all of them. According to the philosopher Gilbert

Simondon (cf. *L'individuation psychique et collective*), our individuation must be achieved at two different levels: a basic individuation, one could say an ontological one, in which sexuality—I prefer to speak of 'sexuate identity'—plays a part and another level, which is more dependent on the environment and on more or less contingent events of our existence, that Simondon designates as individualization, which pursues the process of individuation but in a way that could be viewed as more ontic. This manner of conceiving of individuation clearly distinguishes the individuals from their environment, an aspect of our being to which most philosophers do not lend a sufficient importance, viewing the world, besides also nature, as a whole, either in front of us or of which we are a too little differentiated part. Now individuation is that which separates us from the world, with which it allows us to enter into relation in a specific way. Moreover, human individuation is a universal process, even if that universal is at least dual, and it is not basically dependent on some or other environment but on a natural origin. And if such individuation separates and differentiates each of us from a natural or cultural whole, it also creates links between distinct, in particular sexuately different, individuals.

Achieving an interpersonal relationship thus asks us to distinguish individuation and individualization in/for each subject and to establish a connection between the two levels of our present identity. Our personal evolution, as well as that of a human community, requires individuation and individualization to be harmonized with each other.

Unfortunately, individualization more often than not supplants individuation; that is, the more empirical, occasional and aleatoric aspect of our identity prevails over its more ontological, fundamental, lasting aspect, an aspect necessary to the development of individual and collective life. In order to solve problems regarding secondary differences, for example between cultures, we do not hesitate to forge a standardized and neuter individual, extraneous to any living existence. Instead, we ought to favour the aspects of individuation which correspond with the most basic, irreducible and universal characteristics and differences of life. It is thanks to a communication at the level of our 'deep' being, and not through a sharing of the most familiar and superficial level of our everyday life, that we can preserve both the individuals in their singularity and the human community. Sexuate belonging is the most universal, irreducible and creative element relevant to the participation of the individual in a community. It also contributes to the individuation of each notably through relationships with the other(s) as different. Cultivating our sexuate identity contributes to our development as individuals as well as to that of those with whom we are united, and it also takes part in the elaboration of the milieu in which it is possible to coexist, each and together, as living beings.

Our environment is not only a datum to which we must adapt ourselves, it is also a world that we must create in order to live, communicate or commune with the other(s) and generate a favourable future for each one and for all within it. Such an environment cannot get itself organized simply through rational considerations, abstract pieces of information or moral requirements. It must include emotional elements which ensure the cohesion of the community thanks to motivations which are shared by/between the individuals who form it. Passing from the individual to the collective levels without caring about an ethics regarding the physical and affective relationship between two naturally different individuals does not enable us to constitute the emotional elements capable of ensuring the cohesion of a group. It is in the relation between two naturally different individuals—wrongly confined by patriarchy within the private dwelling and the family unit—that the transition between the role of our sexuate belonging in individuation, a role that it must retain in sociocultural individualization, must be carried out. And man cannot do that all by himself, as Hegel still would like, because it is in the relation between man and woman that such a transition can be achieved without abolishing individuation for the benefit of individualization. Indeed, sexuate identity represents a decisive part of our individuation and it cannot vanish into a collective individualization. Unfortunately, such a process is too often at work in our current societies and it leads to the destruction of the individual and of the community.

Beyond the natural environment, the community must be a milieu which takes the sensitive dimension of the individual(s) into account, as Simondon asserts. It must respect the values which correspond to it and permits their not only passive but also active development at a collective level. The emotions have a share notably in our pre-individual potential which needs to be preserved and actualized at the level of the community.

The society can neither exploit nor repress this potential; instead it must offer the means of living it individually and collectively. According to Simondon, this could correspond to spiritual values which are shareable and to proposals of commitments involving community stakes aiming at the development and blossoming of the individual, or at harmonizing individualization with individuation.

An emotion needs the possibility of becoming enacted. For lack of that, the emotion can turn into aggressiveness, resentment and critical mindedness, which are beneficial neither to the individual nor to the community. And, for example, the revolutionary intentions which express themselves in our times are generally more reactive than affirmative and, thus, do not gather the citizens towards transformations which are favourable to their individuation. The political leaders mobilize affects against what already exists more than towards what ought to exist. For want of emotions likely to combine external action(s) with internal experience(s), social cohesion goes no further than an alternation between adhesion and opposition, something which does not contribute to individual becoming and a positive sociocultural evolution.

All that is not good for the development of the individual, notably through a passage to the trans-individual. Certainly, religions attempt to create some trans-individual but it is often by interrupting a process of personal individuation, particularly the one relative to our sexuate belonging. And yet, the latter is in reality trans-individual. Indeed, if sexuation represents a for-oneself, it is also a for-the-other and for the community. Our sexuate belonging does not confine itself to sexuality, as it is too often imagined, but it determines a basic modality of our way of being, of our individuation, which needs to express itself in community and not only within the family and the family home as a sort of natural datum, which more often than not remains without cultivation, as patriarchy decided on it. Our sexuation must contribute to the formation of the community as an emotional dimension of the individual but also, and first, as faithfulness to the real and its truth.

Our sexuate belonging must be able to, and even must, manifest itself as a modality of individuation with a for-oneself and a for-the-other which differ according to whether we are man or woman. It corresponds to a structure with which we are naturally endowed and which must become incarnate at every level of our individual and collective life. This structure ensures for the individuals that we are a differentiated unity which is necessary for the personal development and for the exercise of our relational life. Such a structure exists from birth, but it will become effective and will determine the different stages of the becoming of being—Simondon would say—in/for which sexuation plays a crucial role. It is not only a question of sexuality strictly speaking, but of sexuate identity and sexuate subjectivity, which entails a specific way of relating to ourselves, to the world and to the other(s).

Passage Through the Relationship Between Differently Sexuate Individuations

Simondon, as most philosophers, takes an inadequate account of the stage of the sexuated intersubjective relationship. Hence, the passage from individuation to individualization means passing, at the collective level, from an individual who is sexuate by nature to a neuter or neutered individual, which divides human being into a natural belonging which lacks cultivation and a cultural belonging constructed regardless of the natural belonging. Sexuation, which is a determining factor in individuation, seems to be absent from individualization, depriving it of the corporeal and sensitive dimension which is essential for the individual development and the formation of a living community.

Sexuation, which represents a crucial aspect of our individuation, is not considered enough in the passage from the individual to the community. Instead of being disregarded in that way, it ought to be cultivated, and even subjected to a dialectical process so that individuation and individualization should be articulated with one another in a personal development, that of the couple, but also in the constitution and the cohesion of a community. Indeed, the body and the mind, materiality and spirituality, sensitivity and relationality must not conflict with one another but determine one another, making the body spiritual and the spirit fleshly in order that a positive evolution of our individuation could happen. Then desire is the main driving force behind human becoming and not a more or less artificial resolution of oppositions, conflicts or contradictions which often ends in a status quo. When these arise, they must be considered the means of discovering the possibility of a relationship more respectful of difference(s), of a communication or communion in difference rather than the necessity of surmounting obstacles in a merely individual evolution.

Merely reasoning in terms of the individual and milieu, the individual and group or community, our tradition often failed to take into account a stage which is decisive for individuation and individualization as well as for their connection, the one in which individual and milieu or individuals between them interact with one another in the present. This interaction continuously links nature and culture together and allows culture to remain also physical without any fixed substantiality because it is in constant transformation. The continuation of such transformation, its maintenance as an ongoing process, necessitates a dialectics which, in a way, proceeds conversely in comparison with the Hegelian one. Indeed, it retrocedes towards our natural origin and energy in order to preserve their relational character without its becoming set in any essence. The relation between nature and culture is thus constantly evolving, which prevents the substantification of the one or the other of its polarities. The relationship between two naturally different human beings who attempt to communicate, to commune and unite with one another, while remaining faithful to their own natural belonging, is a fundamental stage where such an evolution can and must happen. We cannot leap over this moment of the process of individuation. It is the one which can ensure a passage from the individual to the milieu, from the singular to the collective, even the universal, without freezing one of the natural or the cultural polarities in a substance or an essence, a structure or an energy laying down the law on the other. To keep each and all of us truly alive, these transitions and evolutions have to retain their fluidity and metastability.

This also makes it possible for information to be received without harming individuation, which is unfortunately too often the case with our current pieces of information, particularly those passed on by the media. Most of them not only do not contribute towards our individuation and, thus, have no meaning for us, but, moreover, they are toxic because they constrain us to be passive receivers of pieces of information without any possibility of acting in accordance with them. Without yet alluding to the fact that they are generally negative and have an influence on our sensitivity so as to dull it by their intensity.

As for desire, it is a sort of information which contributes to individuation. In order that such information should not turn into a fixed substance or an essence, desire must be continuously shared between two naturally different human beings with an individualizing relationship in mind for both but also for humanity itself. Such a subset of society or community cannot be confined to the private life, it must shape and in a way irrigate all of the sociocultural order. And a dialectical process must constantly work between self-affection, hetero-affection and that which ensures the communication between the citizens. Their gathering cannot be considered to be homogeneous and organized or governed by laws extraneous to their affects. They must participate in the formation of the society through a cultivation and a sharing of these affects.

Such culture calls neither for a subjection to supra sensitive ideals or their ideological substitutes nor to divine figures decreeing the values to which everyone ought to submit, but for being in charge of a continuous process of individuation by each one and for each one. This requires a constant invention of new norms, even of new values, which are not defined once and for all and presumed to be universal but which result from the actualization of their being by everyone and their relationship with the other, with others. It needs a never-ending passage through and a dialectical relation between interiority and exteriority, in particular regarding the other, which contribute towards the incarnation of their being by each one and for each one. All that which is a priori laid down on us thwarts such a process and imposes a becoming which is cut off from life.

It is on/in the relationship between living beings that our being must be found and become incarnate through the relation to oneself, to the world and to the other(s). The process of individuation, for which we are responsible, cannot be the work of only one. It requires a relational practice, beginning with the cultivation of the relationship between two living beings differently sexuate, a place where the relation between body and spirit can be elaborated, so avoiding the split between these two parts of us. It is also in this relationship that a relational ethics must become to be worked out in order to pass from the pre-individual to the collective levels without losing something of our individuation. Nature is not only outside of us, we are nature and its cultivation is that which allows us to carry out a transition from the pre-individual to the individual and the trans-individual. Our sexuate belonging plays a great part in such an evolution—it determines our pre-individual origin, it permits our individuation to be shaped, it contributes to our relationship with the other(s) and with the world. It is at once nature, structure and energy which participate in our individuation through the acknowledgment of our origin and a trans-individual relationship which does not abolish the individuation of each but, instead, preserves and favours its becoming true and its evolution.

For lack of taking account of the individuation between two human beings who are differently sexuate, we cannot achieve a passage—a 'trans-duction'—between the pre-individual and the trans-individual. In this connection, Simondon speaks of expansion and limitlessness as criteria of the morality of an action, which runs the risk of making impossible the linkage between our body and our consciousness that only an ethical relation between two naturally different beings can begin to shape. This relation necessitates a reciprocity without hierarchy, which fades in community belonging. Nevertheless, such a reciprocity does not presuppose the return of the same but the sending back of each to its own being and its becoming thanks to the relationship with a different being in mutual respect. The being to which is then sent back is enriched by the flesh generated in and by the relationship.

Neither things nor a relation to the community can give or give again to us a flesh enriched by a sharing with the other, whereas an amorous sharing can generate such a flesh. It opens and closes again the structure that my body is as sexuate and brings it back to it fertilized by the communion with another flesh. Instead of indefinitely expanding ourselves into an outside of ourselves, the amorous relation brings us, or ought to bring us back to an inside of us towards a rediscovery or a regeneration of our being as fleshly.

It is between two human beings differently sexuate that such an ontological intimacy or communion can happen at the most fundamental level. The sociocultural milieu must preserve this possibility. It must also propose as values and actions to the members of the community, those which do not sacrifice the ontological to the ontical—individuation to individualization—but invite them to carry out the task of becoming human as individuals, couples and community.

What Does the Necessity of an Onto-Theology Mean?

Because of the lack of a sufficient consideration for sensitivity, our traditional ontology is necessarily an onto-theology. Theology will take charge of the affects and what concerns the body more often than not to try to surmount them, but sometimes to attempt to elaborate a spiritual economy which makes their cultivation possible—this ought to be especially the issue at stake in a theology of incarnation. But be that as it may, it is surprising that it is within a theological horizon, and even in connection with God, that the themes concerning our will, appetite, irascibility, love and, more generally, affect are above all approached. It is also in some religious discourse, in particular Christian discourses, that the question of touch is most broached.

What is then said concerning affects includes relevant and subtle analyses, but generally they incite us to dominate, even to cancel the affects at the sensitive level, particularly for lack of the possibility of their becoming incarnate. Indeed, any affect needs to become effective and brought in play, notably in the relation to and with the other(s). And yet, apart from the importance of love in certain theologies, the affective relation to/with the other is little taken into account in theology except as a moral duty quite disembodied, with which love itself is usually confused. Thus theology cares about that which our traditional ontology neglects but often to be its accomplice by keeping sensitivity on hold in supra sensitive ideals. Self-affection is even extrapolated in God, who is said the one 'who love himself' (cf. Eckhart, *Traités et Sermons*, in 'Toutes les créatures se rassemblent dans ma maison afin que je les prépare toutes à retouner à Dieu', p. 245; in All the creatures gather together in order that I could prepare them for returning to God). Theology tries to compensate for a sort of sensitive death imposed on us by ontology by providing us with an absolute of life. But life, then, has often lost the link with our natural life, our life here and now, and the absolute is situated in a beyond of our terrestrial existence, aiming at another life that only our soul, which is presupposed to feel itself, but is now thought as purely spiritual, would be capable of imagining and reaching.

It was possible to clear another path by considering the soul as a reserve of breath. This could be conceived as a medium with a fluid consistency that we could preserve, animate, cultivate and share. I could take charge of the soul which potentially becomes mine by my first breathing. I could care about it by cultivating my breathing and by developing its properties—for example its possible mobility and also its ability to be transformed by the fire and the light of the sun, as well as by those but of desire, the mediator of which is touch.

Air is a diaphanous medium which can be endowed with movements and with more or less subtle qualities according to their natural, material and bodily nature. Thus the soul can be more carnal or spiritual depending on whether our breath is more dense and warm or more ethereal and fresh. This can result from a personal will, but above all from a relational experience. The soul can evolve in accordance with the more sensitive or mental, more amorous or more social character of my relationship with the other(s). The soul is also more wide-awake and moving with desire or more appeased and motionless in love. These are only a few indications which bear witness to the fact that we can act on our soul through cultivating our breathing and our relational life, with the touch that it entails.

To believe that the existence of my soul is only dependent on its relation to God means that I have failed in taking charge of it and in cultivating it both individually and in the relations to/with the other(s). Consequently what ought to correspond to the soul becomes, on the one hand, 'the depth of a bodily pre-constitution' according to Merleau-Ponty, and, on the other hand, it is extrapolated or enraptured in what is called God. Eckhart would then be right in affirming that our soul must free itself from God in order to get neither paralyzed in an inanimate substance nor taken on hold in a supra sensitive ecstasy. Indeed, in that case our soul no longer perceives itself and it is in search of itself outside of itself, unless it is buried in an unconscious physical materiality. Hence its potential is both hidden in the opacity of a primitive experience or transferred to a supra sensitive divinity.

The same goes for the soul as for love and touch, which cannot confine themselves to a solitary sensation. And it is not by chance that Aristotle speaks of touch in connection with the soul. This is both memory and longing which have to do with a touching-being touched which escapes our mastery while lying in the heart of our being and of its truth. Desire or grace can arouse such a touch, summoning our soul to wake up and to revive our flesh by breathing and the way of being affected of which it is capable, which corresponds to its nature. Cultivating such a touch can contribute to uniting in us, and between us, the most physical with the most spiritual of our fleshly being(s), to making the body more subtly alive and the spirit more sensitive. This can, and even must, happen first in the relationship between two different bodies, two different fleshes and, then, be transformed in order to unite with each other the different members of a community.

Indeed, in the relationship between two differently sexuate humans, and only when the two subjects long for it as a path to transcend themselves towards their accomplishment, touching each other can transform the materiality of the bodies, so that they could be shared. This relation is able to unite us with ourselves thanks to the respect for the difference of the other and to unite us with one another by a desire which is both material and spiritual—a physical desire which becomes spiritual in/by taking the difference of nature between us into account. Viewed in the radicalism of what is at stake such a relationship asks for a negative ontology; it must carry out an *epoche* regarding the being of each—the being that each has already become—and the absolute for which each is longing in order to have access to a way of being and an absolute which were not yet perceived and barely sensed.

The structure that sexuate belonging represents contributes to a transformation of the perception and of the content of each being, and of the absolute for which each longs, into a kind of generation of the subjective and the objective, which happens thanks to the dispossession of only one self in order to reach the carnal sharing of which desire is in search. Then the soul—as Eckhart comments echoing the Song of Songs—as the place of gathering of the self capable of moving, goes outside of itself in search of itself through the other, an other capable of taking charge of his/her partiality so that they could send back this soul to its own search for transcendence and the absolute.

Such a quest is a way of becoming if being is not split in itself, if a continuity exists in its evolution. This possibility depends on the nature of the soul, of its consistency, on its remaining faithful to a natural belonging, which it can keep and transform if the breath of which it consists has become fleshly. The cultivation of breathing, which our being alive needs, must be accompanied by a fleshly presence that touching oneself and touching one another can ensure. It is through a tactile experience that the soul can become divine—like God who delights in himself staying in himself. However, the itself of the soul, like the 'himself' of God, takes place beyond any identification with a precise and definitive affect or knowledge. They amount to the sensitive perception of a potential which can evolve, but which corresponds to the totality or, rather, the unity of being. This potential is at once particular but without particularity in its perception; it is a sort of sensitive substance lacking qualities save that of sensitivity itself. As such it can suit to being in relation to/with an other naturally different, but also to an emotional behaviour contributing to the formation of a community.

16

Importance of Touch for a Democratic Culture

Citizens Lacking Identity

To situate my words in the context of Maurice Merleau Ponty's inheritance, I will introduce them with two quotations. The first is of Machiavelli and it is drawn from the book of Merleau Ponty *Eloge de la philosophie* (*In Praise of Philosophy*): 'Men generally judge with their eyes more than with their hands. Every man can see, but very few men can touch. Everyone easily sees what one seems, but almost none can identify what one is really, and this little number of penetrating spirits do not dare to contradict the multitude which has, as shield, the majesty of the state' (cf. 'Note sur Machiavel' in *Eloge de la philosophie*, Folio Essais, p. 296; cf. 'Note on Machiavelli' in *In Praise of Philosophy*). Merleau Ponty comments on these words saying that it is thus a fundamental condition of politics to be practised according to appearances (idem). Be that as it may, it is on a 'communion' between citizens that Machiavelli intends to found a republican community. Now a communion has more to do with touch than with sight. The second quotation is drawn from the treatise *De Anima*, in which Aristotle claims that 'the sense of touch is (…) the only one the privation of which leads to the death of animals' (*De l'âme*, III, 13, Nécessité du toucher, p. 97; *De Anima, III, 13, Necessity of Touch* (435 b)). And, for Aristotle, 'animals' means all living beings endowed with locomotion, thus also human beings.

This warning of Aristotle seems to be particularly relevant in our epoch, in which not only appearances prevail but also the techniques of communication from a distance, which more and more supplant being in relation through touch, be it immediately physical or expressed through desire and emotions.

I want to clarify another aspect of my words by resorting to the distinction that Maurice Simondon makes between individuation and individualization (in *L'individuation psychique et collective*). The political discourses and programmes generally are situated at the level of individualization, an individualization which is presumed to be the empirical and ontic expression of a more original, transcendental and ontological individuation. However, a more and more important interval, not to say a break, today exists between the individualization about which the persons in charge of politics speak and they intend to govern and the individuation of citizens. Undoubtedly, if one believes in Simondon, such a dissociation has existed for a long time, but it becomes more and more effective and crucial not only for the autonomy of citizens but even for the survival of living beings. Thus if, according to Simondon, sexuality—I prefer speaking of sexuation or of sexuate identity when it is not a question of sexuality strictly speaking—is a basic element of our individuation, the neuter or neutered citizens, whom we are presumed to be, are deprived, by our political culture, of their individuation and we have to deal more and more with a so-called democracy to which any real people correspond. The artificial character of the citizens' identity would explain the volatility and changeability of their votes and even their disaffection with politics as well as the feeling that they are misunderstood and extraneous to the city and the society to which they supposedly belong. And it is rightly. Indeed, 'the affective and emotional factors which constitute the basis of the intersubjective communication' (Simondon, op.cit., p. 101), beginning with those relative to sexuate identity, are generally absent from political life, to which they represent a sort of taboo. Thus a truly democratic politics requires individuation and individualization to be reconciled in each citizen and between citizens so that it could regain validity, coherence and credibility. My suggestions attempt to contribute to that.

Beyond the fact that our epoch, still more than that in which he lived, constrains us to give meaning again to citizenship, it seems that Merleau-Ponty himself has not really succeeded in linking together individuation and individualization, respect for singularity and collective commitment, ontological and ontic dimensions of the individual, including in and for himself. To give only an example of that, his way of resorting to self-affection does not allow a fleshly relation to exist to himself and to the other as different from himself. Rather it is a question of fusion-confusion with the environment and the milieu, from which only a relation to/with the same would allow us to emerge. And yet, every individuation and every relation to another living being, thus every intersubjective relationship, requires us to assume our particularity and difference with respect to nature, to the world and to the other(s). How to form a democratic community, what is more of materialist nature, without each taking on its own being and being able to enter into relation with the other(s) with respect for not only social and cultural but also natural mutual difference(s). The ambiguous, and even contradictory, character of some of the decisions and commitments of Merleau-Ponty seems to be the result of a sort of getting caught up in or lacking differentiation regarding a natural or sociocultural environment which bears witness to his failure in reaching an individuation of his own. This is perhaps due, among other things, to the fact that he had not succeeded in completely freeing touch from its being 'colonized' by sight whatever his attempts in this respect. Does he not speak of himself seeing, instead of experiencing, touching himself?

Be that as it may, our epoch is no longer the same as his, and it constrains us to face questions which did not impose upon him with a similar urgency. The current distress of our world and the danger in which we are today force us to think about the way according to which life itself can be saved, beginning with human life. Is not human being henceforth subjected to a more radical exploitation than the exploitation denounced by Marx? Indeed, it is no longer merely a question of the exploitation of the workers by the factory owner but of the transformation of human beings, and even of all living beings, into resources to keep the universal, economic and political mechanism that the world has become in working order.

How can we try to still secure a lasting development not only for nature as earth, water, air and sun as well as vegetal and animal worlds, but also for our own nature, for us as nature? Instead of letting us be only a cog in the technical mechanism which governs the whole world and instead of letting us be moulded by discourses, including pseudo materialist and democratic discourses, which more and more uproot and divert us from our living belonging, it would be urgent to discover a way of behaving in which a certain degree of autonomy and freedom still exists for us. What then matters is to mould ourselves from the given material that our natural belonging is, with our lasting development and that of all living beings in mind. This requires us to be faithful to ourselves in each step forward, and to verify if a return to our own natural belonging remains possible. Our becoming then corresponds to a work that we shape by ourselves without letting us be shaped by external requirements which are imposed upon us from an outside and gradually remove us from our original nature.

In other words, we could wonder whether humanity is coming to its end or if it reaches a stage of its evolution which needs radical changes, in particular in culture and politics. These changes cannot amount to the blindly forging ahead, which is too often suggested to us, not to say imposed upon us, but demand us to return to what can still grant us a birth, a development and a blossoming about which we too little cared until now.

For What Do We Feel Nostalgic?

Together with the estrangement from ourselves as living beings, we find, in Western culture, an insistence on the theme of the return. And it is not a pure coincidence if the text given as a reference to the origin of our cultural tradition tells about the departure of a man going to war and his eventful return home. After many and great trials, this man, Ulysses, goes back home. But does he return to his self?—I am not sure. Perhaps, he comes back to what is called the hearth, to his marriage, but not to intimacy with his self and with the other. With this first epic of Greek culture love is already becoming an institution in the service of the city. And lovers are already subjected to laws foreign to their own feelings. Then love splits off from natural belonging, from physical sensitivity, even from sexuate determination of the individual, except with regard to reproduction and the foundation of a family.

The departure of Ulysses to go to war and his painful return home happen before the construction of Western metaphysics and, in a way, announce it. After the end or accomplishment of metaphysics, the theme of the return is insistent again. I could allude to Hölderlin and Nietzsche, for example, and comment on their feeling nostalgic for an impossible return. Both of them have been removed from their own self by Western culture and they do not succeed in turning back to this self, their attempt ending in a sort of madness.

In the era of globalization which is henceforth ours, we can observe two tendencies: that of the stay-at-home who try to preserve at all costs their own home, country and culture as they are, on the one hand, and, on the other hand, that of people who denigrate any home. All of them neglect to consider and cultivate their own self and the relationship with the other as other. Indeed, this requires the ability to stay in oneself to open up to the other, while remaining capable of returning home, to and within oneself. Such a capacity for opening up to the outside and turning back to the self, within the self is absent from our tradition. Man has searched for himself outside himself and not through making his way in himself. He did not apply himself to the discovery and the cultivation of an interiority, including as affective and fleshly.

What does the insistence on the theme of the return mean today? In particular, what does the present turning back to Greek culture mean? And to what Greek culture do we want to return? I think that we are trying to find the crossroads in which we have taken a wrong path, notably with regard to the elaboration of our subjectivity. My interpretation is supported by the disappearance of some morphological forms and lexical terms which still exist in the earliest Greek culture. As examples in connection with the theme of this chapter, I can cite the word *heteros*, the forms which express the dual, as well as the verbal form called middle-passive or middle voice, but also the evolution of the meaning of the word *genos* and of the value of certain elements relative to a culture in the feminine (cf. on this subject, and some parts of this text, the chapter 'The Return' in *In the Beginning, She Was*).

In the early stage of Greek culture, the word *heteros* means the other of two, two which form a pair and are both similar and different: for example, the other lip, the other hand, the other eye, but also the other sex. We find the dual form too for the verb, the substantive and the adjective which correspond to a duality. These forms appropriate to a relation between two have been supplanted by the term *allos*, which designates an other in a group or a series, and by a plural which no longer takes account of the specificity of the relation between two. In that time, we also find the verbal form named middle-passive or middle voice which expresses both activity and passivity and supposes an involvement which is physical, sensitive and not merely mental as is generally the case with the reflexive form, which already obeys the subject-object logic. Unfortunately, in later cultures the active-passive couple as opposites and also the reflexive form will substitute for the middle voice. Such a substitution makes self-affection, but also the reciprocity of affect, which can correspond to hetero-affection, impossible. The division into activity and passivity entails a split of subjectivity in subject and object—which is often shared out between man and woman—and prevents self-affection from happening as well as reciprocity between subjectivities, which has become the norm in our tradition. Now self-affection and hetero-affection are necessary for the functioning of a true democracy.

With regard to the term *genos*, we can note that originally this word refers as much to sex or gender as it does to generation and genealogy. However, the meaning 'generation' or 'genealogy' has gradually supplanted the meaning 'sex' or 'gender', for which the word '*heteros*', the dual forms as well as the middle voice can be used.

It is interesting to observe that the disappearance of these terms, meanings or grammatical forms is accompanied by an change in the representation of the feminine lips—a thing that I discovered when looking at the sculptures of the goddess Korè in the archaeological gallery of Syracuse in Sicily. In the most ancient sculptures, the lips are closed, touching one another, which can illustrate self-affection in the feminine. In later sculptures, the mouth is open and the lips no longer touch one another, and, afterwards, they are even distorted. At the same epoch, we also can notice an evolution in the value attached to feminine genealogy, at natural and cultural levels. And yet, how is a democracy possible if an equivalent, which does not mean an equal, value is not attributed to man and woman?

A Necessary Return to Self-Affection

The nostalgia that we experience today for a return, particularly a return to the Greek culture, could thus express our want of a return to our own self, within our own self through self-affection. Self-affection—which does not amount to a mere auto-eroticism or narcissism—is as much necessary for human being as bread is and it represents the condition of a real human dignity. It ought to guarantee the foundation of our subjectivity, to ensure the structuring of our individuation and allows us to relate to one another with mutual respect. A human culture and a true democracy cannot exist without the preservation of self-affection from and for each one.

Self-affection, above all in our times, needs a return to the own self, especially to the living body, to the natural belonging, and to a concern for life from each one.

Self-affection is what allows us to be present to ourselves without asking an other for this presence. It represents a necessary transition between a dependence on the other and a sharing with the other—in other words, between the relation which exists between parents or other adults and children and the relation between lovers or friends, but also between citizens, that is, between adults.

Self-affection allows us to discover and cultivate an internal dwelling, a place where staying in ourselves in whatever time or space as regards our own life, the world where we live and the unfolding of history. Self-affection intervenes, or ought to intervene, before all the modes or configurations in which we become incarnate or into which we project ourselves. It corresponds to a structure with which we provide ourselves by and towards the perception of ourselves as a whole. So thanks to our lips, our eyelids, the palms of our hands but also the soles of our feet touching one another, we can create and perceive a place in which to dwell in ourselves. Hence we no longer need supra sensitive essences external to ourselves to acquire interiority and unity. We provide ourselves with them thanks to the different borders of our bodies touching one another. And then interiority and unity, contrary to those which are dependent on constructed essences, are living and can evolve. They are of use for constituting a frame and a medium, the consistency of which is in a way diaphanous, but a diaphanous which is tactile and not merely visual, and which can receive all that which does not destroy it (cf. Aristote, *De l'âme*, II, 7, Le diaphane et la lumière, pp. 48–9; Aristotle, *De Anima*, II, 7 (418 b)). This diaphanous nature can be considered to be the first state of our flesh.

In reality, our first home is our body. It is the first place in which we must learn to dwell. And this dwelling cannot exist without the existence of a link between the body, the soul and the spirit, and our deciding on its creation. In that way, we get a place for ourselves in a conscious manner, a place in which to stay with limits which preserve us from being lost in an indefinite expansion or outpouring into the space or into an appearing, but also in that which Merleau-Ponty calls, in his comments on *The Prince* of Machiavelli 'the vertigo of a life in several' or 'the fading of life through the passage to thousand other lives' (cf. *Eloge de la philosophie*, Note sur Machiavel p. 297 and in Lecture de Montaigne, p. 278; *In Praise of Philosophy* in Note on Machiavelli and in Lecture of Montaigne).

Man has built dwelling places outside of himself without first dwelling in himself by taking charge of his incarnation. Thus he is in search of the most intimate of himself in the most distant. He spreads outside of himself, and he imposes himself upon the world and upon the other(s) even without being aware of that. Hence the necessary resort to more or less artificial sociocultural or juridical limits which are presupposed to bring back everyone to and within oneself, but this so-called oneself rather amounts to an exile from the self. The neuter, or neutered, individual that we ought to be, and our fictitious identity which must be guaranteed by laws supposedly being also neuter, is an example of that.

Consequently, no one is truly oneself and the relations to/with oneself, to/with the world and to/with the other(s) become, at least in part, artificial and extraneous to reality. Our culture, with the support of philosophy, teaches us that the real limit for us is death. It has not acknowledged the limits with which life itself endowed us. It has not attributed to us an identity of living being—an individuation which allows us to gather with ourselves within the limits of our body. This body is thus reduced to the materiality of a corpse animated by an energy external to it, and it is no longer a body which corresponds to the dwelling and the world thanks to which we can live, develop, love and share, including as citizens.

For us, as humans, roots from which we can grow and develop are lacking. We are not trees—we must create a framework and a milieu which allow us to be and to become while remaining living. Self-affection can be such a framework which can compensate for our lack of roots through the borders or limits of our body touching one another. It is not in our genealogy, our culture or our language, what is more as they are, that the key of our being nostalgic for a return—notably to a soul?—can be found nor that of the mystery of the origin of our being. For us, to be born means a rupture regarding our origin: we were born a man or a woman from a union between two, and two who are different, a man and a woman. As humans, we must give an origin to ourselves. We must everyone take charge of our existence without any continuity with respect to roots or a prior environment. Self-affection is a gesture which is able to create a place—made of flesh, of breath and touch—from which we can and must take roots to exist, develop and share as living beings, including at the civil level.

The Functioning of a Real Democracy Needs Hetero-Affection

Self-affection is also what makes co-existence and co-presence between different citizens possible, with respect for their respective natural belongings and their individuations. Indeed, everyone must be able to open up to the other while staying in oneself in order that a meeting, a communication or a communion could occur. Everyone must be able to be faithful to oneself, to remain the same as oneself, in space and time, so that he or she could welcome the otherness of the other without losing oneself. If one subjects oneself to the other, to a sameness which corresponds with the other, meeting and sharing between the two cannot happen. And the same goes if the two subject themselves to a same foreign to both. And yet our culture offers only this alternative to us: either a culture of the same in the masculine to which woman must subject herself, or a culture in the neuter to which man as well as woman must subject themselves. And that allows neither man nor woman to gather with themselves, to self-affect, thus to be able to preserve their own individuation while coexisting with the other as different—a thing which is necessary in order for a community to be truly democratic.

Coexisting with the other as different can take place through touch—be the latter merely physical or mediated by desire or affect. The insurmountable interval or distance between two differently sexuate individuals can be crossed only by a touching, a touching which is reciprocal and does not obey the traditional distribution of activity and passivity, in particular between the sexes. Indeed, in that case the desire for or of the other, and even every relation to/with the other, runs the risk of leading to the loss of one's own self instead of bringing to the latter rebirth, growth and individuation thanks to a meeting and a union with the other. Born of two, and two who are naturally different, we search for being born again of such duality through desire—a desire which is sexuate before being sexual, thus which preexists sexuality strictly speaking, and does not amount to mere instincts or drives—which presupposes the acknowledgment of a fundamental difference between individuations. Desire aims at what transcends us. The other is a sensitive support, here and now present to us, which keeps our desire alive, notably thanks to a touching and being touched which entails passivity and activity, emotion but also action. Desire aspires after a beyond. To such a beyond the other calls us without our being able either to reach or to overcome it if he or she keeps their difference.

The transcendence after which desire aspires can thus be embodied by the other as different—and the most basic and irreducible paradigm of otherness regarding our individuation is the one relative to sexuate difference. The beyond for which we long is mysteriously revealed to us by a touching-being touched which awakens or re-awakens in us an impetus towards an objective which is still to be reached, a future which has not yet come to pass, a being still unknown to us. Because we have been touched and moved, we want to attain another stage in our development through a union or an action with the other, but also through an emotion or an action which is shared at the social level. Our way of moving as humans is never a mere somatic growth nor a mere locomotion, it is also a psychic or spiritual becoming which is achieved thanks to a relational process or an individual or collective work.

In fact self-affection itself aspires to transcending itself, to evolving, in particular through hetero-affection, that is, through a touching which unites us with the other and allows us to communicate or commune with the other as other, at an intimate level but also at a community level. Being touched by and touching one another provides us with impetus and information regarding the path to be cleared towards such an accomplishment. But we do not pay attention enough to this sort of message or we subject it to tendencies of our culture which prevent us from perceiving a sensitive language—and yet it is necessary for the union with the other, the social cohesion, the personal or collective motivation of the work. First, we try to appropriate what touched us, reducing it in that way to an object that we can seize somehow or other. Then, instead of respecting the transcendence of what or whom touched us, we relate it to a same—a same as ourselves, a same as that culture imposed upon us. Moreover, we subject touch to sight. By such gestures we render the communication or communion with the other as other impossible. Indeed, this asks us for being touched and touching one another in a manner which differs from the activity of seizing an 'object' or from the passivity which the fact of reducing ourselves to an 'object' for the other presupposes. However, the discourse on touch in our tradition amounts only to that.

And yet, as is the case with self-affection, hetero-affection does not tolerate activity to be dissociated from passivity. Only their connection allows us to relate to ourselves and to the other in a way which does not fall again into fusion or appropriation of an object but gives access to a communication or communion which transcends each of the selves while remaining rooted in each of the selves. This could be said: gives access to a coexistence, and even a union, which is both ec-stasis and in-stasis, an ec-stasis with respect to one's self which contributes to the becoming of each and a relation between the selves with respect for their difference. This could also be said with these words: which grants us a communication or coexistence which makes possible us to transcend ourselves, individually or collectively, in a way which remains sensitive, incarnate, instead of submitting ourselves to supra sensitive ideals or political ideologies, as our Platonic tradition accustomed us to doing.

If self-affection already entails surmounting the mere materiality of the body through animating it by a conscious sensitivity, hetero-affection allows us to transcend the loneliness or the solipsism of a oneself by achieving our individuation thanks to relating to/with the other, the others. But this is possible only with the acknowledgment and the respect for the difference of the other at the level of individuation, beginning with sexuate belonging, but also at the level of individualization, thus of culture, languages, and even opinions.

The touch about which Merleau-Ponty speaks does not make all that possible. It takes place between a taking, which amounts to a seizing, on the one hand, and a merging into a whole which lacks differentiation, on the other hand. For example, when he alludes to a touching between his two hands, it is a question of a gesture in which his right hand takes, not to say seizes, his left hand, which does not correspond to what happens when the palms of the two hands touch one another, each being both active and passive in a manner extraneous to any seizure. Moreover, when Merleau-Ponty alludes to the colour as to what can ensure a passage from the world to himself, he views that as a continuum and not as a relation between two differentiated elements between which colour is transmitted not only by sight but also by a touching which acts through the diaphanous of the flesh. Besides, Merleau-Ponty maintains that we can touch and be touched only thanks to similarities—for example, similar bodies or similar perceptions—that is, thanks to that which is common to those who touch, thanks to systems of equivalences, and even thanks to a sort of mimicry (cf. on this subject *La Nature, Notes de cours au Collège de France*, and to the book *Le visible et l'invisible; Nature, Course Notes from the College de France* and *The Visible and the Invisible*). However, all that nullifies the mediating potential which corresponds with touch as such and permits relations in difference.

In the discourse of Merleau-Ponty, touch means really other than that to which I allude when I speak of self-affection and hetero-affection. For Merleau-Ponty—as for Sartre, Lévinas, but also Jacques Derrida and Michel Henry—the communication, communion or union which can happen between us thanks to touch does not really exist. Indeed, it is precisely touch which can mediate between oneself and oneself, but also between oneself and the other as other. Touch as the most crucial mediation for the constitution of a living subjectivity of one's own and for intersubjectivity is lacking in the work of these philosophers.

Besides, the way in which most of them speak of sexual intercourse proves such a lack. They perceive this relation as a sort of master-slave conflict in which woman would be destined to assume the role of slave. Unless they consider the carnal union to be doomed to an insurmountable failure, given the impossible union between those who embrace one another. It is true that without self-affection and hetero-affection, in which activity and passivity are indissociable, a mediation is lacking which allows the communication and union between two beings different by nature to happen. Hence the fact that violence is too often at work in this relation— a violence which spreads on other relations, including at the community level. Hence also the reduction of the amorous embrace to an energy release, of which procreation would be the only positive meaning or redemption. And yet the carnal union is, or ought to be, a gesture which gives access to humanity, and to a human community, as the passage from the satisfaction of needs to the sharing of longing for transcendence that desire represents, at an individual but also at a collective level.

It is neither the discourse already known nor the logos as it is which can ensure such a passage. Rather they make it impossible by the subject-object logic which founds them and that they perpetuate. As it is now, our language, whatever its democratic claims, does not allow us to achieve our humanity and its sharing. This language serves above all our needs, including when these appear to be transcendental or common. Unfortunately, philosophers themselves favour the relation to object(s) more than the relation to subject, especially as other, as the means of transcending oneself. However, this leads to competition, rivalry and conflict and does not contribute to coexistence between us. Politicians do not seem to be aware of that and they continue to establish democratic issues and programs from the acquisition of objects or possession of goods. And that does not make a culture and a practice of sharing possible, notably at the level having but also at the level of being, as giving access to humanity and community coexistence with mutual respect.

In Search of Self-Affection and Hetero-Affection in Supra Sensitive Ideals

Our tradition has kept desire on hold through supra sensitive ideals, including in political ideologies and divine figures. We have not yet truly incarnated our humanity. We are still expecting to acquire our real individuation, a condition which is necessary for a community sharing. We still entrust such a task to some belief, some iconic figure or some divinity. Yet we ought to endeavour to finally become adults. And, whatever our ideal or our longing for the absolute, we ought to attempt to discover or find again by ourselves the fecundity of touch for our incarnation, our individuation and our community sharing. About God we know nothing or very little. We can only hope that he will reveal to us something of him through the touch of a grace. But do we not then fall back into the alternative between activity and passivity—if God can touch us, can we touch him? Could a reciprocal touch really take place between God and us? Unlike that, such a reciprocal touch can exist between an other, different from us, and ourselves and it can provide us with the experience of a sensitive transcendence irreducible to any object but favourable to the communion between us and to a common work, including at the social and political levels. We then perceive what a meeting between different longings for transcendence means, a transcendence that can become incarnate here and now thanks to the respect for the otherness of the other regardless of a common ideal or ideology sharing.

Viewed in that way, the amorous union can represent the approach to a human being or becoming which is not reducible to some or other being, even some or other 'object', imagined according to our needs, whatever their transcendental character. Such an approach has the advantage of being able to transcend the particularity of the differences, in particular between cultural, notably religious, traditions. Touch makes possible such an approach because it is without being something—it exists before or after any singular being. It calls on the transcendental matter of our 'to be', of which both of us obtain the experience thanks to a sharing of desires respectful of our difference(s). Instead of searching for appropriating the divine by the knowledge of good and evil, man and woman can attempt to reach their own becoming divine through an amorous union between their 'to be' and the mediation of their desires.

Our longing for the divine is, indeed, a longing for self-affection, and even for hetero-affection, that we situate straight at an absolute and supra sensitive level without clearing the path which could render this experience possible. If we are not first capable of self-affection, and next of hetero-affection, how could we perceive something of the union with an absolute transcendence? Touch can lead us from the mere physical to the most subtle spiritual experience, but this needs a culture of sensitivity that we still lack. We ought to learn to join our hands, our lips, our eyelids and to unite the transcendental longings which correspond to our respective desires and individuations before we claim to experience an absolute transcendence, in particular that of God.

Thus the cultivation of touch, understood and acknowledged as mediation, must be first a personal one in order to reach and preserve our individuation. Then, it requires us to learn how to relate with desire and love to one another as two, two who are different by nature and whose individuation, and even individualization, are different. Our culture has neglected these stages, especially the second, even though they are necessary for a relational cultivation, particularly of touch, towards our personal, but also collective, accomplishment. We have passed, one could say we have leapt, from the one to the multiple, from the individual to the group or the community without considering nor developing sufficiently the relationship between two different individuals, beginning with two who are naturally different. This relation was only of use for the family unit and procreation, on the one hand, and, on the other hand, it was nullified by the reduction of the living person to an individual in the neuter—which corresponds with no real individuation—who cannot experience nor share any affect and for whom touch has no meaning.

Such an individual amounts to an abstract construction which lacks a sensitive body and for which self-affection and hetero-affection cannot exist. It is a sort of automaton or robot which is animated by a mechanism, an energy or an authority almost exclusively external to it, and which is unable to assess by itself what drives it, towards what it makes its way and to what it devotes itself. Hence even touch reaches it/us only from the outside through various creations, at best through works of art.

And it is not by chance that the traditions which are most concerned with incarnation are also the ones in which art is the most developed. The artist tries to affect him- or herself and to affect others through the mediation of a work of art. But this does not yet amount to a cultivation of touch through self-affection and hetero-affection, a cultivation which protects us from the exploitation of our natural energy as well as of our sensitivity, and from the destruction of our individuation by resorting to technology as mediation between us, but also by the impact of cultural or political ideologies which divert us from faithfulness to ourselves and from the individual or collective responsibility towards nature, humanity and the world.

By Way of Conclusion

Without a culture of touch which allows us to dwell in ourselves and to unite with the other, with others, we wander during all our life, exposed to whatever influence or pressure. We lack self-affection which grants us the possibility of returning to ourselves, of dwelling in ourselves, of experiencing by ourselves and, then, of deciding and acting with faithfulness to what and whom we are. In philosophical terms, one could say that we lack the possibility of withdrawing from all our modes of being to gather with ourselves in our own 'to be', without for all that renouncing the physical, sensitive and relational qualities of our existence. We lack a place—Aristotle would say a *topos*—in which we can collect ourselves within limits which preserve our longing for limitlessness, for the ideal and the absolute. We lack a shelter in which our presence can gather with itself and ·restore itself thanks to a return to a natural belonging and an energy of our own.

Such a place is both sensitive and spiritual as long as it is freely wanted and assumed by us. This place is also ethical because it corresponds with the condition for our opening up to the respect for the otherness of the other, in a permanent and in a way virginal manner, given that it is capable of distinguishing our own self from the self of the other. Thanks to such a return and such gathering in ourselves—perhaps Aristotle would speak of a return to our soul—we can also pay attention and remain open to the world, to the thought, to the future and to the absolute, that is, to that which transcends us, without running the risk of losing ourselves in them or merging with them.

Self-affection, as a way of our experiencing ourselves, is a gift of us to us which makes the respect for the difference of whatever otherness possible. We can face it because we are rooted in ourselves by a touching one another of the borders or limits of our self, and by the perception of a threshold between the inside and the outside of ourselves. This also means between the invisible and the visible parts of us, or between the tactile intimacy of mucous tissues and the part of us which is more immediately exposed to the other and to the world like, for example, our skin but also our mode of behaving.

Following, but differently from, Descartes, I could say: 'I am' because I am capable of self-affection, of a self-affection which is sensitive and not only mental, that is, of an alternation, in time and space, between opening up to or unfolding outside of myself and returning to and in myself. Such a movement characterizes the natural life, as *phusis*, but, as humans, we are able to ensure it by ourselves in a free and conscious way through alternating self-affection and hetero-affection.

Part VI

Approach to Touch as Such

17

An Immediate Access to the Transcendental

The Innocence of Childhood

According to our tradition, and notably Hegel, communion would take place between humans and God, or in God, but not between two human beings naturally different. Faith would be that which, apparently, can abolish a quantitative difference, by rendering it absolute, in order for a union to happen between the same ones—a union between the finite and the infinite corresponding to a sacred mystery. However, does not life, as well as the union between the same ones, then lose their innocence by resorting to a third external to them? Hence a necessary return to childhood, when a union between humanity and divinity would exist almost naturally. Could this be because understanding has not yet caused the split of our being—of our soul?

Why does Hegel not keep silent before the 'mystery' of the desire between two naturally different beings? Why does he not consider this union to be divine because understanding cannot arbitrate about it, 'which cannot think simultaneously of absolutely different substances and their possible unity' (*L'esprit du Christianisme et son destin*, p. 88). Could it be because he did not experience desire as a link between

© The Author(s), under exclusive license to Springer Nature Switzerland AG 2024   **283**
L. Irigaray, *The Mediation of Touch*, https://doi.org/10.1007/978-3-031-37413-5_17

naturally different human beings? Because quantitative difference is the only one that understanding acknowledges, a difference which is less familiar to the sensitive nature of incarnation? It is faith which ought to culturally unite that which desire already carried out almost naturally. But the divine could not be present in a body in order to be completely recognized. Hence the necessary disappearance of Jesus so that the Holy Spirit could happen, this being represented as the return of fire to/in each, a fire underrated as desire between fleshly beings. Could that not testify to a failure in the fulfilment of subjectivity, which needs a/its resorting to an external dynamism under the quasi-object form of tongues of fire?

What happens with the ardour which is awakened in us and between us by the amorous desire, and its possible contribution to our spiritual becoming? Does this desire not answer a longing for a return to the divine in us and between us, notably by overcoming the split that the child does not know? Is not the amorous union the most absolute of prayers at a subjective level? At least if it is a living union, not yet reflected—including as beauty or even incarnation of a God—which takes place on this side of or beyond any visible perception, but is, nevertheless, present and giving life to our existence. If it is a union which grants us being born or being born again as spirit, an incarnate and fleshly spirit, which is not limited either to a solely material and mortal body or to a merely formal and abstract spirit. A union which gives us or gives us back us to ourselves, gives or gives back to us our being, while exceeding the being that we already were, or the one that union itself could become by settling down in only one unity. A union which allows us to be thanks to our difference, a difference which is henceforth qualitative and not quantitative and which the passage to the absolute cannot abolish.

Then the emphasis is not put on the entity itself but on a quality that subjectivity perceives and is likely to establish a relation, including between subjectivities. This property possibly can console for what has been lost in the passage to another state, which cannot be only a quantitative progress. This state has more to do with a lost union which determined the way in which our being experienced itself. The only valid quantity would be the one which bears some relation to completeness, but it is not dependent on a quantity, at least relating to object(s). For example, the fact that love is more absolute does not result from a quantity but of an ability to correspond with the whole of being, with a being not yet previously revealed. This could mean an ability to restore our integrity, our innocence—our virginity. Love which brings us back to our being consoles us for any attachment to what diverted us from fulfilling this being. Does it not restore in this way the divine which existed, not yet developed, in the child?

Does not a pure amorous desire restore to us the innocence of childhood that we had lost? An innocence which still longs for a development of life which does not define itself by opposing incarnation. An innocence extraneous to the logic of opposites, and which is instead a naïve search for oneself in the encounter with all that exists. An innocence which seeks, through physical experiences and an approach to that which transcends them, what is good for the body but also for the soul. An innocence which aspires after becoming, and even after the absolute, without an internal split of being, will and knowledge being still conjoined in it. Hence the will to life prevails over experiencing distress, a will of one's own that parents and masters often destroy by imposing customs and laws in which the perception of life is lost, even forgotten. In that way, a form of slavery is instituted by those who claim to handle life but divert children from it, interrupting its dynamism and its development. Innocence is thus removed from what guided life itself and its becoming incarnate in the external nature but also the inner nature of human beings. Indeed, nature is not only the world in which we are and which surrounds us, it is also the world, including the internal world, that we are.

Hegel does not seem really to know and acknowledge such an internal reality. He seems to ignore that it could be the place of incarnation of the divine without an object external to oneself being necessary. The same goes for the objectivity of the subjectivity of the other—our link with this other ought to exist through an 'object' external to us. Hence the fact that the relation could be opposed to the elements that it unites, according to Hegel (op. cit., p. 114). If this union is founded on/in the respect for the respective subjectivities, no external object or objectivity is needed, which would remove each from itself while intending to determine a possible reciprocity.

There is no doubt that a religion of incarnation cannot take our pecu-liarity and sensitive existence away from us. It is from them that the divine can become incarnate and communed between us—a Christian community cannot exist from a being put on hold by an objectivity for-eign to subjectivity. It is the objectivity of the latter, its way of transform-ing its natural belonging into a spiritual determination, which remains fleshly, which bears witness to the presence of the divine in human beings and its possible sharing between them. A Christian community does not need an 'object' or a representation to gather. This happens through its works, the first being the practice of love, a love which must be singular while being shareable, and potentially universal regardless of the verdict of understanding. It is not understanding which can decide on love, but the way in which the link between the divine and human beings and between human beings themselves becomes incarnate.

This link can be neither objectivized nor subjected to an object. Its objectivity corresponds with the subjectivity of those who enter into rela-tion and with the truth and fecundity of their relationship. This raises a question about what God himself represents, rather than about his neces-sary representation as an 'object', to found a divine relation. The only way according to which our relating to God does not split our subjectivity is when his divine nature is compatible with human subjectivity. The true pertinence of a relation to the divine—and even of a religion—depends on its ability to contribute to human becoming. This does not require the mediation of an 'object', but the acknowledgment of the natural belong-ing of the human being and of its aptitude for transforming itself—in particular as soul?—in order to be able to become one with spirit. Thus every opposition between body and spirit, and every condemnation of the sexuate, and even the sexual, desire as that which can unify and unite them goes against the becoming divine of human beings. The split, in particular that of the soul, which is then carried out, and even conse-crated, deprives them of uniting with the divine—a divine which both needs this unity and contributes to its development.

The Dialectical Relation Between I-Myself and You-Yourself

The divine is made inaccessible by the split between the unity of a merely organic nature—as the one postulated by the young Hegel—and consciousness. Indeed, an organic unity has in itself a will to grow without a determined infinite that it could oppose to consciousness. It is sexuation, and the desire for and of the other, which is associated with it, which could correspond with a good infinite, an infinite which includes its limit while longing for the absolute. Sexuation can ensure a link between nature and consciousness, nature and subjectivity, and keeps alive the desire for a good infinite—for an absolute which is both natural and spiritual, which respects life while transforming it.

Sexuation reveals what nature itself can achieve, can produce without resorting to another negative than the one which exists due to the partiality of every human being. Nor does it require an exteriority other than that which is entailed by the relation to a naturally different other—its for-oneself goes together with a for-the-other, an other who is different. The interiority of the sexuate desire does not exist without the exteriority of the other and its subjective dimension cannot do without the objectivity of a physical and spiritual difference between oneself and the other.

The reconciliation of which desire is in search is the one which is the cause of our being, and it is not reachable by consciousness. We aspire after a union between different beings which is out of reach of a single being, or Being. The absolute, which underlies the desire and its transcendental intuition, is inaccessible as such, but it contributes to the accomplishment of our whole being. It corresponds to a relation, and therefore to a syntax and a logic, which underlies or ought to underlie all the others as expression of our reality. However, it is often only through its lack that something of it is revealed, is remembered. And a some lexical contributions could not compensate for the absence of an appropriate syntax or logic. Rather, it could be the acknowledgement of the necessity of taking account of the negative of a difference as well as the search for a logic capable of that. This disrupts our conception of truth and even of the real that truth is supposed to guarantee.

Indeed, the relation between two different but not opposite elements is that which, henceforth, determines the search for meaning and invalidates the pertinence of categories such as finite-infinite, empirical-transcendental, particular-universal and so forth. More generally, opposition itself is no longer relevant because nature does not really know it. But it admits that each particular being has a real essence which does not oppose the others, but is different. Hence essence is no longer the matter of a more or less abstract universality of a concept, of a subjectivity or a consciousness, but the matter of the finiteness of a sensitive existence which must achieve the absolute of the potential of its 'to be'. This sensitive being and its knowing are always particular, even if they are claimed to be universal. This irreducible particularity explains why a consciousness which is supposedly capable of universality must undergo personal, cultural and historical crises. Such universality is the other side of the abstraction or the void imposed on consciousness—one concerning extension and the other comprehension. In fact, a limit to extension and to comprehension can be provided by the acceptance of one's own particularity.

Assuming the latter delimits a framework within which consciousness can act. It also allows consciousness to perceive, even to imagine the particularity of other beings, or 'to be', without having previously to integrate them into a totality. The fact of viewing itself as partial enables consciousness to do that. And a great part of the philosophical work consists in re-broaching what consciousness had denied. But this resulted from an a priori: consciousness is capable of cutting itself off from sensitivity. And yet it is not the case, and such an a priori deprives it and all that it perceives of a dimension corresponding to sensitivity, that is, of its belonging to life. Besides, the knowledge which is determined by a subjectivity which is supposedly abstract and void is itself partial because sensitivity is a supplier of knowledge. Consciousness becomes partial because it underrated its own partiality. It can experience this partiality through self-affection which, better than self-consciousness, can provide consciousness with a framework which does not constrain it to forego a sensitive knowledge.

Self-affection is not an irrational behaviour but is a way of founding subjectivity that traditional metaphysics has ignored. This foundation is not representable by reason but it objectively exists as a substratum of its content(s) and even of its form(s). What is objective cannot merely be laid down by reflection, it must also be respected as the reality of that which exists regardless of it—an existing reality that cannot be subjected to reflection as living but the existence of which must be acknowledged, including as a subjective a priori. Consciousness cannot exempt itself from this a priori, even in its relation to transcendence—be it a question of the existence or becoming of the subject or of its relation to the other as other.

The objective a priori of subjectivity—of which self-affection can supply a perception, including a sensitive one, without splitting the subject—cannot be ignored in the search for and the determination of what concerns the truth and the absolute. Be it recognized or not, this dimension intervenes. It can act in a more conscious way through a dialectical process between the 'I' and the 'me'—of the subject itself but also of the other—the 'me' appearing as a sort of 'thing' or 'stance' in order to subject to a dialectical process that which of subjectivity is the concern of objectivity.

It is above all the relationship with the other which allows a dialectical relation between the 'I' and the 'me' to be practised. If it does not take place between two subjectivities, such a relation freezes in opposites in order to position or seize the polarities from which it must operate. It can preserve the dynamism if it acts between two different living beings for whom and between whom the 'I' and the 'me' must both come into play and evolve.

In a sense, they really exist as such only thanks to their relation. In order that it should be effective, the sensitive and the rational must participate in it—this relation cannot exist without being physical and metaphysical. It necessarily allies nature with liberty, generation with creation, intuition with reason, visible with invisible, notably as/through touch. It gathers all that the human being is and of which it is capable towards its becoming, and in a way that does not close in one system but contributes to the evolution of the human being in which the relationship of the couple has a share. Indeed this requires and causes the production of life, of beauty, of imagination and ideas which represent a transmissible legacy. This can happen if any 'I', any 'me', any world or logos freezes into an entity, and that everything evolves in a manner which supports becoming towards an absolute accomplishment.

If the becoming is achieved at the level of the comprehensive being, activity and passivity must intervene in a dialectical mode in each and between each other. Activity, at least apparently and punctually, is on the side of the spirit, but what energizes it is above all that which it accepts receiving in a passive way. The deed of the spirit stops the dynamism under the form of an idea or a concept more than it supplies impetus to it. It is rather from the 'me' and its sensitive belonging that the spirit receives a surge which, as 'I', compels it to act, notably to think of this 'me'. As it has a more important relation to the physical belonging, the 'me' also relates more to an expanse, that the 'I' tries to shape. In order not to be flooded, submerged, blurred by sensitivity, the 'I' attempts to capture it into forms that it can master.

The relation between the 'I' and the 'me' explains in large part what culture allows and favours but also what it represses and paralyses. For example, there is no doubt that our western tradition attempts to weaken the sensitive 'me' and its relation to another sensitive 'me' with a constructed subjectivity which is determined only by opposition and which behaves in an abstract, technical and meta-physical way. Hence the physical exhaustion that we experience today but also the lack of dynamism of the spirit, of spiritual creativity and the resort to technique and machines which are supposed to compensate for them. Hence also an unbridled activity without real meaning, on the one hand, and a powerless passivity, on the other hand. The content of activity is henceforth lacking as well as the meaning of passivity as a condition of the dynamism, of a sensitive contribution to thought, of a sensitive relation to the other(s) and to the world, but also of an extent which allows us to live in ourselves, inwardly, and to coexist in difference. Even imagination and beauty, which traditionally act as intermediaries between the physical and the meta-physical, seem to have forgotten such a function. This leaves them still more divided than in the past, and raises questions about the present status of the human being.

Forgetting a Conjunctive Potential

What humans have not yet accomplished of their being must also be questioned—for example, a resort to touch which could allow them to unify themselves and to unite with one another. This quality of touch is mainly due to its relation to mucous membranes. It is thanks to them that the mediating function of touch is the most effective in relating to oneself and to the other. Whether it is a matter of our lips or the palms of our hands touching or of letting them touch one another, it is a contact between more or less mucous tissues which contributes to the conjunction in both an active and a passive way, in particular between the outside and the inside of one's own body but also between one's body and another body.

The words on touch, notably of the last philosophers, generally confine themselves to a touch on the outside of the self or of the other, a touch that, consequently, often reduces the body to an object. If the qualities of the object can be perceived in a tactile way, the communion between two bodies or, rather, between two fleshes or two souls, seems to be unknown to these philosophers, and it is even said to be impossible by some of them. They ignore the conjunctive potential of the mucous membranes, which cannot seize an object but can unite living organs or bodies. The mucous membranes join and conjoin—they join me to myself and conjoin me with the other. Hence the name of conjuncts which is given to those who are presupposed to unite with one another in the intimacy of the mucous membranes. Hence also the difficulty for them to remain two because one and the other are both touching and touched in such a way that the difference between them finally vanishes, even though it is that difference which permits the reciprocal touch. For lack of such an experience, touch remains foreign to the intimacy of the self and the union with the other.

Then touch no longer corresponds to a free gesture in comparison with orality and the lack of differentiation from the mother. The lips of the nursling open up to take the breast of the mother, the mucous tissues of its mouth touch-embrace the breast, of which the texture is more mucous than the skin. A tactile communion exists between the infant and the mother, but it serves to feed and not merely to unite with one another.

The space of freedom is not yet opened in order that such a communion should take place, either for the nursling or between it and the mother. Certainly, this space exists from the sexuation of the fetus, but it cannot yet be lived as such. It is assuming sexuate belonging which will make that possible. It is this assuming which will allow us to return to the touch and the touching one another of orality, and to overcome it towards an amorous, reciprocal communion in the intimacy of the mucous.

The insuperable spacing of sexuate difference opens a place in which a tactile communion can occur, a communion which now answers a desire and not a need. Indeed no material or spiritual object could fulfil it, and only desire can aspire to reach a communion thanks to it. This is made possible through each assuming and proposing or offering a nothing of being—nothing if not the search for a union as a longing for a being or being born again to/of a being in which the split body-spirit, nature-freedom no longer exists. The desire for the other is henceforth a desire for a soul as well as for a body, a desire for a body made flesh and which is a dwelling for a soul. And this desire is desire for oneself as much as for the other thanks to freely assuming their difference—a difference which opens the place where a communion can happen thanks to the nothing of its own that each has the generosity of acknowledging and taking on.

There is no doubt that a certain union of the body and the soul already exists between the infant and the mother, but it is still dependent on need—which the amorous desire ought not to be. Furthermore, it is not reciprocal as the desire can be. Thus touch has not the same meaning and does not correspond with the same dynamism—the need to be fed, on the one hand, and the desire for a communion, on the other hand. In other words: moving to abolish a distance in order to survive, or preserving it, notably through a return to the self, in order to keep desire alive. Or even: to clear an external space or to elaborate an internal place. And also: a space already vectorized, inhabited by a more or less reciprocal relationship between two living beings, or no a priori space but the actualization in the present of a potential natural space. In such a space, touch intervenes in all the senses and most basically as touch itself. At least it is so if touch is not subjected to the traditional subjectivity and logic, through which it becomes a tool to seize, more or less peculiar to the human being. In that way it loses its most radical property or function—to unite two different living beings, two different subjectivities—to become an instrument serving a subject who wants to seize everything, transforming everything into objects.

The main property of the hand would then be to know the forms of an object and not to unite two subjects with each other. The hand would be human provided that it obeys a metaphysical logic which favours the creation of form(s), the making and the appearing, to the detriment of its most human aptitude, to ensure a sensitive mediation at a transcendental level. Does touching the hand of the other, especially with the palms touching one another, not mean building a bridge between the sensitive and the transcendental? There is not yet form(s) but a sensitive contact which opens up to communing—that is, a sort of word before any articulate language.

Perhaps, through this gesture, we regain a certain perception of our soul—of an intimate experience which corresponds to it and of the necessity of a wording, which takes care of it, so as to remember and cultivate it by relating to another flesh. Are we not compelled, when we touch the palms of our hands, to touch not only our bodies but also our souls? Would the amorous union not be the limit, always evolving, of a communion between souls? Something which gives access to an internal space where all differences for a moment vanish—the space the most intimate, the one of the deepest in-stasis as well as being also ecstatic, which is experienced only in a communion with the other but remains always transcendent to both.

Such a space does not seem to be known to the philosophers and, for example in the book *Le toucher, Jean-Luc Nancy* (*On Touching : Jean-Luc Nancy*) by Jacques Derrida, it remains always in the future, possibly past but never present, in a sort of abeyance which evokes the one resulting from the dependence on supra sensitive ideals but, henceforth, has no other meaning than being kept on hold. Indeed, there is no communion in that text, even no mediation as that which is most peculiar to touch. The spacing that difference opens, the insuperable spacing between two different living beings is no longer mediated by touch towards their union. They remain remote, sorts of more or less sensitive things for which touch is of use for seizing, knowing, and configuring, filling the space between them with objects and beings, or even with words and a style which closes up it, making any communion impossible.

The reduction of touch, and even touching oneself or one another, to a transitive or reflexive process renders communion impossible too. Instead touch must create a place of self-affection and hetero-affection, or of reciprocal self-affection, that the middle voice can express prior to division into activity and passivity, subject and object, verb and complement. Touching oneself or one another does not presuppose any object but a return to the self, a perception of oneself and of the other, prior to such splits—as a subjective and objective substratum that our logic has neglected, and even forgotten.

Touching One Another as Bodies and Souls

Our logic has also forgotten the importance of our sexuate belonging in the constitution of the 'I' and the 'me' and of their intra-subjective and inter-subjective relations. This is not extraneous to the importance of touching-touching oneself in such a constitution which involves the intervention of our physical belonging not only as a soma but as its most original, dynamic, structuring but also moving part—the most relating to the soul?—which is not foreign to our sexuate belonging and difference and their ability to unify our being, not foreign to our germ cells. Touch can carry out this unification, a touch for which the sensitive can be transcendental, something that our traditional logic—traditionally masculine—does not succeed in thinking. But how could a caress touch my/your body without touching also my/your soul? This seems to be impossible, at least to me as woman. And that, perhaps, explains the meaning that the word 'virginity' could have—the fact that a woman is an indissociable body-soul before she becomes divided, torn up, ravished and perverted by the meta-physical insensitivity of the spirit. Forgetting that the human being is sexuate and, therefore, that a body is never merely somatic and a soul merely spiritual, that the one and the other are animated, from the most intimate of the flesh to the most subtle of the spirit, by the desire for a union which transcends them, the other as different, also acts in this way.

There is a radical aporia in our metaphysical and even onto-theological tradition: on the one hand, because of the ignorance of the mediating quality of touch, notably thanks to its relation to mucous membranes and, on the other hand, because of the loss of the middle voice as a means of expressing self-affection and hetero-affection regardless of reflexiveness and even transitivity, of objects of representation. The communication or communion which takes place thanks to the mediation of touch is on this side or beyond this predicative and basically egalitarian logic—as is, or ought to be, our presence to one another.

This requires us to respect one another as different, and not by comparison. On this condition, touch can affect us in an immediate way as bodies and souls. We can be in communion through it as, otherwise, we can commune through air. Moreover, breath and touch are not without relation, in particular with regard to the soul. However, in order that a communion between us should be possible, we must assume them personally through our own breathing and self-affection. We must also assume our qualitative difference, which makes the immediate perception of touch possible, whereas our subjection to a culture of sameness blurs it. The boundary or the horizon of sameness exiles us from life, deprives us from being affected by touch in an immediate way. Then touch, as solitary or solipsistic, becomes suffering or enjoyment, but it no longer acts as mediation between us, ensuring an immediate and reciprocal experience of touching and being touched between us.

For lack of that, the western man resorts to God, and to the existence of a presumed reciprocal communion between God and him. But how could we decide on the reality of it without first knowing a communion between us as different human beings, between us as men and women? How to speak of an incarnation, and even of a divine incarnation, while ignoring this carnal experience?—an experience which has to do with abandoning ourselves to the passivity of touch, including a mucous touch, more than having confidence in the acting ability of the hand.

Touch is the sense of incarnation, and also of the divine incarnation, something to which Jesus himself bears witness (cf. my 'Epitre aux derniers Chrétiens', dans *Amante Marine*; 'Epistle to the last Christians' in *Marine Lover*).Touch can carry out communion, a communion which can happen without the mediation of an 'object'. The bodies can commune with one another if they have become flesh—grace sometimes acting as mediation. But such mediation can modify the nature of touch.

Obviously, touch does not stop at skin. It unites us more intimately than skin can do, it reaches the mucous membranes and the heart as what unifies us and unites us with one another. And, no more than it can be restricted to skin, can touch, as communion, confine itself to an object. It is capable of unifying without objectalizing. It is from the inside and not only from the outside that the unity comes, touch acting as that which wakes or re-awakes a sap which rises and gives living forms to us. The embrace is the deed of a touching which gives us to ourselves while giving us to one another. It can have some similarities to grace and vice versa as a call or a recall for a presence to ourselves and to the other.

Touch cannot confine itself to words of language either—it is above all syntactic. It is that which, in the present, links together that which has to be said, even concerning the past or the future. And it unites it once and for all as presence. This link, as what concerns touch itself, always occurs once and only once time. To repeat it amounts to reducing, even nullifying its meaning—to giving to it another meaning than the one which is most peculiar to touch. Unlike words of the glossary, the meaning of touch does not increase by repetition or tautology. The same goes with a metalanguage about touch: touch always acts in the present. In a way touch corresponds to a verb, and never to a substantive. It is even a verb which gives rise to other verbs—it moves, it awakens, it fills with wonder, it amazes, it shakes, it opens and so forth—all that without object, transitivity, reflection. Touching has no other 'object' than the mediation that it carries out, always in an indirect way.

Indeed, I never touch you: I touch to you, and you never touch 'I', not even 'me': you touch to 'me'. It is always indirectly, including in an immediate way, that we touch each other as subjects. And a dialectical process is needed between 'I' 'me' and 'myself' before I am able to really sense and approach what could be a communion between us. 'I' represents the more or less conscious and active emergence of what or whom I am. 'Me' refers more to my substantial, material, physical, sensitive and historical existence, to a part not immediately conscious which joins with 'I' in a pronominal verb. Then this 'me' does not correspond to any transitive or reflexive object—'I' and 'me' participate in an indissociable way in an act or a process which involves 'me' in a comprehensive manner. For another subject, a 'you', this 'me' is inaccessible without becoming an explicit 'me', that is, a reality partially dissociable from 'I' but which does necessarily amount to the object of a transitive or reflexive process; this depends on the logic at stake. This 'me'—or this 'you' for the other—is a means of approaching me, of coming up to me, of touching me, a means that I will have to subject to a dialectical process between 'myself' and 'me' in order to return to my comprehensive being and to the 'I' which corresponds to it. And the same goes for 'you'.

Only thanks to such a process, can we each touch the other, and even touch one another, as subjects. Indeed, it is rare that two subjects can touch one another. This entails that they have spiritualized their fleshes so that these fleshes could speak to one another and unite with one another without the mediation of a third in/through which they commune. If it is not the case, the communion between 'I' and 'you' needs to subject the relation between 'I', 'me' and 'myself', on the one hand, and between 'you', you' and 'yourself', on the other hand, as well as the relationship between the two, to a dialectical process. This relationship neither can freeze in a transitive or reflexive object nor be dependent on a secondary mediation on pain of preventing the immediacy of a communion from being possible.

The Transcendental Dimension of Touch

We must thus resort to another sort of dialectics, a sensitive and fleshly one, between 'I' and 'you', which links together our physical and our mental part(s), our body(ies) and our spirit(s). The soul, a soul made of breath and touch, is probably that which can act as an intermediary agent between such entities and allow a dialectical process between them to take place—a soul which remembers a touch other than similar to a haptic knowledge, a seizure by hand, that is, a soul which is still free from any appropriation of/by a metaphysical touch. A soul which is capable of being in communion regardless of the tactile grasping of an object. One could speak of a soul which has faith or confidence without seeing—trusting in, abandoning itself to what or whom touches it, welcoming a sensitive and fleshly truth, concerned less with having than with being. A soul which knows only the grace of touch, of which it will have to value the invigorating or deadly property. A soul which is insensitive to the more or less manipulative logical, linguistic or stylistic approaches intervening in, or even substituting for, a between two allowing us to touch one another. A soul which remains indifferent to any seduction which might remove it from a communion which is a source of life, of breath, of transcendence.

The reciprocity of a touch of/from the other who is different from us by nature cannot happen without respect for mutual transcendence—without innocence with regard to an appropriating knowledge or representation, even an imaginary one. Those who want to be in communion must approach one another in the absence of any knowledge. Only the call for transcending themselves thanks to one another can guide them in the abandon of any reflexivity towards a comprehensive transformation of themselves—a birth or rebirth of their beings.

The action of touch consists in transforming us. Touch always amounts to a verb—not to a substantive or a logos already constituted—and often to a pronominal verb that the middle voice can express before the scission between subject and object, active and passive, verb and substantive. Touching (to) the other is always touching (to) their transcendence, crossing the border or the limit between the body and the spirit, in us and between us. Hence our fear and our withdrawal from such a gesture, which makes us lose the intuition of the transcendental just when we reach it. We enter another world in which transcendence is lived and shared—is communed—here and now between us without being kept on hold by a physical or metaphysical beyond. We touch one another, and we no longer are the same, both lost and brought back to ourselves without any knowledge to which we could cling, not even the resort to a syntax.

There is never a mere contact between living beings, this only exists in relating to objects. Touching the envelope or external limit of a living being spreads, diffuses, radiates towards the inside, the intimate, notably of the mucous membranes. Such a touch is limitless unless it gives up sensitivity to become a supra sensitive knowledge—if it refrains from feeling the other, or if it merely consents to that in order to feel or know oneself. Hence an autistic imaginary develops, more or less narcissistic and powerless, which compensates for the lack of a comprehensive being. This deprives us of a communion with the other, which probably corresponds to that which is most peculiar to a human being. Indeed, is a human body ever our own? Are man and woman not made, woven and mingled with one another as body(ies) and soul(s)? And are they not in search, in their union, of the origin and the end of what is peculiar to them, of which each inherited only one part, of which he or she is in charge and to which they must give life, that they must develop and make blossom without it becoming ever totally their own. It is not only by and for me that I live. And it is no more merely for a community, a people or an ideology. Rather it is with the hope of uniting with what or whom allows me to be, which I do not and will never understand, the other part of humanity. From which I am separated by a distance—which makes the communion between us possible.

Indeed, we never are in communion through a mere touching. Each of us must commune with oneself, with one's irreducible peculiarity, in order for a communion to take place between us—touch being both sensitive and transcendental. It happens in a physical immediacy which is not foreign to the spiritual, even to the idea, that it transcends through the advent of another world, another meaning, another truth. Perhaps it is what the evangelical message announces or senses when it asserts that to love one another amounts to loving God.

In other words, the sharing of sensitivity, the reciprocity in touching one another, which cannot happen without love and which has to do with love, would be of the same nature as the love of the transcendental, the love of God. But what could be a reciprocal touch between God and us? Could it be a question of grace? There is no doubt that grace touches us, and in a manner which is also physical. But how could we touch God? Could incarnation aim at overcoming such an aporia? Touch has then a privileged function to create a link. Is the latter truly reciprocal? If Jesus touches and let himself be touched, does a mutual touch really exist between the other and him? Or does it remain at least a temporal split between the one who touches and the one who is touched, and a necessary resort to the intervention of a third to make their linkage possible? For example, a woman touches Jesus, who feels that he is touched and cures her in the name of her faith. Is there a communion between them or a communion of both in a faith which exceeds one and the other.

How to establish a connection between such a touch and the one which takes place, or at least can take place, in the amorous embrace, in which touch is sometimes such that the one and the other perceive it/them in an indistinct way. This renders their link indissoluble without the one and the other being themselves dissolved. Indeed, the matter is no longer of reaching proximity but of experiencing it until one is immersed in communing—which does not last but exists, at least can exist, and is as much in-stasis as ec-stasis, or is perhaps an in-stasis of our being that we only live in the ecstasy of the embrace. This experience asks us to reconsider the metaphysical foundation of our tradition, with all the pairs of opposites which prevent having access to a communion, of bodies and souls, between two different living beings. It is thus a question of building anew our existence from an unrecognized, neglected, and forgotten background or *upokeimenon*. All is to be improved, and above all to start to live anew from a union which, even as indissoluble, is the place of a limitlessness inscribed in the flesh as a transcendental potential, which remains unrevealed without the desire for/of the other.

18

The Communion Between Beings

The 'Here' of a Communion Between Different Living Beings

Touch between living beings is without boundaries given the porosity of skin and the permeability of membranes. If touch makes us perceive limits, it also provides us with an experience of the infinite—an infinite which can be good or bad according to whether the experience is solipsistic or it corresponds to a sharing, to a communion opening up to an endless exchange. For touch, reciprocity is crucial and its lack brings about repetitions, tautologies saturations or suspensions which cause irritation, exasperation, pain or distress and even the fading of touch as such. The same goes with every discourse, especially metalinguistic, which thwarts the action of touch, which tells by itself. Touch is even syntactic by itself, linking subject and predicate in a unity of being, which revives or restores its potential of life, of energy and its irradiation through the flesh and the soul. Hence the birth or rebirth of intimate movements which gives rise to a becoming still to come—to a physical and spiritual growth which makes blossom and flower what has been perceived of touch in each and between the ones who shared it.

L. Irigaray, *The Mediation of Touch*, https://doi.org/10.1007/978-3-031-37413-5_18

The communion with the other as ontologically other—basically the sexually different other—happens after the assumption of a negative relative to an insuperable natural difference. I am not the other and it is that which allows me to commune with this other. Certainly, at first, a lack of differentiation from the other exists. The infant still perceives itself thanks to and through the body of its mother—it even perceives the body of the other before its own. It is the body of the other which enables it to begin to perceive its own body, and to unify in a 'here' its different perceptions. The relation of its own body is not completely distinguishable from the relation to the body of the other. Far away from its mother, the infant feels so lost that it sometimes lets itself die. Hence its need to seize something, a part of her or a part of itself, to continue to feel itself.

The same does not go for the amorous embrace, at least it ought to happen differently. It is then necessary for each to assume his/her singularity, to gather himself or herself together, in order that the bodies should unite with each other thanks to their specific fleshly belonging. Sharing the same 'here' is no longer due to a lack of differentiation but to a communion between fleshes.

Whatever our difference, or instead thanks to it, it also happens that the other can give or give back to me a 'here' not by a palpating hand but by arms which hug me, by a warmth diffusing in me or by an union of breaths, of souls. My 'here' can thus be given or given again by the other thanks to the respect for its otherness. Perhaps, there is then a recall of my origin, an origin which does not correspond to a reflection, an introspection, a palpation or a caress of skin between a subject and a quasi-object or a quasi-thing, but to a conjunction between chromosomes and between subjects who more or less knowingly take on their subjectivity and their difference—which nevertheless exists and which could not be replaced with any possession of an object. The desire for the other does not long for having but for being—thus for no appropriation, apart from appropriating to oneself.

Desire expresses an intention, it even underlies every intentionality, the end of which is more concerned with being than with having. And if syntax is used to establish a link in order to fulfill the will to be of a subject, the subject-object pattern is not the most adequate. Anyway it cannot supplant the subject-subject relation as is too often the case in our tradition. In the same way, seeing cannot prevail over feeling, the former having more to do with having and the latter with being, at least the being of a subject. For this, the main function of touch is not of seizing but of ensuring a connection, a mediation which can lead to a communion—a gesture or a state which goes beyond a parataxis, and even beyond the 'with' of a common action, belief or perception. Then there is no longer the intersubjective relation which prevails, and it is an object more than touch which supplies mediation, as it is generally the case at the level of the community. In the amorous relation, the objectivity of subjectivity, guaranteed by the respect for the, at first natural, difference between the subjects, suffices to create another syntax, another logic and another dialectics in which the subject-subject relation is determinant.

Failing to take account of the intersubjective stage, and of the difference between natural beings which permits it, discourse, particularly the discourse concerning touch, becomes a sort of self-production and linguistic inflation, a capitalizing use of language as a productive tool to the detriment of a meaning expressing and ensuring the relation—in which touch is the fundamental mediation and must determine the syntactic connection. This is then established through a dialectics acting on the sensitive and fleshly level, and which is not only regulated by co-existing or co-belonging in community, for which touch, as a present mode of relating to oneself and to the other, must be itself mediated by ideals, moral requirements, political rights and duties and so forth to supply a mediating function. Such a mediation has too exclusively been imagined as likely to form a society of the between men for whom, as their writings bear witness, touch has more to do with the seizure of an 'object', be it even mental or metaphysical, than with a sensitive and fleshly communion between different subjects.

Hence the fact that—for example for Merleau-Ponty—touching and being touched cannot really coincide with a touch at the bodily level (cf. *Le visible et l'invisible*, Annexe, Notes de travail, mai 1960 (toucher-se toucher etc.), pp. 307–8; *The visible and the invisible, Appendix,* Working notes, May 1960 (to touch-to touch oneself)). And yet it suffices to put one's hands together or one's lips to touch one another for that to happen. And such touching cannot merely amount to a reflective or a specular process because that which is touching or touched does not correspond to a plane surface or a mirror but to living tissues which make an inter-permeability of physical but also psychical fluxes possible as sensitive impressions which do not stop at any image, repetition, reproduction, reflection. The permeability of living tissues allows me to re-touch myself in the double reciprocity of a touching-being touched but also self-affection to be exceeded by the other. Indeed, the latter can give access to an intimacy that I cannot reach only by myself. From that results a diffi-cult return to the 'myself' and the difficulty, even the impossibility, of distinguishing respective feelings—a phenomenon that masculine phi-losophers apparently do not know. Would they be irremediably con-demned to solipsism, to narcissism and to infinite debates about what is the concern of the body or of more or less prosthetic techniques, begin-ning with the one of their insuperable constitution by the logos?

And yet touch and touching one another between living bodies—that women experience in various ways—differs from that between a living being and a prosthesis as the permeability of a membrane differs from a space or a gap between objects or things which touch one another. Certainly theoreticians exist who reduce the male sex, and why not also the fetus, to a prosthesis. Hence the dread of castration, and the interpre-tation of the desire to be pregnant as a phallic substitute. This does not take account of the fact that the permeability of membranes makes com-munion or hetero-affection possible thanks to a reciprocity between touching and being touched. And that corresponds to a more plenary, and not specifically Christian, experience of our 'to be' than that of a more or less intense pleasure which is accompanied by a release of energy.

Then the matter is not of adapting our bodies to one another, like a technical assemblage, but of them harmonizing with one another. This way of relating is more appropriate to living organisms and means that their touching themselves or touching one another can neither amount to nor coincide with touching things of the world (cf. Merleau-Ponty, *Le visible et l'invisible, Annexe, mai 1959* (*Visible et invisible, deuxième par-tie*), pp. 239–40; *The Visible and the Invisible, Appendix, May 1959* (visi-ble and invisible, second part)). Obviously reciprocity between touching and being touched cannot exist between my body and things of the world.

The fact of remaining in an economy of sameness—same objects or things, same actions, but also same space and time—renders the reciprocal touching which can exist between living beings impossible, a touching which is prior or posterior to any more or less conscious reflection and does not take place in a logic of sameness. It is the other as other, and already 'me' as different from 'I', which allow this sort of touch to take place—or at least to take place regardless of any metaphysical perspective which reduces it to the seizure of an object or a thing by resorting to a technical skill, be it only that of a language which is articulated according to a certain logic. Then touch and touching one another is deprived of its own meaning—a present experience of life that resorting to inanimate being and technique thwarts. One could also say that such an intervention opposes the internalization which characterizes touch. It prevents touch from reaching the intimate, notably of the soul, without confining itself to an alleged surface of the skin, or from being bypassed by a mental process extraneous to sensitive feelings. Another living being, especially a human who naturally differs from me, is likely to provoke such an affect in an experience which is both natural and spiritual if I recognize this other as different. The sensitive immediacy is then transformed into a transcendental experience while keeping a sensitive and immediate quality. The nature of that which touches has acquired a materiality or a consistency such that the body and the soul can be touched by it—which opens to a real life experience which differs from those which are allowed by our tradition.

Intersubjectivity Needs Distance

Does Husserl introduce us to such an experience? Recently rereading the part of *Ideen II : Recherches phénoménologiques pour la constitution,* I have been surprised by some comments on the connection between touch and the soul, on the unity that intentionality can procure from a 'hyletic' background, of which it would be a more subtle and spiritual shaping (*Ideen II, Recherches phénoménologiques pour la constitution,* Deuxième section, Chapitre III, § 39 pp. 216–17; *Ideas,* Second book, *Studies in the Phenomenology of Constitution,* Second section, Chapter III, § 39; reference to the German edition (153)), by allusions to psychosomatic questions, by the affirmation that our body would be originally constituted by touch, that is, by words which seemed to share my way of conceiving of touch.

Nevertheless, are not these words contradicted by others? For example, the fact that one's body could be perceived as a thing, even as an object, and the subject as a sort of counterpart of the object, or the fact that sensitive impressions would be without expanse, and that intentionality could not be physical, or even the allusion to the surface of the hand and so forth (op.cit., § 40, p. 219; op.cit., § 40; (154)). Could a living body really be perceived as a thing or an object? Is not desire a form of intentionality which has its source in the body and is capable of uniting our body with our psyche? Does a physical perception by touch not exist other than that by the hand? Is it valid to affirm that touch is merely immediate as physical? Do mediations not exist in the body itself given the complexity of its composition and the mediating quality of some tissues or membranes? Why cite certain sensations and not others? Is it because they are less localizable? Indeed, where can I localize what the other awakens in me? And joy? And does what I experience not open a space and even a space-time in me? Where does Husserl situate it?

The main question is: How does Husserl conceive of subjectivity? If he apparently lends to it a greater importance than most philosophers, does he not imagine it as a participation in a same world, and even in a same subjectivity, more than what allows us to communicate or to commune with respect for mutual differences? Could that, once more, result from a split between body and spirit and a domination of the latter over the former to the detriment of life itself? And if the body can be viewed by Husserl as a 'thing' or an 'object', could the same apply for the spirit? In order to broach what intersubjectivity means, is it not necessary to consider the objectivity of our global being, both the physical and psychical objectivity of a 'me' but also of a subject? For lack of that, does not intersubjectivity run the risk of being reduced to a relation between numerous individuals which is determined by an intentionality and an energy which is external, and even extraneous to them? Is their consensus not settled a priori in such a case? Does a real 'inter' still exist between them?

Besides, to what does the reality of such subjects correspond? Is not the relation to another subject of a different nature from the common perception of a real presumed to be objective because of the agreement on its subject of many people who are similar? Can the subject and the inter-subjective relation be reduced to the perception of a real external to them, on the one hand, and, on the other hand, is the objectivity of the real dependent on a consensus between subjects, what is more who are alike, or on the effective existence of a specific and autonomous being regardless of such evaluation?

Moreover, after having stressed the importance of the soul in our sensitive impressions and experiences, Husserl seems to ignore it at the level of intersubjectivity. The soul, as sensitivity itself, appears to be subjected to a logical construction from which life as such is absent. If Husserl, through his glossary, lets us glimpse a change in the philosophical horizon, does he not finally remain captive to a vicious circle in which the objectivity and the subjectivity indefinitely determine one another without the perspective that another subjectivity could supply to such circularity? For example, when he describes the objective criteria defining a space of orientation, he confines himself, regarding a possible 'there', to elements which privilege the outside: left and right, high and low, before and behind, as if inside and outside, interiority and exteriority, intimacy and superficiality would not represent important objective dimensions of a subjective space of orientation, individual but above all intersubjective (Husserl, op.cit., Première section Chapitre III, § f-g, pp. 125–27; op.cit., § f-g; (83–85)). What then happens with the latter? Are we still living beings in it apart from the ability to move in order to have different angles of views regarding things and, in this way, can objectively assess them with a shareable 'idealization' in mind? A robot could do that as well as and perhaps better than us. And does what would remain to us as 'intropathy' potential in the service of an absolute objective not finally abolish the 'inter' space-time of a relation between us?

Do the geometrical and physical criteria, too little differentiated in my opinion, that Husserl proposes to define and institute a common objectivity not forget the objectivity of life and of its irreducible sensitive dimension—the one who questions them being suspected of suffering from pathological solipsism? These criteria also neglect to take account of the qualitative properties inherent to life itself, properties which are not situated at the surface of beings so that they should afterwards be penetrated. This would presuppose that they do not belong to living beings themselves and are crucial for their entering into relation, but they are attributed by a subject.

According to Husserl, intersubjectivity would be possible only by reducing any relativity in the approach to things or objects, but also to space and time. Intersubjectivity would exist through the establishment of an absolute objectivity, thanks to an ideal perception shared by the subjects. Is that not a quite radical way of closing again the traditional metaphysical horizon, in particular with regard to the different ways of living a sensitive experience, in spite of the approach to themes that metaphysics generally left outside its field? What then remains living in subjectivity, intersubjectivity, and even in nature itself? Is not everything inexorably defined as interrelations and energy movements or modalities inside a system which is constructed for 'normal subjects with a similar sensitivity' who have decided on the meaning of 'nature' as 'intersubjective reality'? (op.cit., p. 129; op.cit.; (86–7)). What could then be said about my perception of a living being—an oak, a birth, a naturally different human—which does not require such a consensus to correspond to a real existence? Do I need an 'intersubjective identification' to perceive its objectivity? Am I trusting an appearance when I perceive it by myself, an appearance of which only a social consensus could define the real objectivity?

Is it not instead a social construction which prevents me from perceiving the physical reality of living beings? Does it not deprive me of a current sensitive link with them? Does this link really need a previous common 'comprehension' to be objectively perceived—by my body but also by my soul? And do these sensitive perception and lived experience not represent a truth different from that of 'our passive life, our life of animal in the world' (op.cit., § h, p. 132; op.cit., § h; (89–90)), a truth that I must acknowledge and respect, especially when relating to living beings? Such a truth does not lack some schematization—for example, that of our sexuation, and even that of our point of view—which contributes to unifying our being and structuring our physical and psychical relationships with other living beings. These cannot be reduced to things or objects through which we could deal with others thanks to ideal form(s) or statuses, instituted by a social consensus. A living being provides itself with its own forms, and these evolve and cannot be fixed once and for all. It is by respecting it as irreducible to any preliminary definition that we can perceive the objective reality of a living being.

Logos as Prosthesis

Touch also would need an *epoche* in order that its meaning could be perceived. Jacques Derrida writes 'I cannot fully experience touch and the meaning of touch' (*Le toucher, Jean-Luc Nancy, X,* Tangente IV, p. 257; *On Touching: Jean-Luc Nancy, in Tangent IV*). Does not such an interruption deprive touch of its meaning? Indeed, the mediation through feeling that touch carries out no longer occurs because of an intervention, in fact solipsistic, of consciousness. Such a way of thinking about touch, while abolishing its most specific property, perhaps explains the important role that repetition plays in the work of masculine philosophers. They attempt to appropriate the mediating function of touch by means of a logos presumed to be capable of expressing or saying life. Are they then not implementing a widespread *epoche* regarding life itself?

If the mediating role of touch allows different living beings to enter into presence, does not the reduction of touch to a phenomenon of/for consciousness prevent its taking place by sending back each, or one of them, to a specific and extraneous to life way of being? This would be necessitated by the necessary distance, and a 'differance' making the contact possible, Derrida argues (idem). Is it not to forget the distance which exists between living beings—a distance that touch can clear either though a physical contact or through an affect, through a communion which is experienced regardless of any reflection of consciousness, and which feeds it before it can appropriate it? Perhaps one can then suggest that it is a communion of souls or of fleshes which is more often than not unrecognized by the metaphysical tradition of the West. Is not this, consequently, getting bogged down in the facticity of a being there—even of a *Dasein*—or kept on hold outside a living and fleshly intentionality and transcendence of which touch is in search in its attempt to reach the other as other? A touch which is capable of weaving between the immediacy of a physical contact and a communion of souls, between two sorts of immediacies and two sorts of transcendences that our traditional—masculine?—philosophy has neglected.

Our past metaphysics left this unthought touch to religion—to the fall of sin or to the longing for a union with God. It lacked a thought of touch, of a touching one another, and a phenomenology irreducible to one subjectivity and an appearing favouring one sensitivity, visible or haptic. It lacked a phenomenology of the advent of a being which can neither belong to itself nor be dependent on one sense, which happens at another level of our constitution, as an archi-ipseity or archi-existence which is still unthought. Could it be possible to speak on this subject of a prosthesis which takes place outside the domain of consciousness and is not free of borrowing from the other, from the environment and from the world?

In what our becoming incarnate originates remains unknown. The philosophers, the culture in general, resort to various techniques and prostheses to fill that in, beginning with logos itself. This distorts both the experience of natural immediacy and the relation to transcendence. This also renders the philosophers irresponsible for the constitution of subjectivity, which leaves outside the domain of consciousness a part of its origin. How could it thus be possible to decide on what subjectivity is, on the consistency of the ego and on the nature of otherness? Is not an ontological difference buried in an ontical archi-facticity? Hence the resort to many sorts of strategies to emerge from the latter by introducing a distance, an interval, a difference and so forth. And yet all that originally exists between living beings and also, although differently, between skin and mucous tissues, and even between the various strata of the skin, which are more or less epidermic, conjunctive, permeable, because the skin does not amount to a mere surface.

My hand cannot know the other, and no more myself, through a simple contact of the skin, not even by palpating the whole body. Touch is never merely epidermic and superficial. The fact that philosophers attempt to reduce it to that can probably be explained by their desire to seize without being affected, and their will to be active without either giving way or having access to the knowledge that a passive welcoming of the other, and already oneself, can bring. They ignore the power and the truth of such a sensitive experience and know only that of a touch which remains only prosthetic. This 'pro' can have diverse meanings: 'before' but also 'towards', and even 'in front of', and it covers, without our knowing, and before any hypothesis regarding it, the field of a constitution, including temporal, of being.

Could it be possible to suggest that this touch imperceptibly transforms a natural body into flesh? This possibility escapes the consciousness of the western man and exiles him from his natural belonging as well as from his fleshly subjectivity or intersubjectivity. Then, is he not torn between body and spirit, and short in soul and flesh? Could the latter be another way to refer to a sharing of souls? Or to embraces in which breaths and touches commune with one another in a fullness of meaning unknown to understanding, and that all the stylistic and rhetorical contortions cannot reach, trying to substitute, with a lot of fuss, for a fullness of meaning which cannot be mastered by the logos. Hence the necessity of a silence thanks to which each gives to the other a place to be from a sensitive transcendence that they grant to one another—a call or a recall of being the ones who they are in a pause during which longing and inspiration calm down by trusting or confiding to test their truth and regaining their real dynamism. This requires no sacrifice but to assume a negative that allows us to return to our self, a living self, in charge of the becoming of our being.

In order to hear such a call or recall, we must practice an *epoche* as regards the whole logos and its regulation by understanding. The way in which it separates us from one another, depriving us of communing through touch, is showed by Husserl in an exemplary fashion. According to him, it is by an analogy, established by intropathy, at a subjective level, and by reduction to an object of 'nature', which can be substituted for any other because it is ideally constituted, that intersubjectivity can exist. Each 'man', as well as the relation between 'men', result from physical-mathematical elaborations which are extraneous to a living being and the relation between living beings. Husserl's analyses and proposals concerning the constitution of 'man' and of 'intersubjectivity' are like a programme of science fiction amounting to a world turned into robots. A common subjectivity reigns over it, with intersubjective relations which are objectively determinable and in which sensitivity—if one can still speak of sensitivity—would be the same for all 'men'.

Origin of the Dynamism

It remains to define what drives the whole in which the souls are supposed to follow the bodies, 'to move together with it, to make one with
it' (Husserl, *Ideen II,* Deuxième section, Chapitre IV, § 46, p. 236; *Ideas,*
Second Book, Studies in the Phenomenology of Constitution, Second
Section, Chapter IV, § 46; (167–68)). Will it be a 'central organ' capable
of animating the 'somato-objective' as well as the psyche? If nature itself
is already a sort of interpersonal cultural product (op.cit., Troisième section, Chapitre I, § 52–3, p. 289; op.cit. Third Section, Chapter I, § 52–3;
(289–90)) perhaps this is conceivable. But what could be the cause of the
dynamism of the entire system? Where is it situated in the absence of life,
on the one hand, and of God, on the other hand? Are we not staying in a
closed universe the mechanism of which is self-regulated by a play of
mimicry and intropathy between 'things' of nature and consciousnesses?
Are we not in a world in which our making is motivated by what we
heard spoken and what we know about behaviours of the other? (op.cit.,
Chapitre II, § 56, c, p. 310; op.cit., Chapter II, § 56, c; (225)). Could we
call that 'reciprocal actions', as Husserl does? Beyond the fact that these
actions are motivated by a mimicry from a seeing and hearing, the energy
origin of which poses a problem, what place remains for a reciprocal
motivation and touch such as those which can exist in desire and love? Is
my want for your hand other than wanting to appropriate the potential
of this hand, wanting to appropriate your 'I can' whereas instead I long
to touch your hand to feel the warmth of a living being and share life
with it/you?

This requires me to be able to distinguish your effective presence from
your imaginary presence and you as well as me not to have lost our experience of this primary quality of the presence of the living: their warmth.
Certainly, my approach to you then remains natural, but with the meaning that I give to this word and not as 'a cultural interpersonal production' but as a presence which lives by itself and is animated by a dynamism
and a will of its own. Could it be because I am still naturally living that
most, in particular philosophers, do not acknowledge my presence and
do not succeed in touching me intimately either? My presence would

escape their logic and the physico-mathematical evaluations which alone can still motivate them.

And do they not take it into their head to 'press hard' a place of my skin, even to resort to 'blows', notably in order to observe my intimate reactions (p. 233). A thing which succeeds in irritating, wounding and even annihilating me without moving me. Indeed, what moves me is rather that which awakens and communes with my mucous and conjunctive tissues at the deepest level—which perhaps corresponds with what Hegel calls the 'fabric', including that of the soul. Do these tissues not lead to producing a serum which could have some properties thanks to some chorion, this wrapping membrane of the embryo which, through its permeability and its contact with the uterine mucous, has a nourishing role for the fetus? Such a contribution of touch is really little known and acknowledged, including in its questioning the discourses on touch which are limited to the surface of the skin, and even endeavour to perceive the inside of the body 'through' its surface. This relation to touch has also little to do with a reflexive, analogical, mimetic and even comprehensive attitude as a means of achieving intersubjectivity.

In the horizon of our traditional metaphysics, touch remains at a somatic level: it reaches, it fingers, it seizes, it presses, it apprehends getting around and so forth. But it does not know the communion between fleshes thanks to the transcendence of otherness. The philosophers seem to ignore that, before they can seize, their hands have received their form from a union, at the most intimate level, between two living beings—that before we become somas, we have been the fruit of a union between two germ cells. They underestimate the generative potential of germ cells, which does not lie in the seed of one alone but in its sexuate nature which is effective at the level of life only by uniting with the germ cells of a naturally different other. For lack of such a conjunction, this potential remains infertile except—and could this not be what happens with the philosophers and their thinking?—as a soma which is short in differentiation and to which mind incessantly must give form(s), or as an inanimate body already frozen in death.

In the beginning, the soul still animated this formless body, already or still cadaverous, a soul or dynamic principle made of breath and touch, both remembering and waiting for a union which gives or gives again strength to it, notably to return to itself in order to inhabit and animate the body which corresponds with it—in a way which serves it as a sort of shaping, and to which it must return to enliven it and so be able to unite with the other again. This can occur not by giving oneself up and becoming the other, but through a union with this other thanks to the permeability of physical membranes, the fluidity of breath and the mediation of touch itself. The soul must subsist as life and sensitivity appropriate to the body that it suits—a soul cannot be transplanted in another body. Souls can be in communion with an other but cannot be substituted for one another—this would amount to transforming them into mechanisms which drive robots.

Indubitably, the soul can be more or less naturally living or produced. As products of morality or of belonging to the same community or ideology, souls can be the same and substitute for one another. Are they still the dynamic principle, made of breath and touch, which animates the body? Can I live thanks to allegiance to a morality, to an ideology or to belonging to a people? Supposing that that can help me to survive during a moment, can this really be called living? And how then to call that which unites me with the other—an other who is, henceforth, the same as me, defined by a constructed essence unable to commune through touch. Instead, the body animated by a soul can do this and it receives life from such a communion if it is faithful to its natural origin—born of a conjunction between two different germ cells and not of the dissemination of one and the same seed, which is unable to beget without being united with an other. Does the innocence of the child and the movements of the infant seeking, thanks to the warmth and the more or less mucous nature of the skin, for the breast capable of sustaining its life, not remember that? The spirit deprives us from this touch when it pretends to dominate the soul and to prevent it from finding, in the communion with another soul, what it needs to be resourced, to be reborn and thereby discover a word faithful to life.

Indeed, the soul still keeps a physical belonging, which is not arbitrary with regard to nature. It is woven by breath and both a physical and a spiritual touch, which cannot be determined by an already existing meaning defined within the horizon of our traditional metaphysics. Its meaning belongs to another logic, in which sensitive immediacy still has a sense. In it, the body is not reduced to the soma but it exists as flesh, a flesh made of a tactile relation to oneself, to the other and to the world, in a sort of immanence of life which can be communed, and even be given in part to the other—for example, in pregnancy but also in motherhood. Of course this relates to the soul and cannot last without it—a soul which has more to do with silence than with a linguistic mastery. A thing which could explain why a woman can live in a sensible way without resorting to the logos—she silently tells herself. It could also be understood in this way why her limits have little rapport with surfaces but aim at safeguarding the soul and a self-affection extraneous to narcissism. The latter, as the reflexiveness of which it is a mode, already makes a distinction between subject and object and amounts to an appropriating transitivity regarding the self and the other in which soul cannot subsist—the middle voice or pronominal form can better preserve its existence. The soul, as the natural life, can neither be objectivized nor possessed, and it exists before any split due to a technical intervention. There is no possible transcendence with regard to the soul, except though the communion with another soul.

The Touching of Our Lips

If philosophy can speak about the soul—as, for example, Aristotle does—it cannot tell the soul, at least in the current state of the logos. Sometimes, the touching of our lips tells more, if touch communes in this way with the breath of the other, with their life. This requires us, first, to acknowledge their otherness, which can give access to an immediacy otherwise out of reach. I can commune with your life only if I do not make it mine while I touch you at the most intimate level—which allows us to long for an absolute without limits. If touching your skin can, in part and mistakenly, give to me the impression of touching a limit, the same does not go with your/our lips. Their porosity and their humidity blur every limit. Besides, in them, the outside and the inside pass from the one to the other without limits—in us and between us.

The lips are the threshold of the passage to the limitless, the place where immanence and transcendence combine and even merge together—in me, in you and between us. Hence a sort of dazzling effect that no glance can master. In a way, it is blindly that we can commune with each other. But, from such blindness, a light, unknown to metaphysics, arises, the meaning of which is more essential regarding our being. We begin to live it when bringing our hands together. Then we are already beyond every limit and we must learn to move in the impenetrable mystery of our embraces—where it is a question of our body and our soul, but also of the human destiny. This destiny is still unrecognized, still to be achieved, and we can accomplish it only together and in the reciprocity of a communion of beings—a reciprocity which gives nothing if not life and being, which are different for each. From such a communion we will be reborn and, so, find or find again a measure which fits another relation to the terrestrial, another look and even another way of touching to find our bearings. Indeed, we have given up any measure to abandon ourselves and be in communion with one another, a communion in reciprocity which only the touch of our mucous tissues can grant us, overflowing us with the limitless of a union.

We can grant each other such a communion without something having to disappear in order for it to become spiritual—as is the case with the host, according to Hegel—because it happens without the mediation of any object. When our lips touch, we offer ourselves in communion to one another. Nothing must be abolished if both of us have consented to that. Nothing can be substituted for that either—no object, no discourse, no other life. And the linguistic overstatement, notably the one which resorts to the glossary and the semantics concerning touch, must fade away to let communion be. To subordinate the latter to the conception of a child also deprives us, but also the child, of a source of meaning for our humanity.

Such a communion requires us to still have a soul. The heart alone cannot manage to do that; it is too active to give itself up to a communion. It can help to reach it, but it is too somatic and muscular to commune. It is also too neuter and able to be substituted for or exchanged with to commune with the other as other. The heart must remain an assistant and a servant of the soul, a soul which is never indifferent to the body that it animates, and is always singular. The spirit cannot commune either—it lacks the property of mucous tissues which can interpenetrate.

Besides, it intends to be universal, like the logos from which it takes form(s), whereas communion exists only between particular individuals without resorting to any object. It is particularity that, in it, becomes the place and the support of the existence of universality, a different one. And if we cannot commune through the peculiarity which is defined by the logos and corresponds to a constructed essence, we can commune through that which corresponds to a natural essence.

In order that souls could commune with one another, it is necessary that they still exist at a natural level as breath and touch, a touch which does not stop at a surface and does not hang on to a metaphysical knowledge but gives itself up to the limitlessness of permeability. The soul is not a solid with an invariable consistency; it can have a certain density, but this must remain variable and porous—to light, to warmth, to touch, a touch either immediately physical or mediated by affect. Accepting the variable and permeable nature of the soul presupposes that we give up the active, overbearing and appropriating way of knowing privileged in our culture. The soul is not for all that without knowledge, but this is the fruit of a certain passivity which does not merely oppose activity. Such a passivity entails a wait, a welcome, a receptivity and acceptance of the transformation which notably results from uniting with the other. This union, or communion, is never exclusively physical; it is mediated by the respect for the transcendence of the other while remaining physical through breath, touch and flesh. Nevertheless, the soul must remain faithful to the body which is its own and it must remain virgin or become virgin again and again. It can do that by retouching the epidermic but also mucous borders of the body—a gesture which is capable of restoring its diaphanous consistency and its permeability with regard to a touch external and extraneous to it.

The soul must remain virgin, but it must also will to subsist, to grow, to become—something that I seek in uniting with the other as a food both vital and spiritual. The touch of the soul is not without intentionality, but what it wants has often been kept on hold by supra sensitive values, which deprived it of its nature which aspires after a transcendental which remains sensitive. The soul has also been subjected to the spirit, which appropriates it, feeds on it without reciprocity or communion, at least traditionally and until now. Intermediary between the body and the spirit, the soul has been underestimated by the latter, although it had acted as substratum—*upokeimenon*—for its constitution. Nevertheless, it has not acknowledged its existence and its knowledge, in particular the 'knowing of the self' of the soul of which Aristotle still speaks. But does he not misjudge tactile properties of the soul when he considers that it is 'impassive'? Is touch ever impassive? And is a living body ever insensitive? Unless Aristotle alludes to a self-restraint, a safeguard of the receptive quality of sensitivity, one could say to the preservation of a natural inno-cence—thus not to the permeability to/of touch, but to the maintenance of its purity freshness, virginity, and a gathering of the soul with itself. Indeed those who are touching or touched must be able to gather them-selves together and to experience themselves as different to commune with one another—a thing about which Aristotle cares little in his epoch. For lack of that, communion can happen only though a third, and it loses the physical quality of a union between souls, each of them belonging to a particular body. Touch has then another status. And it can no longer contribute to knowing oneself, but to knowing the other and the world either. It becomes a sort of feeling, what is more a common feeling, a belief or an ideology which gathers the subjects otherwise than through a sensitive present experience, in them and between them.

Hence each needs to remember life by the existence of a natural or symbolic object to be shared—an apple or a host. And yet to be in com-munion with one another creates a link, both natural and spiritual, more absolute than any object could do. But one must be able to assume the negative of an insurmountable difference to give up being satisfied with a defined absolute and to run the risk of living in an open space without the shelter of a closed horizon, world or system. This requires one does not long for the absolute as for a form at which one stops but as the efflo-rescence of a living matter to be developed again and again, in oneself and with the other. This corresponds to an absolute without limits, fruit of the communion between two living beings assuming the negative of their partiality, their limitation to one and only one identity, which transcends itself by acknowledging a mutual difference from the other.

Such a communion well answers the desire for a return to and the assumption of the origin of our being. We were not born of nothing but of the union between two different human beings, an origin from which our subjectivity cannot cut itself off if it intends to respect the real, the objectivity of the real, beginning with the real that it is. Our subjectivity is a transcendence which takes root in nature or it is only a theoretical fiction. Acknowledging this truth is assuming a finiteness other than that of death, the one of our natural identity itself, a finiteness in part surmountable by a sexuate desire. Belonging to a genus allows us to transcend our mortal condition by a union, also spiritual, between different germ cells.

Touch can contribute towards that. First the touch that desire entails as mediation between the one who touches and the one who is touched. Perhaps this could correspond to the language of the soul, of a living soul. A soul of which the original and final word is to be in communion—a verb which can articulate two others: 'to touch' and 'to be' in a process never definitively accomplished, staying always between the present of an 'I am' and 'you are' and an infinitive which, paradoxically, corresponds to an absolute in becoming which cannot settle on any substantive.

The infinite after which two desires aspire, becomes still more immeasurable because of their union, a union never definitely fulfilled on condition that it is not fixed on any word or any view which could externalize our touching one another, remove it from its intimacy, its communion—which would amount to a sort of meta-physical rape by the spirit. This in that way keeps on hold the intimate of the flesh in an outside which prevents it from becoming internalized by a touching—of the lips, the hands, the eyelids but also of/with the other. The conjoined self-affection and hetero-affection of a communion is then rendered impossible by a third which interrupts touching oneself or one another, bodies and souls. Such a union happens without the subject's knowing, at least that of the incorporeal subject that our tradition favoured. In the horizon of the latter 'I' cannot touch itself. 'I' can attempt to be itself and, in this process, a still physical and sensitive 'me' intervenes, which cannot be objectified nor reflected, through which 'I' affects itself and which is both distinct and inseparable from it. This can be expressed by the middle voice or a pronominal verb when the pronoun does not amount to a reflexive, even if it apparently resorts to the same grammatical form (for example, in French: je m'étonne, je me promène, je m'émeus, forms which are generally expressed by the passive in English or the resort to 'self').

When I self-affect, the 'me' or 'myself' is not an object and cannot be an other, it is indissociable from 'I' as an integral part of its reality which is irreducible to an 'object', which cannot be captured in/by a 'me' or an other and is not convertible into a theme. This 'me' is that to which or to whom I give existence or I destroy, I grant life and becoming or subject to forms, even to substances, which are foreign to it, and thus annihilate it. Between 'I' and 'me' a reciprocal link and dynamism must exist, touch acting as a mediation thanks to which they cannot dominate one another. This happens as soon as activity prevails over passivity and the middle voice becomes a reflexive. Then the spirit appropriates, or imagines to appropriate, the sensitivity. 'I' no longer gives existence to 'me'. The dwelling of being, even of 'to be', that self-affection and hetero-affection of the middle voice can preserve then vanishes. Could one say that the soul vanishes?

19

Elements of a Culture of Touch

The Crypt of Our 'To Be'

Why has philosophy, in particular phenomenology, so little considered what our sexuate belonging lets appear? Could it be because this appearing cannot be disclosed, at least in part? Or because this disclosure is the fact of nature itself and we do not perceive it because it is not dependent on our mastery? Because it is not the result of a production on our part although we contribute to it, but in a way which remains, at least partially, foreign to us. Indeed, what happens is not immediately nor merely a from us and for us because a from and for the other has a share in our own unveiling—which corresponds to a phenomenology almost ignored by our tradition. Nevertheless, all that takes place, but in a manner which escapes an active and visible operation. If it was not the case, the disclosure might fix and freeze what nature itself discloses, beginning with the ones who we are.

The disclosure of/by nature itself gets complicated, for us as humans, by the intervention of consciousness. We cannot only appear as natural beings, and in order for such appearing to be possible, we must remain hidden. This already exists in the vegetal world—the process of its growing as such remains hidden, and we do not know if a vegetal consciousness exists which intervenes in the becoming visible of this growing. What is incumbent on us, as humans, is to take account of our own consciousness without, for all that, giving up our natural belonging and becoming. Touch is probably that which allows us to ensure the junction between these two dimensions of ourselves.

Thanks to self-affection—that I sometimes call re-touch—I give or give back to myself my natural being. I perceive it; in a way, I am conscious of it. And yet, what I perceive and of which I am conscious is not visible, including to me. I am present to me while being hidden from myself. And that, perhaps, constitutes the most irreducible core of my being, the one which allows me to pursue my natural becoming while appearing to the other. What the other sees does not reach the place, or the presence to me, through which I preserve my own self.

Yet thanks to my appearing to the other, this can unveil to me something of my being that I cannot perceive only by myself. The other can reveal that to me with words which are likely to give me back to myself or to exile me from myself. The other can also reveal that to me through gestures, in particular through a touch which sends me back to the invisible closeness to me that self-affection provides. But the closeness that the other brings to me cannot substitute for or make me forgetful of the closeness with which I can provide myself.

In such a proximity to me, a withdrawing within myself, a hiding myself and disappearing into myself, takes place that I need in order to be able to appear outwardly. Opening up to the other, appearing to the other, somehow or other, is not possible without a return to me to shelter myself, hiding myself in order to pursue becoming in faithfulness to my 'to be'. This withdrawal, this reserve, allows me to continue to grow—phuein—and to appear to the other while dwelling in myself. I disappear within myself in order not to disappear into an external production which leads to an evanescence which ends in an emptiness of being.

To preserve myself from this emptiness, I must resist the risk of being merely produced by the other and the risk of appearing without a sufficient withdrawal so that this appearing could correspond to an efflorescence of my being which does not paralyze the continuation of my becoming. My relation to 'to be' must remain a verb which never fixes on a substantive. To be must mean a perpetual becoming which escapes any stasis in a being or a state presumed to be appropriate once and for all.

There is no doubt that meeting the other runs the risk of one or the other becoming 'a being' for the other or being reduced to 'a being' by the other, that is to say, to a 'to be' which could be unveiled. Desire, which aspires after transcendence, compels us to preserve our 'to be' in meeting the other. The perpetuation of desire asks us to dwell in ourselves while opening to the other—to shelter and save ourselves in a secrecy which permits a desirable appearing.

That for which we long is probably the most hidden, which the appearing must reveal while maintaining it invisible. What appears must express the hidden while also keeping it hidden. Is it not such a will that our desire tries to find in the other as other in order to pursue our becoming? That of which our desire is in search does not appear to it, it senses it as the need of a living being to transcend itself to continue to be—*aeizoein* necessitates *aeiphuein*. This requires the participation of the other but also the maintenance of the difference between the two. Each must withdraw within itself and remain hidden there so that the desire for and of the other should live on. However, it also matters that withdrawing into oneself does not amount to sinking into oneself. The withdrawal must keep going and contribute to an appearing and an opening up to the other, as these appearing and opening must contribute to preserving and enriching the withdrawal. Desire cannot live on without a dialectical process between these two movements, or states, which themselves require the existence of desire—as a both active and meditative fire being careful to maintain a dynamism which does not harm or destroy life but rather cultivates it as human.

Such a cultivation cannot happen, first and exclusively, at the community level. Fire is then transformed into a sort of abstract and anonymous energy, extrapolated from a relation to and between living bodies. Even light, that fire provides when it arises from flesh, becomes a quite cold and barely differentiated light, which spreads from an outside more than it arises from an inner intimacy and its sharing.

In order that fire, and the illumination that it can bring, could support a becoming faithful to our natural belonging, it must arise from a relation of desire between two different living beings, the blossoming of which can radiate and spread over the community. But this propagation cannot result from a submission to the inspection of judgment or from that of reason in accordance with it. The manner in which it diffuses and has influence on the environment is more physical, tactile, fleshly. It touches, penetrates and impregnates regardless of mastery and appropriation by the spirit. It is not, for all that, a question of empathy, irrationality or collective passion but, rather, of the revelation of what a human being could be by experiencing and cultivating a relationship between two different singularities. Undoubtedly, what happens contributes to their own becoming, but it also escapes from them, extends beyond them and happens to the world, leading to an imperceptible evolution of humanity itself and of its environment.

What occurs in the desire between two different humans may be transformed into intentionality, that is into a more mental form of energy. But, the latter, then, loses a part of its sensitive and fleshly immediacy, and of that through which it allows life itself to be experienced, to develop and to appear—which takes place thanks to simultaneous relations of various parts and properties of our body. For example, in self-affection, the more fleshly, blood and conjunctive mucous tissues are united with the skin which, while being physical, is more related to the brain and the nervous cells.

The human being could and ought to live simultaneously some aspects of the embodiment and the expression of being which, for other living beings, for example vegetal beings, are lived at different moments. Appearing of life in the flower corresponds to a material appearing of the plant, as Michel Henry underlies, but this appearing amounts to only a short while of the development of its being. This cannot be embodied in only one appearing, which varies according to the evolution of the flower. The human being can appear in the present as the one who it is more than a vegetal being—for example it can flower, through its skin, a mucous belonging which remains invisible. This asks it to harmonize various parts of its being. Self-affection is a gesture, a frame, which allows it to do that. It requires hetero-affection in order to be fully perceived— communing with oneself is more fully experienced thanks to communing with the other. However, it also runs the risk of being wasted, notably by privileging either mucous tissues or the skin. The amorous embrace ought to give access to a beyond of the skin to reach a communion in the mucous intimacy and, then, allow each to withdraw within its own skin.

There is not, for all that, a transcendental body which allows the empirical body to exist, as Michel Henry maintains (cf. *Perspectives sur la phénoménologie matérielle*, p. 70 and sq.). The sensitivity of my body becomes transcendental through its intentional relation with the other as other. A transcendental dimension is already effective in my desire for this other, not as a mere transcendence of 'the immanence of Life' (idem) but as the presence and the mediation of the other in the appearing and existence of life itself. Such a phenomenology of life cannot concern the visible alone; it must take account of the invisible interiority or intimacy of the flesh, and not only thanks to my power and that of 'Life' in me but because of the presence of another life in myself and in my life.

In order that this fact be acknowledged and inscribed in a long-lasting way, a modality of thought must intervene. Self-affection and hetero-affection do not occur independently of consciousness, but this must serve sensitivity instead of living on it in order to emerge from it by repressing it. Consequently, consciousness becomes mediation and not mastery and domination. It permits the truth of sensitivity to express itself without pretending to subject it. This will make the incarnation and the communication or communion—which does not mean the fusion—between two fleshes possible.

'Life' does not become incarnate only by itself, except, perhaps, at the level of needs. Desire needs the mediation of consciousness. Incarnation is neither the matter of 'Life' itself nor the mere result of the intervention of the 'Verb' in a body. It requires listening to sensitivity by a consciousness which grants it a human status—in oneself and for oneself, in oneself and for the other, the two being ever easily distinguished from one another.

The Asymmetry Needed by the Living

The effects of asymmetry have something to do with a negative entropy. Unlike nihilism, which could result from a saturation short in order, negative entropy means a release of energy and a possible reorganization of a whole by the modification, notably the fluidity, of the outlines or edges of its elements and of its/their horizon(s). So it is the porousness of our/ the being which allows us to commune with another being. Hence our/ the being does not need to disintegrate to evolve, it can do that through its relationship with a different being, which reopens the world in which it was enclosed, including by its mirror image. Then it is not the invisible as such which can reopen the horizon of a world, rather it is what is perceived other than by sight—by touch.

Touch can compensate for the void or the gap which results from a lack of symmetry. But this touch takes us into a completely different economy, that of flesh. In such an economy, it is no longer mastery which inspires and governs logic but the possibility and fecundity of being in contact, with oneself and with the other, of self-affection and hetero-affection, without any of them abolishing the other. For example, the mirror image does that, but also the subjection to one another, notably by the distribution of the active and the passive between one another.

As living beings, we must 'combine equilibrium and growth' (cf. Alexandre Koyré, *La dissymétrie*, p. 30). This constrains us to alternate between self-affection and hetero-affection, which can correspond to an alternation between symmetry and asymmetry. Asymmetry, as giving up a previous symmetry, gives rise to a property (op.cit., p. 36), which necessitates a return to symmetry to become integrated into a transformation.

Our evolution requires a dialectical process between symmetry and asymmetry. Only 'the lower organisms (…) possess the most numerous and the most complex symmetries. Rising in the scale of beings seems to consist in being freed from them' (op. cit., p. 39). For human beings 'the last bastion, the last residue of symmetry lies in the fact that the left half of the body appears to be the mirror image of the right half, and vice versa' but this 'is no longer the result of a rotation but of a reflection' (idem). Such a symmetry is nevertheless called into question by the non-equivalence of the lower limbs to the cerebral hemispheres. Whatever its origin, this bears witness to an evolution by ' progressive elimination of symmetry' (op. cit., p. 50).

According to Pasteur, asymmetry or dissymmetry would be a symptom of the existence of life (op. cit., p. 55)—it would testify to the passage from the inanimate to the animate. Pasteur also claims that ' the system of the whole world is asymmetric' (op.cit., p. 56), and to find a comple-ment to it would amount to opposing the action of life. If the 'mysterious influence to which is due the dissymmetry of natural beings changed sense or direction (…) perhaps a new world would emerge' (op.cit., p. 57). What could it be if the change, instead of being only between right and left would also involve between outside and inside? And between man and woman and their face-to-face?

However that may be, symmetry appears 'as the inertia which slows the production of phenomena, whereas dissymmetry triggers them' (op. cit. p. 59). Nevertheless, symmetry is generally favoured because it has more to do with the visible and it fascinates sight, redoubling its ten-dency to give form, to surround, to encircle.

Symmetry is also priviledged because it seems to be a synonym of order and it exempts us from a constant effort to surmount gravity by a trans-formation of energy. Immobilized, even paralyzed, the latter can express itself as connotations. All our logical dichotomies can result from a lack of conscious effort to surmount gravity. Indeed they always include a valuable pole, which relates to the higher and to the more forward, and an underprivileged pole, which relates to the lower and the more behind—the good and the bad being one of the most paradigmatic examples. Supposedly objective and neutral, these dichotomies are deeply influ-enced by an unrecognized relation to gravity that the more or less effica-cious intervention of a symmetry endeavours to temper, to remedy.

Because of its standing upright, the human being must constantly fight against gravity. Whatever this permanent effort, it is also the one who most frees itself from symmetry, even if it continues being fascinated by it. There is no doubt that its aspiring after spirituality, as taking over from a natural growth, plays a part in its necessary opposition to sym-metry. However, the human being has not sufficiently considered the role that desire, in particular the desire for the other which differs by nature, can play to compensate for the terrestrial attraction—that is, the resort to levitation as a means to surmount gravity. Proofs of such a phenomenon exist but, strangely, the human being fails to cultivate it, at least con-sciously. And yet the 'little death' that man endures after having expanded, instead of increasing, his energy in sexual intercourse is a symptom of his falling back into a gravity of cadaverous nature that desire allowed him to overcome. One could also interpret all the equality, similarity, parity attempts to reduce the difference between the sexes as a difficulty or a refusal of evolving—as a manner of clinging to a physical gravity and its metaphysical counterbalance instead of becoming more and more light through the transformation of flesh thanks to desire.

As attraction to the other who is naturally different, desire is the best agent of an asymmetry serving life. This must not be understood as the production of a new life, with its physical gravity, but as the ceaseless passage from a bodily survival to a spiritualized and/or deified flesh, including by a language which is appropriate and is not subjected to connotations more or less amounting to dichotomies.

Our culture constantly forgets the importance of difference, of disparity, of dissymmetry, notably at a physical level, for the becoming and the evolution of a living being. So sexual, and more fundamentally sexuate, difference ought to mean, for human beings, a possibility of surmounting the need of symmetry, whereas it too often becomes a sort of 'hypnosis of symmetry' by the transformation of the attraction due to difference into a fascination for a supposedly same. Hence the saturation and paralysis of energy, which must be expended to not become harmful instead of giving rise to an additional development and creativity, in particular of life and love.

It is true that society, and culture in general, favours symmetry as an organizing principle. 'A symmetry of equilibrium and exchange (…) governs the entire social interplays' (op.cit., p. 84).The sociocultural order imposes a certain stability on a becoming which, as for it, necessitates asymmetry to take place. The natural belonging and the asymmetry, notably incarnated by sexuate difference, that it requires to evolve has been locked in the private house in order not to perturb the established order. Only some creators and thinkers are allowed to do that, but their infringement is generally tolerated with a delay which makes its assimilation possible without a weakening of the order. What they bring that is new through their infringement can thus correspond to a development of the natural order thanks to a dissymmetry which compels it to evolve, unless, on the contrary, they provoke a removal from this natural order by a return to a more symmetric order, which could end in a chaos because of an excess of entropy.

The public order as well as the order called private have not yet discovered the resource that difference can represent to overcome the symmetry-asymmetry dilemma. Sexual, or better sexuate, difference has a really particular role to play as a possible link between nature and culture. This role has been unrecognized, and the importance of this difference to grant access to another logic has been weakened by dividing the real into dichotomies. This could appear as a way of mastering difference, but favouring a term in relation to the other refutes such a hypothesis. The apparent symmetry between the positive and the negative is then called into question as well as the unity that the two poles are supposedly forming. In fact, the logical dichotomies keep a part of the real on hold and paralyze thinking.

Moreover, the opposition at work in dichotomies transforms the logical operation of the negative into connotations. Thus it is never acknowledged and assumed, and the real is subjected to an affective economy which is not envisioned as such. It serves a logic of sameness and oneness which misjudges the importance of difference to elaborate a culture respectful of the real.

Our tradition has not truly taken account of the becoming of an attraction for the different being or between different beings, an attraction which does not aim at reducing all to the same. And yet does this possibility not represent that which could express the human as a living being? Does it not correspond to a way of pursuing a human development beyond a mere naturalness? Does it not mean serving life instead of subjecting it?

Vilma Fritsch (in *La gauche et la droite; Left and Right in Science and Life*), like some other authors, considers that lingering on duality amounts to a refusal to pass to the multiple. It is true that she little envisions, and she even negates, the existence of psychosomatic correlations (op.cit., p. 164; op.cit.). And yet, if the touching one another of our lips, of our eyelids, but also of the palms of our hands or the soles of our feet is likely to produce a state of self-affection, is that not due to the fact that a bodily symmetry-asymmetry takes place? This provokes a unquestionable psychic affect: a harmony with oneself which does not exclude an opening up to the other and to the world. Unlike a mirror image, which artificially shuts off a living being in a representation, self-affection gives a unity to us as living without closing us to the communication or communion with an other living being. It allows us to escape the alternative between yes and no, between the positive and the negative. Such a property of our flesh seems to be ignored by Vilma Fritsch as well as the reality of the difference between the sexes and their irreducible duality. What happens when sexuate difference is acknowledged in its both theoretical and practical effectiveness? Can a logic founded on dichotomies still exist?

Work of Art as a Projection of Touch

Commenting on art, Maldiney describes many attitudes which could apply to relations to/with the other. However, this constrains him to ascribe to the work of art qualities that meeting the other as other naturally involves—for example, the incompleteness of forms. A co-presence of/with the other implies that we do not live in a closed world, that we constantly reopen the horizon—not only the personal horizon but also the historical and cultural horizon in which we are situated—in order to perceive the presence of the other in a sensitive way. My 'other half' then no longer belongs to 'the mist, the night, the void height or the great castle' (see Maldiney, 'Comprendre' in *Regard Parole Espace*, p. 81). Assuming the negative of a difference makes possible our perceiving ourselves as a whole while being capable of sensitive perceptions regarding what is outside of us. The assumption of a negative in regard to a human being who is different from us by nature allows us to perceive every other living being, and also the world, as sensitive beings. It grants us the capability to unite the passivity of feeling with the activity of acknowledging and reciprocating difference. This reverses the priority of our being in the world over our being with the other. Through such co-presence we have access to another way of being present at/in the world according to which each is approached as a autonomous living being.

About the painter Tal Coat, Maldiney writes ' we are at/in the world before things exist for us' (op.cit., p. 54). One could also say that we are with the other even before being at/in the world, not only from our birth but because of our origin. And if we so much need to make the world thematic, is it not because we fail to cultivate the relation to/with the other as that which permits us to acquire an identity of our own instead of trying to reach this individuation by objectivizing beings or things of the world? And yet if the individuation that we gain thanks to the relation to/with the other, in particular the other different from us by nature, can remain living, the same does not go with the one that we acquire through relating to the world and things. Whatever the sensitive potential that this relation can preserve, it does not entail reciprocity of touch and communion between two human beings. Indeed, these unify each of us while uniting each with the other in a way that exceeds sensory perceptions and concerns our whole flesh, which becomes unified thanks to self-affection and remains open to the other thanks to hetero-affection. In that way, we can be ourselves without being separated from each other.

It is not art which must and can send us back to ourselves but the other whose flesh can perceive ours, of which it can return a structure to us if the other takes on his or her human being—that is, the autonomy of their own existence and the necessity for a relationship with the other as other to fulfil their becoming. This asks that the origin of each, its particularity and singularity, but also its desire be respected, and that the other remains a real after which we aspire without being able to anticipate in what it consists, at least in a thematic way. It is that which happens, as a grace which feeds our existence and helps us to incarnate our being. The other is that which touches us without our being able to seize, appropriate or assimilate him or her. And if this other can nourish us, it is thanks to an irreducible difference. The other is and must remain unknowable and inaccessible in order to truly affect and sustain us without annihilating us.

We cannot unite with one another by abolishing our respective forms but by making them meaningful for the other. In order to commune with the other, we must appear to this other with forms, but forms the borders or limits of which are permeable and do not enclose us in ourselves. These forms must not define us in a definitive way, like the outline of fabricated things, but surround the medium which corresponds to our flesh, a medium which can evolve, notably though its sharing. These forms tell and let themselves be told by the energy which animates them—which cannot occur in the relation with a thing unless it acts as a mediation between the other and us.

This could happen when it is a question of a work of art. Nevertheless, the latter cannot carry out, in the present, the reciprocal touch or communion which can occur between two different humans. It cannot implement the crossroads between 'to bes', and not only between beings, which can exist between two humans—a crossroads which can generate not only being but also 'to be', notably through the meeting between two modes of being in the world, which questions the way of conceiving of 'to be' itself, unveiling what our conception of 'to be', then put into perspective, entailed being.

The meeting between two human beings, in particular as naturally different, challenges the way of conceiving of the human being as neuter, which prevents us from perceiving its real nature. Hence the insistence on denying its possible existence because it questions the foundation of our world. One could say that the meeting between two naturally different humans acts as a negative ontology which can lead us to intuit what or whom a human being could be. For lack of such an experience, various strategies are necessitated to approach what a human being could be from a sociocultural foundation and background. However, if this way of reaching individuation makes a certain coexistence possible, it does not permit a co-presence—the presence of each to itself, to the other and to the world remains impossible. Co-presence is a mode of participation in being which does not require resorting to Being but corresponds to an attempt to share being, the 'to be' that each succeeded in incarnating in the name of what would be a human being.

Such an attempt can be more imaginary or more real. The respect for the difference of the other and for the state that the relationship causes are subjective and objective criteria which can assess its nature. In art, otherness is above all the one that the artist projects and/or has introjected. But the negative that the respect for the otherness of the other presupposes means that my relation to this other does not confine itself to operations which are only mine. And if the value of a work of art is appraised according to its unveiling of an expression of the real, the worth of a relationship with the other cannot be limited to such unveiling but is also reliant on the generation of a 'to be' and/or a being still to come. The effectiveness of a relation to/with the other cannot be limited to an appearing, even minimally thematic. It exceeds the aims, including artistic, of our philosophical tradition, which is little concerned with the production of the invisible and the elusive, that is, with a production of our being that we cannot seize but only let be as a transcendence that we have ourselves almost unknowingly generated, and which cannot amount to the most beautiful landscape, as Maldiney would say following Ervin Straus.

Some artists, especially some painters, have sometimes transformed woman's body into a sort of landscape. Did they not introduce it in this way into a metaphysical horizon by projection and introjection without caring about reaching a co-presence, a co-knowledge and a co-generation in difference? It is likely that the artist intended to pay the most beautiful tribute he could to the woman. He even agreed to stay outside of the landscape to let her carry out it. Unless he tried to possess her otherwise by appropriating her/the most intimate touch, which is destined to be shared and to give rise to another 'landscape', which is henceforth inner and produced by human beings through a mucous touching one another, that Cézanne could imagine to be composed of colours before any other shaping. Then other forms could appear from tactile perceptions lived as diaphanous but that desire—perhaps awakened germ cells?—lights up with colours, sending us back to a chromosomic genesis where space is generated as a result of a meeting in difference.

Such a space is not imaginary, at least not originally, if it arises from a reciprocal touch between two humans beings who are naturally different. It is close to the one which exists in oriental art, notably in the byzantine mosaics that Maldiney endeavours to approach (notably in his text 'L'équivoque de l'image dans la peinture' in *Regard Parole Espace*, pp. 275–322). Indeed, this art expresses an emanation from nature, including that which is presumed to be divine, more than a human creation, which is privileged in Western art. The natural production then turns into an imaginary world for lack of a communion between the subjects or their want to appropriate it with a personal work in mind, denying the duality of its origin and of that of the environment and the medium that it generates. A personal imaginary nullifies in this way the transcendence of the meeting with the other and converts touch, which made it possible, into an operation of sight. But if the action of touch includes many potentialities, the same does not go with sight because the image reduces them.

Why to give up the richness of the potential of touch for the benefit of its nullification by image? Does that not amount to transforming the ontological and transcendental potential of touch into a more ontical seizure, and thereby make the co-presence between two ontologically different subjects impossible? Indeed, these can be present each to itself and to each other only through the mediation of touch. A culture favouring sight has not taken that into account, resorting to the invisibility of a God or that of supra sensitive essences to save the transcendental status of being. But what being is then at stake, whereas touch could preserve its belonging to the real? This has been depreciated for the benefit of representation, thus of a relation to the other from which this is absent or in which the other is reduced or subjected to an 'object'.

The presence of a living being ought, first, to refer to itself, which shields it from our usual way of using sight. Ultimately, we cannot see the other, his or her presence deprives us of perceiving them visually. It corresponds to a real, and even to a sort of medium, which touches us but we cannot identify as an image or a representation external to them. Presence and image or representation are in a way antagonistic to each other. The world of the former does not belong to the world of the latter. Approaching the other is possible only by immersing oneself in a fleshly universe in which it is no longer eyes which individualize but touch.

What art could express such a presence, which is in any way representable? Could it do more than introducing us to an experience of intimacy from which we are constantly removed? This intimacy does not amount to a falling back into a mere naturalness. Rather it gives access to a sharing of flesh which culture is still lacking and which has to be invented each time by and between those who desire and love one another. Its working remains intimate, and it is expressed outwardly only indirectly and independently of a usual perspective. It is an experience of our 'to be' and not the production or the appearing of a phenomenon. But this expression does not bear witness to a pre-existing essence but to the fact that our 'to be' reaches an existence still free from defined form(s). Desire can be a path which conduces to such a genesis. It can lead us to an embrace which has to do with how to be because it asks us to return to the most original presence of our being—to the elusive proximity from which it arises. Hölderlin reserves such proximity for a god, a god who is perceived or seized with difficulty because it is too close.

We sometimes experience this elusive, in a way this inaccessible approach to proximity in the reciprocity of an amorous embrace—in a letting go, or be, in which the absolute of proximity can take place without our being able to seize, name or represent it. How can it express itself? It is through that which it produces in us, between us and in the world. What is revealed by such an absolute proximity is an energy as much as absolute. We experience, barely knowingly, a pure power, the mode of actualization of which is not easy to perceive. It is a matter of incarnating 'to be' itself, leading it to exist as perfectly as we could. But we do not know much about this 'to be'.

Such autophany is a manifestation which remains sensitive while transcending an/our immersion in being(s), including the one(s) we are. This way of expressing itself of 'to be' arouses amazement because it always corresponds to a surprise in the monotonous organization of the world. It animates it, transfigures it by a presence which provides it with a new space-time which transcends the merely natural space-time. This space-time is neither flat nor linear but enveloping and tangible like a fleshly medium which in a way wraps us. It preserves us from an expansion and a withdrawal without limits, acting as a sensitive surrounding which touches us, keeps our forms living, forms which do not enclose us in a fixed identity or definition without for all that leaving us amorphous. These forms speak to us and speak to the other without being mere signs coded by culture. They ensure a passage between our skin, the part of us which most resembles a surface, and the most intimate of the mucous tissues. They radiate our desire and bring it back, enriched by another desire, to the most intimate of us, from which it will transform us. These forms procure a horizon to our world even before we can assume it. They invite us to inhabit it in a truly living way—with the other. They mean themselves and mean us before we give meaning to them. They show that our being in the world is always already a how to be—our *was-sein* a *so-sein*—and not a mere emergence of Nature or Being to which a meaning must be attributed. Present at the surface of us, these forms tell something of the mystery of our being through a both centrifugal and centripetal movement in which our presence must take its basis.

The Incarnation of the Divine

Incarnation is the presence of the transcendent in the sensitive, of the spiritual in the physical. This presence has more to do with touch than with sight. Incarnation is a self-disclosure of the transcendent thanks to touch. This revelation cannot happen without a tactile dimension. For lack of it, experiencing transparency to oneself and transparency to the other could not exist. Hence every truth becomes dependent on supra sensitive values, and we cannot become solely by ourselves but only thanks to a Truth, a Truth to which we can become more or less appropriate, to which we can become more or less equivalent without ever being able to be it.

Incarnation allows us to be by a re-touching ourselves and touching one another—even a touching the Other. The ban on touching means a prohibition on entering into a world where truth is in us and perceptible to us thanks to a self-affection which is free from its being under the hold of being(s) or Being. Self-affection must be 'virgin', also spiritually, to perceive flesh as both sensitive and a place where transcendence expresses itself. Seeing oneself needs a mediation—a mirror reflection, an image or verbal comments—that touch does not need. Touch as such is mediation, in the relation to oneself but also to the other, and even to the Other.

For sight, the non-being is nothing or nothingness, whereas for touch the non-being can favour the discovery of our/the being and its fertilization by another being. Finiteness is, for touch, a condition to experience and live the infinite. The non-being does not represent a danger for touch unlike appearance, that is, an appearing through which the mediation of touch cannot take place because it has lost its living quality. To exist and to communicate between them, the subjects, then, must resort to a truth external to them and not to their own truth, in particular their sensitive truth. Indeed, the latter is more revealed by touch than by sight and, in intersubjectivity, the mediation of touch is more decisive than that of sight.

The Greek culture paid little attention to touch because the subject was not yet considered as such. Consequently, this will become afterwards dependent on sight more than on touch. Hence the resort to the supra sensitive, to the meta-physical, as to the guarantor of truth, whereas our truth as living beings is first physical and relational. For lack of perceiving that and taking that into account we are compelled to make truth dependent on logical rules which have a more or less arbitrary connection with our own truth. Our traditional logic does not really correspond with our truth as living beings. It subjects us to a representation of ourselves, to that through which we can objectify ourselves with images and language. And this removes us from ourselves as living beings, and even as subjects. Indeed, as subjects we are always more than what we can objectify of ourselves.

As living, we are also constantly evolving. Our first requirement is, or ought to be, to grow, to evolve, to pursue a development which arises from us but also from interactions between us and the world or the other(s), the most efficient of them being the interaction between us and other human beings who differ from us by nature. Indeed, it is the one which makes us most evolve physically and meta-physically, which leads us to transform a merely material body into a spiritual flesh. The interaction between two spiritualized fleshes can produce a sort of miracle or grace—a non-predictable event which remains a mystery but of which we cannot deny the effect on ourselves. This sort of miracle or grace is necessary for our becoming, and opposing that which allows it to happen interrupts our evolution and makes us fall back into a mere materiality—into death.

Redemption could mean the re-establishment of the link between our body and our soul or our spirit. It reopens the way towards spiritualizing our body and our soul or spirit becoming fleshly. Viewing our nature as subjected to a blind determination amounts to a kind of nullification of our possible redemption by the reduction of our natural belonging to an inert materiality irrelevant to its development. In fact, the only determinism which is imposed on us by our nature is to grow, to develop in accordance with what or whom we are. A spiritual evolution cannot contravene such a requirement. This asks us to understand how our nature can develop as human. From this stand point a religion of incarnation, seen as a possible deification of our natural belonging, represents an important contribution. By reconciling body and spirit, incarnation of the divine in human being opens up the way to a human evolution, especially by the existence of a sensitive transcendence.

The main issue is not to overcome evil—as Hegel stresses it speaking of Kant—but to change towards developing the spiritual which exists in our physical belonging itself. This calls for that which is described as religious serving the fulfilment of human beings and not being substituted for it, induced by theoretical and practical requirements which thwart its evolution—for example, those which are the concern of supra sensitive ideals extraneous to our natural belonging but also to the functioning of our reason.

Indeed, in that case, belief and reason determine one another in a sort of closed circle. And yet, belief can mean the faith in possible access to a beyond of what already exists—thus an opening in comparison with reason, which cannot be the judge of what exceeds it, as Kant seems to want. Then religion is interpreted as a sort of complement of reason on which this could pass judgment and not as a beyond of an already existing being, which is inconceivable by reason. Such a beyond could contribute to a becoming which is not dependent on supra sensitive ideals but amounts to a progressive incarnation of humanity, in us and in history.

Touch is a crucial moment in the relation to transcendence. It has not been thought of as such although certain religions, among them Christianity, give examples of touching as that which can transform the materiality of the living. For instance, Jesus cures by touching or being touched—a recovery which is more often than not attributed to God as his Father, whereas it could be interpreted as the power of a touch which emanates from a spiritualized and loving body.

Touching is a gesture through which either we sink into the facticity of a body or we transcend it especially by our desire for the other. Touching is also the gesture at which the amorous attraction aims. Touching the other and being touched by the other is what supports the transcendental aspiration of desire or disappoints it by a falling back into the mere materiality of a body and at the level of needs. It is the moment—Hölderlin perhaps would say the caesura—when the divine faces human beings.

Touching is a mediation towards a becoming divine or the gesture through which the transcendence withdraws and is projected onto a beyond unattainable by sensitivity. By touch, the divine comes to/in us or turns away from us. It is the key or syncopating moment of our relation to the divine.

This event, or advent, first takes place between two beings, and two beings which are different. It is there that the god—and even God—becomes incarnate in/among us or withdraws from us. At the community level, the divine is expressed at least in part by images and representations, but 'God' no longer can manifest himself as it is possible between two different living beings. This partial incarnation of God through a people is perhaps why this people runs the risk of being sacrificed. God no longer can be immolated as the spirit of the Father incarnate in the Son. He is no longer begotten as spirit made flesh and flesh becoming spirit between two different living beings. He is incarnate and diffuses in a people and cannot be abolished without abolishing this people.

In fact, the divine can exist only by becoming. It can never be appropriated or possessed by anyone, but must constantly be generated by a desire to fulfill oneself, notably towards and by communing with a different being. A people is divine only if it saves the transcendence which ensures the becoming of human beings from being objectified. Hence the orthopaedic, but never absolute nature of the law, which cannot imprison the spirit in/by categories, but instead must preserve it from settling in any being, even in the supreme Being.

Could it be possible to suggest that the forgetting of 'to be', including in its presumed universality, does not only presuppose the forgetting of the air as a condition of life but also the forgetting of touch as the basic mediation between living beings, which respects them and allows them to be revealed in their own 'to be'? In that case to be cannot amount to any being or Being, but it corresponds to the incarnation of life and of relationships between living beings. To be cannot amount to the ground or the representation of the accomplishment of a finality or an absolute, notably as Supreme Being. To be means the constant incarnation of a life of our own by breathing air and touching one another as living beings.

Touch provides limits and limitlessness. It wraps and oversteps borders. It seems to stop at a surface but acts in depth. Touch grounds what is experienced as groundless. As mediation, touch brings us back to us, but this mediation in a way is immediate and cannot be perceived. Under every this or that, touch acts as mediation between living beings—a mediation that no existing logic could express because it isolates more than it mediates. As Heidegger writes, words are sorts of 'cover' which keep by dividing. They intend to ensure the unity of each element of the world but without their communing between them as living beings remaining possible.

The operation of touch does not aim at reaching the greatest or the highest, the 'supreme', but the most original, the most innocent, the one who lets mediation act without other determination than itself. This, perhaps, corresponds to the positive meaning of the word 'virgin', that is, to a virginity which is not merely physical and depriving but is also spiritual and can be gained through a negative ontology and self-logic. Only that or the one who would be able to keep themselves 'pure', which does not signify 'abstract' but capable of simply uniting, could act as mediation.

At the physical level, touch can work as a link, notably thanks to the permeability of membranes. This link can be more or less intimate according to the nature and the situation of the conjunctive tissues. Woman seems to be more able to ensure such mediation given her greatest penetrability. However, this role of mediating has little been explicitly acknowledged by culture, except sometimes by religion. Mary would be the 'Mediatrix' between the human and the divine. She would be that to such an extent that she would be 'the mother of God', and she would have brought into the world a divine 'Son'. More generally, Mary would be mediating at a spiritual level as the one who is able to ensure a link between humanity and divinity.

In reality, the role of every woman is to carry out a mediation, but how to articulate the mediation between humans and the mediation between divinity and humans? Does Hegel solve the question by considering woman to be the one who ensures the mediation as regards the family unit and is the guardian of the religious dimension—man being the guardian of the civil community thanks to a more strictly human spiritual order? Does Hegel not separate in this way woman and man especially by two different conceptions of the relation to the divine? What then occurs to amorous relations? Is it not the place where the two ways of relating to the divine must join to one another? The place where 'God' becomes human and the human being becomes divine? The place where to be becomes incarnate and flesh becomes 'to be'? Is not the amorous union the place where the mediation becomes flesh in order to become divine in a dialectical process always in progress—a sort of crucible in which grace can be conceived, kept and shared?

A Potential Revealed Thanks to Difference

Acknowledging the difference of the other, we create a space in which our tactile potential can be revealed. The latter is generally repressed, covered or invested in sociocultural structures or contents which, under the pretext of educating us, reduce or nullify it. So we are dispossessed of a means of perceiving ourselves, the other(s) and the world, and of gathering ourselves together in intimacy with ourselves, an operation which necessitates the intervention of a touch freed from references other than to itself.

Desire for an other different from us by nature is likely to give back to us such a virginity in feeling if we listen to them as to an appeal for a human becoming. This other can act at the level of sensation as a revelation or re-appropriation of the truth regarding feeling. If the difference corresponding with a natural ontology is respected, the other can represent a path towards an epiphany of feeling. I cannot perceive the other as different, but I can perceive this other through a sensation. The truth of the existence of the other can be revealed to me by feeling. It is a means to approach him or her. However, in order that it could really approach the other as other, touch must be subjected to a dialectical process which does not abolish it as such but, on the contrary, restores to it its own nature.

In reality, touch can be a means of being aware less fallible than the mental understanding when it is a question of another living being. This requires touch to be freed from any structure and content other than the sensitive perception of the other in the present, a state that we do not reach easily but which makes a co-experience and co-rebirth with the other possible. It is the aptitude for perceiving the impact and the meaning of what touches us and for answering it with a suitable touching which can open this path. It cannot be opened without our putting on hold every representation or will of our own, and even every hypothesis. It is probably thanks to the existence of a soul that we dare to venture into it—thanks to an inner place made of breath and touch which allows us to blindly make our way without losing ourselves. Only the rhythm of our breathing and the tactile mediation remain as guides in the absence of any knowing, including an imaginary knowing.

Such a soul permits us to stay centered in ourselves, to continue to live, move and even take sustenance without being exiled from ourselves. It safeguards a specific link between our body and our spirit which makes it possible for us to respect the other as other without subjecting him or her to ourselves or being subjected to them. The soul acts as a heart which is peculiar to us and enables us to enter into relation with another heart without losing the perception of ourselves. It is even the existence of a different heart which helps us to perceive and distinguish our respective qualities without any resort to a means extraneous to our tactile sensitivity. Touch as such is capable of perceiving the qualitative difference between two living beings—it experiences it before any assessment by the understanding. It creates a state which corresponds to a mode of apprehending which is more revealing than any abstract grasping.

This requires an environment in which touch can express itself—for example, that of the soul. The difference between two bodies and two souls appropriate to them brings us back to a sensitive perception of ourselves of which a solitary becoming deprives us, favouring judgment as the referee for our evolution to the detriment of the quality of our state. This difference also opens a breach in our horizon thanks to which we can recover a natural virginity of our breathing, and even of our touch, by their disinvestment from already existing relations to the world and to the other(s) which determined their way of perceiving. The opening of the horizon acts as a unveiling and a possible interpretation and transformation of our being. It also reveals to us that each being corresponds to a qualitatively determined 'to be', a *so-sein*, and not only a *was-sein*, that is, a substance or a structure which stills lacks differentiation and peculiar qualities, and could be substituted for any other.

This could transform the relation to every other into an objected relation, which prevents a dialogue between an 'I' and a 'you' from taking place. Without a *so-sein*, that is a determination of the respective subjectivities, such a dialogue cannot occur but only exchanges or comments about an 'it', a 'he', a 'him', the human being that 'there is', to whom 'that' testifies but who never enters into presence as such. One speaks of it, and even one ascribes a presence to it but as to one who is absent, an idea or an essence, the incarnation of which is still to come—unless it already happened in a past existence. To give priority to being-in-the-world over being-with-the-other means that human being remains a being or a figure of the world the entering into the presence of which is at best hidden in the organization of the world when it is not reduced to a thing, thus doubly deprived of a possible existence.

In fact the human presence can exist only as a co-presence from which the world itself arises. Before it refers to 'the couple that we form with the world', the real corresponds to the couple that we form with the other, particular the other who in differs from us by nature. It is this relation to/with the other which 'founds all our behaviours and judgments. It is what underlies all our perceptions and gives their tone to them' (cf. Maldiney, *Regard Parole Espace*, p. 50), prior to our relating to the world. And even the painters cannot exempt themselves from such a truth. In the privilege that they grant to the world and its modalities a relation to/with the other is already present, of which they are unaware but which gives their style and tone to their works. One could allude on this subject to the impact that an awakening or a pain of love can have on our perception of the world. One could also wonder about the possibility of a co-presence when the relation to the world prevails over the relation to the other. Is not this co-presence made impossible by the fact of reducing every other—and in a way also oneself—to a being as an 'it', a 'him', a 'that' or a 'there is' in the world?

And what happens to interiority, an interiority which is essential to artistic production, without a relation to the other before all relation to the world? Is it not from interiority that a world can be formed for a human being, an interiority—a soul?—which can transform the natural universe into a human world which takes account of nature without reducing it to a world constructed by man with beings or things placed side by side or bond by an order extraneous to them, lacking their living roots and life which circulates between them, feeding their becoming and their mutual co-presence and relationships.

Interiority cannot for all that close up out of submission to constructed essences or a narcissistic self-sufficiency. It must remain welcoming to the other and to the world, notably thanks to the breath and touch of which the soul is made according to Aristotle. This being welcoming to the outside is that which allows us not to cut ourselves off from an elementary life, from the air and the sensitive perception of the body and the flesh of the other. This means the possibility of a constant discovery of the real, which moves us beyond what we could imagine and gives impetus to a becoming still to come. Such bringing us back to the innocence of life leads us to transform ourselves, to provide ourselves with a new existence, to differently animate forms which were already ours towards more transcendence and profundity—so giving rise to a new conception of the human being.

Opening our being to difference, being welcoming and listening to what another human being can reveal to us, represents an opportunity to rework the already existing story regarding humanity and the world towards a new telling, a new coming into the world, the emergence of a new incarnation of human beings. This allows us to decompartmentalize all that a culture of sameness defines as reality or truth, to free the real towards a perpetual astonishment before the other and the world, in particular regarding the being and existence that we can generate together, of which we barely glimpse the potentialities.

Difference between us also opens a space within the space in which we were placed by history, culture and society. This space is not the plane space to which we are accustomed, but a place endowed with a perspective thanks to the difference, the negative, including with regard to our natural identity, which we each assume and assume towards each other. The existence of such a space allows us to shape or re-shape our way of being and being present. We are no longer assigned to certain places or certain forms by a natural or sociocultural environment nor paralyzed in/ by them without being able to free ourselves from them. Questioning and distance resulting from taking into account and putting into practice a real difference makes it possible for us to shape or re-shape forms which were familiar to us, including, to a certain extent, those which are dependent on our nature. The split between our natural and our cultural belonging in that way can be perceived and reduced. The ground and the background or the horizon from which the human being emerged and was individualized can thus be modified and supply it with a possible different incarnation.

Then the work is no longer a making into which human being projects itself; it is a work of which it is the matter, the intention, the worker and the finality. This can be carried out only through a relationship with the other in search of the fulfilment of the human being who each is and of that of humanity itself. The absolute for which each longs no longer corresponds to an objective reality elaborated by human being, mainly by man, as a sort of incarnation of itself—a sort of double of a subjectivity, that it cannot appropriate, which allows it to refer to it and tackle it. Instead it represents the possibility of the generation of human subjectivity, more generally of human being, by a relation to/with an other faithful to his/her natural belonging, a generation which is also a creation.

By Way of Epilogue: The World Born of Our Embraces

The subjection of the real to the logos brings about a general objectivity, and even objectality, which deprives us of our sensitive experience and removes us from our presence—to ourselves, to the other, to the world. Certainly, our sensory perceptions return to us a part of our sensitivity, notably through an aesthetic experience. But this does not correspond to the sensitivity of our whole living being and entails a stage of reduction to an 'object' perceptible by our senses. Now perceiving a thing does not amount to perceiving an other—a reciprocal sensitive communion can exist with the latter but not with the former. The sensitive relation to/ with the other goes beyond any perception of an 'object', even by our senses. Phenomenology, even a phenomenology resorting to *Da-sein,* cannot truly take such an experience into account, which questions the foundation and the ground which is implied in the perception of a phenomenon. The structuring of the world that desire and love can carry out is lacking, a world in which the reciprocity of desire and love makes the sensitive experience both active and passive, bodily and spiritual, physical and meta-physical.

L. Irigaray, *The Mediation of Touch*, https://doi.org/10.1007/978-3-031-37413-5

The presence of the other cannot be compared with a presence of things or of the world to which a 'direction' gives its meaning (cf. Maldiney, *Regard Parole Espace*, pp. 131–147). The other also brings a meaning that no one can attribute only to oneself without objectalizing, without one knowing, the relation to/with the other. The non-thematic character of this relation—the fact that it remains extraneous to a traditional phenomenology—in part results from its dual direction, which regulates the truth of the affect and its existential potential.

Touch, as a mediation towards communing with the other, takes part in this non-thematic dimension of transcendence, a dimension which, in a sense, no longer has a direction because it is immersed in a co-presence, and not a mere coexistence, from which we can be born again and again. Touch acts as a generating, even a germinating, process on which we cannot decide a priori and the meaning of which escapes the reach of our understanding. It arises from a union between us without our being able to grasp or comprehend it, we can only long for it as for a beyond which does not remove us from our life but allows us to accomplish it. This happens in a certain blindness for which touch compensates by giving to us an access to another perception of the real, an access which allows us to become the ones who we are not only through appearing but as being born from a conjunction between two different beings.

Thus the phenomenon, at least as it is usually imagined, cannot express the truth of touch, which has more to do with a link the efficiency of which is not visible and can even remain imperceptible. Appearing does not belong to the action of touch as such—differently from what happens in art. Art, except sometimes music, still takes place in the world of representation, whatever its modes. The importance which is attached to art, an importance that, for example, Maldiney still grants it, can be explained by the fact that art, at least in part, keeps sensitivity in a subject-object logic irrelevant to a subject-subject relationship, in particular a relationship between subjects who are different. Our traditional metaphysics knows only one subjectivity, which becomes appropriate by relations to/with the world, without being originally determined at an ontological level. It does not take account enough of the natural belonging of the subjects and of the co-belonging or co-presence of different subjects, from which forms can arise other than those the genesis of which is dependent on a single subjectivity or a single 'object' or objective. Now this is still the case in the beautiful reflections on art by Maldiney in which forms are constituted in space in an ecstatic way without their genesis happening in the secret of a union between two different dynamisms through a dialectical process between immanence(s) and transcendence(s). Such dialectics is not always lacking in intentionality. But the latter is different from that relating to only one subject, whatever his giving up the object as such.

The meeting between two intentions, which a reciprocal desire can intend reaching, is of another sort. It is surprising that a phenomenology regarding aesthetic experience has shown so little interest in it. It generally confines itself to a solitary sensory, more generally sensitive, feeling and neglects the nature of the affect which results from a relationship with another living being. Then to feel is not only a for-oneself and its impact is not merely instantaneous; rather it takes part in the unfolding of a reciprocal relationship with the other. It is not only a question of an instantaneous event occurring in only one world but of the intertwining between two worlds with their peculiar spaces and times. Thus it is no longer appropriate to say 'I become only because something happens, and something happens only because I become' (Ervin Strauss quoted by Maldiney in *Regard Parole Espace*, p. 192). Indeed, I become thanks to the meeting with another living being and the fact that something happens between us, a sort of invisible genesis of which our culture too little takes account because it escapes the making of man and does not take place in the space-time of his world.

But if forms, for man, amount above all to an appearing, it is not the case with the forms which are produced between living beings through the mediation of touch. Forms then emerge from matter itself and are neither images nor representations shaped by sight. If art, in particular painting, often contents itself with these latter and their evolution, the formers exist only thanks to desire and love. That is not to say that the artist does not experience them, but they do not entail a reciprocal communion between living beings, except in his imagination, memory or intention. Now what happens in the sharing of desire and love is both real and present. And the 'moving' which is joined to the 'feeling' does not aim only at an external action but at an intimate becoming of life and flesh which can give rise to a new real—not merely to 'the running of a work' but to the evolution of being, including the being that we are (op. cit., p. 210). Henceforth, the work concerns human being itself and its being in the world. Desire and love contribute to the self-genesis of the being that we are as our own work—a work that we must not only do but also let be done through a constant process of self-affection and hetero-affection, which is not only dependent on our hand and our sight but on our whole being.

This does not happen automatically when each enters in the presence of one another. But when it occurs, it matters to pay attention to that event of an ontological nature and to bring off its development. It is the meaning that faithfulness to a relationship, in particular of desire and love, between two persons can have. It represents the opportunity for an individual and collective evolution which requires both activity and pas-sivity, and the outcome of which must be preserved without it being spread or scattered into other meetings on pain of losing its fleshly and ontological nature. And, as the advent of a landscape in painting needs heterogeneous elements according to Cézanne, the advent of being in the meeting between the living needs their difference. In Aristotle's thought, that could mean: only the dissimilar is able to feed the living being, that is, the 'animal' that we are.

To perceive such a food, we must go further than a mere sensation or a communion with the world lacking differentiation. We must transform these original feelings by acknowledging and assuming the difference between the other and ourselves. Nevertheless, this must not end in 'object(s)' but must aim at identifying the quality of the real and its abil-ity to contribute to the development of our being, notably through the evolution of the state that we experience. This could also be said: its abil-ity to carry out our individuation, that of the other and of the relation-ship between us from a ground that we form with the whole of beings, thereby mistaking ourselves for one another without being able to relate to one another.

We go no further than such a stage for lack of incarnating ourselves as a whole, of taking shape according to our nature, and of acknowledging its own forms—which ends in a split between body and mind to which our traditional culture has led. One way to surmount it is probably to admit that the female germ cells have a specific potential relative to embodiment. If their taking shape from matter depends solely on the male germ cells, the forms do not have a life of their own. They arise from a ground but cannot truly evolve, and their appearing amounts to a death. The forms which arise from a conjunction between different germ cells are different and act otherwise. Their beings do not correspond to their appearing and their value is due to their arising and developing while refraining from cutting themselves off from life, from the sap of what appears, from their germinating origin, the fertility of which does not stop at any definitive form(s). The female germ cells have the power to give birth to living beings and forms. This necessitates the ability of woman to give herself up to welcoming and uniting with male germ cells while remaining able to gather with and within herself, notably, but not only, to feed the fruit of such a conjunction towards its autonomous becoming incarnate.

Images and representations suspend such an alternation. They prevent the passage from the outside to the inside, from the inside to the outside. They fascinate, interrupting in that way the perpetual becoming of life. They substitute themselves for the fluid consistency and the irradiation of a presence—with which another presence can communicate or commune without being able to determine it as a 'thing'. They submit the world and the other to the subject or the subject to the world and the other without a communication or communion remaining possible between them. The world, the other and we as living are forgotten in their images or representations, in a confinement in which all are enclosed, isolated from each other. Every presence is alienated in them, as is ours in our mirror image, which allows us to perceive ourselves by cutting ourselves off from our living belonging, apprehending ourselves as a sort of 'object' capturing in its reflection the living being that we are.

We less need images and representations to become than generating, including between us, new forms that we can inhabit as living. Love allows us, and even incites us, to do that—love as the place of a possible genesis of being that an appearing, frozen in appearance(s), interrupts. Such alternation of being born and perishing belongs to a logic of understanding that can be overcome by a growing which involves a vanishing of appearing towards a transformation of the background and the emergence of new forms. Our sight does not know this sort of evolution of the living and, by favouring seeing, our culture has deprived us of it. Touch is that which allows it to happen anew. What touches us moves us forward towards what brings about and feeds our growing. We need touch to live and not merely survive. We need it as we need a soul, a place in ourselves, as both a memory and a source of touch and of that to which it invites us, for which it calls us, to develop and blossom as living, instead of going no further than the satisfaction of needs to survive, our longings holding on to supra sensitive ideals.

Living forms spring from the germ cells. They shape life through their dynamism. The germ cells relate to the flesh and the soul, whereas the constructed forms, which the mental and the spirit aim to conceive, belong to a world which, even if it draws inspiration from the germ cells, ignores them, trying to substitute for them; that is, a world in a way already dead. Then forms live on flesh and abolish it for lack of breath and dynamism, which correspond to properties of the living and of the soul. They act as a split between a living sensitivity and an artificial sensitivity, which can be both fusional and wounding. They lead to a fusion or a lack of differentiation, which gives no possible access to intimacy.

So Hegel's way of conceiving of sensitivity does not know a real intimacy—his dialectics fails to deal with fleshly sensitivity and its sharing. Then what is sensitive becomes illusory and what is artificial becomes true. This could result from the forgetting of the germ cells. It also entails the substitution of an object for another subject and a status of intuition which seems to respect sensitivity but not respect it, at least as far as touch is concerned. But if our senses can deal with object(s), it is not the case with touch, at least a communing touch. It is not a sense similar to the others—it is the mediator of the sensitive. As such it truly fulfils itself when it relates to another touch. Its ideal deed is the sharing of the sensitive as the language of the living before any language coded in a way parallel to the living.

Touch is a sense the efficiency of which can be immediately transcendental. In fact, it acts in a way which is extraneous to our traditional logic for various reasons. First, it presupposes our passivity, a passivity capable of welcoming what it experiences—a thing which is possible only if our subjectivity remains sensitive. Moreover, the mediating potential of touch is fully efficient between two beings which differ from one another by nature. And yet our culture has favoured sameness as the means of knowing and relating, leaving difference to be a mere means of survival and of physical growth, as Aristotle asserts. Our tradition has also confined the relationship between two human beings which are naturally different within the family home without wondering about its potentialities and the means of cultivating them. Besides, it has subjected this relationship to procreation without considering the other positive aspect that the difference between germ cells can represent. Indeed, before any negative at the disposal of human beings, their germinating potential has imposed a negative on all claims to universality: it has determined every human being as ontologically particular by its sexuation.

But the negative which corresponds with specific germ cells enables human beings to overcome a particular destiny through achieving it by uniting with different germ cells. Through such a union, every human being accomplishes itself while overcoming him- or herself and generating an other human or an other destiny by the advent of a being or a world arising from the conjunction between different germ cells. What determines a human being as particular is also that which allows it to surmount this destiny by questioning the peculiarity of one being or one world, and even the necessity of resorting to death to individualize its existence. The germ cells lay down a limit, a specific sexuate belonging, which acts as the origin of a development which does not confine itself to a mere particularity while being faithful to it at a natural level. In that way, the spiritual no longer separates from the natural, it no longer asserts itself by dominating the latter but by assuming a genetic potential which determines us, in a way negativizes us, in order that we could take charge of our being as human. The genetic inheritance of germ cells differs from the somatic, even from the psychic, traits inherited from ancestry. These determine us ontically whereas the germ cells represent an ontological potential.

Aristotle speaks of the soul as a doctor. As such, it is remarkable that he acknowledges the existence of the soul as a place where the living being that we are can gather with itself by internalization. However, Aristotle little considers what a psychic and spiritual human growth means—which requires desire and love as driving forces taking over from needs and mere individual intellect, and relating to the other, especially the naturally different other, as a source of affect(s) and development. And yet Aristotle in fact notices that feeling and feeding oneself necessitate the dissimilar, but he broaches these things above all as a doctor, at the level of the body and the needs, in an epoch where subjectivity and intersubjectivity do not represent a theoretical stake and, perhaps, not even an existential datum. Besides, what does a woman mean for Aristotle? How could a man long for the one who lacks peculiar forms and an autonomous germinating potential with which he would desire to unite? Must he not, instead, care about fertilizing her, even feeding her, without being himself fed by her at all?

If the living being is a being which moves by itself, how to ensure this motion beyond what motivates the satisfaction of needs? Is it not by its desire that the human being is compelled to a fulfilment which is not only somatic but also psychic and spiritual? And does longing for another human not mean transcending a mere natural belonging by imparting to it a spiritual destiny?

The language of touch is without metaphors. It makes known and gives sense to the real, in particular that of the flesh, before any coded language. It is a word which silently unites the physical with the metaphysical, through a return to the being that we are and which we try to make exist and achieve. This requires us to be faithful to our origin without disowning it by 'being in the world only through not leaping from anywhere' (cf. Maldiney, in *Regard Parole Espace*, p. 169). The fact that our origin is elusive does not mean that we come from anywhere. The world into which we come is opened to us by a meeting between two different living beings. It is within such a horizon that we take place and it determines the space in which we live. Even if we do not perceive it, this horizon is present and it participates in the truth of what we perceive, which is never completely objective nor dependent only on 'things' that we meet. A meaning is attributed to them by our way of perceiving, which is never totally neutral nor neuter. So our approach to things is not extraneous to the desire that we experience for an other. The depth of our relationship with an other, especially an other naturally different from us, has an impact on the size and the quality of our way of experiencing the world and things. It joins the inside and the outside of us even before the forms of our body compel us to incarnate this passage, a passage which succeeds or not in weaving together our horizons, building in this way a habitable world, which doubles that of nature itself.

If such a horizon is lacking, a horizon which is formed by various modes of fleshly embraces, we wander in the world without discovering our path and the place in which we can live. Art can help us to discover them but it cannot substitute for them. Is it not too often the aim of the works of art—notably in their beautiful analyses by Maldiney? Do they not embody outside of the artists something of the incarnation of their beings, particularly through the meeting and the union with the other, although these could give flesh to space-time itself? This flesh is invisible but it is real and its absence removes consistency, depth and quality from the world and the things that it comprises. This flesh lives in the space between us, which requires neither 'tearing' nor 'jumping' or 'leaping' to exist (cf. Maldiney, op. cit., p. 174). To respect the difference between our horizons is sufficient for its opening.

Instead of a superego repressing instincts and drives, taking into consideration the natural difference of the other can open up a passage from the natural human being to a human being which is cultivated and takes place in history. The negative, of which the superego was the guardian and the guarantor, is then ensured by a difference between beings existing from birth—being who I am implies that I am not the other. This permits us to surmount the alternative between to speak and to remember because the word that I address to the other can, and even must, be faithful to the natural being that I am. So I can keep remembering for love of the other and with a view to the development of our relationship. The respect for our difference acts as a sort of culture of the immediacy of affects and emotions, in that way granting them a cultural status.

This asks us to use another language the syntax of which is structured in accordance with the body, the flesh and desire. The assessment of the meaning, its being put in perspective, is no longer dependent on a vertical hierarchy for which sight and understanding are mainly responsible, but on the quality of energy and of its generating and transforming power regarding our evolution and that of our relationship with the other, the others and the world. This is possible thanks to a dialectics of sensitivity in which the motion is not determined by the search for a truth parallel to the living but by the transformation of the real towards the constitution, the existence and the blossoming of our living being.

The meaning that our tradition has favoured is not the one which is suitable for love. What matters for our existence is not to prioritize understanding but to discover a dynamism which can contribute to our becoming and the constitution of a presence which corresponds to the flowering of our state. The quality of our state must prevail over the acquisition of a presumedly appropriate truth, and the meaning which is at stake henceforth concerns the state of our being and not the acquisition of a truth more or less arbitrarily elaborated in relation to the real of our nature. Communication with the other and with the world has more to do with a sharing of state(s) than with exchanges within a horizon already culturally constructed.

The state of our being is in search of itself through relating to/with the other. We have too often ignored such a truth, mistaking our human condition for the acquisition of mental performances. This has led to the automation of the human being. To be a human would amount to becoming a machine capable of performing certain programs, or even of inventing some which are of a higher performance. Our body itself is invited to conform to such an economy according to various modes: sporting, intellectual or sexual. The living and sensitive contribution through which our body can supply quality to life, its rhythm and its evolution, ought to be sacrificed and forgotten for the benefit of performances, the quantitative assessment of which retains mainly competition as a relational element, the importance and the number of productions as a positive aspect, and a possible return to homeostasis as a condition of well-being. But this return is more and more compromised by the threat of cosmic disasters, of world epidemics, of the collapse of economic mechanisms. We, powerless, undergo all that as a sort of apocalyptic advent, if not an apocalyptic show, which would be caused from elsewhere without our intervention and which would be extraneous to us— in a way as the logos to which we have agreed to subject ourselves. All that would depend on a 'they', a 'one', a 'there is' or a 'That' in which my 'I' no longer takes place as the foundation and the horizon of a living speech and world thanks to our faithfulness to a real origin and a co-presence of different subjects, each having charge of the incarnation of its own life.

A cultural chaos has succeeded to a supposedly original chaos. No sub-ject still governs meaning, which results from an education and a culture which impose forms which are defined regardless of life itself and which no longer have matter or flesh in which they could find resources.

Our touch has lost its power of mediation between different living beings and, even reduced to a way of seizing the world, it has no longer very much to apprehend. And yet it is touch which could save us from a nihilistic disaster. Touch which has been the means of discovering our first food, could help us to sense that which, today, could give back life to our being. This cannot happen through any sort of possession but by providing us with a food which can fit our current state. It is probably in an ontological communion with the other that we can find it, a commu-nion which is both bodily and spiritual, which is no longer dependent on already constructed metaphors and from which a new meaning can arise thanks to a reciprocity of sensitive nature, which soothes our thirst for the absolute without seizing anything. We must let it bring relief to us, bring us into the world again in a complete ingenuity and innocence.

This way another 'I' can emerge who can tell the other its self and be with him or her more than by apprehending things or elements of knowl-edge. An 'I' who is born, or born again, in/of an amorous embrace through which the mystery that we are is passed on. We will have to care about it in a new way, trusting the meaning of an embrace, the nesting wrapping of amorous arms more than any self-logical or solipsistic knowl-edge or power of a body or a spirit which hang on to the success of a hold, to the seizure of some possession. We mistakenly abandon to that the elusive character of our being, forgetting that our first touch was of use for entering into relation with the other and not for appropriating some-thing. It is to this original touch that we must return as to a path leading us to a possible co-presence with the other, the style of which must aim at rendering us human, which needs a culture of touch. Indeed, touch can make fall back into a physical opacity, into the illusory transcendence of the appropriation of things or it can give access to a sensitive transcen-dence through the respect for the otherness of the other. This allows us to reach a human status, between animality and divinity.

The experience which makes possible such a becoming is in a way uni-versal but the presence which can carry it out is unique and no one nor no thing can be substituted for it. The mystery of our being lies among others in the absolute singularity of its incarnation. For lack of it, we fail to be and we wander in the dark among beings made by man. In the co-presence to/with the other, especially an other which differs from us by nature, a space-time is opened up for the discovery of the ones who we are. No doubt, our being cannot be apprehended as a thing—it escapes any seizure. However, we perceive something of it through what moves us in the touch of the other and our touching this other in turn. This touch, both physical and meta-physical, fits out a space in the common space in which we can shelter, repose, curl up in order to prepare our birth or rebirth. It acts as a place in which we can nestle—in part as in an incuba-tor—a place that our amorous touch creates and which allows us to iso-late ourselves from the appeals and noises of the outside. Then we can be listening to the most intimately alive of ourselves and to the desire that we experience for one another, which lies in it and calls for being lived, and thought, in a constant development towards the absolute. Wrapped by our mutual horizons, we transform the space into an environment in which to breathe, to warm ourselves up, to touch one another without any infringement, preparing us in that way to receive from one other the awakening of the sap of our being and the surge which compels us to incarnate it as far as it is possible to do.

Bibliography

Generally, the quotes come from a French version and I translate them into English. I also try.

I also try to provide the references to a publication in English. They come from an English version to which I have access and I can indicate the page(s) or, if I cannot consult the work, I furnish all the details that I can (part of the book, chapter, title and subtitles etc.), starting from the French version or even I indicate the code referring to the original version of the text.

Aristotle. 1980. *De l'âme,* texte établi par A. Jannone, traduit et annoté par E. Barbotin. Paris: Les Belles lettres (*De Anima*, translated by Mark Shiffman. Indianapolis/Cambridge: Hackett, 2011).

D'Aquin, Thomas.1961. *La Grâce,* dans *La Somme Théologique,* traduction française Ch.V. Heris. Paris: Ed. du Cerf (*The Grace,* in *Summa Theologiae*, Ed. Joseph Rickaby, 1822, J.M. Ashley, 1888).

Derrida, Jacques. 2000. *Le toucher, Jean-Luc Nancy*, Paris, Ed. Galilée (*On Touching: Jean-Luc Nancy,* translated by Christine Irizarry. Standford University Press, 2005).

D'Hondt, Jacques. 1984. *Hegel, Textes et débats*. Paris: Le livre de Poche, Librairie Générale Française.

Eckhart, Maître. 1942. *Traités et Sermons*, traduit par F.A. et J.M. Paris: Aubier, Ed. Montaigne (*From Whom God Hid Nothing: Sermons, Writings and Sayings*. Ed. New Seeds, 2005).

Freud, Sigmund. 2019. *Oeuvres Complètes*, avec le conseil de Jean Laplanche. Paris, PUF (*Standard Edition*, ed. by James Stracley, 1999).

Fritsch, Vilma. 1967. *La gauche et la droite*. Paris: Flammarion (*Left and Right*, Barrie and Rockliff, 1968).

Guillaume, Paul. 1937. *La psychologie de la forme*. Paris: Ed. Flammarion, Champs (cf. Gestalt Theory and a PdF version on internet).

Hegel, G.W.F. 1966. *La Phénoménologie de l'Esprit, Tomes I et II*, traduit par Jean Hyppolite. Paris: Ed. Aubier Montaigne (*Phenomenology of Spirit*, translated by A.V. Miller, edited by J.N. Findlay. Oxford: Oxford University Press, 1979).

———. 1970. *Encyclopédie des sciences philosophiques en abrégé*, traduit par Maurice de Gandillac. Paris: NRF/Gallimard (*Encyclopaedia of the Philosophical Sciences in Basic Outline*, translated and edited by Klauss Brinkmann and Daniel O. Dahlstrom. Cambridge: Cambridge University Press, 2010).

———. 1972. *Le droit naturel*, traduit et préfacé par Albert Kahn. Paris: NRF/ Gallimard (*Natural Law*, translated by T.M. Knox. Philadelphia: University of Pennsylvania Press, 1975).

———. 1973. *Principes de la philosophie du droit*, traduit et annoté par André Kaan. Paris: NRF/Gallimard, Tel (*Hegel's Philosophy of Right*, translated by T.M. Knox. Oxford University Press, 1997).

———. 1979a. *Les orbites des planètes*, traduit et annoté par François De Gand. Paris: Ed. Vrin, Librairie philosophique.

———. 1979b. *Esthétique II*, traduit pas S. Jankélévitch. Paris: Flammarion, Champs (*Lectures on Fine Art (?)*, translated by T.M. Knox).

———. 1988. *L'Esprit du Christianisme et son Destin*, traduit par Jean Martin. Paris: Vrin, Librairie Philosophique (*The Spirit of Christianity and its Fate*, in Early Theological Writings, 1970).

Heidegger, Martin. 1958a. 'La question de la technique' dans *Essais et Conférences*, traduit par André Préau. Paris: Gallimard, Tel ('The Question Concerning Technology', in *The Question Concerning Technology and Other Essays*, translated by William Lovin, New York: Harper and Row, 1977).

———. 1958b. 'La chose' dans *Essais et Conférences*, traduit par André Préau. Paris: Gallimard, Tel ('The Thing' in *Poetry, Language, Thought*, translated by Albert Hofstadter. New York: Harper Collins, 1971).

———. 1962. *Chemins*, traduit par Wolfang Brokmeier. Paris: NRF/Gallimard.

————. 1964. *L'Être et le Temps,* traduit par Rudolph Boehm et Alphonse De Waelhens. Paris: NRF/Gallimard (*Being and Time,* translated by John Macquarrie and Edward Robinson. Oxford: Blackwell Publishers, 1962).

————. 1966. 'Lettre sur l'humanisme' dans *Questions III,* Paris: NRF/Gallimard ('Letter on Humanism'. In *Basic Writings,* ed. David Farrell Krell. London/New York: Routledge, 1993).

————. 1967. *Introduction à la Métaphysique,* traduit par Albert Kahn. Paris: Gallimard, Tel (*Introduction to Metaphysics,* translated by Gregory Fried and Richard Polt. New Haven/London: Yale University Press, Nota Bene, 2000).

————. 1968. *Questions I,* traduit par Henry Corbin, Roger Munier, Alphonse De Waelhens, Walter Biemel, Gérard Granel, André Préau. Paris: NRF/Gallimard (cf. *Pathmarks,* translated by William McNeill, also editor of the volume. Cambridge: Cambridge University Press, 1998).

————. 1973a. *Qu'appelle-t-on penser?,* traduit par Aloys Becker et Gérard Granell. Paris: PUF, Epiméthée (*What Is Called Thinking?,* translated by Fred D. Whieck and J. Glenn Gray. New York/London: Harper and Row, 1968).

———— et Eugen Fink. 1973b. *Heraclite,* Séminaire 1966–67, traduit par Jean Launay et Patrick Levy. Paris: NRF/Gallimard (*Heraclitus Seminar, in Studies in Phenomenological and Existential Philosophy,* 9780810110670 amazon. com. books).

————. 1976a. 'La fin de la philosophie et le tournant' dans *Questions IV,* traduit par Jean Beaufret, François Ferdier, Jean Lauxerois et Claude Roels. Paris: NRF/Gallimard ('The End of Philosophy and the Task of Thinking' in *Basic Writings,* edited by David Farrell Krell. London/New York: Routledge, 1993).

————. 1976b. *Acheminement vers la parole,* traduit par Jean Beaufret, Wolffang Brokmeyer et François Ferdier. Paris: NRF/Gallimard (*On the Way to Language,* translated by Peter D. Hertz. San Francisco: Harper and Row Editions, San Francisco, 1982).

————. 1977. *Réponses et Questions sur l'Histoire et la Politique,* Interview avec *Der Spiegel,* traduit par Jean Launay. Paris: Mercure de France (*Only a God can still Save Us,* translated by William J. Richardson in *Heidegger, The Man and the Thinker* edited by Thomas Sheehan. New Brunswick, Piscataway: Transaction Publishers, 1981 or in *The Heidegger Controversy: A Critical Reader,* Edited by Richard Rolin. Cambridge, MA: MIT Press, 1993).

————. 1998. *Pathmarks,* ed. William MacNeill. Cambridge: Cambridge University Press.

————. 2007. '*Ma chère petite âme*', *Lettres à sa femme Elfride.* Lettres choisies, éditées et commentées par Gertrude Heidegger, traduit par Marie-Ange

Maillet. Paris: Ed. du Seuil (*Letters to His Wife Elfride*, selected, edited and annotated by Gertrude Heidegger, translated by R.D.V. Glasgow. Cambridge: Polity Press, 2008).

Henry, Michel. 1990. *Phénoménologie matérielle*. Paris: PUF, Epiméthée (*Material Phenomenology*, translated by Scott Davidson, Perspectives in Continental Philosophy, 1990).

———. 2000. *Incarnation; Une philosophie de la chair*, Paris: Ed. du Seuil (*Incarnation: A Philosophy of Flesh*, translated by Karl Hefty. Evanston: Northwestern University Press, 2015).

———. 2010. *Pour une phénoménologie de la vie*, Entretiens avec Olivier Salazar-Ferrer, suivis par 'Perspectives sur la phénoménologie matérielle' par Jean Gregori et Jean Leclercq. Ed. Corlevour.

Husserl, Edmond. 1982. *Recherches phénoménologiques pour la constitution*, traduit par Eliane Escoubas Paris: PUF, Epiméthée (*Ideas II:Studies in the Phenomenology of Constitution*, translated by R. Rojcewicz and A. Schuwer. Dordrecht: Kluwer, 1989).

Hyppolite, Jean. 1983. *Introduction à la philosophie de l'Histoire de Hegel*. Paris: Ed. du Seuil, Points.

Irigaray, Luce. 1974. *Speculum*. Paris: Ed. de Minuit (*Speculum*, translated by Gillian C. Gill. Ithaca: Cornell University Press, 1985).

———. 1983. *L'oubli de l'air: Chez Martin Heidegger*. Paris: Ed. de Minuit (*The Forgetting of the Air: In Martin Heidegger*, translated by Mary Beth Mader. Austin/London: Texas University Press and Continuum, 1999).

———. 1984. *Ethique de la différence sexuelle*. Paris, Ed. de Minuit (*An Ethics of Sexual Difference*, translated by Carolyn Burke and Gillian C. Gill. Ithaca/London: Cornell University Press and Continuum, 1993).

———. 1987. *Sexes et parentés*. Paris: Ed. de Minuit (*Sexes and Genealogies*, translated by Gillian C. Gill. New York: Columbia University Press, 1993).

———. 1993. *J'aime à toi, Esquisse d'une félicité dans l'Histoire*. Paris: Ed. Grasset (*I Love to You, Sketch for a Felicity within History*, translated by Alison Martin. New York/London: Routledge, 1996).

———. 2011. 'Perhaps Cultivating Touch Can Still Save Us' in Journal *Substance*, vol. 40, no. 3, taken up again in *Building a New World*, Palgrave Macmillan, 2015.

——— (and Michael Marder). 2016. *Through Vegetal Being, Two Philosophical Perspectives*. New York: Columbia University Press.

———. 2017. *To Be Born: Genesis of a Human Being*. London/New York: Palgrave Macmillan.

———. 2019. *Sharing the Fire, Outline of a Dialectics of Sensitivity*. London/New York: Palgrave Macmillan.

———, ed. and contributor. 2022. *Challenging a Fictitious Neutrality*. Other contributors: Mahon O'Brien; David Farrell Krell; Emma Reed Jones. London/New York: Palgrave Macmillan.

Koyré, Alexandre. *La dissymétrie*. Paris: NRF/Gallimard.

Levinas, Emmanuel. 1961. *Totalité et infini*. La Haye:Martinus Nyhoff (*Totality and Infinity*, translated by Alphonso Lingis. Dordrecht: Kluwer Academic, 1991).

———. 1979. *Le temps et l'autre*. Montpellier: Fata Morgana (*Time and the Other and Additional Essays*, translated by Richard A. Cohen. Pittsburgh: Duquesne University Press, 1987).

Maldiney, Henri. 1973. *Regard Parole Espace*. Lausanne: Ed. L'âge d'homme.

———. 1993. *L'art, l'éclair de l'être*. Seyssel: Ed. Comp'Act, Collection Scalène.

Merleau-Ponty, Maurice. 1964. *Le visible et l'invisible*. Paris: NRF/Gallimard (*The Visible and the Invisible*, translated by Alphonse Lingis. Evanston: Northwestern University Press, 1968).

———. 1989. *Eloge de la philosophie*. Paris, Gallimard, folio essais; existe aussi dans le recueil *Signes*, Gallimard, folio essais, 1960 (cf. *In Praise of Philosophy and Other Essays*, Northwestern University Press, 1988 or *Signs*, translated by Richard C. McCleary. Evanston: Northwestern University Press, 1964).

———. 1995. *La Nature, Notes de cours au Collège de France, par Dominique Séglard*. Paris: Ed. du Seuil (*Nature: Course Notes from The Collège de France*, translated by Robert Vallier. Evanston: Northwestern University Press, 2003).

Nietzsche, Friedrich. 1971. *Ainsi parlait Zarathoustra*, traduit par Maurice de Gandillac. Paris: NRF/Gallimard, Idées (*Thus Spoke Zarathustra*, translated by Graham Parkes. Oxford: Oxford University Press, 2005).

Patanjali. 1979. *Les Yogasutras de Patanjali*, Commentés *par Swami Sadananda Serasvati*. Paris, Le Courrier du Livre (New York: North Point, 2009).

Piaget, Jean. 2003. *La représentation du monde chez l'enfant*. Paris: PUF (*The Child's Conception of the World*. London/New York: Routledge, 1929).

Sartre, Jean-Paul. 1980. *L'être et le néant*. Paris NRF/Gallimard (*Being and Nothingness*, translated by Hazel E. Barnes. New York: Citadel Press, 2001).

Schelling, F. W. ou G.W.F. Hegel. 1986. 'De la relation entre la philosophie de la nature et la philosophie en général' dans *La différence entre les systèmes philosophiques de Fichte et de Schelling*, traduit par Bernard Gilson. Paris: Ed. Vrin (*The Difference between Fichte's and Schelling's Systems of Philosophy*, translated and edited by H.S. Harris and Walter Cerf. Albany: State University of New York Press, 1977).

Simondon, Gilbert. 1989. *L'individuation psychique et collective.* Paris: Ed. Aubier, L'invention philosophique.

Spitz, René. 1962. *Le non et le oui,* traduit par Anna-Marie Rocheblave-Spenlé. Paris: PUF (*No and Yes.* New York: International Universities Press, 1957).

Wallon, Henri. 1973. *Les origines du caractère chez l'enfant.* Paris: PUF.

Index[1]

---

[1] Note: Some words - for example, 'touch', 'germ cells', 'flesh', 'supra sensitive', 'presence', 'body' etc; - are so much used that they cannot appear in the Index with references save when they intervene in a particular expression.

© The Author(s), under exclusive license to Springer Nature Switzerland AG 2023
L. Irigaray, *The Mediation of Touch*, https://doi.org/10.1007/978-3-031-37413-5

Intend (to)
 intention, 6, 22, 61, 63, 64, 76,
  89, 302, 345, 349
 intentionality, 29, 302, 305, 306,
  309, 317, 324, 349
Interiority, 14, 15, 26, 27, 31, 33,
  46, 72, 73, 89, 95, 106, 108,
  119, 139, 147, 151, 155–158,
  161, 173, 225, 241, 256, 267,
  269, 270, 287, 307, 325,
  343, 344
Intermediary, 207, 241, 297, 317
Internalize (to)
 internal, 7, 33, 102, 107, 117,
  155, 157, 172–174, 202, 250,
  253, 269, 285, 292, 293
 internalization, 3, 4, 45,
  305, 353
Interpersonal, 7, 11, 251, 312
Interpretation, 29, 42, 72, 132, 133,
  135, 138, 149, 214, 245, 267,
  304, 342
Intersection, 19, 21, 190
Interval, 25, 27, 54, 203, 264, 272, 310
Interweave (to), 76
Intimacy, 14, 33, 41, 60, 72,
  139, 143, 145, 155, 161, 217,
  257, 266, 279, 291, 292, 304,
  307, 319, 323, 325, 334,
  341, 352
 intimate, 5, 40, 61, 62, 72, 73,
  95, 96, 101, 106, 107, 112,
  141, 144, 161, 174, 211, 213,
  220, 237, 270, 273, 293, 294,
  298, 301, 305, 313, 315, 319,
  333–335, 340, 349
Introject (to), 332, 333
Introspection, 173, 302
Intuit (to), 332

intuition, 11, 29, 36, 38, 50, 141,
  287, 289, 298, 352
Invisible, 19, 43, 61, 130, 139, 144,
  146, 152, 156, 157, 161, 162,
  167, 248, 249, 274, 279, 289,
  303–305, 322–326, 333,
  349, 355
Isomorphism, 172

Janet, 173
Japanese, 208–210, 213
Jesus, 25, 119, 235, 284, 295,
  299, 338
Join (to)
 conjoin (to), 26, 31, 74, 112,
  291, 314
 joint, 20, 70
 jointly, 35, 223
Judgment, 3, 134, 144, 165, 193,
  324, 338, 342, 343

Kant, 36, 172, 338
 Kantian, 38
Kingdom, 60, 100, 177
Kiss (to)/kiss (the), 2, 5
Korè, 268

Language
 metalanguage, 296
 sexuate language, 229
Law, 37, 53, 89, 105, 123, 175, 229,
  249, 255, 256, 266, 270,
  285, 339

Printed in the USA
CPSIA information can be obtained
at www.ICGtesting.com
LVHW021104270324
775628LV00009B/318